By Antoni Gronowicz

BIOGRAPHIES

Garbo
Béla Schick and the World of Children
Modjeska: Her Life and Loves
Sergei Rachmaninoff
Paderewski: Pianist and Patriot
Gallant General: Tadeusz Kosciuszko
Tchaikovsky
Chopin

NOVELS

An Orange Full of Dreams
The Hookmen
Four from the Old Town
Bolek
Hitler's Woman

POETRY

The Quiet Vengeance of Words
Polish Poems

PLAYS

The United Animals
Shores of Pleasure Shores of Pain
Chiseler's Paradise
Forward Together
Recepta
Greta
Rocos
Colors of Conscience

ESSAYS

Polish Profiles
The Piasts
Pattern for Peace

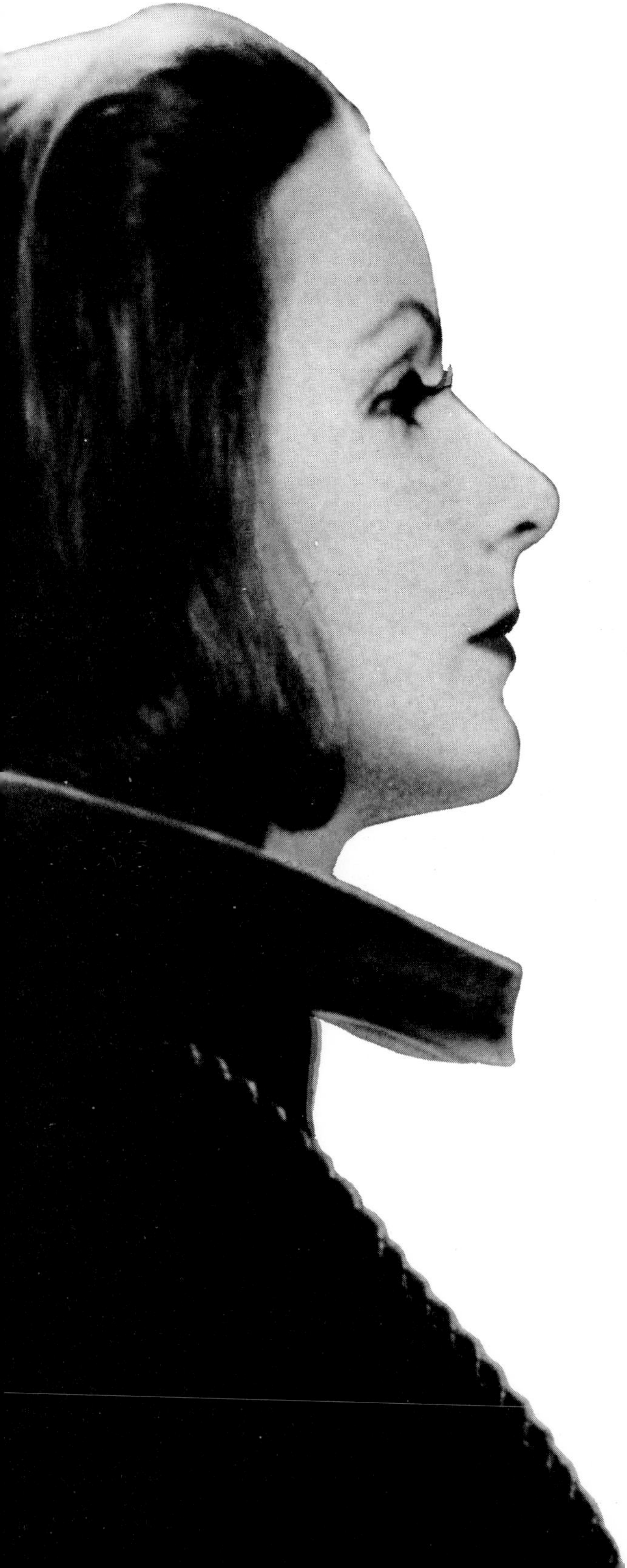

G

arbo

BY *Antoni Gronowicz*

Publisher's Afterword by RICHARD SCHICKEL

SIMON AND SCHUSTER

New York • London • Toronto • Sydney • Tokyo • Singapore

SIMON AND SCHUSTER
Simon & Schuster Building
Rockefeller Center
1230 Avenue of the Americas
New York, New York 10020,

Manufactured in the United States of America

10   9   8   7   6   5   4   3   2   1

Library of Congress Cataloging in Publication Data

Garbo, Greta, 1905–1990
  Garbo

  1. Garbo, Greta, 1905–1990.   2. Moving-picture
actors and actresses—Sweden—Biography.
I. Gronowicz, Antoni, 1913–1985.   II. Title.
PN2778.G3A34   791.43 028'0924   [B]   78-15998
ISBN 0-671-22523-5

Unless otherwise credited, photographs are from the
Lester Glassner Collection.

Garbo

Contents

Prologue

A relationship between two people can gradually be transformed into friendship, into love—or into a book. This book began in chance acquaintance and developed through many decades of my life.

In the 1920's I heard about Greta Garbo from Mauritz Stiller's relatives who were my neighbors in the Polish city of Lvov. During my frequent visits to their modest home, I often looked at photographs of her and Mauritz in family albums and read letters he had written in Yiddish from Stockholm and Hollywood. These letters were full of praise of Greta and her talents. Although his parents thought Moje, as they called him, a megalomaniac, he rarely wrote about his theatrical and filmmaking successes. Whenever Moje did refer to his films, it was in a postscript, as if to emphasize that his greatest success was the discovery of Greta, on whom he spent so much of his creative energy.

In one of his last letters, Moje announced how happy he was that Greta was now in accord with him on everyday matters and also shared in his outlook on art. Then he added, "I spent the best part of my life bringing her to this state of being."

The day after the telegram arrived from Stockholm announcing Moje's death, I wept along with his family. That a forty-five-year-old man of great heart and equally great innovative film genius had committed suicide was beyond all comprehension. The legend he had molded so successfully had shunted him aside. He had returned alone to Stockholm, his career shattered by the Hollywood moguls, steadfastly maintaining that he could live without them. But he could not live without Greta.

When you think about his career, it's not easy to believe in justice. And justice was in short supply all over Europe in those days. A second world war was approaching. The forces of fascism came to power in Italy and then in Germany. To me, to Moje's family, and to most of Lvov's 300,000 inhabitants these events were ominous. Lvov was Poland's second city, after Warsaw, not only as a cultural center but also in commerce. It lies on the ancient trade route from the Near East to Western Europe, and among its population, in addition to Poles, were Ukrainians, Jews, and Armenians. With fascism on the rise, differences among Lvov's inhabitants grew.

In the fall of 1935, as a youthful poet, I approached Polish intellectual circles with the idea of organizing a nationwide committee to sponsor an international conference against fascism. The committee sent letters to five hundred outstanding cultural figures. Most of those invited sent papers expressing fear about the impending world tragedy or telegrams supporting our cause. Some of the writers were Nobel Prize winners Romain Rolland, André Gide, and Thomas Mann, as well as Jules Romains, Lion Feuchtwanger, Ernst Toller, and Joseph Roth. Among the many film notables who responded were several who had played in Garbo's films, including Lionel Barrymore, Douglas Fairbanks, Fredric March, Maureen O'Sullivan, and Robert Montgomery. But the Sphinx herself did not send any communication. When, years later, I asked Garbo why she had not responded to our appeal, she replied, characteristically, that she had not received our invitation.

This international meeting, held on May 16 and 17, 1936, had a great impact, even without Garbo. Although I was not yet twenty-three years old, I became the focus of attention, especially among the highest Polish authorities, who forced me into political opposition. Later on, the president of the Polish Senate delivered a furious denunciation damning me and the conference. Even before this attack, I had made up my mind to leave the country. A helpful hand was extended me by many prominent people from outside Poland, including the world-renowned musicians Ignace Paderewski and Leopold Stokowski, friend of Greta Garbo.

"We should have our eyes wide open before love, and half closed during love." The thought crossed my mind as I continued our conversation. "An author who writes glowingly about women doesn't know them well; but an author who writes disdainfully about women doesn't know them at all."

She, looking fixedly at the mountains, nervously brushed blond hair out of her eyes and said, "Every one of us lives his life just once; if we are honest, to live once is enough." Again brushing back her hair, she added, "In view of our short lives, it is not important who is writing or talking about others in derogatory terms. Death will crush the good and the bad, but history"—she paused—"history will select whom she wants."

It was the summer of 1938, and we were sitting on the upper terrace of the Chalet Riond-Bosson. It was a sunny afternoon, and before us lay serene Lake Geneva, behind which rose majestic Mont Blanc. The chalet was enveloped in greenery—trees, bushes, all kinds of flowers, well attended by a gardener and his six helpers. The owner of this magnificent place was Paderewski. On the morning of this memorable day he had left for Lausanne and had promised to return for tea.

"I don't know why Mr. Paderewski is trying to convince me that you should write about me," Greta Garbo said, turning her white face toward me. And at that moment her blue eyes, blue as the quiet sky, were touched by the golden sunlight.

"He asked me here to arrange his papers," I said, as I watched her face develop more color. "Because he's past seventy and has played an important role in the life of his country, there are many interesting papers. Eventually I might even write a book about him, but that would be difficult and time-consuming."

"I'm sure he'll pay you well."

"He's very generous."

"Perhaps he suggested that you write about me," she said, "because I'm famous and wealthy."

"I haven't decided yet."

She pushed back her creaking chair and abruptly asked, "How much money do you want for writing a book about me?"

Without thinking, I said, "Nothing!"

Her oval face with high-boned cheeks immediately gained some extra dimension of beauty, and her eyes opened wider in a bewildered gleam. "Nothing? How can it be nothing?"

"Absolutely nothing. Besides, I don't know if I could write something real and honest about you."

"That means I'm a liar and not worth writing about."

"I don't think you're a liar, but I don't know if I'm capable of writing about you."

"Why do you doubt your capability? Mr. Paderewski said that you are a talented writer, and he praised you so very much."

"He is a musician. Like most musicians, he doesn't know anything about writing."

She looked at me and started laughing in the voice of a first tenor. I laughed too, but with a growing appreciation of something deeper in her than her humor. It was not simply her beauty that attracted me; rather it was the strangeness, the special quality of her beauty that fascinated me: the way in which her movements and her manner were touched with masculine shadows. And at this moment I imagined that God had first created a man, then a woman, and at last, after a long rest and a few mishaps, the unique creature sitting next to me. I was thinking of saying something clever on the subject, but she said, "We have not known each other for long, but we are already good for each other."

"I understand you."

"You understand me! I doubt it. We have to have some resemblance to understand each other truly or to develop a friendship. But we have to be really different to love each other."

I wondered what she was saying. Then I suddenly recalled the gist of an article in a French newspaper that I had read a few days before. It was about the conductor Leopold Stokowski, a good friend of Paderewski's, and his romantic involvement with Greta Garbo. I didn't have the courage to ask her point-blank about Stokowski, so I generalized instead. "I know how it is," I said, "with men and women."

"What are you talking about?" She stood up and moved toward the corner of the terrace as if she were trying to catch some sunbeams. There she said to herself, "The sun is shining the same way on flowers and on mud." And to me she said very loudly, almost spelling out every word, "A man gets married because he is in love."

"But a woman?"

"A woman?" And here she paused a moment. "A woman pushes herself into love because she wants to get married."

I was feeling much more confident. "Let's say openly what we're thinking about instead of playing with abstractions."

"What are *you* thinking about?" she asked.

"You won't be angry?" I said. "I am thinking I really may write a book about Paderewski—or possibly," I blurted out, "about you. I should know, however, how this Stokowski affair is going. I read in the papers that—"

Her laughter—descending from soprano to baritone—broke off my sentence as she beckoned me to the western end of the terrace. Gesturing wildly with her arms, now like a bird, now like a windmill, and finally as if she were pushing an evil spirit from her, she continued to laugh almost hysterically. I stood spellbound. Was she expressing an emotion she felt, or was she acting? Unable to distinguish her acting from her feelings, I could do nothing but admire her.

I don't know how long this moment would have lasted had it not been for the appearance of a white-haired woman servant in a black uniform. As soon as she noticed the old woman, Greta was immediately still. Our faces turned to the servant, who quietly said that Paderewski was staying overnight in Lausanne and would not be able to join us for tea or supper. She suggested that we go in and have our tea at once. Like good guests, we followed her. On the way to the sitting room we learned from the servant that Paderewski was visiting his sister, Madame Antonina Wilkonska, who was ill.

For some reason, we didn't eat anything. We did drink a little tea, though. And later, when Greta was looking at the walls full of pictures, I managed to sneak a piece of ham and black bread. We did not say anything during the whole time when we were supposed to be having the meal. We just looked at the walls, at each other, and at the display of cheeses, fruits, and cold meats.

When we had had enough of this polite companionship and no food, we silently rose from the table and went out to the garden. I first spoke on a neutral subject. "During some nights in Switzerland," I said, "the sky looks magnificent and as it does nowhere else. It looks, I might say, holy."

"Why do you think so?" she asked. She was keeping about two feet ahead of me, and I wondered if she wanted to play hide-and-seek or to run away completely. I replied, "Because on such nights, on such holy nights, the gods are christening new stars."

She stopped and turned around fast, almost tripping on a dead branch. "You are peculiar," she whispered to me. "You are young and you are peculiar."

"What do you mean?"

"I don't know myself. I am lost today. I feel at the same time unreal and crazy."

"To be really crazy is to believe in something you want while disbelieving in all those things around you others say are important." I took her hand and we started toward two huge spruce trees. Under those trees and surrounding bushes we saw dozens of birds making noise and fighting for some worms. Each was desperately trying to feed itself before going to sleep. Her eyes went from the birds to the sky, which was obscured by thick green branches. "The sun's going down," she said. "It's getting dark. Let's go back."

"That's only because the trees are covering up the day," I remarked. "Look. The birds are still foraging for food; everybody knows they don't eat at night. Then they sleep."

"You mean birds don't have supper?"

"Your naiveté is disarming." At this moment I observed that suddenly she looked more interesting. "Don't you know anything except playing in films?" I waited for her unpredictable reaction.

She smiled and replied, "Probably until this time I haven't had a good teacher."

"Your genius doesn't need teachers."

"If this thing goes further, I will have to pay a lot for your praises and attentive attitude toward me."

I again took her hand and we walked deeper into the park. The woods were redolent with the fragrance of flowers, and the needles and leaves of trees grew darker. We were walking in a silence interrupted only by the occasional murmur of birds preparing for the night. Her blond hair was gradually losing its artificial curls and was shining more against the pink skin of her cheeks. I noticed that the lobes of her ears stuck out a little through her hair and thought of what the Swedish peasants believed: that large lobes were a sign of thriftiness. This thought vanished when I read on her face that she was thinking about something, perhaps even making decisions about important matters of life. Her nostrils began to move delicately, absorbing as much park fragrance as possible. Her breaths came faster and faster as she grabbed my hand and we doubled our pace.

After a few minutes we slowed down again, and we walked for another hour or two in silence through the park's labyrinths; a sense of nature's profound peacefulness grew upon us. We began looking for the shortest path to the chalet, but it seemed as if we would never find an exit from the park. I kept saying to myself, "When we subdue our inner desires, it does not necessarily mean we have strong character; more often it is that our desires are not sufficiently strong."

Finally we reached the chalet, which, with its columns supporting the bellies of two terraces full of light, looked like a fairy-tale palace lost in deep forests. Inside, we were greeted by complete silence.

She pulled me by the hand toward her room. I didn't expect this from a woman who, according to the press, was cold and had little interest in men. I didn't know what to think, and in such cases it is better not to think. Was it the enchanted and quiet park that had excited her, or the memories it might have evoked of her experiences with men and women? I could not concentrate on the answer as she led me by the hand, with her head down and her hair covering her face.

On the walls of her room there were paintings by Monet, Cézanne, Wyczolkowski, and Kossaks; but I hardly had time to glance at them before she pulled me onto a bed covered by a quilt decorated with flowers just like those we had seen in the park.

Since her blouse didn't yield to my fingers, she helped me. I began to kiss her breasts, but I did not feel her shiver. I pulled down her skirt, unwrapping perfectly proportioned legs. Pressing my lips to hers, I began feverishly to undress. She was lying obediently and returning my kisses. I took her in my arms, and her body started to tremble as if an electric current were coursing through her. She whispered, "I don't want to have a child." But I did not think about that. And finally she abandoned the thought also.

A twenty-four-year-old man normally thinks that pleasure will last forever, but a woman is always curious as to how long a man will last with her. Although she didn't show a special ecstasy, I felt that she gradually began to like my lovemaking, which lasted minutes or hours.

Because either the rhythm or her inner feelings had become too intense, she abruptly pushed me to one side, jumped off the bed, and started doing some forceful dance exercises while singing a Swedish peasant song whose melody—but not the words—I recognized. I was startled and asked, "What are you doing?"

Without interrupting her dance, she replied, "I don't want to have a child."

"This is the way it's done?"

"They say it should be done this way. Anyhow, I don't know any other way. I saw my mother doing that." With these words, she sat down on the edge of the bed.

I don't know why, but I returned to the previous subject that had bothered me and asked her, "Did you dance in front of Stokowski too?"

"No, never."

"Why not?"

She bounded off the edge of the bed and started dancing again. "Because he didn't have enough strength and nothing came out. He was embarrassed. He was crying."

"He was crying?"

"Yes, he was crying and saying that he was a martyr to pure love and the conditions created around him and me, a martyr to the press and the crazy world."

She stopped her dance again, returned to the bed, and embraced me. "I was even more embarrassed, and I was crying too. And since it wasn't too far, I escaped to old Paderewski."

I asked, "Who was your best and most fulfilling lover?"

She became very much embarrassed and was silent for a few minutes. At last she said, "Many men and, after Moje, many women have tried to please me." Once more she fell silent, and I sensed it was difficult for her to talk. Finally she succeeded: "But first and only was Moje . . ."

"Moje?"

"You don't know who he was?"

"Besides your films I don't know much about you or your lovers," I lied.

She leaped on me and started kissing me. This eruption of intimacy greatly excited me, and I asked, "Why are you trying to please me so much? Why are you doing so much?"

"I am trying to forget."

"Forget what?"

"I don't remember anymore."

It took me quite some time to gain Greta's confidence and break down her resistance to speaking about herself. I even developed a new method. I always began by talking about my own life in all its intimate aspects. I spoke of the period when I had lived in Lvov and was close with Stiller's relatives. After an hour of this kind of conversation she would open up and speak of her relations with Moje.

My next step was to uncover her inner views about her mother and father. For that purpose I cast about in my mind for a few colorful stories about my own parents. When the moment was right, I told her details, especially intimate ones, of my family life. Greta was startled, but looking at her face, I knew she was searching for similar incidents. I was happy my approach was working, although I don't know if such a method would have been successful with a more sophisticated person.

It was rather more difficult to discuss sexual matters. I had to build upon my presumptions concerning her sexual interests, and I worked out in advance a half dozen stories about my supposed relations with women and men. On late evenings when we sat with the lights dimmed and drank champagne, I told them to her. She timidly responded with stories of her own. I would leave it at that.

It was a delicate, time-consuming operation, requiring mental agility so as not to oversell or repeat myself and provoke suspicion. Later, when I needed a fuller picture of a particular part of her life, I concentrated on small incidents, one at a time. For example, when we walked in the park, or sat in a restaurant, I would inquire about her excursions to the country and ask about her parents' arguments. From there she would go into their other habits. By creating the right atmosphere and sharing my experiences, I was able to gain even more insight than I had expected.

I told her of my relations with publishers, writers, editors, and literary agents. She reciprocated with her views on filmmaking and Hollywood. I purposely played down my role as a writer. In response, to show her superiority and feeling of achievement, she grew more open in describing her professional life. This was the only technique by which I was able to reach the depths of her soul and fathom the inner activity of her character.

As early as our second or third conversation, Garbo had emphatically opposed having any book written about her. Consequently, she did not permit me to write down anything she said; nor, later, would she allow any mechanical transcription of our conversations. I always complied with these rules. But as soon as I had said good-bye and was alone in a taxi, train, or plane, I feverishly began making a complete record of all our dialogue. Over the years I amassed a tremendous amount of basic fact and psychological observation which I tried to shape into biographical form.

Garbo often lamented that more than anything else it was the boring trivia in life that killed her time. I, as always, tried to provoke her into confessions by opposing what she said. I told her that time destroys all trivia, even that which illuminates our character, and that time is the greatest evil because it destroys human beings without offering any apologies. Then I would add, "Only a book can preserve your life and your achievements for posterity. A long time after you're gone, it will continue to fight for you." She would listen, but on her smooth alabaster face not one muscle would move in favor of my project. Instead, I saw the stubbornness she manifested at all times and in all places. This stubbornness came from her peasant background, and against such resistance ironclad logic must yield. But I was patient, very patient, and patience, they say, levels even mountains.

When, at the end of the 1950s, I came to the conclusion that I had taken enough notes and had collected enough trivia and other petty detail as well as written some pages, I started to give her biographies of great figures in science, politics, and literature of the eighteenth and nineteenth centuries. I wanted to show her that only a book can capture the past and hold it up to merciless time. She seemed to read the biographies with enjoyment. I believe she suspected nothing. I then gave her biographies of famous women with special emphasis on those who had appeared on the European stage. I waited for her reaction. I was certain that my plan would collapse if I again started pressing her about a biography of herself. She waited a long time before calling me up to say that she had exposed my sinister plan.

"What kind of plan?" I asked.

"You are writing a book about me. And I don't want any book to appear during my lifetime."

When I said nothing, she poured out some more of her soul in rougher language: "I will deny that I talked with you, I will deny that I know you, I will deny that I have even heard of you . . ." She waited for me to respond. When I again said nothing, Greta demanded, "Are you there?"

"Yes, I'm here."

"Nobody would believe you. Who are you?"

Cruelty overcame her. I knew what Moje had suffered. I gathered my thoughts together and patiently replied, "If you imagine that you will always be great, I am warning you now that you will gradually sink below the horizon of remembrance and be gone forever."

"I live as I want to," she yelled back.

"If thou livest slapdash," I said, trying to confuse her, "as thou wantest to live, thy life is trivial, thy life is flimsy and paltry."

A long pause and great silence ensued.

Even her breath could not be heard. I was certain that some very strange thoughts were roaming through Greta's head. She knew I had received nothing from her in return for my time, that I had never asked her for anything, and that I had run after her like a dog with a hanging, tired tongue. This whole business really did concern her, and I had no more words. Yet I did not wish to hang up on her.

Suddenly, after what seemed ages of waiting, I heard a faint voice: "That means that nothing will be left if I don't put everything down on paper?"

"Your films, yes, but nothing of your life; and your life is you—not what appears on the screen."

She seemed thoroughly confused, but did not wish to lose me.

"Come tomorrow," she said apologetically.

It is difficult to believe that all this began with my knowing nothing about Greta Garbo and that now, after all these years, I have completed this book—her book—the story of her life, as she told it to me, in that voice I will never forget.

Book One

PART ONE   *Keta*

1

Father

Karl Alfred Gustafsson was born not far from Stockholm in 1871 to a small Swedish farmer. The eldest of four children, he began helping with the farm work as soon as he could walk. Later he hired himself out to richer farmers in the neighborhood. Not many peasants were able to give their children an education—the children were needed to work on the farm. With Karl, it was a different story. He didn't want to study and thus barely finished third grade. He was interested in practically nothing, except making money. With his simple mind, he didn't realize that without an education or a big farm he would never get the wealth he wanted.

He grew up to be an exceptionally handsome and likable person. A little over six feet tall, he was rather thin, with short blond hair and blue eyes set close to a Grecian nose, well proportioned to his round face. He seldom laughed, but when he did he displayed a healthy set of teeth well polished by hard bread and fresh vegetables. He was a quiet, reticent person, but was especially sensitive to other people. Greta has always said that she resembles her father.

Perhaps she understands that by any standards, Karl was an attractive man who appealed to women.

As a young man Karl discovered that he could not support himself—even in a village—on character and good looks. He was capable of hard work and eager for it. Therefore at twenty-five he left for Stockholm, telling a friend who could appreciate his humor that he hoped to make his way by catching a girl from a wealthy family. Alas, to wish is easier than to achieve. At that time Stockholm was full of boys from the countryside looking for work and girls, both of which were in short supply. Karl's first job was as a butcher's helper. Soon, however, he got tired of seeing the blood and carcasses of animals he had loved in the village, and he found employment as a janitor in a poor section of the city.

Stockholm was a city with two faces. The prosperously smiling section was modern, while the ancient section wore the ugly look of poverty and exhaustion. Karl lived in Södermalm, one of the oldest, and certainly the poorest, sections, occupied by the lowest class of workers. Södermalm was famous not only for dilapidated buildings and uncollected trash, but also for its peculiar jargon, which was recognized all over Sweden.

Götgatan, the borough's main street, was its heart. In the morning the shops were full of gossiping old women and young mothers examining the day's bargains. At midday the workingmen's restaurants up and down the street threw open their doors to the hungry. After dark, dance halls rioted with the music, songs, and celebrations of people trying to escape—if only briefly—the drudgery of their lives. Karl often was among them, looking for fun or companionship or, in his drunker moments, for that rich girl he had to find. Of course he didn't find her on Götgatan, but he did discover friends, a group of men for whom drinking was the highest, almost the only, mark of sociability. "When I see a friend drunk and crying," Karl would say to himself, "I don't want him to get more upset, so I drink with him." Soon his drinking started to interfere with his work, and he was forced to change jobs frequently.

Karl was working as a street cleaner when Anna Lovisa Karlsson, a peasant girl, came to Stockholm for the same reasons as he had. She was of medium height, plump, with a head rather too large for her body. Like Karl, she was blond, but her blue eyes were deeply set and small, suggesting, according to popular belief, shrewdness and determination. And like him, Anna Lovisa was uneducated. The single job for which she was qualified, and from which she would never move on, was that of scrubwoman, laundrywoman, and general servant in the houses of the wealthy. Every evening she would return to sleep in her shabby room in the Södermalm. Often she fell asleep thinking how cruel and pointless her life was. Yet just as often she awoke the next morning with renewed determination to marry a man who was as rich as he was handsome.

Karl met her through a friend in January 1896, and in the same year they were married. Or rather, as the story goes, she forced him into marriage because she was panicky over the thought of being an old maid, and she had found a handsome and willing man. They rented a one-bedroom apartment on the fourth floor of a five-story walk-up in Södermalm. The building, off Götgatan at Blekingegatan 32, was sandwiched between two light-brick four-story buildings. In winter, when snow covered the sight and smell of the garbage, the buildings didn't look bad, but in the summer the decay and negligence were unbearable. Karl helped the janitor of his building with the cleaning, so that the house looked better than the rest on the street. He knew how much his wife cared about such things.

Indeed, Anna Lovisa was a wholly dedicated housewife, who kept their modest apartment spotlessly clean and well organized. She hung fresh white curtains on the three front windows and got some old furniture from her employer to furnish her new home. At her insistence, they started to save for a home in the country. She also persuaded Karl to cut down on his drinking. But when the children started coming, Anna gave up her attempts to save money for the country house and to save Karl from drunkenness. The first to be born, in 1900, was a healthy son, Sven. Next came a daughter, Alva, in 1904, and on September 18, 1905, the last child, a girl, was born. She was named Greta Lovisa, but for no good reason she became known at once as Keta.

Since his wife could no longer work, the responsibility of supporting the family fell completely upon Karl's shoulders. In his simple, honest way, he started to save on his own food, occasionally going for days without eating, so that he could buy *brännvin*, an inexpensive whiskey. Once again Anna used all kinds of persuasions and arguments to discourage him from drinking. Meeting with no success, she finally abandoned her reeducation efforts. Instead she concentrated on raising the children and making a little extra money for their shoes and clothes. Now and then she would leave the children by themselves and go to her former employer to pick up some linen to wash and iron overnight.

Anna's efforts didn't solve her problems with her husband. Many times the children witnessed quarrels and even physical violence between their parents. Soon they thought up a scheme for avoiding their parents' violent altercations. Sometimes Sven, at other times Alva or little Keta, kept watch on the stairs listening for their father's footfall. If he sounded unsteady, the alarm would be sounded and the three of them would dash out of the building. When Karl appeared upstairs drunk, his wife would take whatever she had in her hand at that moment—a pot, rolling pin, or frying pan—and begin beating him. Throughout this ordeal, Karl would make his way to the bedroom, where he would collapse on the bed and thrust his head under the pillow. His wife would throw herself on his body, flailing her arms, and then fall to the edge of the bed in tears.

The Gustafsson children spent all their free time in the street or in a nearby square. Alva usually didn't have any difficulty finding someone to play with, and most of the time she led the other children gently in play. Sven spent his time playing ball in the square, which was full of broken bottles, rusty iron, and piled-up garbage. Keta was different. She avoided children of her age and looked for the friendship of older people. She often walked down the street observing passersby. One day she noticed two half-drunk men who were going home after a day's work. Out of curiosity she started to follow them, listening to their conversation, which gradually developed into an argument. Keta noticed that a few children and adults were walking behind her. The two men, not content with shouting at each other in loud, sharp voices, started pushing each other. The onlookers were quick to take sides. One group was urging the tall younger man to beat up the short, fat older one. The tall one threw three or four hard, fast punches and the short one went down. When he got up, his face was covered with blood. His supporters egged on the short one. Keta, who had been watching this incident with tears in her eyes, ran to the tall man. Pulling his jacket, she asked in a pleading voice, "Why are you hitting him?"

"He insulted me and my wife," he said, spitting the words at his opponent.

Keta's courage did not fail her. She saw that everybody was looking at her, and she said, "Don't you see him bleeding? Don't you see that he is weaker? Don't you see that you are the victor?"

Losing patience with Keta, the tall drunkard shoved her aside; she fell to the ground. When she had regained her footing, the crowd had begun yelling at the fighters, "Stop it! Stop that!"

A group of boys and girls followed Keta's lead and started to pull the tall man off the short man, who was lying in his own blood. The victor, although drunk, sensed the danger of confrontation with the young people. He took one look at them and another at his victim and started to move away. The hisses and insults of the onlookers followed him.

Keta leaned over the beaten man and began cleaning his face. She felt the eyes of the admiring crowd on her back, but she didn't have the courage to meet their gaze.

Many years later, Greta Garbo said that this incident made her realize the tragic situation and misery of her parents for the first time. She realized that her parents' plight was not an isolated tragedy, but that many people's lives were filled with sorrow. She didn't know how she would free herself, but she did know that she had a strong will.

Karl Gustafsson loved his three children, but the youngest, Greta, was the apple of his eye. He always played with her, talked to her more than to anyone else, and showered her with all kinds of toys. Anything she asked of him he did—except to stop drinking. By begging and crying, Greta could get him to stop for a day or two; the following day he always returned home drunk. Karl never told Greta how disillusioned he had become with his life. He didn't have to—she could read it on his face by counting the early wrinkles.

After finishing public school, the two older children went to work. Sven, who resembled his mother very much and who, like his mother, loved sweets, worked in a candy shop. Alva, afflicted with tuberculosis, was often bedridden. When she was able to, she worked as an office girl. Each week they gave their salaries to their mother, who allowed them to keep a few kronor as pocket money. Sven and Alva were closer to their mother than was Greta, who took her father's side and tried to adopt his paternal role toward her brother and sister. From her own meager earnings and the salaries of the two older children, Anna managed to buy the food, pay the rent, and dress the children. She dressed them well, because she made many of their clothes. But Greta was not satisfied. Again and again she accused her mother of favoring her brother and sister. Whenever she quarreled with her mother, the question of Greta's attachment to her father would arise. Her mother would insinuate that Greta was not acting as a daughter to her father, but as something more.

Karl himself was indifferent to such insinuations. He had become indifferent to almost everything and everyone except his children, especially Greta. When he wasn't drinking, he slept. In his youth he had dreamed of success; nothing came of it. Instead he had three children, a nagging wife, and dreams of failure. Without an education or special training in a trade, he had moved from butcher's helper to grocery boy, from janitor to street cleaner, from one menial job to another. His only good fortune had resulted from an accident. Despite a history of childhood tuberculosis, which briefly recurred in adolescence, he had been drafted into the army during the First World War. During his first week in the army barracks, he was accidentally wounded by a fellow soldier. He was retired with a small invalid's pension, which also entitled him to buy rationed food for his family.

Karl's life had a deadly monotony. After a day of hard, dull work he would stop in at an inexpensive bar and have a few drinks. He knew that once he got home he would face an exhausting quarrel. Then he would fall into bed and sleep until the next morning, when it all began again. And so this went on, day after day, week after week, with the routine broken only when he was too sick to get up from his bed.

Her father's aimlessness was reflected in Greta's inability to excel in her studies. She loved her father and could not concentrate when he was drunk or ill or in poor spirits. She was not really interested in school, finding it boring and humiliating. The only thing she enjoyed about school was the reading of novels by Swedish authors, and often when she stayed home, her father would ask her to read to him. The work they admired most was Selma Lagerlöf's *Gösta Berling's Saga,* a two-volume collection of stories which portrayed the life of the 1830s in Värmland. In Greta's eyes Selma Lagerlöf, who received the Nobel Prize for Literature in 1909 and became the first woman member of the Swedish Academy five years later, was the greatest woman in a thoroughly male-dominated world.

When her mother discovered that Greta was not doing her best, she tried to shame her husband into a sense of responsibility toward his daughter. "If she does not do well in school, nothing will come of her as nothing has come of you. She will be a drifter and might even become a drunkard like you."

He did not reply to his wife's tirades, but when he talked to Greta, he tried to encourage her to study.

"Mother is right," he whispered to her one day. "Try to learn, try to get an occupation as soon as possible. Maybe some day you will be famous like Selma Lagerlöf."

Thirteen-year-old Greta listened to what her father said, but he could not change her attitude toward school, which had become just a series of unpleasant experiences for her. Once she came into the classroom late. The teacher was asking what were the four elements. No one raised his hand, so the teacher, seeing her sit down, asked her for an answer. Greta was seldom called on by the teacher, who was a good man and didn't wish to embarrass her. But Greta's peers were cruel and enjoyed her discomfort. When the teacher asked what were the four elements, she replied spontaneously, "Water, fire, air, and *brännvin.*"

Though sympathetic, the teacher could not help laughing with the class, although he was able to get out one question: "But please tell me, why *brännvin?*"

Greta answered, "Because when my father comes home drunk, my mother yells at him, 'You are in your element!' "

Such humiliation drove her to depreciate the value of a

formal education. "I don't have the talent or desire for learning," she told her father. "But I love to read stories and act out the characters."

"Why do you do that?" he asked, moving off his back and on to his side.

"Because I hate the life around us."

"But it is not so easy to change things. . . . You know, everybody says that I am stupid, and I have nothing to show that I am smart." When Greta tried to protest such self-disparagement, he dropped the subject of himself to talk about her: "But you are very stubborn, and because you are stubborn you will select the thing you like best to follow. Anyhow, I'm not going to be long in this world. And I have no influence on anybody, including myself."

Throughout his last winter, Karl Gustafsson spent many days in bed. One day, however, he got up and dressed. A heavy snow had immobilized Stockholm, and the city had called up every available street cleaner. Karl worked a long day, and then he stopped, as usual, at a nearby bar before facing his wife. He sat by a window, sipping his drink slowly. As he watched the silent snow fall in the blue-black night, one thought kept recurring to him— he should take his family and return to farm and village life. He was not old, and he had enjoyed working in the soil. Instead of running from his wife to bars, he might run to the fields and drink spring water. He ordered more *brännvin*, and the picture of future life in the village glowed. He thought he had solved all his problems. Outside, it had become completely dark, and the snowflakes' dance grew more frenzied.

That day Anna had returned early from her chores as a housemaid and had started supper right away. The children noticed that she looked especially excited. Sven and Alva asked her for an early supper. She glanced at them and then seemed, almost out of spite, to slow down the preparation of the meal. She was probably waiting for her husband to join them but didn't want to tell the children. She brought out the white tablecloth, and Sven and Alva concluded that there would be something special for supper to celebrate their father's return to work. Now there would be more money for food and clothing, and perhaps they could eventually buy a little cottage in the country.

While the others were dreaming about the good days ahead, Greta slipped quietly out of the apartment. Pushing open the outer door of the building, she stepped into the blizzard through which two figures were moving like ghosts. As they passed by her, she—though wrapped in her coat—shivered to see how their faces were covered with frost and snow. Then she wondered which way she should go, or to which bar, to find her father. Her eyes rested on the square in front of the house that looked so desolate and dirty in summer; now it was blanketed in clean white. She recalled how her father, coming back from work, used to pick her up in the square and take her to buy some candies or magazines full of photographs of theatrical and film actresses at Agnes Lind's tobacco shop. He always let her have all the magazines she wanted, which meant as many as she could carry. Sometimes he hadn't had enough money to pay for their purchases, and he would make an arrangement with the shopkeeper to pay for them the next day, saying to Greta, "Don't deprive yourself of things you would like to do or enjoy. Who knows, you might find your real future in them."

The currents of rushing snow momentarily swirled back from the middle of the square, revealing a prone figure. She ran forward, but even before she reached the fallen body, she knew who it was. She grasped her father by the hand and began to tug at his arm. She knelt down and placed his limp arms over her shoulders and wrapped her arms around his chest. Several times she tried with all her strength to pull him up. At last she got him to his feet, though he clung so tightly to her that for a moment she thought they both would fall. His face was blue and his eyes were closed. Greta was frightened.

"Please, Father, please try to come with me," she pleaded, not knowing whether he could hear her. "Please try to walk."

Her father said nothing, but he was leaning less heavily upon her and had opened his eyes. The snow whirled against them as they began to move, Greta dragging him on step by step.

The distance from the center of the square to the door of the house, which she usually covered in a couple of minutes, took them together perhaps fifteen minutes. At last they reached the hall, and sat on the bottom step to rest. Greta put his head on her shoulder; his heavy breathing scared her. Her first thought was to leave him there, run up the four flights, and call mother, Sven, and Alva to help her bring Father into the apartment. "Oh, no," she thought, "as soon as Mother sees Father she will start yelling and cursing and the whole building will be on the stairs. They will laugh and jeer." So she helped him up and placed his hand on the rail; she put her arm around his waist, and with all her energy she started to push him up.

It was a long and painful climb, one she felt would never end. On each landing they stopped, sat down, and rested. It took them ten minutes to climb the stairs. When Greta opened the apartment door, she saw Anna, Alva, and Sven sitting at the table eating supper.

Anna looked at her husband and daughter and yelled, "You are drunk! I hate you!" She turned back to the table and resumed eating. She always began her tirades with those two sentences: "You are drunk! I hate you!" After that she usually started beating him. But not this time. Neither Alva nor Sven moved from the table to help Greta. Alone she dragged her father to bed, put him down gently, removed his wet coat and shoes, and covered him with a blanket. With her last remaining strength, she sat down on the edge of the bed and started sobbing. Anna and her two older children remained at the table and finished their supper.

The next morning the snow was still falling. Karl Alfred Gustafsson did not get up to go to work. He was dead at forty-eight years of age. The year was 1920, a most important and tragic year for Greta.

2

The Dream

"K-e-t-a! Ke-ta! Keta! . . . Greta!"

I tried to ignore my mother's voice. I was dancing in an orange garden full of flowers and exotic aromas and lovely songs and soothing sun. I looked around, and instead of the thick features of my mother, I saw the delicate faces of many beautiful women who were dressed in colorful silk gowns; they were dancing with me to the music. Among them I recognized Sarah Bernhardt, Eleonora Duse, and Helena Modjeska. But my mother's voice grew louder and beat harder against my brain. Suddenly a quick jab knocked me off the bed to the floor, and I woke up. My mother stood over me yelling, "Keta! Keta! Greta! It's getting late. You have to go to work. Nothing will come of you!"

I opened my eyes and said angrily, "Why did you wake me up from a beautiful dream?"

I was angry at my mother. I was mad at my life. I never had time for myself or my dreams.

As far back as I can reach with my memory, I dreamed about oranges, which were my ideal fruits and the source of good things. Perhaps I was enchanted by them because they were scarce and expensive; or there may be other mysterious reasons for their charm. I do know that in my childhood oranges were a symbol of wealth, success, and exquisite taste. They excited me when I noticed them in vegetable stores. I would imagine that I saw them guarded so closely by the storekeeper that nobody could possibly steal them. When I did manage to steal or buy an orange, I would take it home right away and hide it under the bed. After everyone had gone out, I would take it out, place it on the floor, and observe its texture and color for many minutes. I would caress it with my fingers and look for a weak spot where I could pierce the skin, which was full of sun and the fragrance of faraway countries.

When I was peeling the thick skin, I would feel on my face a mist of juice which invigorated me. Peeling the fruit was like searching in a mysterious forest for castles or digging into your soul for undreamed dreams and fascinating stories. But the greatest experience was when I quartered a naked orange. On each quarter I would see the faces of actors from the past or of those about whom I had read in newspapers and magazines. I thought they would eat oranges for breakfast, dinner, and supper. And if they were very famous, I thought they would have baskets and baskets of these fruits. I identified the oranges themselves with females, never with males. Once I saw my father on an orange quarter—he was dancing with me in a garden; we were surrounded by flowers and beautiful women. I told no one about my experiences, except my family; I thought other people would think that something was wrong with me and would laugh at me.

I regret most talking to my mother about my world of oranges. Soon I felt that she had repeated my dreams to her pastor and to our neighbors. When I thought they had started to look at me in a strange manner, I stopped telling my dreams to my family, since I could not trust them, particularly my mother. Oranges became more and more a part of my secret life. I decided to have at least one every day. Each time I went out I would carry an orange in my pocket, touching it from time to time for assurance. This talisman gave me strength to live and the feeling that someday I would be famous and have hundreds and thousands of oranges.

I will never forget the first time my mother interrupted

my dream about oranges. I think I began then to develop a real hatred for her. I began to believe that she wanted to thwart all my aspirations and plans. Unlike me, she lived completely in the present. Perhaps she never thought about my future; I don't think she ever thought much about her own. For her, dreaming about fame and recognition was a stupid and sick way to live. She was always saying, "The most important thing is how much money you get for your work. Don't think about your future. Kronor! Money is the source of happiness!"

I remember that when I was about four years old, we all spent a few days in the village of Finnaryd, where my father was born. It was a very dry summer. Vegetables in the gardens were dying of thirst. And everybody was saying that some cataclysm was approaching, since no one ever remembered such a dry summer. During midday dinner my mother said to Father and us, "Rain is money, money is rain." As always, Father said nothing. He kept his head bent over the bowl of soup, waiting for more wisdom from my mother. Alva repeated what mother had said, "Rain is money, money is rain," and like an echo, Sven followed. Being so young, I didn't understand.

The next morning when I got up it was pouring. I ran to the kitchen, grabbed an empty pail, and went to the garden to catch some rain. Outside I discovered that it took only minutes with the help of a gutter spout to catch a half a pail of heaven's money. It took some strength to bring the pail inside. When I appeared in the kitchen, completely wet and with mud-coated shoes, Mother was standing in the middle of the room, holding a stick. I approached her smiling, but she yelled, "Why did you ruin your dress and your shoes? Why are you so stupid?" And she began to hit me with the stick.

I was confused and hurt, and with a bitter smile I said, "I went out to get money. Now you will be able to buy a new dress and new shoes and clothes for all of us."

When she heard the word "money," she stopped hitting me and asked, "Where is this money?"

"In the pail," I said.

She glared at me and in an angry voice yelled, "In the pail you have nothing but water!"

"But, Mother, it's rainwater, and yesterday you said that 'rain is money, money is rain.' "

She didn't even smile before she started beating me again. I withstood the beating without crying or saying a word. And all the time my mind was bursting with three words and inwardly screaming to my mother, "I hate you! I hate you! I hate you!"

Imagine a simple, ordinary orange: how could it create so many problems for me and hold so many secrets and mysteries?

3

Tvålflicka and the Pastor

Einar Widebäck, the owner of the barbershop on Horns-gatan in Södermalm, was a friend of Karl Gustafsson's. After Karl's death, Einar offered his widow, Anna, a loan. Instead, Anna asked him to help her get a job as a cleaning woman in the home of one of his rich customers. And she suggested that he hire Greta to work in his barbershop as a soap-lather girl, or *tvålflicka*.

Greta's work consisted of soaping the customers' faces, hanging towels, and cleaning the barber's tools. For a long week's work in Widebäck's barbershop, she received seven kronor and tips amounting to less than two kronor. She would give her mother the seven and keep the two for herself. She used this small sum to purchase theater and movie tickets and, above all, magazines about the lives of actors and actresses, which she studied more earnestly than she had any schoolbook. Above her bed, which stood in the northwest corner of her room near the window, were pictures of many actors and actresses. Among them were Norma Talmadge, William S. Hart, Clara Kimball Young, Thomas Meighan, and others, both American and Swedish.

Her frequently changing fancy resulted in a glue-stained wall that became the subject of many arguments between Greta and her mother. But Greta stood firm, and her gallery remained.

At fourteen, Greta was already five feet six inches tall. She was physically, except for her small breasts, well developed, and she acted in a mature fashion. Despite her mother's opposition, she went out each night after work and a light supper and stood in front of two neighborhood theaters, the Mosebacke and the Söder, to look at the displays of photographs. Sometimes she was able to slip backstage. She was determined to learn the craft of acting through reading, observing, and talking with theater people. Indeed, since her ninth year she had promised herself that if she could not be a princess, she would be a famous actress. In pursuit of her own career, she would follow a famous actor for miles to observe him. The time was slow in coming when she would have the courage to speak to the illustrious man; usually she would lose her power of speech. But occasionally the actor, seeing the bashful girl watching him, would initiate a conversation. And often enough to thrill Greta, he would invite her to his theater.

But though she occasionally met people prominent in the theater, Greta grew more and more frustrated. She wanted to share greater intimacy with the actors she admired. Now and then she could achieve momentary and vicarious closeness to her favorite actors by enjoying herself sexually as she hid under covers with their photos. If she could not perform with them on stage, at least she could act out a private and fantasized role with them. When her mother discovered what she was doing, she tried to reason with her. She suggested that she see a doctor or the pastor, but Greta refused. Rather, whenever her mother caught her, she would run from the apartment to the house of a girlfriend, Eva Blomkvist.

At last her mother decided to take more drastic measures. One day, when Greta went out into the corridor to the toilet, her mother waited to see how long she would be. After ten minutes she walked quietly into the corridor and abruptly threw open the door to the toilet. There sat Greta, one hand holding a photograph and the other hand between her legs. Her mother grabbed her by the hair and pulled her down the corridor to the apartment, yelling, "You have to go to church! You have to go to church!"

When they were inside, her mother started beating her with both fists. Greta made no response; she did not try to defend herself or run away. She stood erect as her mother struck her, almost as if she were proud of her humiliation. Her mother's anger subsided into exhaustion; with sore fists and perspiring face she moved to the nearest chair. Without any feeling whatsoever, Greta watched her mother slump into the chair and hold her head in her overworked hands. She was relieved, however, that Sven and Alva were not home, because they might tell their friends what had happened. But she was afraid that her mother would tell Mrs. Widebäck about her sexual "problems." Mr. Widebäck would tell his customers, and eventually the whole neighborhood would know. So Greta found herself a new barbershop job, and then one in a vegetable store on Götgatan.

One morning, on her way to work, she met Pastor Hjalmar Ahlfeldt on the street. He had confirmed her, and he always had a kind greeting for her. "Good morning. I see you are no longer working at Mr. Widebäck's establishment."

"Good morning," she replied, averting her eyes. "I prefer the smell of vegetables and fruits to that of men."

"But I also see that you are not coming to church."

"No. God left me because I am poor, and if I am poor I am not needed in your church."

"Keta, Keta," said the gray-haired pastor, taking her by the arm, "I see your mother was right when she said that you are impatient and arrogant."

"Please tell me what is wrong with me," she asked.

"Probably very little," he replied. "I know you want to be an actress. Just remember that the road to the theater or to the films will not be paved with fights with your mother."

Greta listened to this wisdom in silence. When she had to leave, he gave her arm a little squeeze and said, "I'll try to help you. I know many people in various walks of life."

She suddenly looked up and murmured, "If so, help me get a job at Bergström's department store."

"You mean you don't want to be an actress, but a salesgirl at PUB?"

Unafraid to confirm everyone's belief in her arrogance,

she replied, "First, I have to have bread, and money enough to get my mother off my back. Then I can think about acting."

"That's a sensible approach. The one thing I have against you is your sharp tongue—although you do not speak much—and your rude behavior."

"Everybody tells me that," she said gaining confidence. "But for some reason everyone takes pity on me, promising everything, and after that there is nothing."

"You are right. You have to judge people by their actions."

Pastor Ahlfeldt understood her, not only because she was simple and direct but also because her mother had talked with him about her many times. He had realized from these conversations, however, that Mrs. Gustafsson was primarily interested in sympathy and only secondarily in getting help for Greta.

"Paul Bergström and his family come to my church regularly. I also see Captain Lars Ring, who makes all kinds of films. Next Sunday I will speak to both of them about you. Maybe something will come of it."

Greta turned skeptical. "Please don't bother yourself, Pastor. As I said, many people have promised to help me. But here I am. I can only rely upon and trust myself; even my father taught me to depend upon myself."

"You know," said the pastor, "it's good to have strong faith in God and less faith in people."

"A beautiful philosophy, Pastor, but where does it get me?"

He let her arm go. "I think I have lost this argument with you. In a few days I shall let you know what I've been able to do. In the meantime, God be with you."

Greta and the pastor politely nodded to each other and walked in different directions. He turned and looked back until her shabby black coat disappeared around the corner. He had known thousands of people in his long life of pastoral service; he had helped hundreds of them solve their problems. And yet this simple girl had made a special impression on him. "When we are young," he thought, "we try to change the whole world. When we are old we try, for no particular reason, to change the young." But rather than attempt to change her, the pastor decided to help Greta.

4

"Kalle"

My first real contact with the theater—or at least, with a professional actor—occurred when I was fifteen. It happened without anyone's help.

The Mosebacke Theater, in the working-class district where I was born and lived, was presenting a very popular revue, *The Count of Söder,* with Carl Brisson in the leading role. Almost every girl in Stockholm was collecting photographs of "Kalle," as we called this elegant and handsome actor. Many girls loved him secretly, and I was not an exception. Born Kalle Pedersen, he was a Dane who had started his career as a boxer. As I remember him, he was tall, with curly blond hair and big blue eyes. He was a good dancer, piano player, and singer. He was also an exceptionally fine dramatic actor.

Every krona I saved was spent on tickets. Dressed in my best white blouse and well-pressed dark-red skirt, I tried to attract Kalle's attention by sitting in the first row and eagerly joining in the applause for him. Before the show began and after the final curtain fell, I stood at the backstage door to catch a glimpse of him. When he emerged, he smiled radiantly at the sea of girls awaiting him until a path opened through our midst. I never doubted that he was smiling at me alone.

One evening I decided that I would have to do something drastic in order to meet him. I bought my usual first-row seat, and when the curtain went up and he appeared on stage, I started clapping loudly and nervously. I lost my head and clapped for what seemed like a long time. He looked at me and smiled. I smiled back and yelled, "I love you, Kalle!" The whole audience turned toward me and started clapping. At that moment I thought it would be better for me to be swallowed up by the earth than to be sitting there. I was so ashamed that I stopped clapping, put my head down, and placed my hands over it. Throughout the entire performance I remained in the same position with my eyes closed. Only the sounds of Kalle's voice and the music comforted me.

A few minutes before the play ended, somebody tapped me on the shoulder. I looked up and saw the old backstage doorman. He whispered, "Please follow me." The audience was spellbound by the performance, but I followed the old man with eyes fixed on his black uniform. I was humiliated, because I thought the management was throwing me out and would warn the attendants not to let me in again.

After walking slowly through corridors and up and down stairs, I was led into a dressing room. The doorman said in the same hushed voice, "Please wait here." I didn't ask why I was there. I hadn't had much time to think the matter through, and the attendant was already on the other side of the door. I sat on the edge of a chair, again with my head down and almost touching my breasts, which were padded with cotton. At that moment I discovered that my "breasts" were not even. I tried to adjust them, first with my chin, next with my hands. Just then, the door opened. I jerked my head up and saw "my" Kalle beaming.

"Good evening," he said. "Good evening." I replied in a voice that I could barely hear.

"You said you loved me. Is that true?"

Putting my head farther down, I felt my cheeks burning. He approached me, delicately stroked my hair, and said, "Put your hands down. Show me your face."

I did what he asked. He looked at my face, my shoulders, and then he said, "You are strikingly beautiful."

I didn't say anything, but I felt goose pimples over my whole body. And yet I was gaining courage. This was my first chance, and perhaps my last, to talk with this famous actor; I felt I had to say something.

Then he asked me, "You want to play in the theater, I presume?"

"Yes," I replied.

I was thinking he hadn't heard me when he said, "If you want to act, you have to have courage. That is the first prerequisite of being a professional actor."

"Don't I have it?" I asked.

He pulled his chair over to face mine and sat down. "You may," he responded with some hesitation, as if he didn't want to discourage me; "but yelling doesn't mean you have courage."

"I read, I study various plays, and I go to the theater." My boldness was overcoming my timidity.

"This is something else. I like your seriousness."

"My girlfriends say that I am arrogant and shrewd."

"I haven't noticed those traits, but they are important ones for an aspiring actress to have."

He was quiet and kept observing me with a look of ironic detachment. Finally he said, "At least you are very honest. That's a good beginning, though I don't know what will happen later."

He went to a table and picked up a book. I watched him leaf through it for a few minutes until he found the passage he was looking for.

"Read this, please," he said.

I took the book from him with shaking hands. It was Shakespeare's *Merry Wives of Windsor*. I glanced very quickly through the first pages of the play. I could see that he was impatient. He must have been trying to put me under stress to see how I would react.

"What are you waiting for?" he said. "Read. Read!"

In a subdued voice I began to read the dialogues between Mistress Ford and Mistress Page, Robin and Falstaff. I varied my voice to indicate differences of character. I thought that I was doing pretty well. Suddenly he interrupted me. "You have talent," he said. "Despite that, you still must go to dramatic school."

I fell silent again, holding the book in my left hand and keeping my eyes on the floor. Then, for no apparent reason, he began singing. "Here is the girl from Södermalm, / Slender and gentle as a desert palm . . ." He stretched out his hand and pushed my chin up, and I looked into his eyes for the first time. He stopped singing and started to laugh. Although I felt there was distance in his mirth, it was nevertheless friendly. Cutting short his laughter, he said, "Perhaps you would like to have supper with me?"

"I am not hungry, and since I have to go to work tomorrow, I must go home and get to bed."

"What kind of work do you do?"

"Practically nothing. I am ashamed to talk about it. It's like any work that doesn't have something to do with the theater. Just work."

"Won't you change your mind about having supper with me?"

"No, thank you. I have to go home."

"Then leave me your address."

"For what?"

"I may be able to help you."

"I will be in the theater tomorrow. My name is Greta Gustafsson," I said, rising from the chair. As I walked toward the door, he approached me and kissed my left cheek. Before I realized it, I was running through ugly streets that I imagined were meadows near the hamlet, where I had visited my relatives last year. The hard sidewalk seemed soft with flowers and grass, and in the distance I saw the shores of Årsta inlet. The cold wind which bit my face seemed to carry the fragrance of the countryside in spring. It was winter in Stockholm, but an altogether different season in my heart. A cold night was coming on, but for me it was an early summer morning.

When I reached Blekingegatan 32, I leaped up the stairs, two at a time, to our apartment. Opening the door, I quietly entered the dark silence in which my mother, sister, and brother were sleeping. But there was neither darkness nor silence in my mind. As I took off my shoes, I could hear the murmur of applause—for me. I got into my bed, and there across the room, across the lighted stage, stood Kalle. I improvised a marriage scene with him. I closed my eyes and found myself in a luxurious apartment and, moments later, on a yacht. Gradually all these scenes, full of color and laughter and drama, flowed together to give me an exhilarating sense of joy and satisfaction. As I drifted into sleep, dreams completely superseded reality: I was a rich and married actress.

But reality would come tomorrow, when my mother's shouts would wake me. After a hurried breakfast and a few more barks from her, I would be on the street rushing into another meaningless day. She would call me back to monotony, to boredom, to the anxieties of my real life. And that is why I have often thought that children should have no mothers.

5

A Threat

Despite the arrogance and distrust Greta had displayed toward him, Pastor Ahlfeldt helped her get her first bit part in films. He knew that her sister, Alva, was also interested in acting, and so he recommended both girls as extras for *En Lyckoriddare* (A Soldier of Fortune), directed by John Brunius. Each sister received twenty kronor, something like five dollars, for her work. More important to Greta than her salary was the discovery that she was extremely photogenic. Brunius assured Greta of this when he gave her a few dozen of the best prints, saying, "These could prove useful to you in securing future jobs in films." Nothing more, however, came from the goodwill of Brunius.

In July 1920, Pastor Ahlfeldt found work for Greta as a salesgirl at PUB, Bergström's department store. He had spoken highly of her to Lars Ring, the retired army officer who was very active in the Swedish film industry and at the moment was directing promotional shorts for this huge Stockholm store. Captain Ring told the pastor that he would speak with his producer, Hasse W. Tullberg, about finding work for Greta in one of his films.

Meanwhile, Greta made many friends among the sales-girls and department managers; her quiet air and her diligence won the admiration of her co-workers, who also thought her special because she was an aspiring actress.

In early 1921, Captain Ring came to the department store accompanied by the actress Aga Andersson. He announced that he would be making an advertising film. A few minutes later his technical crew arrived. The salesgirls hurried to put on fresh makeup. Some of them tried to get as close as possible to the camera, hoping to be in the film.

Greta was different. She handed a photograph of herself to her girlfriend Eva Blomkvist and then disappeared into the stockroom. But Eva was not successful in reaching Captain Ring. However, to everyone's surprise, Ring asked the store manager to bring Greta Gustafsson to him. The manager, with the help of other salesgirls, started to look for her, but she wasn't to be found at her counter. She was not in the ladies' room or the stockroom. The manager, David Fischer, had in his youth played some minor acting roles; he went himself to look for Miss Gustafsson. He thought that if he was the first to find her, all the girls and Greta would remember him as the one who had transmitted her first offer to act.

Finally the elusive Greta suddenly appeared. "Captain," she said quietly, "one of the girls said that you are looking for me." Glancing at her alabaster-textured face, he noticed two things: large wide-open blue eyes and shiny white teeth with the front two sticking out.

"The girl will be good in our films," he whispered to Miss Andersson.

"Almost every girl is good for you. It is something else to play in one of your films."

"I will use her," he said.

Miss Andersson continued to object: "You have no part for her."

Captain Ring didn't listen to his jealous companion; he ordered Greta to change quickly into a costume suitable for riding in a motorcar and return to the set of his promotional film, *How Not to Dress.* She turned around and disappeared. The captain said to those nearest him, "With such a face, such eyes, and such movement of the body, that girl could play the role that Lili Ziedner usually takes in her variety shows. We must help her go to the Royal Dramatic Academy. And I must introduce her to some theatrical people."

Aga broke in, "In other words you are taking her under your wing—and your blanket."

There was no time for more comments and arguments, because Greta appeared in her new costume. All eyes turned toward her. Aga Andersson remarked that Greta was fat and clumsy, but Ring ignored her and began shooting right away. In two minutes Greta's outfit for motoring had been wire-pulled into a habit for horseback riding, much to the amusement of the audience and to the discomfort of her character.

"Remember," he said to Aga, "this is only an advertising film. The girl's face will come out beautifully; it will be fine."

Greta had overheard their conversation and felt sick, since she realized that jealousy, conniving, and bitterness poisoned not only family life but also other human endeavors. Once again she was learning that in order to have any success in life she would have to swallow bitterness, abuse, and even degradation. Although she didn't allow this realization to show on her face, Ring sensed her mood.

"Please don't mind us," he said. "We always talk like this. Remember, when you succeed in getting into the acting profession you will hear many negative things about yourself. To develop strength you must listen to those critical remarks and remain quiet. After you have gotten the upper hand and have become stronger and more secure in your position, then you can start talking against other people. If you don't talk and relieve yourself of the tension, you will go crazy. And then, good-bye to your career."

Greta kept an astonished silence. Ring changed the subject—"Hand me a piece of paper and a pencil." She reached to the counter and picked up her pad and pencil.

"Give me your address. We will send you payment for this appearance. I would also like to give your address to certain people who might prove helpful to you."

He took her hand and thanked her, and Greta went back to her work. A few months later Ring asked her to appear in *Our Daily Bread*, an advertising film for the Co-operative Society of Stockholm. Aga Andersson, seeing a competitor in this inexperienced girl, became upset.

"I have to act quickly," she must have said to herself, "before anything serious arises between her and Lars." The situation soon grew urgent. Aga discovered that her lover planned to employ Greta in a full-length feature film. She was to have an important role along with Aga. Aga knew, however, that she could not compete with an attractive young girl. She therefore decided upon drastic measures. First, she hired a detective to spy on Lars. Second, she sent a letter to Greta asking her to come to her house to discuss a new film.

Knowing that Miss Andersson was not her friend, Greta read the letter with surprise and suspicion. At times she thought that Miss Andersson wanted to stop her advancing career; at other moments, she was not so sure. Nevertheless, Greta was curious; she would go to see Miss Andersson, who lived near Björns Gardens. It was a cold fall day, but Greta, though lightly dressed, did not feel the chill.

Aga Andersson's apartment consisted of four rooms exquisitely furnished in the Louis XVI style down to the smallest detail. When the door opened, Greta saw before her a middle-aged, blond, plump woman attired in a gold-embroidered green dress. She was so professionally made up that she could have stepped onto a stage. With the friendliest of greetings she ushered Greta toward a small table where food and wine had been laid out.

"Let's have something to eat and drink," her hostess said.

"Not now, thank you," Greta replied.

"Aren't you hungry?"

"Yes, I guess I am, but I cannot eat now," said Greta, handing her her coat.

"Why not? Do sit down and have something to eat."

Greta obediently sat down and said, "I am extremely curious about what you want to discuss with me."

"We will eat and we will talk. Would you like some wine?" asked her hostess, reaching for a bottle.

"No, thank you, but you shouldn't deprive yourself."

Aga poured herself a glass of wine, and after taking a few sips, she began, "When I was your age, I wrote in my diary."

"I don't keep one," Greta said softly.

"Older women like me collect the addresses of men," Aga continued.

Greta wondered what this small talk was all about, but she decided to play along with her hostess. Smiling, she said, "I don't know any men well enough to keep their addresses."

Miss Andersson filled her own glass again. "Won't you change your mind and have a drink?" she said. "And do have some sliced beef or fish."

Greta felt that Aga had something important to say but did not know how to begin. She thought that if she agreed to eat something, a real conversation might begin. She took a piece of bread and, ignoring the serving fork, picked up a slice of smoked salmon with her fingers. When Aga saw that Greta had taken her first bite, she started to talk differently. "I used to collect the addresses of many men. It was my great hobby; it was almost an occupation. But now I have only one address in my book."

"Lars Ring's?"

"Yes. Greta, please, may I call you Keta, as your friends do?"

Greta could not respond, since her mouth was full of bread and salmon. The hostess pushed a glass of wine toward her. "You are just eating bread and fish. Why don't you have a drink?"

"I don't drink before a revelation."

"In love there is no such thing as a revelation, only stubborn faith and trust. I am faithful to Lars!"

"I believe you. But what does this have to do with me?" asked Greta, sensing that her hostess was getting drunk.

"In my grown-up world they say that a man is admired for all the good things he does, while a woman is admired for all the bad things she refuses to do." Once more she filled her own glass, insisting, "Have a drink with me."

Finally Greta lifted her glass, touched it to that of her hostess, and slowly took two sips.

"Although I have tried many men," the older woman said in her nasal voice, "now I am faithful to Lars. But I am not saying what I wanted to say." She started to stutter. "Lars, after meeting you, is becoming more and more cool toward me. He is always saying that he must help his 'poor Söder *flicka.*' "

Greta stopped eating and murmured, "I haven't asked him for anything."

"I know. You didn't have the opportunity to do so, but I noticed how you were shifting your behind in front of him when we were getting dressed for the film."

Greta rose from the table with the intention of taking her coat and leaving. Suddenly her hostess grabbed her by the arm. "Sit down!" she commanded. "Don't go! I haven't finished yet."

Greta yanked her arm from the grip of the older woman and, without moving, said, "I do not intend to listen to insulting talk."

"That was not an insult. That was the honest truth. You have encouraged him."

"It is not my fault that he was looking for me at PUB. I was not looking for him."

"I know that. Pastor Ahlfeldt was responsible for that. He wants you, your sister, and your brother to be independent; and he himself would like to take your mother to his home as his housekeeper and mistress."

Greta was astounded by this revelation. She had neither the words nor the strength to respond. She stood like a dead, dried-out tree in the middle of an enormous field. Tears welled up in her eyes. Trying to hold them back, she barely prevented herself from collapsing to the floor. Aga continued to yell, "I know! I've checked and rechecked the whole story. I know!"

Greta regained her composure and quietly said, "Why are you attacking me?"

"You're a Söder *flicka,* and a Söder *flicka,* if she goes after a rich and famous man, will always get him."

"That's ridiculous."

None of these things were her doing, she thought. She hadn't asked Lars Ring to help her, and she hadn't asked Pastor Ahlfeldt to help her. Both men had had their own motives for being interested in her. She sat down again, put her hands over her face, and sobbed. Aga knelt before her and started comforting her in a hoarse voice. "Perhaps it isn't your fault," she said, "but please avoid Lars. If you need money, I will lend it to you. If you need any kind of help, I will go out of my way to help you. Just avoid Lars. I am afraid of being alone, and Lars is my whole life."

Keeping her head in her hands, Greta said nothing. She didn't move, but she did stop crying. All kinds of thoughts came to her head about her mother and the pastor. She had very little feeling left for anyone. Now she understood the situation in which she found herself: her mother quarreled with her because she wanted to get rid of her. But why did she quarrel more with her than with Alva and Sven? That was a mystery. Then there was Pastor Ahlfeldt, who, while pretending to be a man of God, was like any other man. Did everyone run after money and sex? It appeared so.

"Why are you silent?" asked Aga, struggling up from her knees. "If you do not accept my offer, I will destroy you." Her voice was dry, tight, and full of hate.

Greta thought, "I guess I want to escape from people and live with the wind and the rain and a crackling fire. Yet even in this dream I hear my mother's harsh voice."

"Say something! Say something!" shouted Aga. She staggered to the table, poured herself another drink, and in a single gulp, fortified herself to return to her victim. "Why don't you open your mouth? Say that you agree to my proposition!"

Aga waited for a few seconds and then grabbed Greta by the hair and dragged her down to the floor. Greta jumped to her feet and ran to the door, but Aga caught her and pulled her down again. They started rolling, and Greta attempted to free herself. She began to beat Aga back. For a moment she thought she was fighting with her mother. However, this time, instead of being on the receiving end of a beating, she was administering one. Feeling the pain of Greta's fists, Aga doubled her blows. Both women groaned and breathed heavily as they tumbled into chairs; each tried to get onto her feet.

Aga felt that she was losing the battle. She lurched to the table and grabbed one of the bottles. Seeing her chance, Greta leaped to her feet, snatched up her coat, and ran to the door. She opened it and sprang into the empty corridor.

Aga, bottle raised, appeared at the doorway and shouted loudly, "Evil bitch! I will kill you. I will kill you."

Greta, impelled by the force of these words, ran even faster. In seconds, the sharp, cold wind was once again biting her face. She did not feel it much; the sting of Aga's words hurt more.

6

The Fledgling

I was perhaps four or five years old. Sven and Alva were not home. I was pretending to be asleep in my corner bed. My mother, complaining of the heat, had stripped herself completely. She began walking around the room, shaking her fat body and swaying breasts. Father was lying on the bed fully dressed and didn't pay any attention. He was not excited by the idea of having intercourse with a woman who was always quarreling with him. But my mother was stubborn. She went to the kitchen cabinet, pulled out a bottle of *brännvin*, poured a glass, went to Father's bed, and handed it to him with two words: "Drink this." He did not need encouragement. He grabbed the glass and finished it in one gulp. "Give me another."

Mother ran to the kitchen cabinet. She filled the glass, this time almost to the brim, and in the process of a quick delivery, spilled a third of it. I was peeking from under the covers, feeling that something important was about to happen, maybe even a reconciliation between father and mother. Again Father gulped down the *brännvin*; Mother picked up the empty glass and walked the few steps to place it on the kitchen table. When she returned, she discovered that Father had turned his face to the wall and was snoring.

"Wake up!" yelled Mother, hanging over him with her breasts touching his back. "Wake up!" she shouted louder. Although Father stopped snoring, he didn't move. Mother started hammering on his back with her fists. His body rocked under her strong fists, but he continued to lie with his face to the wall. Suddenly Mother jumped off the bed, grabbed a chair, and hit him on the back and head. The chair broke into pieces, and Mother became hysterical. She ran through the house, screaming, "You are a drunkard and a fraud! You can do it with other women but not with me!" Again and again she repeated, "You are a drunkard and a fraud! You can do it with other women but not with me!" As she became more hysterical, she ran around the room in circles, all the time rubbing her stomach, her breasts, and her head. Finally I decided to rouse myself and sit on the edge of my bed. I wasn't sure how to react to such a scene, so I stared motionlessly at my father. I had seen my mother nude many times, and her nakedness was of no interest to me. I was curious, however, about my father's reaction to this peculiar situation.

I didn't have to wait long, because almost on my command, he got up. There was blood on his face where he had been hit by the chair. As blood trickled down his forehead to his left cheek, he moved toward the door with unsteady steps and disappeared. Mother, standing in the middle of the room, kept looking at the walls and avoided my gaze. Her eyes were red and full of madness. She didn't cry. She stood there for a few minutes and, in a trance, went to the chair on which her dress and other garments were spread. She started putting them on. Having dressed, she took an empty coal sack and went around the room collecting pieces of the broken chair. When she had finished picking up even the smallest splinters, she tied the top of the sack in a knot and put it under the bed on which Father had been lying just a little while before.

Sven and Alva returned home and asked about Father. Mother replied, "As always, he hasn't arrived yet. He's probably out drinking."

I yelled from my bed, "You're lying!"

She rushed toward me and started hammering on me with her fists. I don't know what would have happened if my brother and sister had not pulled her off. In such moments she always seemed to need someone to prevent her from committing more violent acts.

About this time Mother began her other sexual career. I noticed that she began to work only for the rich. In order to convince herself and us that she had good reason for preferring to work in the homes of the wealthy, she would say, "In wealthy houses they don't bargain about salary." Although she had always worked with her hands, she held in contempt other people who had to do so. The rich were different; they were smart, good, and honest. She always urged my sister and me to marry rich men. That was why she tried to prevent us from going out with neighborhood boys. Her reasoning was simple. "Don't lose your virginity," she would say. "When you marry a rich man, you will be able to bring your innocence as a dowry." This philosophy she repeated two or three times a week. My sister always agreed with her for the sake of keeping peace in the house, but she let me know that she didn't really believe in Mother's way of reasoning. Despite this, I never liked to hear Alva agreeing with Mother. When I heard them talking about how to get a rich man, I would recall my mother's vain efforts to arouse my father.

I don't know whether there was any real connection between Mother's philosophy and that scene. I do know that the scene stayed alive in my imagination for years and influenced my attitudes toward both males and females I liked. I was ashamed because I had seen it. I was ashamed for Mother because she had to dance nude and beat Father with a chair. And I was ashamed for Father most of all. I felt pity for him, and my pity was mixed with guilt and with a sense of feminine superiority. Furthermore, after I discovered that Mother was having an affair with Pastor Ahlfeldt, my attitude toward religion changed. I quickly lost the little appetite for holiness I had had. This trinity of father, mother, and pastor weighed heavily upon my mind. I started to develop feelings of disgust about sexual intercourse. When I thought about it, I felt pain in my stomach, weakness over my whole body, and a desire to vomit. But I was never bothered by the fact that I had similar sexual feelings for both boys and girls. On the shores of Årsta inlet, which I managed to visit for a few weekends each summer, I would watch with fascination the play of nude boys and girls. I admired the boys as they ran along the shore. I equally admired the girls lying on the grass, and I would sometimes imagine that they were waiting for me, my companionship, my tender kisses. In these fantasies I imagined that I was receiving caresses from both boys and girls. But when it came to real situations, I would lose my nerve and run away to hide. Girl friends and boy friends quickly noticed my bashfulness.

One summer day my sister, Alva, asked me to help her build a tent with blankets. I loved to play with her, so I agreed to help. We used two big gray blankets, which we spread over bushes and then pinned to the ground. When the tent had been set up and the inside covered with soft grass, Alva went in and pulled me after her. We were both dressed in swimsuits, and almost at some mysterious command we simultaneously started to pull down our black suits. We said nothing to each other because as sisters we knew everything we were supposed to know about each other and about our bodies. Alva drew me to her side and embraced me with her left arm while her right hand tickled me between the legs. In a sweet whisper she urged me to do the same to her. I followed her lead. Our experiences in the blanket tent were a revelation to me.

One day, while I was waiting in the tent for Alva, a local boy peeked in. When he saw me naked, he said, "I know what you do with your sister, but I will show you how to do the real thing." I was very much embarrassed, and a mixture of fear and admiration for the boy, who was getting undressed, froze my limbs. I didn't say anything, and I didn't move when he jumped on me and started pushing his penis between my legs. But he was clumsy and spilled everything on my stomach. Then I discovered that he could caress me in the same way that my sister did. Although it was a pleasant experience, there was not much intimacy, because he was a stranger to me and I didn't know what to expect.

From then on I dreamed many times about a mature man with experience who would have the vigor of a boy but an adult's polished methods. Strangely enough, I also dreamed about women of my mother's age who were ideal lovers. These dreams came superimposed one on another. Sometimes the masculine element was dominant, sometimes the feminine one. At other times I wasn't sure. And many times in dreams, I saw a female body with male organs or a male body with female ones. These pictures, blended together in my mind, occasionally brought pleasure but more often pain. I can use only one word to describe my sexual attitudes: confusion. I have never thought about sex as the means of increasing the population. For me sex has always been a source of pleasure, though I have approached this source hesitantly. Confusion causes reluctance, and feelings of sexual confusion engulfed my body from early childhood to old age. I don't think I could ever live with either a man or a woman for a long time. Male and female are attractive to my mind, but when it comes to the sexual act I am afraid. In every situation I need a lot of stimulation before I am conquered by the forces of passion and lust. But confusion, before and after, is the dominant factor. When I was with a young girl I dreamed about a young man, and the reverse. After the final act, I always felt empty and unfulfilled. If I were to analyze myself, I would say that the source of all this confusion was the relationship that existed between my parents.

To make up for my sexual shortcomings, or, if you wish, my double desire, I had a tremendous urge to act on the stage or in films. This brought my mind, my subconscious, some sense of balance, order, and happiness. What is more, and however foolish it might sound, acting on stage and in front of cameras was a sexual experience for me. Because of this I feel I acted fantastically for the public. When I touched my partner's face, or hand, or leg, I felt great. When a partner hugged or kissed me, I felt pleasure in my stomach. Directors, cameramen, technicians, actors, looking at me sweating under the hot electric lights, were thinking, "Here's how Garbo plays." But for me it was a sheer sexual experience, and my complete secret. Maybe this pure emotional experience mixed with deep sexual satisfaction is the basis of my creativity.

I started early in advertising films, and Lars Ring liked my work very much. However, Aga prevented me from developing a professional relationship with this enterprising man. There was no way out for me but to keep my job as a salesgirl in Bergström's. But since I spent long evenings hanging around the Dramatic Academy, I found it hard to go to my job in the morning. Sometimes I would not show up for work at all. My friends in the school, Mimi Pollak, Curt Andersson, and Lena Cederström, were constantly occupied with dramatic study. I was jealous of both their freedom to do so and their great opportunities. In the meantime, the manager of my department, Mr. Fischer, noting my increasing absenteeism, began to warn me of dismissal. Finally it came. "I cannot tolerate you any longer in the store," he said. "I have to cover up your poor work, your tardiness, your long lunch periods, and the days you take off. I might lose my own job because of you."

I will never know why, but three days later I was called back to the store and told that I could have my job back on the condition that I become a more diligent employee. I said I would try. However, by that time I had decided that nothing was going to stand in the way of my own dramatic education—not even a job that I needed. I continued to go to the academy every day, occasionally during a long lunch period, most often after work, to gossip with friends, to observe the coaching sessions, and to listen to a bit of dialogue between young actors. I was especially attentive when they were being directed by the head of the school, Frans Enwall, or his daughter Signe, a dramatic coach. Gustaf Molander, who later became the director of the school when Mr. Enwall was taken sick, was another great teacher. Moreover, in the corridors of the school I often saw professional actors and directors who played nights in Stockholm theaters. During the day they visited the school to share their experiences with the young aspirants.

One day, while walking through the corridors, I caught a glimpse of the tall, slightly stooping figure of Mauritz Stiller, who was soon to become the center of my life. I had admired his face, and his strange eyes, on posters and in newspapers and magazines; I had attended plays that were shaped by his mysteriously commanding direction. But I had never seen him as closely as I did that day in the corridors of the dramatic school. I could even smell the eau de cologne he applied so lavishly.

Frans Enwall saw me many times in the school. One day

he approached me and said, "You spend much time in the corridors, and it seems to me you are interested in everything going on in school. I do not know your name, but I'd like to."

I was startled by the forwardness of this illustrious director. Before I had an opportunity to respond, he said in a most pleasant voice, gently touching my arm at the same moment, "Don't be upset or scared. I just want to know your name. You look as if you should become an actress."

"Greta Gustafsson," I replied, looking at the group of girls and boys in heated discussion a few feet away.

He repeated my name as if he were thinking of something else. "Oh, I recall that Carl Brisson mentioned your name. You intend to begin courses in our school soon, don't you?"

"Yes. But during the day I have to work, so I cannot attend school regularly. I must work to eat."

He noticed that I wanted to say something more; perhaps he sensed the self-pity in my voice. So he took me by the arm, saying, "Let's go into my office and talk about it."

As I obediently walked beside him, the students turned to watch us, wondering why the great Frans Enwall was showing interest in me, even though I had not yet officially auditioned for the academy.

When we entered his office, he asked me to sit down and then said, "I don't know why you didn't come in sooner to get some advice." Turning in his chair, he reached for a book on the shelf behind him. "Here," he said, "select a scene from this and read for me. Brisson told me you have talent."

Paying no attention to the compliment, I took the book and started leafing through it. It was *Madame Sans-Gêne*, by the French dramatist Victorien Sardou. Fortunately, I had read the play twice before, once with Mimi Pollak and a second time when I couldn't find a novel by Selma Lagerlöf at the library. Naturally, I acted as if I had never seen the play before. I was still looking for an appropriate scene to read when he took the book from me and impatiently pointed out one to me, saying, "Read this."

The reading trial went well, and Enwall said to me, "You have talent and a beautiful voice." I felt happy inside, but said only, "Thank you. Thank you."

"I will give you private lessons at your convenience," he continued. "When I do not have the time, my daughter Signe will substitute for me." I wanted to thank him again, but he had more to say. "You should work in acting. Last week I talked with Erik Petschler, a film producer who is looking for young actresses. With your permission, I should like to recommend you."

I was so overwhelmed by Frans Enwall's words that I grabbed his old hand and kissed it. He was extremely moved and said, "You don't have to do that. You don't have to be apologetic for your talent. Your talent doesn't need to beg. And my duty is to help you. Otherwise I should not be running this school."

During the spring of 1922, the time when my real acting career began, I went to Enwall's office or home for private lessons. When he could not meet with me, Signe, who normally taught advanced students, coached me. Together they taught me practically everything about acting. They tutored me in reading, diction, stage movements, and singing. We started first on Lagerlöf's *The Fledgling* and *Wedding at Ulvåsa*. When we had mastered these works, we graduated to Sardou and Shakespeare. I worked hard on these texts and spent many sleepless nights because I was determined to keep my job at PUB. This job remained the primary source of my financial independence; it also provided money with which I could buy presents for Signe and her father. The entire business brought me to a state of nervous exhaustion. I knew that I might collapse completely if I continued to push myself, but I felt strongly that I should try to repay them in some way. That was a major reason for my keeping the job at the department store. In the beginning, I bought a pipe for Enwall and a pair of gloves for his daughter. I soon tried to bring him something every month. On their birthdays, I gave a good woolen sweater to Enwall and an Italian lace blouse to Signe. They accepted these gifts readily, but I have to admit that they also asked questions. My reply was simple. I was an employee at a store that gave me a high discount on its merchandise. This was only partly true. Usually I would buy one present with the discount and hide the other on my person. I justified my stealing by telling myself that the Enwalls were generous people who, having done so much for me, deserved the gifts. I would also say to myself, "When I get a scholarship to the Royal Dramatic Academy, I will be more independent of the Enwalls."

Because I understood that I could get the scholarship only if they gave me a good recommendation, I decided to buy them really expensive going-away presents. By April I had selected a cashmere vest for Enwall and a red silk gown for Signe. Then I discovered that those two presents would cost me practically a year's salary, so buying them was out of the question. And yet I wanted to give them the gifts because of the scholarship. So one day I took the dress from the floor and carried it into the manager's office. I hid it behind a bookcase full of account books and papers. I knew the place was safe because even if somebody found the dress, I couldn't be blamed for its odd presence. A few days later I selected a beautiful brown vest and successfully hid it with the dress. The next problem was how to get the items out of the store. At first I thought of asking Sven and Alva to help; they could drop into the store, put on the clothes, and leave. Since they would both be wearing coats, they could get away with it. But then it occurred to me that they would know I was a thief. On the other hand, if they decided to assist me, either one might get caught. If they were arrested and jailed, they would never forgive me for destroying their reputations and careers. And I doubted whether I could forgive myself if that misfortune happened.

David Fischer was the manager of my department at that time. It was said that he was related to the popular stage actor Josef Fischer, and he always talked about the dramatic arts. From the time that Lars Ring started to make advertising films at PUB, Fischer considered me something special. Very often he would stop at my counter to talk with me. Knowing of his interests, I decided to wait until the next time he became sick and his office would be empty. Then I would sneak in under the pretext of taking him a book or a play and leave with the garments hidden on me.

I waited a week or two, but Fischer was more regular than ever. I found myself getting nervous again. This situation bothered me so much that some of my nights thereafter were entirely devoted to thinking about how I would get the garments out. I thought I might ask Fischer to let me have them on credit and that he might agree because of his love for the theater.

I had by now convinced myself that I was being exploited, because I made such a small salary, and therefore I deserved a raise. The raise would take the form of the hidden clothes. Fischer's lunch hour was meticulously regular, and it seemed conceivable that I could perform the little miracle of removing the articles from the store while he was out.

I selected a particularly sunny day, because on such days Fischer took an extra ten minutes for a stroll in the streets. When I saw him go out, I picked up a pair of gloves, pretending that I was going to his office to ask for a discount. I carried the long black coat that I had worn that morning to work. Once in the office, I dropped everything and slipped into the gown. The dress was longer than my coat, and I quickly pinned it up. I slipped on the brown vest and then put on my coat. All the while I was shaking and kept saying to myself, to give myself courage, "They are exploiting me. They are exploiting me. They are exploiting me." My conscience stopped bothering me, and I walked normally out of the office and through the store. When I had reached the door, I was grabbed by a tall man who whispered, "Greta Gustafsson, what do you have under your coat?"

"Nothing," I said, terrified.

He kept a tight grip on my arm and said, "Let's go to Mr. Fischer."

There was no way of getting away from him, so I had to cooperate. I didn't know whether anyone was watching, but my cheeks were feverish and I was shaking like a dry leaf.

The detective knocked on the door, and when there was no answer he opened it and pushed me in. "Wait here," he said, leaving the room. I heard him lock the door. In a couple of minutes I had regained my strength by repeating my litany, "They are exploiting me. They are exploiting me." I took off the vest and gown, folded them nicely, and placed them on Fischer's desk. As soon as I had put my coat back on, I heard the manager and the detective at the door. They entered without a word. Finally the manager turned to the detective and said, "Please leave us alone."

When the other man had left the room, Fischer said to me, "What's happened to you? You've hardly begun your career and already you're ending it." I didn't say anything as I stood before him with my head down. Tears poured down my cheeks and fell to the floor. "You are only seventeen, and yet everything is now behind you; you are finished." I have never sobbed as loudly and hysterically as I did then. I was alone with no one to turn to. My mother would not be sympathetic; neither would my brother, my sister, or my friends.

Mr. Fischer stopped talking, and I saw his worried face through my tears. He was probably thinking, "What can I do? I can't ignore her theft. The store detective might go around and talk." Then I thought, "How can I face my co-workers? How am I to resolve this mess?" Suddenly, despair became strength. There are people who in a tragic situation, one without apparent resolution, come to rely on some mysterious power which allows them to keep their balance and helps them solve their problem. I was determined to be one of them. Although I was still crying, I ran through a little speech in my head. "Mr. Fischer," I said to myself, "I took these two garments and I brought them to your office because I was thinking of buying them for my sister and my brother." This sounded like a good excuse until it occurred to me what he might reply, "You are lying. The detective caught you at the exit when you tried to sneak out without paying."

"Nothing will help me," I thought, watching Fischer get up and arrange some papers on his desk. Lifting his head and turning to me, he said, "Come here and sign this." He put his pen on top of the paper and walked out of the office. I haltingly approached the desk, signed the paper, and returned to where I had been standing in front of the desk. Suddenly the door opened and he appeared with the store detective. Taking the paper from the desk, he handed it to the store detective. "As you can see, Miss Gustafsson signed this paper the day before yesterday. I let her have the vest and the dress for a few days to show her mother and sister."

I was astonished and felt like hugging Fischer. But I didn't move from my place in order to show respect for my superiors.

"But why was she sneaking out with the garments under her coat?" asked the detective.

"Have you ever seen a young girl on the street at noon

dressed in a long red gown?" Fischer asked him in reply. And after a pause, he added, with a trace of a smile on his face, "And on top of the gown, a man's vest?"

"To tell the truth, I never have."

"So you see, the mystery is solved. And if I hear from anyone in the store about this incident, I will know right away that you've been talking. I won't look kindly on any indiscretion."

"I understand," the detective replied emphatically.

"Complete professional secrecy, do you understand? Between you and me."

"Yes, yes, Mr. Fischer."

And with those words he left the office. During this dialogue I stood and searched for a way to express my gratitude to David Fischer. But he didn't wait for my response. Instead he came forward with a new revelation. "I know that from time to time you have taken small things from the store for your theatrical friends. I have closed my eyes to this activity. I know that since you do not pay for your lessons in kronor, you want to pay with something else. But to steal the most expensive dress in the place—this is beyond my comprehension. What do you want me to do? Do you want me to lose my job too?"

We looked at each other in silence for a long time. A ray of sunlight broke through the window and brightened the room. Both of us were surprised. He smiled and, glancing out the window, began to speak. "Let me try to explain why I protected you," he said. "As I have told you before, I have been in love with the theater all my life. When I was very young, I dreamed of becoming a great actor. But dreams are not real life—at least, not all of it. So when I took this job and gave up my hope of acting, I decided to develop another fantasy—that Josef Fischer, a truly great actor, was a relative of mine. In fact, I don't know him and he does not know me. And there are other stories like that which I have told about myself, pretending to be what I couldn't be. I would admit to being a cheat and a thief and worse if doing so would make me more of an actor in the eyes of others. So I can understand stealing when it is done out of a love of theater."

Another long silence, which I was too weak to break,

filled the room. I felt as if this were all part of a dream over which I had no control.

"You know what I am going to do?" he asked, moving around his desk and toward me. I shook my head. "I shall let you go. As far as I am concerned, none of this ever happened."

"Thank you," I managed to say as I started to leave.

"Wait a moment," he said to me. "I believe that someday you will be a great actress. And because I have no family, and no one will remember me when I am gone, I will do something else for you."

I saw that he was excited and breathing hard. I wanted to tell him how much I liked him before he said anything else. But it seemed to me that I had swallowed my tongue. My mind itself was like a blank slate.

"Next week when everything is back to normal, you will come to my office and you will find two beautifully wrapped packages. One will be addressed to Professor Frans, with an 's,' Enwall; the other will be for his daughter."

I opened my mouth to thank him, but I was unable to speak. Instead, for the first time in my life I felt tears of joy roll down my cheeks. He went on, "You don't have to pay for these things because I know that you are learning a lot from the Enwalls, and no money can buy that kind of knowledge for a crazy, inspired girl like you."

I had no idea that he knew so much about my school and my attitudes toward life and art.

"Besides these gifts, you may also select presents for your mother, sister, and brother. When you have selected what you want for them, let me know, and I will arrange it so that you don't have to pay for them. But please do me the great favor of never showing up again in this store after you leave. If you work here any longer, not only will I lose my job, but instead of playing in the Royal Dramatic Theater, you will be acting in jail."

That was the end of my career in Paul Bergström's department store. Years later, when I met some relatives of David Fischer's, I had a tremendous urge to tell them of his kindness. But somehow, as on that day, I could not find the words.

My brother, Sven, tried to help me in my career with advice and sometimes with small loans. He once asked, "Why do you avoid Lars Ring and Carl Brisson? You know that they can help you."

"I know that."

"So why don't you see them?"

"I think they are too intelligent for me."

"What do you mean by that?"

"When I do not agree with them on life and relations with women, they consider me stupid. And when I agree with their opinions about girls, I get panicky."

"You mean they want to sleep with you in return for the help they can give you in the theater?"

"It hasn't reached that stage, but I feel it is definitely going in that direction."

"Maybe it is your imagination. Anyhow, be smart," my brother warned. "A girl like you, who has so much talent, should not do such things. When you start that way, you will end by going with everybody, boys and girls, men and women. In the end you will be worn out, having only a bad taste in your mouth and no career in front of you."

I wondered why he talked like this to me. Perhaps he knew something about my sexual inclinations—maybe more than anyone else. One thing he could not know was that I had lost my job. Alva and Mother didn't know either. Every morning I got up, dressed, and after a hurried breakfast, said I was going to work. Instead I went around the city visiting friends and spending most of my time in Frans Enwall's school. One day I received a letter from Erik Petschler, in which he asked me to come to his house to discuss a minor role in a film. He mentioned in his letter that three people had recommended me: Enwall, Brisson, and Ring. I was happy now, having grown tired of fooling my family and myself. I knew I had been going nowhere.

From the gossip I picked up, I knew that Petschler was a tall, elegant *bon vivant*, that he wore light-colored suits and pigskin gloves and smoked cigars. He had been seen many times and in many places with good-looking young girls. Everyone wondered how he found the time to work on his films. As soon as I appeared in his house that afternoon, he said to me, "I am going to make a film called *Peter the Tramp.* I will play the leading role and direct it myself. I have twenty thousand kronor to start off with, and I will pay you fifteen kronor a day."

I was dumbfounded. No one had ever spoken to me like this at a first meeting, and on the doorstep at that. I recovered quickly and replied, "Thank you. What must I do for my salary, and when do I start?"

"Come inside, take off your coat, and we will discuss the details."

At this point I recalled the conversation with my brother and considered turning around and leaving. But my host was polite, so I sat down on the edge of the couch and waited for the scene to unfold.

"We shall begin the film in Djurgården. Later we will travel to Dalarö to take bathing shots."

"And what kind of film are you planning?"

"A comedy in the manner of the American filmmaker Mack Sennett. I might even try to act a little bit like Charlie Chaplin. I don't know yet. I'm still trying to figure out my own role."

"It sounds very interesting," I said, trying to act as mature as an experienced woman should. But I was thinking, "What role am I going to play? When will you start paying me those fifteen kronor?"

Petschler continued, "I will have adventures with the mayor, his wife, and their three daughters. I haven't worked out the complete scenario, but you'll play one of the daughters."

So I discovered that at least I would not be playing the mayor or his wife. He moved close to me and put his hand on my knee, "You are young. How old are you?"

"Almost seventeen," I replied, moving to the corner of the couch.

"Very young, and even more beautiful. And very inexperienced in films."

"So why do you wish to engage me?"

"I've heard that you have great potential. You have beautiful eyes placed in an Anglo-Saxon face. Your hands are fantastic. Your legs are good too. But your feet are a little bit too large; we will have to avoid them with the camera. . . ."

I didn't let him finish describing me. With unusual

courage, I interrupted. "You don't need an actress. You need a girlfriend." With those words I got up, ready to leave the house. But he grabbed me by the hand and pulled me back down to the couch, saying, "Don't be silly. If I wanted a girl, I can have any one in Stockholm. But I need an actress whom I can mold to greatness."

I decided to remain on the couch, though at some distance from him. "If you need an actress, then why are you talking like this? Why do you talk about physical appearance in such a way?"

"Because I don't know you. Your movements, your body, your coordination, everything in your physical appearance says that you can be a very important actress someday. Besides that, Kalle Brisson, Lars, and even old Frans Enwall say the same thing."

"*Tack*, Mr. Brisson; *tack*, Mr. Enwall; *tack*, Captain Ring; and *tack*, Mr. Petschler. Isn't it enough that I say 'Thank you' to everybody?"

I hadn't allowed him to be fresh with me this time, nor had I given him any hope for the future. Still, I received the role in *Peter the Tramp*. Although the story was trivial and the filmmaking unimpressive, I did enjoy working with the two actresses who played my sisters. I felt triumphant, and also exceptionally happy knowing that I would have some extra money.

The film's premiere was in the Odeon Theater in Stockholm on December 26, 1922. The papers said that I was a good actress with an Anglo-Saxon appearance which would give me a bright future.

As a result of this film, I became popular; people started to recognize me on the street. This first real work, though in a minor role, gave me further incentive to read and study the Swedish classics. I also began to read French and English plays and to digest them one by one. Signe doubled her efforts to teach me as much as I could learn. She went out of her way to introduce me to various people at the Royal Dramatic Academy; through her I met Gustaf Molander, the new director of the school.

Once I had been introduced to the actors' circle in Stockholm, I began to pay more attention to my dresses and especially to my shoes, which I bought in good stores in order to disguise my big feet. Although I suffered a lot because the shoes were small, I shrugged off the pain for the sake of art.

The tight shoes were not the only thing that hurt. I was painfully aware of my need for someone in whom I could intimately confide, someone with whom I could discuss both my successes and my failures. When I tried to talk about my minor achievements with acquaintances, they would often sneer at me. For all I knew, they were jealous. But perhaps I was wrong for taking pride in the few things I had done. I do not understand why I couldn't talk more freely with my brother or sister. I suspected that they too were jealous of me. Therefore I was left completely to myself for advice and comfort. My joys I enjoyed alone; my pains I suffered privately. And for answers to my doubts and questions, I looked inside, believing they could be found nowhere else.

7

Exams

Signe prepared me well for the Royal Dramatic Academy. But despite her training and the study I had done on my own, I still felt nervous about the entrance examination. When I thought about it, I would feel perspiration all over my body. The day of the examination, Signe gave me plenty of black coffee and many encouraging words. I was still in a state of panic, because I thought that if I failed the exam, I would fail at everything. It was August, a sunny day. In my heart, however, there was darkness; in my mind, despair.

I knew that Molander, who was director of the school and liked me very much, would be at the examination. In addition, there would be four professors from the school. I had no illusion that they would all like me. The sixth judge would be an observer from Svensk Filmindustri. Even if all six were sympathetic to me, I knew that they could choose only a few entrants from among the many applicants taking the exam.

"You know Ibsen, Lagerlöf, Sardou quite well, and even some Shakespeare," Signe reassured me. "I am sure they will ask to have you read or act from the first three. And those you know especially well."

I thought that this meant little when I was feeling more faint every moment. Signe kept me in the schoolroom that she had inherited from her father. She tried her best to calm me. "You are in such a terrible state," she said, "because you are waiting. As soon as they call you in, you will gain strength and your nervous system will calm down. I am convinced that you will pass the exam."

Signe walked around me and kept looking at me. She knew that I was on the verge of collapse, and she also recognized that her words could do little. A new thought came to my mind, and I said to this blond, plump woman, "What will happen if I do not pass the exam?"

"Nothing will happen. Svensk Filmindustri will engage you anyhow. You know they are constantly looking for young actresses."

"Why me, even if I fail?"

"You are tall and have a beautiful face and shoulders. Those qualities and your smile will charm them."

"What about my big feet? My masculine gait? My two front teeth that stick out?"

"If you are aware of those things, I am sure you can correct them. Your two front teeth can be replaced by false ones. Your long strides can be shortened if you think about the way you walk. You complain about your big feet. They don't seem that big to me. If the director finds that they are too big, he will order the cameraman not to photograph them."

"I see you have an answer for everything," I said to Signe as she peeked out the door into the corridor. "But you can't convince me."

She was trying to determine how long it would be until I had to go and meet the examiners' eyes. When she turned back, I asked her the name of the representative from Svensk Filmindustri. "Mauritz Stiller," she replied, proud that such a distinguished director was visiting the school.

I was surprised that he was taking part in the examination. Although I had dreamed of meeting him and knew him by sight, I had not expected that I would ever perform before him. I had seen him many times walking on the street, or driving his fast yellow car. And I had seen him in the theater a few times, once at PUB, and once at the academy. He was tall, maybe over six feet two inches, and thin.

His face was taut and ascetic, and under his prominent nose was a well-trimmed mustache. His most striking feature was his black eyes, the right one having a slight cast. Before he asked anyone a question, he always seemed to pierce the person with those eyes.

People observing him on the street or in a theater remarked on his English clothes, which he wore with as much poise and elegance as a British lord.

I don't know why I thought about Stiller in such minute detail at that crucial moment before the examination. However, my musings brought both distraction and relief, and for a few seconds I forgot about the exam. All at once a strange feeling rushed through my body, and I said to myself, "This whole business doesn't mean anything to me." I began to exercise, and Signe looked at me and asked, "Do you always do things like that when you are with people?"

"No. But I've discovered that when I'm upset and nervous, physical exercise brings me release. My body is revitalized and my soul takes courage. Doing this may help me show off my talents better."

I noticed a strangeness in Signe's look. "Do you think I'm crazy?" I asked.

"No. But I do think you are a very religious girl."

"I have never been religious, and although I am simple and even stupid, I don't believe in life after death—if you think that is the cornerstone of religion."

"No, but I think you believe in your soul."

"I have no idea what you mean by soul, but in addition to my body I have desires, emotions, aspirations, and so on. I put these things together and call them my soul. And I try to make this soul the master of my body. Exercising gives my soul room to float around, and I gain more confidence in myself."

Again Signe went to the door, opened it, and looked out into the corridor. Turning back quickly, she saw me jumping up and down in my white dress. She said with a smile, "Stop those crazy gymnastics. You really are an odd girl. Pull yourself together and leave right away. You are next for the examination."

I can't say whether the exercise had worked its spell or whether I was calmed by our silly talk about the soul, but when I entered the examining room I seemed to be in a dream. I approached the dais, which was covered with a green cloth, and bowed my head. Then I looked to its center, where Molander was sitting. He was saying something to me as I glanced to the left and saw Mauritz Stiller, dressed in a gray suit with a red carnation in his lapel. His strange eyes caught mine, and for the first time I had eye conversation with a forty-year-old man. Our eye contact put me into a kind of trance. Thereafter I felt quite strong.

After I finished my exam, I completely forgot what had gone on during our visual encounter. I vaguely remembered that I was first asked to read a scene from Ibsen's *Lady from the Sea*. This was followed by a few personal questions and a general discussion of acting. After that I recited a scene from *Wedding at Ulvåsa*, by Selma Lagerlöf. As a final test, I read with someone I cannot recall a dialogue from Sardou's *Madame Sans-Gêne*. The three-hour experience passed quickly. I was not nervous, for I didn't perspire. Nor did I think about the people around me except as a series of eyes. I had no thought of doing well.

The next day we continued the examination, going from monologues and dialogues to group acting before the jury. There were more questions about my personal life and about my attitudes toward acting and school. Again I was completely cool and indifferent. I attributed my calmness to a long, cold bath I had taken the night before. In the morning I had exercised strenuously for more than half an hour. My roles were usually played emotionally, but now I played them coolly. When the judges looked at me with special attention, I told myself that they were looking at my beautiful red dress. And I went on with my part.

Rather abruptly, all the examinees were discharged by the commission except me. Mauritz Stiller got up from his chair and walked slowly toward me, eyeing me from head to foot. He reached my side and whispered in my ear, "I would like to see you in Svensk Filmindustri." His voice was so forceful that I almost fainted. He returned to his seat with the same slow pace with which he usually walked. I tried to stand still, but I thought I would collapse from dizziness at any moment. My head was spinning, and my body was covered with goose pimples. I knew I would be disgraced if I lost consciousness and fell to the floor. Then I heard Molander saying, "You can go."

Without looking at anyone or saying anything, I walked from the dais to the door. The walk seemed to stretch for miles. Signe Enwall and Mimi Pollak were waiting for me in the corridor. With some envy in her voice, Mimi said, "You certainly had nerve to wear a red dress for the examination."

I came to my senses clearly enough to say, "I did it because I thought everybody would look at my dress and not at my feet."

"You're conceited."

"Don't you remember? You yourself said that I had big feet."

"And you are also shrewd and insulting," said Mimi in anger. She spun around and left.

"Pay no attention to her," said Signe. "There are girls who can't stand competition, even in dresses."

"That doesn't matter to me. I don't feel guilty. I wouldn't go through those tortures again for any amount of money or fame."

"Well, I don't think you should worry. You've gone through them for the last time."

"How do you know?"

"I'm sure you will be accepted by the school."

She was right. A couple of weeks later I received a letter stating that I had been accepted on full scholarship. In September I would go for formal registration.

I immediately started to think about how I would modify the school's curriculum. I felt that fencing, gymnastics, and dancing were not necessary for the education of an actress. I told myself that I would have to do something about those courses, because I needed time to earn money and to read modern plays.

While I gave some thought to my studies, I gave far more to Mauritz Stiller. His eyes were before me day and night, breaking into my waking and sleeping dreams. At times they seemed to invite; at other times they were stern and distant. They were always intensely commanding. And each time I felt his gaze, I said to myself, "I will never forget you."

PART TWO   *Moje*

8

The Birth of a Genius

The man who gave Greta Garbo her name and fashioned her into perhaps the greatest film actress in history was Mauritz Stiller. There are two distinct versions of his origins. One, which has been popularized, is that he was born of Russian-Jewish parents in Helsinki on July 17, 1883. The other is that he was born in Lvov on May 21, 1882, of Polish-Jewish parents.

Questions concerning the origin of many other prominent cultural figures who were born in Eastern Europe before the First World War are unsettled or at best remain cloudy. I myself had an illustrative experience. In the fall of 1938, arriving from Europe, I brought a personal letter to the well-known publisher Alfred A. Knopf from his nephew in Lvov, who begged his uncle to help him come to America just as Mr. Knopf himself had been brought to New York by relatives. When I delivered the letter, Mr. Knopf read it in my presence in his Madison Avenue office and promised to take care of his relatives in Eastern Europe with whom he had spent his youth. I was surprised when I read later in *Who's Who in America* that Alfred A. Knopf was born in New York City.

In the case of Stiller, I am assuming, in these pages, the Polish version of his origins, since I knew some of his relatives and friends in Poland before the Second World War. I feel that the book, being about Greta Garbo, will not suffer if Stiller's place of birth is not settled, even though we are talking about a man who influenced a great actress. His actual origins cannot have had an impact on the future of his relations with Garbo, only on the perspective through which he expressed his art.

I still have hope of settling the question of his birthplace once and for all, because his character and his work in film fascinate me. I feel that through intensified efforts, a complete story of Mauritz Stiller can be presented in the future.

We do know that Stiller's parents died before he was five years old. His Polish mother, Mieczyslawa Kraszewska, commited suicide a month before his father, Abraham, died of an incurable illness. The Katzmann family took him under their wing. When he learned about the circumstances of his parents' deaths, he changed his name back to Stiller and asked that he be called Mauritz instead of Moyshe.

From early childhood, Mauritz was interested in the arts and theater. No inducement would make him take up the family business. He was at the top of his class in school, but his real interests lay in acting. When the need arose to organize a theatrical enterprise, Mauritz was the natural leader and the hardest worker. Everybody liked him, not only because he was tall and good-looking but also because he was friendly and ready to help with schoolwork or any extracurricular activity. Nobody knew why he was learning Russian and German in addition to Polish and Yiddish. Yet it was evident that he learned them quickly. At last, someone asked about his interest in languages. "I like to read plays in their original languages," he replied.

When he was eighteen, Mauritz organized an amateur theater, which he called Maska. With a group of other young people of various nationalities, he presented plays, sometimes in Polish, Yiddish, and Ukrainian and occasionally in German, although he didn't like the German-speaking Austrians very much. The Maska Theater was soon visited by people active in professional dramatic companies, and Mauritz was offered a job in the municipal theater. But he refused the position, saying, "I would like to travel over a larger body of water, over oceans." Not long afterward, he left for Warsaw, and as soon as he had learned everything about theater in the Polish capital, he moved to St. Petersburg, and then to Helsinki.

He discovered that Helsinki was a cultural tundra. To make his living he worked as a messenger, a tailor's helper, and a coal carrier. He lived in a basement where rats were his companions. Dampness and the smell of cooking disturbed his sleep. Unable to secure wealthy patrons, he could not organize the small theater he had planned. Hard work, poverty, and his longing to leave Helsinki made him sick. He stopped working and spent his days and nights lying in bed thinking of ways to escape from Helsinki.

After long deliberation he decided to go to the local Social Democratic Club and ask for help, saying that he was a political refugee from St. Petersburg.

At the club he met Andrei Andreyevich Platonov, a Russian doctor. Platonov discovered that Stiller was a fellow Jew and befriended him. The doctor noticed Stiller's anxious and run-down condition and questioned him. Stiller explained his illness succinctly: "I am afraid of rats."

The doctor answered, "Being afraid of rats is normal, but you are physically ill. You should go to a hospital for an examination."

"I'm afraid of the police, so I can't sign into a hospital. Since you've been kind enough to offer to examine me, perhaps you would come to my room."

Platonov visited him the next day. After making his examination, the doctor told him that he had tuberculosis. He offered to arrange a trip to the Crimea. There, in the proper surroundings, Mauritz could rid himself of disease through rest, good food, and medical attention. Stiller, however, said he would prefer to be helped on his way to Stockholm or Paris, where he could take care of himself.

In subsequent visits, Platonov discovered that Mauritz became panicky and paled when he saw rats. He was also subject to violent attacks of sneezing and incapacitating headaches. The doctor began to think that he was mentally ill and inadvertently revealed his opinion. Stiller calmly corrected him: "You would react the same way if rats slept in your bed and crawled over you at night, if you saw them eating your food, and if you could never escape from their noise and filth."

Stiller took to walking the streets for hours. He would look for restaurants where he could eat in exchange for washing dishes. Late at night he would return to his rat-infested room and dream of a new life. He knew that he could not go on much longer without work or career prospects.

Growing more desperate daily, and faced with the dire prospect, as Russia then controlled Finland, of being drafted into the Tsarist army, he decided that he must go to Stockholm, where theater was flourishing. He had also read newspaper accounts of the film industry that was beginning to develop there, and he thought he might manage to find work in films. Since he had a facility for learning languages, Stiller worried little about learning Swedish. His big problem was raising money. He recalled that Platonov was always bragging about his rich Jewish, Finnish, and Russian patients. "There is no honest way to get their money quickly," he told himself. "They won't give it to me just because I ask. I will have to develop some kind of swindle."

For a week he considered various projects, and then the right one came to him. He would organize a phony film corporation in Helsinki. If he could get financial support from some of the doctor's wealthy friends, he would tell them that he was going to Berlin to buy equipment, but instead he would make off with their money to Sweden. During the next month Stiller spent most of his time in the library reading about filmmaking in Sweden, Germany, and America. He studied the technical aspects of photography and directing. When he was ready, he went to Platonov and presented his plan: "I'm about to organize a big motion-picture corporation, and I'd like you to serve as president."

The old doctor stared at Stiller for a long while, as if he were examining a medical specimen. Then he gently took Stiller's large hand and said, "I don't have a great deal of money. I don't know what to think. Are you mad or are you a genius?"

Stiller smiled, revealing his handsome teeth. "What I am is not important for the moment. And I don't want your money; I want you to be the president of this corporation, nothing more. I will be a mere film director. According to the bylaws of the corporation, you will control me completely."

A long silence followed. From the expression on the doctor's wrinkled face, Stiller sensed that his idea had taken hold. It seemed to him that the doctor was thinking about how he would fit in without investing any money. His judgment was confirmed when the doctor said, "Your idea is certainly interesting, and I do have a number of patients who would invest some money provided I had control over its disposition."

"You would be in complete charge, Dr. Platonov. You will be the president and the treasurer. I just want to make films."

"That sounds fine to me. And if I'm in control, my patients would not lose money."

"You're right," Stiller said, rising from the chair and moving toward the door. "I will stop by to see you again soon. Thank you for showing interest."

Platonov called him back, saying, "Please let me give you a hundred rubles for your trouble and for your kindness in asking me to be the president of your corporation."

Stiller turned around. "I can't take your money without giving you a receipt," he said, pulling a piece of paper and a pencil from his pocket. "I'll use this money to go to Berlin to look at some film equipment. While I'm gone, you can discuss our project with your patients. Then we can sit down together and discuss the entire business. You will, of course, be chairman of the meeting."

"I don't know why you're so honest," the doctor said.

"Please suspend your judgment until the corporation begins to make money," replied Stiller. "When I return, I'll be able to tell you how much we will have to spend on equipment."

"There will be no need to spend money on equipment," the doctor said emphatically. "I have friends in Berlin who can rent us what we need for a small fee."

Stiller could see that the doctor was enjoying his role as president. He waited for him to speak again.

"I'll give you a letter of introduction to my friends in a day or two," Platonov said. "But if you're going to Berlin, you will have to have more money." He went to his desk and wrote a short note. "Take this to Madame Bursukov.

She's a wealthy widow, and she'll give you more money for the trip."

Stiller took the note, thanked Platonov again, and ran all the way to Madame Bursukov's house. She was only too happy to give him nine hundred rubles. So with a thousand rubles in his pocket, Stiller left Helsinki the next morning for Stockholm.

"When I've made a great career in Stockholm," he told himself, "they will read about me in the newspapers and be happy that they helped me. And when I'm a rich and famous filmmaker, I will return their money with interest." After a pause, he added, "Thank God for the naive. Life without them would be unbearable."

As soon as he arrived in Stockholm, Stiller bought two suits of fine English cloth. One was charcoal gray; the other, brown tweed. He then registered at the Strand Hotel, giving his occupation as German filmmaker. That afternoon he bought antique rings encrusted with diamonds to cover his thick fingers. Next he stopped at a foreign-car dealer's, where he considered buying a yellow Opel. At the last moment he changed his mind, because he suddenly realized that immediate financial success was not a certainty.

In the evening he went to Reinhold's Café, which was frequented by theatrical and film actors. He played the role of German filmmaker well—he bought everyone drinks and spoke a charming mixture of German and Swedish. During his conversations with various Swedish celebrities, he nonchalantly dropped the names of wealthy men back in St. Petersburg and Helsinki.

Stiller believed that he had to exaggerate in order to establish good contacts with producers, directors, and financial backers. He felt particularly pressed to find a source of income, because he was uneasy about his health. He didn't think he had tuberculosis, but the doctor's diagnosis still bothered him. He adopted a strategy of trying to startle those associated with the Swedish film industry into recognition of his cinematic genius. He had more faith in himself than he had in God. Success meant money, and the path to fortune lay in the film industry.

In Reinhold's Café he met Julius Jaenzon, a young cameraman whom he promised a job on a film which he said he was going to produce with the backing of a Swedish millionaire. Jaenzon, after tossing down a half-dozen cognacs, urged Stiller to visit him at work the next day. Stiller replied, "I'm not interested in small motion-picture companies. My meetings with my friend take up most of my time. We are planning a whole series of motion pictures."

Jaenzon pressed his offer: "Maybe you'll find time in the near future. We would like to have your advice on our productions. I understand the demands on your time. However, important people from Svenska Bio often visit our company, and I think it would be good for you to meet them. Captain Lars Ring, one of the founders of the Swedish film industry, is a frequent visitor, and just the other day Erik Petschler came by. He's a real eccentric; he hasn't made much money from film productions, preferring to be a production himself. He has grown rich on Swedish widows. Thus, though our film company is small, it is associated with a dozen illustrious names."

When Mauritz heard this, he gently placed his hand on his friend's shoulder. "Julius," he said in a soothing voice, "please call me Moje, as all my friends do."

"Thank you, Moje," mumbled the half-drunk Jaenzon. "You will come in tomorrow, won't you?"

"Perhaps, if I have the time. Besides meeting Kreuger, I want to buy a car. It's inconvenient to have to depend on taxis.

"I've already looked at Opels. You know, Julius, they are fine German cars. If I can find a yellow one, I'll buy it. I love browns and grays, but I adore yellow."

"Well, you'll certainly cause a great sensation if you show up at our studio in a new yellow Opel."

"I'll try to come, but my schedule is so uncertain. Give me your address and I'll let you know by telegram."

Mauritz Stiller was a bundle of ideas and energy. From the day of his arrival in Stockholm to the time he received his first steady work in film, he spent hours each day organizing the avant-garde Lilla Teatern. He acted in and directed Strindberg and Tolstoy plays.

Charles Magnusson, as head of his own film company, was looking for a new director. He had heard of Stiller's theatrical success and had his company, Svenska Bio offer Stiller his first directorial job in films in 1912. The film was

Mother and Daughter; Stiller wrote the script and acted the role of seducer. Stiller often acted in his own films. In ten years he managed to direct over forty films, whose subjects ranged from potboiler romances to folk tales to satires of Swedish society.

The first film to bring him international recognition was a drama called *Song of the Scarlet Flower* (1918). This was followed by *Sir Arne's Treasure,* a sumptuous historical epic with stirring scenes of a wild nature that affects the course of young love. Mary Johnson, whom Stiller considered the greatest contemporary actress, played the leading role in the film. From their first meeting, Miss Johnson was enchanted by Stiller, and she strove to help him in the artistic and financial circles of Stockholm. But although Stiller admired her, he did not return her passion. Hunger and the rats in Helsinki remained vivid in his memory. Those memories killed, or at least becalmed, sexual desire.

In 1920 Stiller directed *Erotikon,* the most influential Swedish comedy ever made. It was this film more than any other that inspired the "Lubitsch touch" which the director of the same name used to great success in Hollywood. Tora Teje played the female lead in *Erotikon.* Like Mary Johnson, she fell in love with Stiller. During the production of the film, she tried to capture his affection by flirting with him and giving him presents. He always maintained that a film's success was assured if the leading lady was in love with the director.

Stiller had become a prominent yet mysterious man-about-Stockholm. Every well-known actor and actress sought his companionship, and financiers were eager to offer him money for new film ventures. It was widely believed that he directed films with the same degree of daring and skill with which he drove his car. Many were willing to put their careers, destinies, and fortunes in his hands.

Stiller the man bore all the personal hallmarks of extraordinary individuality. He was thought to be the best-dressed man in Stockholm; he had dozens of well-tailored suits and four fur coats, and his hands were covered with diamond-studded rings. He owned two cars, an orange one in addition to the yellow Opel, which he kept parked before the Grand Hotel, where he lived in splendor. In cafés, private homes, or the best restaurants, where the elite of the capital gathered, Stiller's eccentricity was a favorite topic of conversation.

Stiller customarily established friendships for a short period of time and on his own terms. But when he broke off a relationship, he did so in such a way that he could return to it later. Two things were clear: he was the one who would initiate the relationship, and he was most interested in relationships that opened new doors for him. Some thought his behavior neurotic. To a friend he once said, "I am not perfect, yet I believe there are many near-perfect human beings. I want to associate with them so that I can help make them perfect. I know I will also ruin some of them. That can't be helped."

To the shrewd observer, Stiller's constant search for new actors and actresses, new cameramen, and new scriptwriters represented different facets of his diamond-hard and indestructible genius.

The most popular turn-of-the-century author in Sweden was Selma Lagerlöf (1858–1940), and her most widely acclaimed book was *Gösta Berling's Saga* (1891). This two-volume work was not a novel in the conventional sense but rather a reworked rendering of Swedish folk legends. Gösta Berling is the main character in this romantic tale. Berling is a pastor, but his inordinate love of alcohol and women causes him first to lose his parish and then to fall into the depths of privation and despair. At the moment of his greatest loss, Elisabeth Dohna, a beautiful and pure woman, comes into his life to rescue him.

In 1917, Lagerlöf had approached director Victor Seastrom and Svenska Bio with the suggestion that they make films of her novels. Seastrom agreed, and a seven-year contract was signed which called for a film a year to be made, based on seven of her works. Although Seastrom had been considering doing *Gösta Berling's Saga* on his own, he turned down this particular project for two reasons. First, Svenska Bio would not allocate enough money to create the lush magnificence necessary for this epic. Second, by the time he got around to seriously considering this work, he had signed a contract with the Goldwyn Picture Corporation and was about to go to Hollywood. He told Lagerlöf that he could not make such a Swedish film in America, and the matter seemed closed.

Stiller immediately grasped the cinematic possibilities. Having become a Swedish citizen in 1920, Stiller realized the prestige that would come to him if he created a national epic for the screen. It was 1923. He had already directed Lagerlöf's *The Old Mansion* the year before, and he felt that he could provide the artistic capstone to the series of Lagerlöf films. To make the *Gösta Berling* film completely his own, he determined that he would use unknown actors. He spent the next few weeks searching the streets of Stockholm and visiting shops and restaurants; he was looking for the kind of people who "do not have mannerisms or established methods of playing. I can mold them in any way I want to suit me and my ideas." Because he was not as successful in this venture as he had hoped, he asked a few established actors if they were interested in the film. The major role would be that of the pastor. He spoke to Carl Brisson about this part, but Brisson's screen test was disappointing. Instead, Stiller engaged a lesser-known actor named Lars Hanson. His chief supporting actress would be Greta Gustafsson.

Stiller said nothing about his plans to Greta, but went about completing the cast. For the role of Major Samzelius he selected Otto Elg-Lundberg; for the role of the major's wife, Gerda Lundeqvist. Sixten Malmerfelt would play Melchior Sinclair; Karin Swanström gladly accepted the role of Gustafva Sinclair. With Greta in mind, Stiller gave the roles of the countesses Ebba and Märta to two friends of hers, Mona Mårtensson and Ellen Cederström. Although he admired the talents of both, the main reason for his choice was his belief that Greta would work better with friends around her. Finally, Torsten Hammaren took the role of Count Henrik Dohna. Most of these actors were unknown; none had appeared more than once or twice in films. During the auditions, Stiller used dialogues from Shakespeare rather than from the scenario; he wanted not only to discover whether the actors had talent, but also to excite them with the notion that he was going to make great performers out of them. Signing the cast was a relatively inexpensive proposition.

Meanwhile Greta discovered, through her girlfriends,

that Stiller was planning to produce a film in which he thought she might play a part. Although the news thrilled her, Greta was disturbed that Stiller had not approached her himself. Perhaps he was reconsidering. She did not know how much to rely upon rumor, but there was no one with whom she could share her doubts. She would wait. Suffering in secret had been her longtime experience. Both suffering and silence had given her strength many times before. She would wait.

9

Protégée

"You will play the Countess Elisabeth Dohna, opposite Lars Hanson, in my film *Gösta Berling's Saga*," Mauritz Stiller said to me as we stood at the entrance to his suite in the Hotel Esplanade. Remembering Petschler, I said to myself, "This is the second time a film man has greeted me at a door with a startling announcement."

"For your work, you will receive from me three thousand kronor." A smile curled his black mustache, and he delicately gave me his right hand to guide me inside. "Please sit down. This is only the beginning. I will work hard and long with you until together we make something great of you."

I was spellbound. I decided without hesitation to allow him to mold me into a great actress. No one had ever before expressed the desire to make of me what I myself had longed to become. I would do everything he asked.

This June day in 1923 was the beginning of a new life. I put aside everything to be near him, to listen to him, to obey him as a little girl obeys her father. The eighteenth year of my life found me deeply in love with him. Almost from the first time I had seen him, about four years earlier,

I had studied the actresses who appeared in his films and plays. I collected clippings of newspaper and magazine articles that mentioned him. I walked the streets of Stockholm looking for his towering figure among the male and female companions who always surrounded him. Sometimes I got close enough to hear him speak to his friends about the production of films and plays. Once or twice I felt his black eyes on me, but he didn't acknowledge me any further. Even then he probably understood me as a teacher understands his students. He was a severe teacher, as people often remarked to me; occasionally he was unjust.

That day in his hotel he said, "You have a good figure, graceful shoulders, fair legs, an unusual face, beautiful eyes with long eyelashes, and a husky voice."

The praise felt like a warm bath. But he was not finished: "You are fat. You don't know how to walk. You don't know how to talk. You don't even know how to smile. What is more, you don't know how to behave among people, nor do you know how to think. In other words, before you can become an actress, you will have to study for months, perhaps years. Every hour of every day you will have to obey me. If you do so, I promise you I will make you great."

He said all this with grand gestures, waving his large hands in the air. I wanted to gulp in air, but I kept my lips tightly closed. I didn't want him to see how my front teeth stuck out. He seemed to know what I was doing, because he said, "I think you will have to have those front teeth removed eventually. They spoil, my Greek goddess, the perfection of your alabaster face. You will need new clothes, and those I will select for you. But you won't have to pay for any of them. If you follow my instructions, I will take care of everything. I don't wish to be your lover, nor do I want to be your father. I will be your mentor and will make you a great film actress. After I die and after you die, our films will survive. People will continue to admire you as the phenomenal discovery of the great Stiller."

"What can I say?" I thought. "A great actress would have something to say to such pronouncements."

"Today you must promise me, you must swear, that you will do everything I ask and that you will never repeat anything that I say to you. Will you swear to that? Will you swear?" his voice grew louder.

"I swear," I said in a subservient tone. I felt as if we had signed a contract in blood. He got up and shook my hand, still staring at me. Perhaps he noticed the tears that I quickly brushed from my face. He took out his billfold and said, "Here's a thousand kronor. Go to the best store in Stockholm and buy yourself some elegant undergarments."

Noticing my surprise, he said, "Don't worry. If nothing comes of our collaboration, I won't ask for the money back. In a few days I will go with you to buy dresses and shoes."

My hand shook as I took the money, and Stiller said, "Look at your hands. They're beautiful but need care. Your fingernails have never been kept properly. They have to be pampered like little children. A woman who plays in the theater must take care of her fingernails every week. You have to look perfect from top to bottom. Yes, yes, your toenails too. You have big feet, and I must choose special shoes that will hide them. Next week I will help you select not only dresses, but also coats, suits, hats, handbags, even your handkerchiefs and perfumes. Everything must be made of the finest materials. Your clothes, your perfumes, everything about you has to be harmonious in color, shape, and fragrance. Day and night, at each moment, you must be charming, mysterious, and exciting to the human eye. And I mean to the eyes of both men and women. The image of a screen goddess is not created for your pleasure or mine but for millions of filmgoers and for posterity."

He looked at me and could clearly see that I agreed with him. He knew that I could not refuse his offer. For me there was no way out; nor did I want one. I had always dreamed that someone like Mauritz Stiller would come into my life.

As he paced the room, I wondered to myself why he had not chosen as his leading actress Mary Johnson, Tora Teje, or Mona Mårtensson. I had no answer to this question, and I doubted whether he would have had a good one if I had asked him. He continued his pacing and said, "You must change your name. There is nothing glamorous about Gustafsson. There must be a million Gustafssons in Scandinavia."

A thought then came into my mind: "How will people recognize me if I have a new name?"

He read my mind. "After this film, your new name will be known all over Europe; you will be publicized in the

Swedish press and in newspapers all over the world. Don't bother about your friends. When I finish with you, you will have no friends, but rather admirers everywhere."

I found these remarks a little disturbing, but I remained calm and asked, "Should I decide on a new name?"

"I have been working on this problem all night," he replied authoritatively.

"What's the name to be?"

"You will be called Greta Garbo."

Upon hearing the words that he slowly pronounced, I felt strange and for no reason leaned over to one side. He saw my discomfort and asked, "Are you sick? Don't you like it?"

"I feel so peculiar; I'm too weak to say anything."

"Don't be upset. The name is simple and hard-hitting, and it suits you. Even though it's derived from Polish, it's pronounceable in any language." He was becoming irritated. "And if you don't like it, I will get another girl to play Countess Elisabeth Dohna," he concluded with a mirthless smile.

He opened his gold cigarette case, but found it empty. "Do you have a cigarette? Mine are all gone," he said in a surprisingly conciliatory voice.

I was still stunned by the name he had proposed, but I managed to open my handbag for the pack of cigarettes I always carried. I didn't smoke at the time, but I usually kept one of the packs that Sven brought home from the tobacco store where he then worked. As I fumbled for the cigarettes, I decided that it would be foolish to reject the name Stiller wanted to give me. If that was part of the bargain, I would agree. When I handed the pack to him, he commented, "These Swedish cigarettes are only good for dogs. From now on you will carry Fatimas, a Turkish cigarette."

"Yes," I replied obediently, thinking about the thousand kronor he had given me.

"Now, Greta, you have to buy yourself combs made of ivory, powder cases rimmed with gold, wallets made from crocodile skin, fine lipstick, and scissors and files for your nails. But you must not use powder or lipstick during the day, except when you are acting."

"Then why must I carry all these things?"

"Every elegant woman carries them and uses them. You

will be elegant but different. You will carry them, but you will not use them."

Nothing escaped his strange eyes. He had probably looked into my handbag while I was searching for the cigarettes. He took several more long drags, made a few smoke rings, and watched until they disappeared. Then he continued to tell me what I must do, how I should act.

"You must have a telephone installed in your house. I will pay for it."

"I don't need a telephone, because no one calls me. I talk with my friends face to face." My thriftiness prompted my words.

"I will be calling you often." I instantly perceived that even in such a small matter as the installation of a telephone I would be overruled.

"As you know, Svensk Filmindustri is located in Råsunda. I go there every day, and from now on I will pick you up and take you with me. When I am unable to do so, you should take a taxi. Under no circumstances should you take a trolley car."

"Why not? I can save money by taking the trolley."

"The answer—since you want one—is simple. An actress with your future must cultivate elegance in all things."

With these final words of direction, he took my hand and walked with me to the door. I realized that his hand was larger than my father's and had been roughened by physical labor. I also noticed that it was covered with black hair.

"Our first lesson is finished," he said, picking up a script. "But here's your homework. Read the whole thing, with special emphasis on your own role. Come tomorrow at eleven and I will discuss it with you. After that we shall have a late lunch. In the afternoon we will go shopping. Agreed?"

"Agreed." And so began my life with the legendary Moje.

At the end of July 1923, I signed my first contract, my first real contract with Svensk Filmindustri.

When I appeared the following day in his hotel suite, Stiller said, "I think you will achieve something in your life because you are a punctual person. In any of the arts you must have tremendous discipline."

In a deliberately cool tone I responded, "I was thinking about being late for you, but at the last moment I changed my mind."

"I see you are gaining courage and are not afraid of me anymore," he said, clenching a cigarette between his teeth and embracing me in those huge arms of his. This embrace was like that of a father for his daughter on her return home from a date before the time set by him.

He motioned for me to sit down in the precise spot where I had been seated the day before and said, "Are you hungry?"

"I have already had my breakfast, and I would like not to eat until supper. I recall your saying that I was too fat."

"Dieting is one thing. Starving yourself is something else. You must choose foods that do not make you fat around the hips. But you must also eat three square meals a day to have the necessary energy for strenuous work. Later today I will give you a diet to follow. For now I have made a one-o'clock luncheon reservation at Bern's."

He took the scenario from me and began to read it to himself. After a few minutes of reflection he said, "Before we start talking of your role in the play, I would like to make a couple of comments about you personally." He picked up a cigarette and started to pace in front of me. "In the restaurant, I want you to watch me as I eat and see how I hold my fork. You should also notice how I hold my wineglass and unfold my napkin. You have to develop a delicate touch at the table. If you are one of several guests at a table, talk about clothing, talk about the weather, but never talk about yourself. Be secretive. Yet, at the same time, be simple with other people. If you are forced to talk about yourself, speak critically. If you talk about other artists, praise them."

I was impatient with all his directives, so I interrupted him. "What will this kind of discipline bring me?"

"Now, don't start to be critical toward me. I will show you what it will do. First things first." He thought a few seconds and then approached me from a different point of view. "You should know by now that most creative artists crave publicity, especially actors. Some of them pay lots of money to create publicity."

"I can't spend money I don't have on publicity."

"You will get your publicity in a different manner. You won't need money. Just listen to me. You must always avoid all reporters and journalists. If you should meet them by chance, say that you have nothing to say about yourself. If they persist, tell them to ask Stiller. In the beginning it will be difficult to maintain this attitude. After a while it will get much easier. Soon reporters and photographers will run after you, while you will continue to avoid them. After failing in direct approaches to you, they will go to your friends and even to your distant acquaintances. Colorful lies will arise around the name Greta Garbo, lies for which you will not be responsible. You will become the center of half-truths, half-lies. And I will manipulate all this gossip to create a properly mysterious image. In a year or so, though it may take a little longer, you will be a truly fascinating woman in the eyes of the general public. Believe me, this method is the surest means of gaining the best kind of publicity. The public will rush to see your films, and everyone around the world will talk about you."

As he spoke, taking long strides back and forth across the room and repeating himself at times, I began to understand the man's immense cleverness. It seemed as if he had thought out every aspect of my career. I listened to him more intently than I had before.

"When you are entertained in large gatherings, never raise your voice. First, begin by praising the host and hostess. After that, go on to actors, writers, and musicians; if you meet some political bigwigs, praise them too—but in such a way that no one can make a fool of you. If you know little about a given subject—and you don't know much about most things—then smile and say nothing. When you find yourself in such a gathering, don't eat, and definitely don't drink. If you must eat or drink, consume very little. Let everyone think that your nourishment is art and your drink is spiritual exercise. Most certainly don't eat if you are in a circle of women. Just talk about them, about their virtues, looking straight into their eyes. Say beautiful things about them. Throw bouquets of compliments. Keep to yourself whatever you may honestly feel toward men and women. Behave in such a manner that people will think they are dealing with an angel of goodness and modesty. Avoid gossip, and do not collect friends. Keep a moderate distance from everybody. Never accept gifts or help from anyone. Be independent and self-sufficient. When you do need something, I will give it to you as payment for your work. When you receive an invitation, tell me. I will decide which gatherings you should attend and which you should not."

I was becoming rather bored by all this talk, but I counted myself smart enough to listen. Stiller, still walking and smoking, continued: "When you do go to a reception or party, I will be there too. Try to keep close to me. I will help you out of difficult situations, and I will enhance your stature in ways so subtle that no one will notice. You alone will know, because you understand my silent language. And if you live according to my instructions, you will learn everything, so that eventually you will swim on your own. Most importantly, you should not involve yourself in romance, because . . ."

At this point in his monologue there was a knock at the door. Stiller stopped pacing, looked at me suspiciously, and then turned the knob. Three hotel porters entered with a dozen packages of all sizes. He asked them to drop the packages anywhere, gave each a tip, and hurried them out. Then he wheeled around and said to me with an air of proud command, "Here is your wardrobe. Get undressed and try on everything."

I was petrified and couldn't move. Seeing my reluctance, he said, "We were supposed to go shopping together, but I took a guess on your measurements, and so as not to embarrass you, I decided to order the wardrobe in advance and to have it sent here." His explanation made no impression upon me; I thought, "All of them are the same."

"If people saw us together in a store, they would eye us and say, 'That old man Stiller is buying gifts for his girlfriend.' This rumor would spread through Stockholm. As you might guess, that would not be good for your career. I am sure you understand that, don't you?" Wrinkles of anger appeared on his forehead. "Get undressed, and don't think for a moment that I am going to touch you or anything like that!" He swung around and, with his back to me, started to rip the wrappings off the packages and toss garments over his shoulder. "First put on this underwear, for I am sure you have holes in your panties."

What could I do? Overcoming my hesitation, I began removing my clothes mechanically. He remained in the same position, tearing open the packages and letting the ashes from his cigarette fly every which way. His timing was good, for I knew that he couldn't see me from where he was standing. When I had undressed myself and put on new panties, he threw me a beautiful pink lace slip. Next I put on a dark orange dress and admired myself in a mirror. To complete the exquisitely designed costume, he tossed me shoes and a box of jewelry. "Put these on. Then tell me when I can turn around to see my stupid virgin."

I wondered what Mauritz was really trying to do in making me dress behind his bed when there were two other rooms in the suite he could have gone to. He was presumably attempting to convince me that his interest in me was genuinely artistic. So, anyway, it seemed at that moment. I nervously adjusted my new garments, feeling proud of my success with him. But when I looked at my panties lying on the floor, I saw a hole in them. I remembered what he had said when those panties were still on me. How could he have known? He didn't have eyes in his feet. My hands quivered as I piled my old clothes together. He was still standing with his back toward me when I opened the jewelry box and saw a necklace. It was gold and in imitation of an Egyptian style. There were also a Swiss watch and two rings. In an irritated tone he said, "Have you finished dressing?"

"Yes, I have finished," I said, waking up from dreamy admiration of the glittering jewelry.

"Now go to the bathroom and comb your hair." He did not move as I went into the bathroom, washed my face in cold water, and carefully combed my hair. Seeing myself in the mirror dressed in the new clothing and jewelry, I liked myself, for the first time in my life, as a woman. When I returned, he was standing in the middle of the room. His eyes gleamed as he studied me. "This," he said, "is how a great actress should look. Dressed simply but with great elegance. Not much jewelry—just enough." He ordered me to walk like a model, turn around, come back, and walk again, saying, "Perfect! . . . Perfect!" Here he paused and said proudly, "And now we can go to lunch at Bern's."

"If I remember correctly, you said that we would study now."

"I've changed my mind. After lunch we will work on your role."

With those words he handed me a coat and a hat. I took them and started toward the bathroom to look at myself in the mirror. But he stopped me and suggested, "Here, use the big mirror by the door on your left. You'll be able to see your coat and hat better."

Not having seen the mirror before, I grew deeply upset. I suddenly realized that although he had been standing with his back to me, he had watched me undress in the mirror.

"Why did you fool me?" I shrieked. He looked at me without a shadow of embarrassment. "I told you I was interested in every aspect of you. I had to see you without your clothes in order to see how I could enhance your figure. Greta, if I had asked you to get undressed in front of me, you would have thought I wanted to seduce you. At this early stage of our acquaintance, nothing could have convinced you of my pure intentions. By using this mirror, we have saved lots of time and I have gained information that will prove helpful in building your career."

I stood motionless and speechless, thinking that this was probably only the first of Stiller's tricks. How was I going to endure him? He touched my back with one finger as a signal to leave and followed me to the door. "You know, this is the first time I have seen a woman who looked a thousand percent better naked than clothed. A great gift has been given you by the Creator."

I cursed myself and him under my breath. I was about to begin insulting Stiller openly and uncontrollably when the chambermaid appeared in the doorway with fresh linen. I put my head down and walked out; Stiller followed.

"You have to remember two crucial things when you play the role of Elisabeth Dohna," said Stiller, sitting beside me, "or, for that matter, any role. First, you must be aware of the period in which the character is living. Second, you must be aware of yourself as an actress. If you play the role and forget about yourself, nothing will come of it. On the other hand, if you project your personality above the role—I mean if your personality dominates the role—nothing will be achieved either."

My first acting lesson with Stiller seemed to be promising. I listened to him attentively, hungry for his wisdom.

"Through intuition you have to find a way of merging your own real character and physical mannerisms with the soul and physical mannerisms of the writer's imagination—with the character he has created. If you succeed, dramatic reality will become for the viewer as authentic as his own experience. He will simultaneously admire the character you are playing and your own character. When the viewer later recollects the character in this particular play, he will associate it with your own personality. You will play hundreds of roles in your career; imagine the millions of viewers who will come to look upon you as a femme fatale. The whole world will be your audience. Remember the Latin maxim *Fama semper vivet*—fame lives forever!"

Stiller lit a cigarette and offered me one also, saying, "Would you like to smoke some fine Turkish tobacco?" I accepted the cigarette and delighted in its rich, strong taste. This was the beginning of my smoking habit. He asked, "Are you wondering why I am trying to teach you so much at once? It's because I don't have much time left. You will outlive me, so I must hurry to prepare you."

This did not seem the right moment for him to talk about the shortness of his life. We were just starting to work together and already he was talking about the end. I remarked, "Who knows how long any one will live? As people say, everything is in the hands of Providence."

"I believe in biology and work rather than Providence." He took a few more puffs on his cigarette and changed the subject. "To achieve a symbiosis of yourself and the role you are playing, you must ponder the differences between your own character and the one you are to portray. Who are you in terms of emotional makeup and physical appearance? And who is the character in the play? When you have all the facts, add them up and draw the appropriate conclusions. These should be simple. It is through your acting, through the character you play, that you will bring forth the main ideas of the playwright. At the same time, you will expose elements from your own character. As a talented actress, you have to know which elements to use in a particular characterization. In the marriage of the two characters—the fictitious one and your own—you can create an unforgettable performance which viewers will tremble upon seeing." He stopped, lit another cigarette, and concluded, "I think I have made myself clear for now. Let's move to something more concrete. Explain to me the character of Elisabeth Dohna."

I recall that I muttered that she was a sacrificing, honest woman, who clung to her man like a leech and who was sentimental in every situation—all characteristics that I did not share in the least. Stiller realized this and laughed between puffs. "It is precisely for that reason that I selected you to play the Countess Elisabeth. And you must act so that the honesty of her character will blend with the coolness of your figure and mannerisms. Thirty or forty years from now when this film is shown, I would like the critics and viewers to say, 'The film itself is a mediocre creation, but Greta Garbo and her acting give it lasting greatness.' I want those people to ask how you came to be a mysterious femme fatale. Do you know what they will think?"

"Yes," I replied honestly. "They will say that I am your creation, that I grew to fame under Stiller's direction."

"Let's not exaggerate. If you did not have a unique talent, I could do nothing for you."

For the next six months each day, seven days a week, no matter what we were doing or where we were, at Svensk Filmindustri in Råsunda or in Öregrund, where we shot exteriors for the film, Stiller coached me on every scene. We went over every movement and every expression on my face and in my eyes. I would rehearse each day's scene—or my part in it—several times before leaving for work. It was usually early when we arrived on location, and Stiller would have me sit on the side and observe other actors. Eventually I memorized the entire film—not only the lines, but also the ways in which every actor played his part.

In the evenings I was taken to Reinhold's Café or to some elegant restaurant where through Stiller I met many important members of Stockholm's cultural set. Among the persons to whom I was introduced were two theater and film critics, Hjalmar Lenning and Bengt Idestam-Almquist, multimillionaire Ivar Kreuger; two Americans, Mary Pickford and Douglas Fairbanks; and also Lagerlöf. He even introduced me to members of the royal family. In a short time I had become a celebrity, although often described merely as Stiller's protégée. I didn't like this description because of the sexual overtones. But what could I do?—I was stuck with it.

When *Gösta Berling's Saga* was finished, Stiller busied himself editing, and I played small parts from Ibsen, Shakespeare, Sardou, and Ibañez in the Royal Dramatic Theater. I received two hundred kronor a month for this work—not much money, but plenty of experience. Quoting my mentor, I would say to myself, "Every talented actress should know how to play all kinds of roles, from tragedy to comedy, on the stage or in front of the camera."

The premiere of the first part of *Gösta Berling's Saga* was held on March 10, 1924, in Röda Kvarn, a Stockholm theater. The second part premiered seven days later. Just prior to this great event in my life, Moje invited me out to dinner. Afterward he took me straight to his home, locked the door, and with a childlike smile said, "You have to be luxuriously elegant for the premiere of this film." He ran to the corner of the room and grabbed a mink coat from a box. As he draped it over my shoulders, he said, "You look exciting in mink."

I carefully slipped into the coat and walked toward the mirror saying, "It is a crime for me to wear this. Such a coat must cost a fortune."

"Do you always have to be a miser? It's not your money, so enjoy it. Besides," he said stroking the glossy fur, "you have been patient with me and you deserve it."

"Even so, I would prefer a well-tailored woolen coat. I think you should take this back to the store."

"Don't be obstinate. I bought this for you and you should wear it."

"I will not take it, because it will burden you too much financially. Besides, people will say that Stiller's protégée was doing something on the side for him because she received an exquisite mink coat."

"You haven't so much as kissed me, and you should realize that we cannot prevent what people think."

I felt sorry for myself and for him. The constant pressure to learn how to act and behave and live had prevented me, and I think him too, from developing a deep emotional attachment. But perhaps we were attached to each other in a different way, on a deeper level. I didn't have the strength to remove the coat; I sat down in front of the mirror and started to cry.

As my chin touched the soft fur, Moje moved closer to me, hugged me, and pushed the collar up to my face. When the collar had reached my lips, I began to kiss his hands. He hugged me more tightly. I got up suddenly and threw my arms around his neck. I think he was surprised at my taking the initiative. As we held each other, a pleasant warmth coursed through my whole body. Then, with his long arms, he lifted me up and we moved to the next room. He delicately placed me on the bed and started to remove my coat and dress. He acted so slowly, so methodically, even phlegmatically, that every movement of his hands excited me. I closed my eyes and was waiting for more activity to come from his hands, from his body, from his lips. His huge figure fell on me, but I didn't feel the weight. I felt happiness. I thought I was floating in the sky—high, near the sun. We didn't say a word. Surely this was because words could not express our feelings, the feelings of one body, the feelings of one soul.

Never before or again in my life have I achieved so much satisfaction as I did then. When the morning sun began to scratch our window, I whispered to him, "I'll never forget you," and he repeated with kisses the same words. When we got up it was late in the day, and neither of us spoke to the other.

Despite our timidness and feelings of guilt, it was good to be with each other, to touch each other, and to have no more secrets. From then on we possessed not only knowledge of each other's character and body but also a shared physical pleasure that gave special mystery and the seal of secretness to our relationship.

10

Rehearsal for Conquest

Both parts of the *Gösta Berling's Saga* premiered within one week. For Stockholm it was an enormous cultural event, attended by not only the most illustrious personages of that city but also celebrities from Paris, London, Berlin, and even America. If I am not mistaken, it was the first European film produced in two segments. Receptions in Saltsjöbaden followed both openings and were attended by members of the royal family. The author of the saga, Selma Lagerlöf, believed that the film was cheap and sensational and distorted her work. Her attitude made Moje angry, and with the help of friends he got her drunk after each premiere and had her safely delivered home before she had a chance to express herself. I do not know whether Miss Lagerlöf influenced the reviews in Stockholm papers, but they were mediocre. I alone received the critics' praise and prophecies of a great career. But they qualified their praise by saying that I was the creation of Stiller and that my future depended upon him.

Despite the reviews, the film was a financial success; citizens of Stockholm waited in line to see it. Immediately after its premiere, the distribution rights to the film were sold for one hundred thousand marks to Trianon, a German film company which planned to present it in Berlin.

Moje had other reasons for going to Berlin. In response to my questioning he said, "Please keep this a secret, but I have special plans. If we go to Berlin, I'm sure I could get a million marks for the production of a new Russian film. I am counting on the services of David Schratter, who is the power in the Trianon Film Company. Like me, he is a Jew from Eastern Europe."

He then spoke of his new scenario, *The Girl from Sevastopol,* set during the Crimean War. The main character was Nina, a Russian girl from an aristocratic family who was searching for her fiancé, a Turkish prisoner of war in Constantinople. Nina was modeled after me. Moje thought that we would succeed in establishing me in the film world more firmly if we made our next film on foreign soil.

"Since no one makes films in Turkey," he said, "there will be an abundance of free publicity in our doing so. Then we can bring the film back to Stockholm."

"So if I play in a film produced by a German company on Turkish soil I will get more recognition?" He didn't answer.

Before we left for Berlin, Moje convinced the cameraman, Julius Jaenzon, who had photographed me very well in *Gösta Berling*, to accompany us. The young actor Einar Hanson and the scriptwriter Ragnar Hyltén-Cavallius also came with us. The pretext of our visit was the premiere of *Gösta Berling.* Officials from Trianon greeted us royally, and we were lodged in the best Berlin hotel. In return for this generous hospitality, we were supposed to appear on stage before the showing of the film. Moje skipped this rather humiliating ordeal; he was running from conference to conference, from Schratter to Pabst, trying desperately to make a deal. When Hanson and Jaenzon questioned him about his constant disappearances, Moje become noncommittal and said, "I know that I should be with you, because we arrived as a group, but I have something good in the works." When they asked him what, he smiled and disappeared again for hours.

As we were about to return to Stockholm, Moje called me into his room and announced, "I have signed a contract with Trianon. You will get five hundred marks a month plus all expenses."

I was speechless as he went on, "Now I will really fashion a miracle for you. You will shine in all the capitals, including Stockholm, and—" I started hugging and kissing him. He gently pushed me to the side. "Let's leave the emotions for later," he said. "We have our whole life—I mean, all my life. It is time we took the Orient Express to Turkey." Accompanying us were Hanson and Hyltén-Cavallius and, of course, the camera crew.

From the windows of the moving train I saw clusters of houses tied together as if out of fear. Under the thin blanket of snow I saw roofs made of straw and disintegrating shingles. Seated in the comfortable compartment of the moving train and looking at those poor houses, I felt frightened. No doubt the people living in them were scared by their miserable lives. My fear was of a different variety; it was both real and ridiculous. I, a Scandinavian girl with some talent and a good beginning in Stockholm, was traveling through southern Germany, Czechoslovakia, Austria, Yugoslavia, and Bulgaria to the poorest country in Europe, Turkey, to make an expensive film.

We had just crossed the Bulgarian–Turkish border when we saw to our left the beautiful sight of the Istranca Mountains. Moje made me eat a sandwich of Bulgarian kielbasa and dark bread and gave me a cup of Turkish coffee. He lit a cigarette, saying, "Very shortly we will arrive in the domain of Mustafa Kemal. Although he has given his country a constitution, Turkey is ruled by his iron hand. Don't forget that Turkey is not Sweden."

Moje announced that we had arrived in Constantinople. I looked out a dirty window on which drops of rain had made intricate mosaics. I tried to clean it with my arm, but most of the dirt was on the outside. We saw many poorly dressed men in black capes and children stretching out their hands and begging on the platform.

On our way in an open car to the Pera Hotel, I saw that the government buildings were in much better condition than those in which the people lived. The rain increased in intensity, and I yearned for the dry warmth of our hotel.

When we arrived there, a swarm of beggars lunged for

our valises, but hotel porters beat them back. It was depressing to see men in rags tangling with men in bright new uniforms. One old beggar with a beard and a long mustache grabbed me by the hand and spoke to me in a strange language. A porter translated what he was saying: "I want to tell you something important." At that moment Moje got between us and began pushing the old beggar away. "Please Moje," I pleaded, "the old man doesn't want to hurt me. He just wants to say something."

Moje read the anxiety in my face and started talking to the man in various languages. Eventually he found the right one, which was a mixture of Slavic and Germanic, and spoke with the old fellow for a minute. He then turned to me and said, "He is a Gypsy who wants to predict your future." Again Moje started to push him away. And again I begged Moje to let him alone. We three moved closer to the hotel wall, over which hung a long roof that protected us from the rain. The old man was making signs to me, protesting that he didn't want money, that he wanted only to talk. Finally I persuaded Moje to talk to the Gypsy, and I asked him to translate the conversation. They began in German. Then he changed to Russian. Just as suddenly, Moje was talking to him in Polish.

"What is he saying?" I asked.

"He is telling me all kinds of nonsense about you."

"Please tell me everything."

"He says that you are an unusual girl full of fears and desires. You will live among many people, but will have no friends. Although everyone will admire you, your life will be lonesome and you will die a tragic death."

As Moje listened further, his face grew pale. The old Gypsy now spoke without interruption, and I noticed that Moje was becoming very much disturbed. Then the Gypsy turned around, took a few steps, looked back at me, and started to walk away into the rain. When the bent-over figure of the prophet in beggar's clothing had disappeared, I closed my eyes to regain my strength. I grabbed Moje by the arm and said, "What did he say to you?"

Slowly he mumbled, "How could he have known that I was afraid of rats? He said I am afraid of rats, and that I will die like a rat, lonely and far away from you. I will die alone, abandoned by everybody."

I was terrified. "What? How does he know? Are you sure?"

"Pure coincidence. Pure coincidence. I don't believe in prophecy. It doesn't matter who he is or where he is from. I don't believe in such prophecies."

"Did he say anything else about you and me?"

Moje avoided my question and my eyes. "Startling, just unbelievable—a beggar without money or shoes. A beggar in rags, and he refused to take money."

I repeated my question. With Moje so shaken, I thought, he would divulge more; if I waited, he would regain complete composure and keep his secret.

"It is not important. He said our Turkish expedition will be full of trouble and nothing will come of it."

"I knew the last prediction myself. I've told you that we should not be here."

The next day Moje hired cars for our entire party, and we traveled around the city looking for picturesque sights. Even though we had protection from the Turkish police, at every place we stopped we were surrounded by beggars demanding handouts. Despite previous permission from the government, we were not allowed to shoot at certain locations. The day was a complete failure, and everyone was discouraged. In such situations, Moje seemed to gain extra strength. He would run about encouraging everybody and engaging them in conversation. The next day would be more successful, he told them. It was Christmas Eve. To cheer me up, he bought me two dresses of Chinese silk and a Russian sable. I tried to put on a show of being happy, but inside I was sad. Dresses or fur coats could not possibly have cheered me up. Rain fell continuously; the streets were cratered with puddles of mud. "I don't know why you are spending money on me in this difficult period."

"Don't you know that it is Christmas, and it is customary for people to exchange gifts?"

But money was getting scarce, and Moje was getting more and more nervous. He sent telegrams to Berlin to ask for additional funds. We didn't get any replies, even though we were scheduled to stay in Constantinople for the next two months. There were nineteen people in our group, and they all had to be housed and fed and provided with expense money. As a last resort, Moje decided to take the

Orient Express back to Berlin and ask for another million marks from the officials of Trianon. After he left, we sat in the hotel eating, talking, playing cards, and watching pennies. After two weeks of waiting, we received a telegram telling us that David Schratter had left Trianon abruptly. At that moment, Moje was trying to persuade G. W. Pabst, who was a director for Sofar-Film, to take over the production of *The Girl from Sevastopol.* He was unsuccessful.

After our return to Berlin, I was depressed and without money. So far, the prophecies of the Gypsy had been fulfilled. For the first time, Moje was in the same predicament as I. He began to smoke and drink more, even though he had to give up his favorite champagne and switch to *brännvin.* The only luxury he allowed himself was to stay at the Hotel Esplanade. "I can eat from a garbage can," he frequently said. "I can be dressed like a beggar. But I must have a decent bed to sleep in."

At that time I was hearing about the achievements of American filmmakers and their studios. When I discovered that Louis B. Mayer, one of the bosses of Metro-Goldwyn-Mayer, was in Berlin, I used every conceivable connection I had to get in touch with him, but I did not get to see him. That may have been just as well, because I don't know what I would have said to Mayer about me and Moje.

One day, on Unter den Linden, I met Asta Nielsen, a Danish actress I knew from Stockholm. She was with Pabst, who kissed my hand and said, "I have seen you perhaps ten times as Countess Elisabeth Dohna."

"He doesn't exaggerate," remarked Asta. "He considers you a great actress and wants you for the lead role in a new film. We were just discussing it."

I then became extremely sly. "Mr. Stiller and I have recently received a request from Svensk Filmindustri to work on a new film. We have also received an invitation from Hollywood. The question now is which proposition we should accept."

As we passed Rumpelmayer's Café, Pabst observed, "I know you are both tired. Let's sit down and have something to drink."

When we were seated, Pabst, like a good businessman, began to unravel his scheme. "The name of the film is *Die Freudlose Gasse.* It will be fashioned from Hugo Bettauer's novel, and the screenplay will be prepared by Willy Haas. The picture will present Vienna after the war, a city sunk in the moral and physical mud of deprivation. You, Miss Garbo, will play the honest girl."

"Even if I could accept your offer," I began, "and your unseen script, I must tell you right now that I have a director and a cameraman whom I trust completely."

Startled, Pabst moved toward me abruptly and spilled his coffee. "Miss Garbo, I would first like to point out to you that you will be playing in a company of excellent actors that includes Asta Nielsen, Jaro Furth, Valeska Gert, Werner Krauss. I am the one who must direct these people in the film! And secondly, my cameraman, Guido Seeber, is a far better technician than your Julius Jaenzon!"

"I don't deny that you have an attractive package," I replied meekly, realizing that it would be a great tragedy for me if this proposition collapsed when I did not have even fifteen marks in my purse. I timidly remarked, "You have to admit that Julius photographs me very well."

"I can assure you that Guido will learn to photograph you even better."

"Let's not talk about that," I said. I thought that if he considered me a great actress, he might find a way out. It was up to him, so I got up to leave. Pabst rose from the chair and folded his palms as if to pray. "Please, Miss Garbo," he pleaded, "don't leave me and my project in such a disagreeable manner."

I sat down and picked up his coffee cup as a symbol of reconciliation.

"I cannot give the directorship or camera work," he said, "to anyone else." And then he moved squarely to the point: "I will pay you two thousand marks in advance. We shall discuss the details later, but mind, you will be working on the film less than a month!"

"Mauritz Stiller is taking care of the financial side of my business," I said. "You will have to talk with him." I read in Asta's and Pabst's eyes that I was as good a businesswoman as an actress.

When I returned to the hotel, I discovered that Moje had already learned about Pabst's offer from Hanson, who had talked that very morning with Seeber. He jumped on me right away, telling me I had no self-control and was arranging business behind his back.

I defended myself. "If you take the trouble to talk with Pabst," I said, "he will tell you that I referred his proposal to you. Besides, we have no money for meals, and I have to walk to save on transportation."

Moje quickly softened. "I know," he said, "that people are dying in different parts of the world. But you and I, who love each other, should hold back our harsh words and inform each other of matters that concern both of us."

I was verging on tears. "I did exactly that," I said. "It was only by chance that I met Pabst and Asta. When he offered me a role in the film, he said they would pay me two thousand marks in advance. I referred him to you."

When Moje heard this he leaped from his bed and started hugging and kissing me. "I knew inside you could not do anything wrong," he said, "but I felt like scolding you anyway."

Naturally, we accepted Pabst's generous offer, and the following week I began working with him. He worked fifteen hours each day in order to squeeze three months' production into six weeks. Because Pabst pushed me so fiercely, Moje persuaded me to play sick and stay in the hotel until he could get two thousand marks more. And he was successful, because the producer had fallen in love with me. When Moje found this out, he said, "It's all your fault. You are too nice to Pabst." My reply was simple: "I have had nothing to do with Pabst. If you don't believe me, go hire a detective. You have the extra two thousand marks."

He calmed down, because he realized that if I had really had an affair going with Pabst, I would not have made such a suggestion. Then he said mysteriously, "I will teach him a lesson. I will put him in his place."

"How?" I asked frantically. I knew that Moje's jealousy would not bring anything good. Years later I learned from Cavallius that Moje had found a prostitute in Berlin who spoke Swedish and also had a venereal disease. He dressed her elegantly and introduced her to Pabst as a Swedish actress. Because she was young and had managed to retain her beauty, Pabst entered into a relationship with her and was soon afflicted with the disease. But Moje didn't stop there. One evening he caught him with the girl in the same hotel where we were staying and he beat him up. So ended our relationship with G. W. Pabst.

Die Freudlose Gasse premiered on May 18, 1925, at Berlin's Mozartsaal and on September 28 in Stockholm. The film later opened in London as *The Joyless Street* and in New York as *The Street of Sorrow.* Press reaction was mixed, mainly because of the film's brutal realism, which was too much for the time. The narrow-minded critics condemned it outright, but even they, and practically everyone else, praised my acting. They also had good words for Seeber, who, under Moje's instruction, photographed me extremely well. Thus ended my career in Europe. I should mention that I never once lost faith in Moje's business genius even when I lost my temper with some of his tactics. I had grown more sure that the world belonged to me and to my talent.

I remember it vividly. It was a sunny Sunday. Thousands of people were strolling on Unter den Linden while Moje and I sat in the Esplanade discussing our future.

"I am sure you would like to have a house in Stockholm and a house in the country, though not my stinking place in Lidingö," began Moje. "But you just cannot squeeze enough money from crooks like Pabst to get even decent clothing."

"It would be better if, from time to time, you would ask me what I wanted."

"I know your wants. As a famous actress you should have expensive furs, dresses, and other accessories. As for houses, let's say that I want them."

"I won't deny anything. I see that you're trying to tell me something, but I can't figure out what you're trying to say."

"From now on I will tell you of my every step. This way we can do away with many misunderstandings. First of all, I've made some contacts with Pathé, the French company. I told them I would direct your pictures, and they coolly made a counteroffer in pennies, because they think that Swedes can work practically for nothing and be happy. Or perhaps there is another explanation. Einar Hanson or Asta Nielson may have told them that we have no money."

"I think they're just good business people. I don't believe our friends would interfere." I was thinking that there might be a possibility that those two would scheme behind our backs, but it was against my nature to talk negatively about people. I was not sure, however, so I said, "The big film companies wouldn't be influenced by anyone's opinion, especially the opinion of two countrymen who might have personal reasons for talking against us."

Moje flushed with anger. "We are the artists, the real artists, and our country is the world. We do not belong to one country. Our country, our real homeland, is art."

"Let's leave the philosophy for some other day," I cut in abruptly, "and examine the realities."

"You're right," he said. He pulled out a German paper and showed me a short article which said that Louis B. Mayer was thinking of engaging Mauritz Stiller and Greta Garbo for a new film. I was very much surprised that such information had gotten into the Berlin paper.

"I didn't talk to Mayer. Did you?" I asked.

"No," he replied meekly. Still unbelieving, I posed the question again. Again he denied speaking with Mayer, but after a long pause he admitted, "I placed the item in the paper through a connection."

"But what will happen if Mayer doesn't see this story?"

"I am sure he will see it, because I asked the manager of the Esplanade to show it to him. And as you know, Mayer and his daughter Irene are staying at the Esplanade. Naturally he is staying in the most expensive suite."

"But what if he reads the item and doesn't approach us?"

"I will go to him and ask him point-blank, 'Why are you spreading false rumors and injuring our reputation? You know perfectly well that Berlin, Stockholm, and Paris are the film centers of the world. Everyone knows that America is just trying to follow Europe.' "

"Yes," I said, "but anyone who talks to you knows that you are eager to collect dollars. Don't you always ask European producers to pay you in American currency?"

"That is true, but Mayer doesn't know about that—at least, not yet. He has been in Berlin only a few days."

Moje always had a ready answer to any question. "Only with dollars can you buy houses cheaply in Sweden. We shall work no more than two years in Hollywood; we will teach those bastards how to pay us and how to direct films. After collecting a few hundred thousand dollars, we shall return to Europe without worries to work on artistic films, to travel, and especially never to worry about hotel bills."

"It all sounds very exciting, but how can you collect huge sums of dollars in such a short period?"

"If I cannot make an arrangement with Mayer, I will talk to other producers in Hollywood. We need just one good deal. And besides, you and I will be working. I also hope to get, for the first time in the history of filmmaking, a percentage from the income that our film will make. We will then invest our dollars in American and European business, and live on a fraction of the salary. We could invest in oil, steel, zinc, and God knows what else."

Moje was excited; he smoked one cigarette after another and paced quickly around the room. I too was caught up in his fantastic dream. And yet I was cautious. "This scheme is worthy of American multimillionaires. But remember, we don't even know Mayer."

"Don't worry about that. Do you know why we're sitting here and aren't out walking on this beautiful day?"

Before I could respond, Moje answered his own question: "We are waiting for Mayer's telephone call."

"It has to be something else, if you are so sure."

"Maybe," he said, lighting a new cigarette from his last one.

I was really puzzled. "What do you mean by 'Maybe'?"

"I will tell you everything, because in a few hours you will know anyway."

"You have another surprise for me?"

"Yes, but a very pleasant one this time. The manager of the hotel is at this very moment asking Berlin's leading theater and film critics to the Esplanade for an elaborate reception. I have promised to give him a couple of hundred dollars as soon as I sign a contract with Louis Mayer."

"What kind of reception are you talking about?"

"A farewell reception on the occasion of our leaving Berlin. Mayer is on the manager's list, so we will see him for sure. He is certain to come, since he is so anxious to meet German critics, actors, directors, and others working in films. You know he is here to hire people. And knowing

Mayer, I am sure he will call me before he goes to any reception."

I was terrified, because I knew that Moje didn't have money for a reception. He didn't even have money to pay the hotel bill. But what good would my anger have done?— I knew he was doing all this more for me than for himself. I ran to him with tears in my eyes and hugged him. "Moje," I said, "what will happen if you don't sign a contract with the American producer? Where are you going to get the money to pay for the reception if you have no money to pay your own hotel bill?"

He took me in his arms and sat me in the chair saying, "Don't worry about it. I am a Jew. And Mayer is a Jew too. I am one million percent sure that he will be at the reception to talk with the luminaries of German art."

"I agree; he might very well come. But to sign a contract with you and me is something else. There will have to be a miracle."

"Then let there be a miracle." He began kissing me on the cheeks, on my lips, and holding me. I didn't respond. I just accepted his affection. Suddenly the telephone rang. He jumped up and in a second was jabbering in Yiddish. I didn't understand a word of the conversation, but I prayed his caller was Louis B. Mayer. I heard my name spoken in connection with three magic words: Metro, Goldwyn, and Mayer. "Half of the miracle has been accomplished," I said to myself.

They talked for a long time in Yiddish. Every minute or so Moje turned his smiling face to me, waved his hand, and even danced around the telephone. I had never seen him so happy. My heart was happy too. I got up and straightened my dress and my hair. My eyes were on Moje talking, responding to questions, and I felt that there had to be interest on the other side of the line because the conversation was going on for so long. I started to move toward him. Suddenly he hung up the receiver, swooped me up in his arms, and carried me over to the bed. He put me down and, standing over me, said, "You know what that *skorwysyn* said about you?"

"Of course I don't know. I don't even know the word you just used. You were talking in Yiddish."

"You're right, we were talking in Yiddish, but the last word was Polish. It means son of a bitch."

"Never mind. Tell me how things went with Mayer."

"All right, all right. Do you know what he said about you?"

"What?" I asked, still lying on the bed and trembling now.

"He said he doesn't know you. He has never even heard of you."

"That means he wants you—not me?"

Moje bent over me and kissed my forehead, saying, "I replied that he should go and see your films and after that make his decision."

"Did you say that to destroy your own chances? You know perfectly well that you can go by yourself to the United States and make a big career directing and that I can manage for myself in Stockholm."

Moje sat up, reached for a cigarette, and almost spilling over his words said, "I would like to live with you forever. I would like to make many films with you. I would even like to die with you."

I had no words to express my gratitude. I kissed his hand. It was the happiest day in my life. I had found a man who wanted to do everything with me. At that moment I was the luckiest human being in the world.

The second part of the miracle was more realistic. It was a financial one. Moje signed a contract with Louis B. Mayer which stated that from the first day of July 1925, he was to receive one thousand dollars a week for the next year. I would get three hundred and fifty dollars weekly with the provision that the amount would be raised to five hundred as soon as I arrived in America. Moje somehow got the money to pay for the reception, hotel, tips, and other expenses connected with our life in Berlin.

During the reception, Moje mentioned to Mayer that Samuel Goldwyn was a distant relative of his and that Goldwyn's name was really Goldfisch.

"When we arrive in Hollywood, I will make a different arrangement with my relative Sam," Moje whispered in my ear during dessert. "I will teach him not to neglect his relatives." He was elated. But as soon as somebody approached him, he developed reserve and inordinate politeness. I was noticing that Moje could be several different people depending on whom he was with.

"I predict that very shortly you will be a successful American director," I said.

"Deep inside I don't think you believe what you are saying. But I, Mauritz Stiller, tell you right now, and vouch with my life, that I will make you there, in Hollywood, the greatest actress the world has ever seen."

Between us at that second there was nothing but faith—faith in each other. There was no basis for anything else.

After signing the contract with Metro-Goldwyn-Mayer, we left for Sweden. Moje was tired, pale, and almost collapsing on his feet. And his hair had become grayer. On the train to Stockholm I kept asking him about his health. He refused to discuss it, and when we arrived in the city, he immediately left for his suburban villa in Lidingö. He invited me to go with him to rest for a week, but I decided to stay at Blekingegatan 32 with my family.

I did not want to remain at home, but I did so because my sister, Alva, who had tuberculosis, insisted that I spend some time with her. It was at about this time that she received a small role in a Swedish film. I do not know why, but I felt that her career was finished or that she had never had one. I also felt that if I went to the United States, I would never see Alva again. People may not believe me, but for a long time after signing the contract I deliberated about whether or not I should remain in Stockholm and avoid a more complicated life in a foreign country. Naturally, the health of my sister was an important factor, though I knew that medical care was more necessary for her than the emotional bond that we shared.

For the first time in my life, I had also begun to doubt whether it was worthwhile to continue my own career. Moje's strenuous negotiations with Mayer had worn me down, and I had found the whole business rather degrading. There had been a time when I believed that the only thing you needed for a career was talent. But now, after my experience with American film-industry representatives, I had completely lost faith in the so-called cultural circles that are supposed to be at the center, at the heart, of our Western culture. These experiences, and my conversations with my ill sister about the achievements of film in the Soviet Union, caused me, in my own naive way, to believe in socialism. I thought over Alva's dream of my going to the Soviet Union with her and making a film career there.

"We will work on films in Moscow," Alva used to say, "and for vacations we will go to the Caucasus Mountains or to the Black Sea."

"It sounds very inviting," I replied, without really knowing anything about the Soviet Union. "What is the state of the artist in that country?"

"I've read a lot," she said. "Artists in theater or in films have steady employment, and they don't have to sleep with producers to get it. Artists and other cultural figures are the state's employees, and they command tremendous respect, more so than in any other country. You go to America and I will go to Russia, and we will see who makes a career first."

"I am sure you will be first," I said. "You are more graceful and more beautiful than I am, and you have greater talent."

"You're just saying that; you're thinking something else."

"Why do you talk like that? I believe more in your potential than I do in my own. I have always believed in you."

Alva started coughing and between coughs managed to say, "Let's go for a walk to Björns Gardens. There's no air in the house, and I'm choking."

Our walks were long and gave us time to discuss our film careers. When Alva got tired of walking, we would go to a *konditori* for pastry. She would say to me, "Do you remember how you used to like pastry, the creamy kind, and how you saved money from your salary to go to the *konditori* where we met well-known actors?"

"Yes, I remember. I remember, too, that when I didn't have enough kronor I would steal from Mother."

"In my eyes, you are still a poor *tvålflicka*, even though today you are known as the Countess Elisabeth Dohna."

During my stay we had many talks in which I confessed my anxiety about leaving Stockholm. Alva encouraged me, saying that I had a good protector in Moje and that I would achieve great fame. I would tell her that when I returned with my riches, all would be spent on her and me. We confided in each other as we had not done since childhood. We shopped together and I bought clothes for us both.

The day I would leave for America was drawing near, and Alva asked if I would go with her to Årsta inlet. She had fond memories of the days we had spent there with Father and Mother. None of the family ever argued in the country. There were never any bad words between us. And when my father confronted nature, he became quiet and calm like a baby satisfied after feeding.

The inlet that June looked beautiful in its peaceful greenery, and because it was a working day, there were few people. I remembered those days with Alva when we had gone fishing, and how after a good catch we had cooked the fish on an open fire. We walked, we ran after birds and butterflies like small children, without giving a thought to the past or the future, remaining in the enchanting present. We shared the pure love that can exist between two people with no sense of obligation, no feelings of regret. We had returned to childhood. True, we had had conflicts, for we had felt that our parents were playing us against each other. But none of those problems were like the ones we had now: Alva's poor health, my great desire for money and fame, and, to some extent, my deep feelings of loneliness and uncertainty.

My thought persisted that it would be our last time together at Årsta inlet, that I would never again see her delicate face or her childish behavior mixed in with those realistic observations about life.

Later, many times, at regular intervals, I dreamed of Alva among buzzing insects and the fragrance of flowers. To my nostrils came the smell of freshly cut grass, and to my ears Alva's gently mocking words, "Keta, Keta, you will never grow out of the simple ways of a Söder *flicka*. You will always like pastry with cream."

TWO PHOTOS: SVENSKA FILMINSTITUTET

Greta at the age of ten in a school photograph. Karl Gustafsson, above right, Greta's father, whom she greatly resembled, and her mother, who was born Anna Lovisa Karlsson.

Garbo's earliest excursions into film included (above left) *How Not to Eat*
and (above right) *How Not to Dress.* Her first role in a feature film was as
a bathing beauty in *Peter the Tramp* in 1922.

Garbo in *The Joyless Street,* a film made with G. W. Pabst as a result of his admiration for her performance in *Gösta Berling's Saga.*

Above and right, two scenes from *Gösta Berling's Saga*, the picture that established Garbo as an important film personality. Above, she is with the well-known Swedish actor Lars Hanson. Below, with Mimi Pollack, a friend from the days of the Stockholm Dramatic School, in 1921.

PART THREE   *America*

11

The First Crossing

In the early morning of June 27, 1925, Moje and I took a train from Stockholm to Göteborg. There we boarded the S.S. *Drottningholm,* which would carry us to New York. A haze covered my eyes even though the day was bright and sunny. Moje was solemn too. To the very last moment my mother, Sven, and Alva could not believe that we were going to a faraway land. Everything was unreal and nightmarish. I could not collect my thoughts, and I had nothing to say to my family.

The S.S. *Drottningholm* had the air of a circus. Crowds of Scandinavian people mixed tears and kisses with words. Some were visiting America for the first time; others were returning from visits. All were excited, and their colorful garments and noisy chatter made my mind reel. The children seemed most adjusted to the ship's circus atmosphere. They ran as freely as wild animals do when released from the confines of three rings.

Finally the noise and the bustle became unbearable, and I went to my cabin. My mother, brother, and sister followed me. Moje stayed on the main deck and talked with the reporters. He was the star attraction. No one paid any attention to me, although, as I heard later, Moje mentioned to them a few times that I was going to Hollywood under contract and that a great career awaited me in America. The reporters did not look for me to deny or confirm this exaggerated story. To them Moje was a great figure in European cinema, going to Hollywood to revolutionize picture making. I was happy that he was able to command their attention because of his creative genius. I was only a working girl striving to be an actress under his direction and trying to develop my creative intuitions.

In Cabin 7, time was slipping by for my family and me. We sat facing each other, staring at the door and waiting for someone to open it and release us from mental numbness. The noise grew louder as it poured through the open porthole. I got up and tried to close the window, but I didn't have the strength. Sven, in a display of masculine force, proved successful. I returned to the edge of the bed and sat closer to Alva, holding her by one arm. Alva didn't react; she didn't move at all. She didn't express any desire.

"Do you have a bad premonition?" My mother broke the silence, turning her face toward me.

"Nothing. Only sadness."

At that moment Alva removed my hand from her shoulder and said, "You don't have to be sad. You have more important matters to confront, for now you have a real opportunity to demonstrate your acting talent."

"I will be alone. That is why I'm sad."

"But Stiller is traveling with you in the next cabin."

Then Sven interrupted with words that went to my soul. "He didn't leave you alone in Europe, and I am sure he will not leave you alone in America."

"Who knows?" Alva added in a monotonous voice. "You might leave him or he might leave you. But one thing you should not forget, never trust a man."

"Ja, ja, ja," my mother joined in, her behind hanging over both sides of the narrow chair. "Ja, ja, ja, don't trust a man. Don't stay longer than a year. Make lots of money and return to Stockholm."

I had chosen a few words of farewell for everybody, but they died on my lips. Then the gong in the corridor and the ship's whistle released me from any obligations. We hugged and kissed each other in the customary family way. We wiped salty tears from our cheeks. But we spoke no words that anticipated joy from future meetings.

Sven opened the door and Mother walked out after him. Alva followed, tugging my hand. As we struggled to reach the gangplank, Moje suddenly appeared.

"Don't cry or be sad. Greta is going to become famous in America."

Sven and Alva looked at him, and then at each other, not uttering a word. But Mother gave him last instructions.

"You do everything possible for her to make a hundred thousand dollars and next year return to us."

"Yes, Mother, I will do that. I will do everything to make Greta rich, happy, and healthy." With these words he kissed her hand. He then kissed Alva's cheek and shook Sven's hand, saying to him, "I will see you soon."

Mother yelled, "I love you," and my family left the ship to a Strauss march that the ship's band was playing. Moje and I searched for a space on the rail for one last look at the Swedish countryside and the hundreds of people standing on the pier. I stood very close to Moje trying to spot my family. It was difficult to see anyone clearly in the shifting mass before us. Moje asked several times, "Where are they? Do you see them? Do you see them?" When I glanced up at his face, I noticed that his eyes were somewhere beyond the crowd. His face was dark and brooding and the muscles in his cheeks twitched. Suddenly he turned toward me. "Tell me," he said, "if we fail in Hollywood, will you return with me to Europe?"

"Are you mad? We haven't started yet and you're already talking about returning."

"For the first time in my life I have a strange feeling that although I have a contract in my pocket, I am not going to achieve anything there. They will not accept my ideas. I will quarrel and return to Europe."

"If you talk like this in Sweden," I retorted, "I can see we will achieve nothing. You must learn to control your temper."

"My temper goes hand in hand with my creativity. It is difficult to divorce one from the other."

"Please try. If you don't, we will return to Stockholm with nothing and the European press will ridicule us. We will be a laughingstock. After that, we could never return to our profession."

"On Swedish soil I can always begin again, but not over there. I suppose I should not talk to you about that."

"Why not? Aren't we partners? Aren't we grown-ups?"

"With an actress it is a completely different story. You can play any role they give you, but as a director I have to search for new approaches, new ways of working with the camera, with actors, and with scriptwriters. I have to experiment because film without experimentation is a dead art."

"I am sure the Americans will give you many opportunities to experiment. They like inventive people like themselves." I tried to cheer him up with words that I had borrowed from him. With one hand I held onto the rail, and with the other I squeezed his damp palm. He said, "I understand you have the same feelings as I do, but sometimes you astonish me with your strong nature. You usually show your strength when I am completely down." I listened and felt good. Moje continued, "You know what I would like to do?"

"What?"

"Make a pact with you."

"What kind of pact?"

"Let's say I will do everything possible. I will try to satisfy the people at Metro-Goldwyn-Mayer, and I will cut down to a minimum my artistic temper—by which I mean my experimentation with filmmaking. Now please tell me, what will happen if nothing comes of it?"

"Nothing. They are not going to break their contract with us."

"But what will happen if they do?"

I looked to the left, to the right, and searched in the center of the crowd as I tried to escape Moje's question. But he grabbed me by both arms, looked into my face, into my eyes, and asked again, "What will happen if they break their contract with me?"

"You want me to return with you?"

"I don't want anything from you by force or even by persuasion!"

"Good. I will say of my own free will that I shall return with you on the same day and on the very same ship."

His face became bright like the sun, and through his clenched teeth he whispered, "Will you swear to that?"

"I will."

He grabbed me in his arms and started kissing me on the cheeks, tears streaming from his eyes. He kissed me again and released me. He took me by one hand and started pulling me away from the mass of people, "We have to celebrate this occasion with champagne in our cabin."

"Yes, we do, we do," I whispered, but in my heart there was a terrible pain.

The orchestra played the national anthem and the passengers burst into song. Moje stopped in front of my cabin and in his loudest, most powerful baritone began singing the "Internationale" in French.

Before he had finished, half of the ship's crew surrounded him, and he began embracing everybody. I thought he had gone berserk. It took me a few minutes to drag him away to the cabin. I never saw a man so happy in my whole life as he was at that moment.

We spent many long hours in my cabin, because Moje's was smaller and mine had two beds, as well as a bathtub and other fixtures that one would usually find in a hotel room. I didn't notice the arrival of dusk, only the taste of salt on my lips. Two portholes were open, through which I heard the energetic conversations of passengers walking on the deck. Moje lay on his side, his hand propping up his head, and presented his future plans to me in an unknown America. I sat opposite him on my own bed; I didn't switch on the light, because I did not want to see his face plowed with ideas. He had lectured me on how I should behave in America. He seemed tormented by the obsession that I might somehow, through my behavior, destroy not only my own career but also his. I remember he again warned me about social contacts and once more told me that I should be secretive and avoid discussion or, for that matter, even conversation. According to him, I would by silence stand out among the chatty Hollywood actors.

"In their country lots of money is paid for publicity and advertising in the press, on radio, and on posters," he went on. "Those clever bastards in high positions in

Hollywood—most of them are Jews—can take an unknown actress without talent and turn her into a goddess in a few weeks. Naturally, if such an actress seizes the opportunity to develop her skills, she might become a Bernhardt, Modjeska, or Duse. Eventually she will get a good contract and steady work. If she is lucky on top of that and her films make money, the motion-picture company will double or triple her publicity budget and develop the more brilliant publicity of hired boyfriends and wild animals that will accompany her everywhere, anytime, day or night. But if her films do not make money," Moje continued in his dry monotone, "then the producer will cut out the publicity, cut out the contracts, and kill the actress."

At that point I interrupted, trying to learn something: "And how should we behave?"

"According to the contract, we have limited rights and many obligations. It has been difficult, as you well know, to squeeze a more generous contract out of Mayer. I have to create a situation in which Mayer will approach us and beg us to participate in publicity and advertising."

"It will be difficult," I answered, and Moje didn't reply. A sudden silence reigned between our beds. I guess Moje was trying to collect some good arguments to conquer my skepticism. "The first thing I have to develop is a good script for you. I already have a few stories in my head, and I work on them constantly. We must be publicized, but we have to convey the impression that we are opposed to publicity. When we land in New York, and later when we arrive in Hollywood, I must find a few intelligent Swedes and ask them to leak ridiculous stories about your past to the press and radio."

"I suppose I have no objections to that, if they also spread some rumors about you."

"My life is not important to the audience. They are not going to see me on film. You are something else. As a matter of fact, I'll make up some spicy tales about you, concerning your beauty secrets, your sexual life, and even your philosophy."

"I don't believe you can develop any interesting lies about me."

"Well-chosen gossip, innuendos, and half-truths can establish a foundation for future fame. Your talent will shield you from damage. Besides, you can always deny the gossip and shift the responsibility to me, or to Mr. Jones or Mr. Brown or some Swede who is in love with you. You will see very soon that the publicity boys from MGM will discover the great potential of such gossip and will themselves feed it to the press and radio, as well as manufacturing their own. When your first film finally reaches the public, you will receive the official studio publicity plus an overflow river of outside gossip."

"And what will happen if my first film is a flop?"

"I don't think about that," said Moje, raising his voice as if to smother my disbelief as we sailed through the night. "If your original beauty does not fascinate men, it will fascinate women. But I am confident that it will excite both. The fantastic intuition and interpretation that you bring to your roles—plus my instructions, which transform your natural primitivism into fascinating, intelligent acting—will intrigue everybody. You will be a sensation in America. Oh, let's not talk about it anymore, because you know very well that I believe in you more than anything else. I am very hungry. Turn on the light, and I'll call the steward for some food."

"Why this 'let's not talk'?"

"Never mind. Turn on the light."

"Not until you say everything that is on your mind."

"You stubborn and stupid girl. You know very well that I am twenty-three years older than you, and my anxiety to make something of you stems from a very simple emotion. I would like to see you famous before I die."

I switched on the light and looked into Moje's face. He was pale, but his eyes shone with strange fire.

"Don't look at me as if I were already dead. Ring for the steward."

I walked slowly over to his bed and hugged him. I felt that I was not only his girlfriend, but also his daughter and mother.

"I'm hungry. For the whole day I have had nothing to eat." With one hand he held on to me and with the other he pushed the button for service. "To think about art, to create art, I have to eat well and drink well. For me luxury is a necessity for creativity. And to have luxury we have to have money. To have money we have to produce films, money-making films. . . . America is in my brain, in my stomach, in my bloodstream, in every breath I take."

I never stopped admiring the vitality and originality of Moje. He represented some sort of miracle that kept coming out all the time with new ideas and observations. Naturally, his knowledge of filmmaking surpassed anyone else's in the field. He also had stored in his brain millions of facts and stories and could speak in half a dozen languages on many subjects. He was a self-taught man, but if you talked to him, you could see right away that his facts and logic were convincing, his observations wise, and his conclusions beautiful. He was also unique in making love. This originality charmed and excited me and was one of the basic reasons for my attachment to him. I always gained something from him at any time and in any place.

12

Impressions of New York

It was July 6, 1925. And it was a Monday—I am sure of that, because every Monday of my life I have gotten up at five o'clock in the morning to wash my underwear for the following week. But that Monday I had forgotten that I was traveling by ship and that the ship had its own laundry. Anyway, I awoke at five A.M. on the dot and looked through the porthole to see a flock of sea gulls against the hazy sky. Far away lay a body of land, and on this body, like a tumor, was a group of buildings. I thought, "That must be New York." The S.S. *Drottningholm* then cut its speed, and I heard the muted whistles of the pilot boat and the tugs. When I looked again, I saw a half dozen small boats cruising around our liner. We had reached our destination.

I took a quick bath and started to dress myself meticulously. First I put on silk underwear; next, a white blouse with a wide collar. Then I put on a blue-and-white-checked skirt, which reached just over my knees, and black, high-heeled shoes. Over the blouse I put on a long matching jacket. Standing before the mirror, I combed my hair carefully and adjusted my white hat. When I had finished dressing, I picked up white gloves and a dark-blue handbag. Then I looked at myself in the mirror again and said, "You look all right: conservative but elegant." I went into the corridor and knocked on Moje's door. He was dressed in a gray summer suit, with a white handkerchief in his jacket pocket. On his head he wore a gray cap; his shoes, as always, were polished to a high sheen.

"We are ready. Are we not?" He kissed me on the cheek, and we went out onto the deck. Behind us now was the Statue of Liberty adorned with an American flag, probably left there from a Fourth of July celebration. Warm air held the haze, and it rolled across our faces as the ship pushed forward.

"It will be very hot," said Moje. "I don't know how we'll endure that cement jungle."

"We will endure everything if they treat us right."

It took the ship two hours, I think, to finally reach the pier of the Swedish-American line. We felt the warmth gradually increasing as we neared land. Buildings grew before our eyes, and streams of people could be seen moving along. My first impression of New York City was that it was a tremendous cemetery full of oversized headstones. Some of them reached the skies. Others stuck close to the ground. Millions of windows looked out at us apathetically. The heat grew with the activity on the pier and on our ship. Automobiles, horse carts, and handcarts mingled with workers in green overalls running every which way. Piles of valises, boxes, and crates, of different shapes and colors, interfered with the movements of vehicles and people. I don't know how long it took us to make sense out of all these lines, color, and movement, but I know when I asked Moje the time, he said mechanically without looking at his watch, "Ten o'clock."

At that moment two men appeared in front of us. One, tall and skinny like Moje, was dressed in a fashionable dark-blue suit. The second one was short and loaded down with a camera and other photographic equipment. The tall one spoke first. "Mr. Stiller? Miss Garbo?" As we nodded affirmatively, he lined us up against the rail and told the photographer to take some pictures. The photographer motioned for me to come nearer and took a few close-up shots with and without my hat. We discovered that two men made up a greeting party from MGM—a publicity man, Hubert Voight, who spoke Swedish, and a photographer, James Sileo.

"Where is our friend Louis Mayer?" asked Moje.

With dignity Voight replied in Swedish that Mr. Mayer was in Hollywood. I detected immediately from his tone that he thought we were stupid to expect an important man like Mayer to greet us. But Moje persisted, "Why didn't he come here to meet us?"

The two of them looked at each other, then quietly, with even more dignity, replied in a well-rehearsed chorus, "Mr. Mayer is a very busy man."

Moje turned to me and whispered, "Don't worry. The day will come when they will all be running after you."

This was difficult for me to believe. The heat had squeezed all emotion from me; otherwise I would have had a good cry. It was not yet noon, and the temperature was already reaching into the high eighties. The smell of rotting garbage glided over the ship's decks.

I asked our greeters to take us to the Buckingham Hotel at 57th Street and Sixth Avenue, which I had read in the papers was the stopping place of Paderewski. I knew it must be a good hotel. They nodded their heads with approval, but I was sure they were thinking of some other place. Finally one of them stopped nodding and announced that he had reserved rooms for us at the Commodore, not too far from the New York offices of MGM. The conclusion was simple: we would dance to our boss's music. I was afraid and said to Moje, *"Mitt liv är ett enda sorgligt misstag."*

"You have to say that in English for the benefit of our two angels here. *'My life has been one sad mistake.'* As you know, they don't speak Swedish here. You must learn English quickly."

At the time I knew very little English, though I had spent every day on the ship practicing. Moje had also tried to teach me some important phrases while we were in Sweden. But now I needed my Swedish. I complained to Moje, "It's nice for you to joke, since you as a director will get far more money for waving your hands than I will. I have to learn my role very well to get a real salary."

"What can we do? We have to fool around a little bit. In the matter of dialogues, you are learning them fast, and if you make a mistake on film it is easy to correct. Most important is your acting, and there you are superb, and you know that."

As I got into a taxi, I replied, "It is not good that you praise me all the time. I must learn to expect the bad also."

Moje pinched my behind and took a seat beside me. Voight gave directions to the driver and sat beside Moje. The other man sat up front next to the driver.

We drove very slowly east on 57th Street. On both sides of the street children played in front of gray and brown buildings. The adults, despite the heat, moved fast. Some of them pushed small carts loaded with fruits and flowers. They waved their hands over their possessions as if they were chasing away flies. We crossed Ninth Avenue, and I noticed that the people there were better dressed. I saw fewer black people. As we passed 57th Street and Seventh Avenue, the taxi driver opened his window, waved his hand, and announced. "Carnegie Hall." I saw a dark-brown building plastered with posters. At that moment Moje remarked, "This is America's greatest concert hall, where the greatest musicians of the world play."

"Paderewski too?" I asked.

The taxi driver said, "Ja."

I turned to Moje and said, "Ask the taxi driver to show us the hotel where Paderewski stays."

The driver must have known Swedish, because he responded immediately by pointing to the left and saying, "Buckingham Hotel."

I looked at the building, whose door was guarded by two men dressed in dark-purple uniforms with gold-trimmed sleeves and caps. When we reached Fifth Avenue, the taxi turned right and I noticed shops with real wealth. Windows shone with jewelry, furs, and colorful dresses. I had heard about American merchandise in Europe. Now to actually see it was quite comforting.

"To get those things, those exquisite dresses, shoes, hats, and furs," I said to Moje, "I have to make ten thousand dollars a week."

"Do you think you have to have all those things?" I didn't reply, and Moje continued, "You have talent. If you work hard, the producers will give you everything."

"Judging from the reception we got today, I don't think

the producers believe we have any talent. As a matter of fact, they don't consider us as people."

"This is the American approach," asserted Moje, trying not to lose his confidence. "Tomorrow the whole affair will be cleared up. I will go straightaway to the MGM office. In the meantime let's not offend these polite gentlemen."

The taxi stopped in front of the Commodore Hotel, and the blond driver got out and opened the door for me. I reached into my handbag, in which I had American change, and pulled out a few quarters and pushed them into his palm. He grabbed them hungrily and said, "*Tack.*" He looked again at the money in his palm and saw that a few kronor had been mixed in and said again, "*Tack.*"

He then stood up very straight and looked at my face, forgetting about the money in his palm and maybe even that he was a taxi driver. In Swedish he said, "I will never forget you."

"If you profess that you will never forget her, at least you should know her name."

"I know it."

"What is it?"

"Greta Garbo."

I felt very good for the first time in New York. I shook the driver's hand and quickly crossed the sidewalk toward the hotel. The driver was still saying something. I turned to Moje and asked, "What was he saying there?"

"He was mumbling in Swedish that he loves you."

"At least somebody loves me in America. Please ask at the desk if our rooms have baths, because if I do not take a bath this moment, I will commit suicide, not from love, but from dirt."

While Moje ran all over New York trying to arrange our business affairs, I sat in our dark fourth-floor hotel room reading about America or soaking in a tub of cold water. When I wandered downtown to Fourteenth Street, Union Square, and the Bowery, I noticed that some people were dressed worse than the people in the worst slums of Berlin, Stockholm, or Constantinople. What puzzled me was that America had the reputation all over the world of being a rich country with hardworking, ingenious people. Then why did this tremendous difference in wealth exist among Americans? My limited knowledge of the English language and complete ignorance of history and current affairs prevented me from drawing any optimistic conclusions. I was scared of the thought of being poor in this great America.

I began to hint to Moje that he should work harder and persuade the New York MGM people to give us some more money and send us to Hollywood to work on a film. When I heard that the president of MGM, Nicholas Schenk, was in New York, I urged Moje to do everything possible to see him. But the great president refused to see us; instead we were to see Edward Bowes, vice-president in charge of the New York office. He later became known as the famous Major Bowes.

MGM wanted to put Moje in his place. The film-company executives hadn't originally wanted me. When Moje insisted, they showed him who was boss by making him sit in New York doing nothing. They were interested in him as a director, but he was pushing an unknown on them and lacked the credentials in America to back himself up. He was just another European their money had enabled them to get.

Close to noon, we went to the MGM office, completely prepared for the appointment with Bowes. We even rehearsed what we would say to him. We had to wait for an hour. Finally we were summoned into a huge office, where all the furniture and paneling was in beautiful mahogany, and Bowes as a greeting said to me, "How can Miss Garbo play in our films if she can't even read English?"

Although Mayer would have agreed with Bowes, Moje took advantage of Mayer's absence and jumped to the attack: "Mr. Mayer thought she could do very well, and that is why he has given us a contract."

"That is not a reply to my question," said Bowes, who sat in a large chair behind a huge desk and stared at the ceiling. I suddenly grasped the situation and concluded, "They would like to get rid of us and leave us stranded in New York—to cool off, as they say." I quickly said, "I can very easily learn any role by heart in a day or two." Moje took the cue. "Miss Garbo has an excellent memory, and I am sure she can memorize even the Bible in a few weeks."

"I don't believe it," replied Bowes.

For the first time I felt that we had no hope. I would

have to put my cards on the table. "If you don't believe us, if no one else above you believes us, we have no choice but to return to Europe."

"And what will happen to the contract? Who will return the money which Mr. Mayer advanced you in Europe?"

"Ask him, not us." With those words I left the office. I looked back and saw Bowes get up from his seat. He was very pale. Moje also stood up, white as lilies on a grave. It was the first time, I guess, that he had witnessed the boldness that desperation gave me. I returned to the waiting room, thinking, "Here's the beginning and the end of the Swedish Norma Shearer"—something Mr. Voight had called me when he first saw me. I took a seat with my eyes fixed on the doors of Bowes's office, thinking that Moje would appear at any moment so that we could go to the hotel and pack.

My waiting dragged on interminably. People went into and came out of Bowes's office, but not Moje. In the split second during which the door was open, I glimpsed Moje's hands waving energetically as he emphasized some point.

It was well after four o'clock when Moje reappeared. His face was red, but he wore a happy smile.

"Everything looks all right. Let's have something to eat."

"How can this be? The same afternoon bad and good?"

"You must have noticed that all the activity concerned you. First he asked his assistant to bring the photographs that were taken of you when we landed. Afterward, his two assistants came to the conclusion that you are very photogenic and have striking beauty. Then Bowes called Hollywood, and they agreed too. They even agreed to give us more money to cover all our expenses in New York, including clothing, hotel, restaurants, transportation, and so on. But when we arrive in Hollywood we will have to submit a detailed expense account."

"It sounds like a miracle," I said to Moje as we left the building and came out onto a Broadway crowded with people coming from work. We moved uptown and went into the closest restaurant. Moje responded to my comment, "It was no miracle. Your anger and abrupt departure from his office and your exquisite photographs performed their task.

As you know, he does not make the decisions himself. He is just a vice-president. He got scared when you threatened to return to Europe."

"Let's have something to eat," I said, seeing the waiter standing near us with menus in his hand. Moje grabbed the menu and said, "Oh, a Jewish restaurant. I haven't had a meal in a Jewish restaurant for such a long time." By exchanging a few words in Yiddish with the waiter, he discovered that both of them were from the same part of Eastern Europe. They were soon talking, one-third English, one-third Polish, one-third Yiddish. Although it was not yet dinnertime, we ordered, on the advice of our waiter, cold borscht with sour cream and after that gefilte fish. Then a piece of carp, potato pancakes, and other Eastern European Jewish delicacies were pushed on us by our eager waiter. Moje was happy after the successful visit to MGM and ate a great deal in Polakoff's Restaurant. It took us some time to discover the name, because there was none on the menu or on the window. The waiter supplied us not only with that name, but also with delicious food, service, and stories about his native town, Lvov.

After the meal, we went for a walk on a Broadway that was bustling with people and rang with the shrieking of trolley cars, taxi horns, and horse-drawn carts. Crowds moved in all directions. In a few blocks I had seen many stores with an enormous variety of products, had heard many languages, and had seen faces of many races—black, white, yellow. My head was spinning, and I felt hot. "Let's stop for something to drink," I said to Moje.

"What do you want to drink?"

"I would like to try American whiskey for the first time."

"Don't you know that there is Prohibition in America, and only in special, hidden restaurants can you have a drink?"

I was very much surprised that in a country where there seemed to be no prohibition on anything, there was a prohibition on alcohol. We started looking for a place where we could have our first illegal drink. Moje used all his languages, from German, Yiddish, Polish, Russian, Finnish, and Swedish, to French and English, in making his inquiries. I, in the meantime, stared at the various theaters. One movie house was playing a Chaplin film. Right opposite it was *The Lucky Devil* with Esther Ralston and Richard Dix. On a side street, a legitimate theater was presenting *Desire Under the Elms* with Walter Huston. And in one across the street Pauline Lord was appearing in *They Knew What They Wanted.* I noticed a few more film titles like *The Freshman* with Harold Lloyd and *Don, Son of Zorro* with Mary Astor and Douglas Fairbanks.

Moje was still intent on finding a speakeasy, but I suggested, "Let's go and see *The Lady Who Lied* with Lewis Stone and Nita Naldi. I heard in Europe that Stone is a good actor."

So our first film in America was *The Lady Who Lied.* And our first nightclub was the Lido-Venice, where we ventured after the film to have our first glass of prohibited alcohol. I remember to this day that we paid one dollar for a small shot of rye whiskey and the same amount for a glass of beer. For free we received lots of noise and lots of drunkards cooped up in these small quarters.

13

Coney Island

"Being in New York and not seeing Coney Island," said Martha Hedman to me in the swiftly moving subway car, "is like being in Rome and not seeing the Vatican."

It was Sunday, and Moje had arranged our meeting with Miss Hedman, a Swedish actress and singer whom he knew. She had been preparing to spend the day at Coney Island with Arnold Genthe, a famous photographer who, according to Moje, had an impressive studio on 57th Street.

I sat with my ear close to Miss Hedman's mouth because of the tremendous noise the subway made. I didn't know anything about the games, rides, or other excitement of Coney Island that she described, but I nodded my head in agreement.

She was wearing a well-cut green dress and looking very beautiful; but Genthe was even more elegant than his Martha. He was dressed in a white suit, yellow shoes, and a yellow straw hat. Moje and I were again dressed in the clothes that we had worn when we got off the S.S. *Drottningholm.*

It took us three quarters of an hour, maybe more, to

reach the last stop. When we got off those shaky subway cars, we were plunged into sticky heat and into the midst of thousands of people of different ages and different speeds. The noise, the crying of children, the yelling and calling, mixed with the heat to create a hell for me.

"Not yet one o'clock and a few hundred thousand people around us," said Miss Hedman, advising us to hold one another's hands or we would get lost in this ocean of people. I didn't know where we were going, but Genthe said, "I feel like having a few dozen raw clams and a bowl of Boston chowder."

"Not a bad idea," yelled Moje over the million other voices. "I see pictures and signs that say 'wienie.' " Is that not the Austrian *Wienerwurst?*"

"*Ja,* Austrian," exclaimed Miss Hedman. "I would like to have a wienie with sauerkraut. But I think Miss Garbo would like to try a Coney Island chicken. Wouldn't you?"

I nodded my head, almost too preoccupied with the sight of all the people pushing one another on the wide boardwalk. We went to a place on Surf Avenue called Lane's Irish House. When we walked in, the waiters' chorus was singing "When Irish Eyes Are Smiling." One of the waiters approached us and pinned a shamrock on each of us. Then the owner himself, Dan Lane, a man with a huge stomach, a cigar in his hand, came forward to greet us. He grabbed our hands warmly and asked us what country we were from. I was very much surprised, because we hadn't yet said anything in any language. Perhaps we were dressed a bit differently from the ordinary Coney Island crowd.

The restaurant was full of men, happy or sad from alcohol, yet there was no alcohol to be seen. Some of the men looked as I had imagined American gangsters would look. Then Lane opened another door and escorted us to a back room where everybody was drinking whiskey or beer. I even heard the occasional popping of a bottle of champagne. The men ordered whiskey for themselves; Miss Hedman had sarsaparilla, and I had a lemon soda.

We asked the owner to bring us the food he considered to be the best in the house. We didn't have to wait long. Singing the "Beer Barrel Polka," three waiters came up with full trays. Among the many dishes they brought were the famous Coney Island chicken and those wienies, which were called hot dogs here. Before they had finished serving us, the owner reappeared with a bottle of champagne. "This is on the house," he said. It was good business on his part, because when Moje finished his whiskey he ordered three more bottles of champagne without even tasting the first one. The three waiters, each carrying a bottle, returned, this time singing "Did Your Mother Come from Ireland?" We probably spent three hours eating and drinking and not seeing the ocean.

From Lane's Irish House we made our way to "Streamlined Follies," drawn there by a poster of a naked girl named Mona Miles. On the urging of Moje, we went into this establishment and saw a nude girl walking in small circles shaking her breasts. Other girls were doing some sort of gymnastics in drawers. In the midst of all of them stood the famous motionless Mona, nude and beautiful. She might have been twenty years old—she was definitely not more than twenty-one—with long black hair which fell over her beautiful breasts to almost reach her knees. She was truly an American Venus. Men hovered around the stage, shouting excitedly and making all kinds of obscene motions. We were all captivated by this scene. On one side, the beautiful faces of these deminudes, and on the other side, the leathery, creased faces of these middle-aged men. I have to admit that I was more fascinated than anybody else, and Moje had to drag me out.

Our next stop was The World in Wax. The effects of the champagne had worn off, and we left this exhibition sober. Genthe, whom I noticed observing me as a good photographer should, finally said, "Someday your wax figure will be here too."

"Is that necessary for famous people?" I asked.

"Yes! All of the famous people are displayed here. And you will be famous in America."

"*Tack,*" I said politely to him, but whispered in Swedish, "You are drunk."

Moje overheard my remark and said to me, "Arnold is very friendly, and if he photographs you and then gets your picture on the cover of *Vanity Fair* it will make you famous."

"What is *Vanity Fair?*"

"It is a magazine which is read by all people of importance in the cultural life of America."

"Ah! Ah!" I exclaimed in surprise.

The next attraction for us was the rides in the amusement park. We began on the Dragon's Pup. Next came the Caterpillar. Then Genthe suggested the new roller coaster which was said to travel at fifty miles per hour. Moje and I took seats in the front, with Genthe and Hedman behind us. The cars moved upward slowly; we could see the quiet ocean to our left, while to our right were the buildings of Manhattan, clouded by the smoke of many chimneys. The string of fifteen or more cars kept moving faster and faster, higher and higher, making more curves. My head was spinning, and my stomach had reached my throat. Moje saw my deadly white face and asked, "Would you like to get off?"

"How can I?" I was gripping the railing with one hand and with the other, Moje's arm. Suddenly a tremendous jerk pushed me forward and I was out of my seat and on top of the car. My head burst and I lost consciousness. Black night covered my eyes; I tried to scream but my voice wouldn't come from my mouth. I also heard voices calling, but I didn't know who would be calling me and for what reason.

I didn't know how long this had been going on, but when I awoke, Genthe and Moje were kneeling beside me, and Martha Hedman was standing nearby. Both men, with the help of the attendants, had pulled me off the top of the car. I saw three pale faces. I got up, stood on my weak feet, and tried to walk from the roller-coaster platform. It was then that Moje grabbed me in his arms. Holding me tight, he kissed me.

14

From *Vanity Fair* to Sinclair Lewis

By noon every day it was unbearably hot in the cement jungle. I thought the heat must be exceptional, but people later told me that this was normal New York summer weather. Nobody talked about it; the poor were busy perspiring with their work and the rich were out of town in the mountains or on the beaches resting.

When I reached Genthe's studio-apartment, the shades were pulled down to the middle of the windows, which were opened to allow the breeze to come in. The apartment was well furnished in Victorian style, with Oriental rugs on the floors. I could see that his photographic studio had the newest equipment and cameras imported from Germany. The walls of the studio were covered with photographs of men and women of different ages in various poses and clothing. Some had no clothes on at all. Genthe had trimmed his black mustache, perhaps specially for me, and he wore a pair of white trousers and a maroon jacket. Eau de cologne emanated from him when he first appeared in the doorway to say, "I am most happy to see you in my humble establishment." His voice was full of coquetry of the Don Juan sort.

I don't recall my reply, but I do remember repeating to my-self what Moje had said to me: "Genthe is one of the best photographers in America, and he is a power in *Vanity Fair*. If he likes you, and submits your photograph to this maga-zine, or to a similar publication, MGM will raise your salary to seven hundred fifty dollars a week or more."

So I played the role of a woman very much interested in Genthe's apartment and his studio, but above all in him. Moje's words were constantly on my mind.

The photographer, of course, knew his own power and after a short conversation began showing me the nude women on his walls. "You have a beautiful Greek forehead, and romantic blue eyes which do not go together with such sudden beauty. Nevertheless, there is something in you which I should like to bring out in the full warmth of a tropical country. Your ears stick out a bit too much, and your hair is curly, far too much so. Your lips are for kiss-ing." As he was saying these things, he touched me all over and danced around me, chattering all the time. "Your hands are delicate, but I would like to see a little more of your body. I would like to make a few portraits from your head to your feet, in clothes and without. Some of them will go to *Vanity Fair*, and some to film studios and theatrical enter-prises. In a short time I will have made a sensation of you."

Seeing surprise on my face, he added, "Naturally, everything must be with your and Mr. Stiller's approval."

With a sudden effort I got up enough courage and po-litely pushed his hands from my body. "Mr. Genthe, please let's start first with the head. I would like to see how my profile will photograph. If nothing good comes of that, I would like to abandon the rest of the project."

"But, Greta"—and here he began to call me by my first name—"call me Arnie, okay?"

"Okay," I replied, "Arnie, let's start, as I said, with the head. We have lots of time for the rest of the body."

"But Moje told me I could do everything with you, so as to create the proper sensation in artistic circles."

"Arnie, you are a very pleasant man and a great photog-rapher, but I assure you neither Moje nor I thought that for you to make a photographic portrait I would have to undress completely."

"I have to know where to begin."

"You mean, Arnie, you have to judge me nude to know where to begin—from the bottom or from the top?"

"Yes, that is precisely what I mean," he said, and he made an attempt to undress me. "I am a professional photographer, and I would like to make an artistic photograph. I have to see the body nude to develop a balanced vision. Look at the photographs on the wall. All those women are famous today, in theater, fashion, or film, and none of them objected."

"All right, Arnie, take my word. My head is the best part of my body," I said, pushing his hands from my shoulders. "If my head does not come out well under your great camera, I would like not to go further."

"But I have to convince myself," he replied annoyingly.

"No, not now; I have to be convinced first. You must give me some time." And I started to button my blouse. "Maybe tomorrow, maybe the day after tomorrow. I am embarrassed."

He tapped me on the shoulder and then slowly moved his hand down my back. "I will make an exception, but under one condition. I will take pictures of your head from all angles, and if nothing spectacular comes of it, tomorrow we shall begin to make pictures of your torso. Agreed?"

"I might agree."

He started to busy himself with cameras and lights. The lights gave off tremendous heat, and I felt uncomfortable. But I sat still on a high stool and waited. He approached me and took my head in his hands. He started to move it slowly in different directions. Holding my chin steady, he started combing my hair. Then he removed his hand from under my chin and put mine there saying, "Rest your whole head delicately on your hand. Open your eyes as if you have been dreaming about your first love, or about your first intercourse with the person you will die with. In other words, be a warm Latin woman, not a cold Scandinavian one."

I listened to every word that he said and followed his instructions precisely.

"Open your lips more, as if you were about to kiss your lover." Then touching my cheeks, "The eyes should be more dreamy and natural." He left me to go from camera to camera, all of them having been arranged around me. I heard the slow, steady clicks.

"Relax for a minute," he said finally. "I have to reload."

I left the stool and began to walk about, all the while exercising myself. He observed my actions. "That's a good idea; gymnastics relax your muscles."

His preparations went on for perhaps ten or more minutes. I kept walking around the room. I could see that he was a prosperous man who knew practically every woman of beauty and wealth in America. I was very much surprised that Martha Hedman was his favorite model. I found a dozen of her photographs, some with clothes and some without. When I had returned to my stool, he said to me, "As you can see from all those photographs on all the walls, beautiful women want to be photographed in very sexy positions—every one of them except you."

I didn't reply. He continued to buzz around me and perform the fingerwork that gave him so much pleasure. In proportion to his pleasure I became cooler and cooler. "How long," I asked myself, "will I have to stay here and suffer in order to gain a secure place in the American artistic world?" I was rather annoyed at Moje for having arranged this photographic session. I even began making up a dialogue with him which I planned on using about this torture at the hands of a sexual pervert who walked in the skin of the respectable Arnie Genthe. But I guess Moje's eagerness was not his fault; I myself was eager to get somewhere on this huge American continent.

The photographs made by Arnie were extraordinary. Moje had a few hundred prints made and sent them all over the country, to every theatrical impresario and film studio. It was made to appear that the famous photographer Arnold Genthe had discovered an original beauty, the "New Star from the North." One of the portraits appeared on the cover of the November 25 issue of *Vanity Fair*. Moje sent copies of the proofs overseas to Europe. We heard that many people connected with the film world were talking about me, but not as they had in the past as the "Swedish Norma Shearer." I had become a person in their eyes, a person named Greta Garbo.

After that, I forgave Moje for sending me to Arnie. To make peace, I even forgave Arnie, who, seeing the impact that his photographs were having, started acting apologetic about his insistence on seeing me nude. I responded, "You cannot fight your nature, but in the future you must take my word that the best part of my body is my head."

Now it was, as I recall, a hot August afternoon, perhaps the ninth or tenth of the month. Moje was lying on the sofa in the living room while I was taking a cold bath. Suddenly I heard a strong masculine voice: "*Jag älskar dig, tvålflicka.*" I jumped out of the tub and called to Moje to see who it was. When he didn't answer, I put on a robe and ran to the door. As I opened it, I saw Victor Seastrom, who repeated his greeting in English—"I love you, soap-lather girl!" Then he embraced me. Irritated, Moje said, "Go back to your tub, or dry yourself off before you flood the whole room." So, like an obedient girl, I released myself from my guest's arms and hurried back, Seastrom's words echoing in my ears.

I had known Seastrom in Sweden, but not well. As a matter of fact, Moje didn't want me to associate with him, because he claimed that he was always chasing young girls. The day we arrived in New York, Moje called Seastrom in Hollywood, but he was not in. In America, he had become rich and famous. Instead of returning Moje's phone call, he arrived in New York four weeks later.

"I know what is bothering you both. You are lost. Nobody is interested in you. I decided to investigate your situation at MGM. I even talked to Mayer, and he promised that everything would be all right. He did say that somebody is spreading silly rumors about Greta, among them that she once worked in a barbershop soaping old men's faces."

When I called out from the bathroom that this was true, he said, "I know, I know. Moje has told me everything about you, more than you even know, but"—and here Moje interrupted, "Let's forget what you know about Greta and me. Just tell me why Mayer said everything would be all right. His office in New York has ignored us for weeks."

As I came out of the bathroom refreshed and decently dressed, Victor was commiserating with Moje. "You don't know how much humiliation and suffering I've been through. I too went through this American method of humiliation. They perform all kinds of tricks on European artists. When the artists become sick of them, the film bosses come and make them an offer. Naturally, after such an ordeal any offer looks good."

Moje agreed, "They spit in our faces, yet we must say that manna has come from heaven."

"That's right, Moje. The most important thing is to keep your composure, to remain strong emotionally, and to ignore them completely. In the meantime, behind their backs, do something to enhance your career."

"How can we, Victor, when we don't know anyone here?" Moje asked.

"Don't worry, you're doing all right. For example, the photographs of Greta are doing wonders. Lots of people in Hollywood now are talking about Greta Garbo."

"You know, Victor, Greta almost threw me out of the hotel room because she accused me of conspiring with the photographer against her."

"I didn't throw you out, but you should have told me about the methods the photographer used to get his pictures."

"How could I know that you would have to put up with his amorous advances?"

Victor broke in, "Children! Children! Don't quarrel in front of me."

"Don't I have the right to object?"

Victor answered, "Yes, you do to some extent, but you should know that the whole theatrical and film world is based on the relationship between man and woman—on who sleeps with whom. For a man this is not so bad, but for a young European girl it is terrible. The young European woman may sleep with everyone and then find that nothing will come of her cooperation.

"In the end, talent is the most important commodity. No producer will spend a million dollars or more on a film with a woman in a leading role because she also has the lead in his bed. Sex you can get anyplace, and cheaper. But a film must have good acting, good directing, good photography, and a good story in order to make money for the company.

"But although sex is not the key to success, every success has some sex in it. Let's not talk about it anymore. Let's go get something to eat. I would like to take both of you to Delmonico's for a good dinner and after that to the New Amsterdam Theater."

"What is playing there?" I asked.

"The *Ziegfeld Follies*, starring W. C. Fields and Will Rogers and plenty of young, beautiful girls. It's a typically American show, and you must learn about America. Fields and Rogers satirize the American upper class. It is very interesting to observe the reaction of the audience. It is also important for us, as professionals in the theater, to see the realization of the harmony between words, music, and dance. After the theater we'll go on to a party."

The third part of our evening was the most interesting for me. After supper and the theater, Victor took us to a private party at the Chelsea Hotel on Twenty-third Street in Manhattan. At that party I met Helen Hayes, who quietly, almost in a whisper, told me that she was old and famous. She was actually not yet twenty-five years old, and was playing Shaw's Cleopatra on Broadway.

Miss Hayes was petite, and her hair was combed back tightly. She was constantly holding a glass, but I don't know if it was being refilled or always contained the same liquid. She listened attentively to all the men who were trying to explain things to her with rich gestures. I approached these men also—or maybe it was they who approached me; I don't really know. Anyway, I found myself in their company and I tried to talk to them in my broken English. But our conversations didn't progress well. I was looking for a way to leave when in front of me appeared Humphrey Bogart holding a glass and a cigarette. He bowed and said, "I'd like to have a date with you." Bogart, not yet famous, was playing in *Hell's Bells*. I followed his film career with great interest; I have always felt that his fascinating voice resembled mine in some ways. As we talked, I saw Victor moving closer with Sinclair Lewis. "Excuse us, Greta, but I would like to introduce to you a very important American novelist." Bogart fired back rapidly, "If he doesn't write detective stories, I'm not going to read him," and after a second added, "We know each other." Almost ignoring everybody else, Lewis took my arm and said, "I would like to spend some time with this lady." This forty-year-old novelist, whose *Main Street* and *Babbitt* were quite popular, was the most important trophy of the evening. As I recall, Lewis was very tall, skinny, with red hair, and had a face covered with terrible pimples which grew purple when he drank. It was he who introduced me to Scotch whiskey.

Holding our glasses, we went into the next room, where Lewis found an empty, soft chair and asked me to sit down, while he took a place at my feet. I guessed Victor had been following us, because I saw him observing the two of us. He disappeared and returned with Moje. They stayed just a few minutes and left. I was sitting on the soft chair, the author of *Babbitt* at my feet. Lewis touched his glass to mine, saying, "To our rosy friendship and your success in Hollywood."

"Friendship all right, but I don't know anything about success."

"Pessimism may become you. But don't let it get under your skin. You have the face to become the mystery of all time." He paused, took a long sip from his drink, and continued, "I know it will be hard for you. I know America is not a just country. It is full of contradiction and misery, but we artists can get our everlasting two bits in. We do have some, albeit a small 'some,' opportunity to reform life, to reform art, to show others that we, with our vision, can fashion reality into success. To help us we have very talented people from Europe like yourself, Mr. Seastrom, and Mr. Stiller, who escaped from Europe and are now trying to help us build."

"I did not escape. MGM gave me a contract, and I came here."

Lewis replied, "Don't be offended. I'm a little drunk, and I've never seen such a beautiful girl with such enchanting eyes under such long eyelashes."

"You flatter me," I said, but my thought was "Here is a new edition of Arnold Genthe."

"I am trying to be honest. I would like to see you tomorrow, and continue our conversation while we take an excursion around New York. I want to assure you that my attitude toward you is platonic. Although I'm not handsome, I have plenty of women around me. They want me because I'm famous and they think I have a lot of money. As you see, I don't have a high opinion of American women."

"One thing I have noticed in my short stay in America—"

"What have you noticed?" he asked, grabbing a full glass of Scotch from a tray which was being passed by a black maid. Her tray was full of oddly shaped glasses of white, amber, red, green, and other colored drinks. I turned back to Lewis. "I have noticed," I said, "that American men are very frank and very often announce their opinions too quickly and too loudly. Most of the time behind their philosophical opinions, sex is showing its teeth."

"That's right. In our country you have to yell very loud to be heard, and you have to have a great amount of salesmanship to be effective. Don't pay too much attention to sex, because sex is the same everywhere. Tomorrow I promise not to speak of sex. Instead I will talk about my country, which is fast losing the flavorful individuality of its human beings. Everyone has become a member of Tweedledee Club and Tweedledum Company. Everyone is trying to make more and more money and be important."

"In one word, 'Babbitt,' " I replied.

"You've read my novel!" Lewis's voice broke with excitement.

"No, I haven't. On the way here, Victor Seastrom told me about the people who would be at the party. When he mentioned the name Sinclair Lewis, I asked him to tell me the story of your life and his opinion about your novels."

"I admire your honesty. In the same situation an American woman would tell me how much she admired my books and would make various stupid observations. And I would nod my head and play along with her."

"I have to hurry up my study of English in order to read your novels, because I have the feeling that besides money, you will receive a few great prizes."

"You are most wonderful, and your English is charming. When did you learn to speak our language?"

"When Mr. Stiller told me that we might be going to Hollywood, I decided to study English day and night. And on the ship I practiced English every day with native-born Americans."

"Allow me to be your teacher."

Just then a group of completely drunk men and women strolled into our room. Our eyes turned to them. Taking advantage of the situation, I got up. "I have to find Mr. Seastrom and Mr. Stiller. I am tired and would like to get back to my hotel."

Lewis slowly got up from the floor and said, "I will take you there."

I saw that he was swaying. To be polite, I said, "I promised those two gentlemen that I would return with them. But I would like to know the subject of your next novel."

"Now I sense a false note," said Lewis with his face like a pickled red beet. "You are exaggerating your interest in my creativity."

"No, I'm not. I can make a bet that you will get the Nobel Prize."

Lewis searched for words in his alcohol-flooded brain and finally said, "I am enchanted by your charming simplicity. I don't know about the Nobel Prize, but my next novel will be about an evangelistic preacher."

When, five years later in 1930, Sinclair Lewis received the Nobel Prize, he sent me a telegram from Stockholm: "Saints alive! How did you know about this? Please join me."

15

Chaplin

Late at night, or maybe it was already the early morning of August 16, Moje returned to the hotel, excited and upset with me. That evening we had gone to the New York premiere of Charlie Chaplin's *The Gold Rush* at the Strand Theater. Moje's anger showed.

"Why did you return to the hotel after the film? You knew that you were invited to a reception in the Ambassador Hotel, where Chaplin is staying."

"It's very simple. I was tired. My head was hurting, and I wanted to take a cold bath," I replied.

"You lost the opportunity to meet Chaplin, who is already a legend in America. You are really stupid. He can be a very important contact in Hollywood," Moje shouted.

"Perhaps you're right, but I would like to meet people whom I like. Chaplin plays only drunks and slapstick, and I am a serious actress."

"You are an idiot!" Moje was shaking. "He has a comic genius and an inexhaustible imagination. He can play any role. Everybody knows that. Imagine, only thirty-six years old and he already has international fame."

"What does all that have to do with me? I don't like his acting and I don't like his adventures with women."

"It's not important how Chaplin lives or how he plays. He is already a millionaire. He has made over sixty films and has a palace in Hollywood. In that palace we can meet all the people who can be useful to us."

"If your talent and mine plus our contract with MGM are not enough—"

"Listen, Chaplin considers you an actress with great talent. He also thinks that I am a great director. Through him I may be able to make a contact for you with Cukor, De Mille, Lasky . . ."

I was lying on the bed, watching Moje. For a while he stopped his monologue, and just paced back and forth puffing a cigarette. A sense of great pity came over me. I knew he was trying to do the best for me, while I was always somehow undermining his way of thinking and acting. Deep down, I felt that I loved him. At that moment he stopped in front of the window, pulled the curtain aside, and looking at the bright young day said, "Do you know what I admire most in him?"

"His ability to have teen-age girls around him?"

"No."

"Money?"

"No, the fact that he has risen from the depths. After Chaplin and I left the reception, we went downtown to a little Greek restaurant. There he told me, 'Life can never defeat me. Nothing matters, only physical pain. Our tragedies are only as big as we make them.' "

"Very clever," I said, getting up from the bed and going to the bathroom.

Moje continued, "A good actor, and Chaplin is a genius, can play any dramatic role. And I will tell you something else. You, who are always talking about dramatic roles, can play comic ones."

"I doubt it."

"Imagine if you were paired with Chaplin in some good role," said Moje. I detected an enthusiastic tone in his voice.

But my opinion was different. "Nobody would like to see a picture with me opposite Chaplin."

"Leave it to me. The first order of business is to develop a scenario. If Chaplin likes it, the next step will be easy."

"I know that you already have two or three completed scenarios which you wish to show to people in Hollywood. Don't you think you have enough projects?"

I always seemed to be dragging Moje from heaven to the ground. "Let's presume that he likes your scenario. For his leading lady he will want Georgia Hale or some other girl who plays in his films like Edna Purviance or Mildred Harris. Why should he take on an unknown Swedish actress?"

"You said yourself that he changes his women as often as other men do their gloves."

"Aha! Do you want me to join Chaplin's harem?"

"Again you are talking nonsense," responded the irritated Moje. "Have I ever told you to sleep with someone in order to get a part?"

"There is always a first time, and I hear that Hollywood has tremendous possibilities for body trading."

"Get dressed!" snapped Moje. "Let's go and do some window shopping on Fifth Avenue. Get up and get dressed!"

I soon found out that Moje was using Seastrom to persuade Chaplin to help me in America. One evening Chaplin invited us to a sumptuous reception he was holding in the royal suite of the Ambassador Hotel. Practically everybody of importance in New York came. Mary Pickford was there, and so was Marie Dressler. Gloria Swanson came and followed Chaplin all over the suite because she wanted very much to play in his next film. Her first and only role in a Chaplin film had been the tiny role of the stenographer in *His New Job*, without any billing. Anybody who saw this film would recognize Swanson, but when asked, she always denied that she had played in any of his films. Chaplin liked her, but he said, "She reminds me of myself. So I don't want her to play in my films."

Edna Purviance, a great friend of Chaplin's who played in many of his films, was also there. She was very friendly to me, but I detected that she was somehow jealous about my starting a relationship with him. Perhaps this was because she was some eleven years older than I. Other guests were Eva Le Gallienne, Carl Sandburg, Douglas Fairbanks, and Max Eastman, a very close friend of Chaplin's. Among the other writers present were Alexander Woollcott and Heywood Broun, whom Charlie called "an old Bolshevik," and there was Sinclair Lewis again, Scotch glass in hand.

I was introduced to Chaplin, and his greeting startled me: "You've signed a contract with a man whom I punched in the face five years ago."

"Louis B. Mayer?"

"Yes. But first I asked him to take off his glasses. And as one good businessman who listens to another's sound advice, he obliged. Thereupon, coolly and with all my force, I hit him. He's an obnoxious man, and I hit him because he was trying to seduce my wife."

Chaplin escorted me through the crowd of half-drunk people and began introducing me. He tried to acquaint me with everyone in this huge gathering, but because of the tremendous noise from the singing, dancing, and music, I could catch only one out of every ten names. Besides, practically everybody was in an alcoholic fog that serious conversation could not penetrate. Finally he gave up his task and drew me aside. We talked intensely about his films and his theories about acting and comedy.

After nearly an hour he turned and said, "Miss Garbo, I must call my family in California. Don't you disappear, now; I'll be back in a moment and we'll stage something for our drunken guests."

Victor and Moje joined me, and Victor said, "I have never seen Chaplin talk to anybody as intently as he talked to you. You have to be proud, Greta."

"For the first time," Moje said, "he has found somebody who is his equal."

"Instead of praising me, you should do something for me."

"We are doing everything possible," Moje reacted in some annoyance.

"Nothing has come of it," I replied.

Victor broke in, "You are both impatient. You haven't yet been in Hollywood, and already you have met the entire artistic world in America. Isn't that enough?"

The argument was cut short by Chaplin's return. Putting his arm around my waist, he asked, "Do you know *La Dame aux Camélias*, by Alexandre Dumas?"

"I do."

"Then let's play the death scene for our guests."

I almost fainted, because I couldn't believe I was playing a tragic scene with this great comedian. Moje and Victor were also surprised, but Moje quickly regained his composure and urged me on.

I began to recall the scene between Marguerite and Armand. In the meantime, Charlie asked Victor to announce our little entertainment to the guests. Somebody pulled a couch to the middle of the huge room and Victor jumped on it, shouting and waving his hands to quiet our public. When complete silence had come over the gathering, Chaplin spoke. "Ladies and gentlemen," he announced. "Here with me is the famous Swedish actress Greta Garbo. She and I will do the death scene from *Camille*."

I was frantically trying to recall the dialogue between the two famous lovers, and Chaplin, as if reading my mind, said, "Don't worry about the dialogue. We will play pantomime. All you must do is be funnier than I."

The end of this adventure was predictable. Instead of concentrating on the dying Marguerite, everybody was choking with laughter at Armand. I lay on the couch in the middle of the huge salon while Chaplin danced about me. After performing all sorts of funny exercises around me, he leaped on me, and I began caressing and hugging him. Suddenly he stretched out completely, shrieked, and died in my arms.

The hundreds of guests roared with laughter. I looked at Moje's face and saw him laughing too. I sensed his thoughts; we both felt that Chaplin would make me his leading lady and I would play with him in many slapstick comedies. There would be no doubt of our success. We would make lots of money, my troubles would be over, and I would be famous. Moje, Victor, and I awaited Chaplin's invitation.

When the cheers and laughs had died down and people had returned to their drinks, Chaplin asked the waiter to bring four glasses of champagne. He offered me one with this toast. "You are a great actress and you play very well in comedies . . . but not with me."

I didn't have the strength to ask why. I looked at Moje and Victor and felt I had had enough of everything.

"The reason is simple. You are too tall for me and I

would get lost in front of you. I need a short actress with ten percent of your personality and one percent of your talent."

All the champagne I drank with Chaplin that memorable evening did nothing to ease my painful disappointment.

16

Across the U.S.A.

It was clear that the MGM executives wanted to keep us in New York, where they hoped the heat, humidity, and waiting would wear us down. Tired mentally and physically, we would know who was boss—an American expression which fitted our situation. But finally the day arrived for our departure to Hollywood.

It was a humid August evening, and Moje and I had just returned to our hotel loaded with packages from last-minute shopping. In the lobby waiting to see us off was a group from MGM—Edward Bowes, Hubert Voight, and Jimmy Sileo. Sinclair Lewis was also there to say good-bye. He kissed me on the cheek and sighed, "The other night we did not have enough time to talk. I would love to see you act out my novels in Hollywood. I'm going there very shortly myself, and I hope we will have the opportunity to discuss such matters more concretely."

I shook his hand and nodded my head in agreement, but I noticed that Moje didn't care for this developing friendship with Lewis. Bowes moved about nervously, warning us that we had very little time before the departure of our train.

"You're only a couple of minutes from Grand Central," interjected Lewis, and turning to Bowes, he said, "Don't make them over into nervous, jumpy Americans. They've come from Stockholm, where life is normal and people behave like people."

Voight, trying to be a good publicity man and please his boss, appeared confident. "Everything is ready. The tickets are made out for the Twentieth Century. The porters are waiting. Miss Garbo must just finish packing and we can board the train."

Bowes glared at his publicity man in annoyance, as if to say it wasn't his job to push me around. I had a few thoughts of my own—on my future, and on my small successes in New York. Those widely circulated photographs by Arnold Genthe, parties at which I had met so many people, bits of publicity in the papers, and word of mouth had done much for me. Already I had discovered that in America nothing is achieved without pushing and maneuvering.

It took us about twenty minutes to pack and reach Grand Central Station, which looked to me like a cathedral built in a hurry, full of people whom nobody knew, going in to pray or to escape the ugliness of their working lives. Voight kept to my right and Lewis to my left. Behind me followed Moje with Bowes and a group of photographers.

We entered the car, with its narrow corridors covered by heavy carpet, and moved to our compartment. A black man in a white jacket made a low bow. When we arrived at our double bedroom, we found a table covered with food and a few bottles of Vichy water—because of Prohibition— in silver buckets. Voight turned to Bowes. "Should we open them?"

The vice-president nodded his head, and immediately two black men appeared to open the bottles and pour the Vichy water. Mr. Bowes took the first glass and handed it to me. At that moment a photographer took a picture. After this quick toast the black men and the photographer left. Then Bowes signaled to Voight, who removed two bottles of champagne from the large briefcase he was carrying and placed them in the silver buckets. While they cooled, we ate the canapés.

Bowes was talking very fast to me, and his publicity man translated. I didn't listen to either of them. I just looked at Lewis. I think we understood each other and our position as human beings in the complicated machinery of American society. One, a pure product, fighting that society tooth and nail; the other, just entering, unaccustomed to it, but prepared to fight just as hard.

Suddenly, the conductor appeared and announced that in four minutes the train would depart. I looked at my American watch and noticed it was four minutes to nine. We did have time for one quick drink, and after that our host left. Lewis then kissed me on the cheek without saying anything. The train started to move slowly. We went to the window to wave our good-byes to Lewis, Bowes, and Voight, who stood talking with the stationmaster.

When they had disappeared from view, we returned to our food and drink. We were both tired, and when we finished our supper, Moje pushed a button near the door. Almost instantly a black porter appeared, and Moje asked him to make our beds. We left the compartment and looked through a corridor window at the dark sky. The train gained speed, breathing heavily and shaking as it went faster and faster. People passing through the corridor pushed one another the way people did on the streets. Most of them were headed for the rear of the train. I ventured, "I guess they are going to have supper. This is the first time I've seen Americans going backward, not in the direction of progress."

Moje smiled. "I tell you the honest truth. I have had too much of this American progress, especially the technical, and most especially the shallowness and insincere politeness. I should like to go to sleep right now. Would you like to go to sleep, Countess Elisabeth Dohna?" He held my face in his hands and kissed me.

"Why did you call me that?"

"Because that name is connected with your greatest artistic achievement up until now."

"Talking about names, you haven't yet convincingly and fully explained to me how you came to call me Garbo. Please tell me the whole truth. I'm asking you once more, wasn't Greta Gustafsson good enough for me?"

"It was all right, but too prosaic and too common. Only one Garbo exists today in the world," he replied, sitting down near me on my bed.

"Once and for all explain to me—how did you arrive at

this name?—because everybody is asking about it and I don't know how to explain it."

"Oh, let's go to sleep. All of a sudden something unimportant becomes important to you."

"I will not go to sleep until you once and for all explain to me the mystery of my name."

"You will not like it."

"How do you know that?"

"I feel it."

"Let's have less feeling and more facts," I said with annoyance.

"When I saw you the first time, you were beautiful, but your beauty was not refined. You were fresh and simple in your behavior and in your appearance. I said to myself, I must *wygarbować* this girl."

"What is the meaning of that word?"

"It's the Polish word for the process of making leather. A fresh animal skin, just removed from the carcass, is smelly and not very useful. It must be cleaned and put through all kinds of processes to produce first-class leather suitable for the most exquisite products." He could see my amazement but continued the explanation. "Very often in my house when I was mischievous or impossible in my behavior my parents would say, 'We have to *wygarbować* his skin.' That was the signal for a good thrashing, a scolding, or at least a tongue-lashing and lecture on manners and the need for a polite attitude toward other people."

"That means that I was just a little calf, simple and ignorant?"

"Speaking exactly and truthfully, I would have to say that you were a very simple and very modest girl."

"Even still, I do not deserve such an ugly word."

"The verb *garbować* is beautiful, strong, and important. I decided that I would have to work a lot on you, so—"

"So you chose a Polish word."

"A word is a word, but this particular word suits you very well. And how beautiful it sounds in English. The great Garbo!" He repeated these three words over and over again and hugged me.

"Aren't we supposed to go to sleep?"

"Yes, we are going." And he started undressing me. The rhythm of the train brought us together, and we held each other tightly to drown out the noise and the constant, monotonous motion. The train sped on while we clung to each other. It was different from Stockholm. It was even different from our New York hotel. We were very close together despite the constant rattle of steel wheels over steel rails. But we were not steel. We were fragile in our emotions. We were so lonesome in this enormous country and were being carried into the unknown. Scared but happy, we felt that this happiness would endure through any bitterness and disappointment.

We were still in bed when the conductor knocked on our door and announced that we were in Chicago. He told us that we would have to change to the train known as the California Limited. To do this we had to travel to a different station. "How confusing," I thought as we got dressed and went to the other station. Chicago seemed as busy and noisy as New York, but newer and less interesting. Nevertheless, we tried to see everything for which this city was famous. But I don't remember what we saw, except that for some reason the stockyards stick in my brain. When we returned to the train, we went straight to bed.

The next day, when we opened the shades, an avalanche of sun poured into our room. We looked out over an enormous carpet of green fields and found that if we looked very hard we could spy an occasional white house. But mostly, it was the vast expanse of green that overwhelmed us.

Moje pulled out of his pocket a map on which he had marked out our trip. He pointed to the towns we had passed in the night.

"What does it matter to me," I said, "that you show me the places we have passed? I would like to talk to the people who live there and smell their fields and gardens. Here we are locked in a cage which races through states and which does not allow us to do anything but eat and sleep."

"The cities will not disappear," Moje said, taking his finger off the map. "When we achieve fame in American films in the next few years, we might take some time off and travel around the country to meet the people, admire the parks, and smell the flowers. The people will still be there, and the parks might even be bigger and nicer."

I was full of doubts. When I was upset, Moje was usually in a very good mood and tried to console me. Without exception this worked in reverse, for when he was upset, I tried to cheer him up. At that moment I said, "I doubt that we will ever take a trip around this huge country."

Moje jumped up from the bed and for no reason started to be rude with me. "You are an idiot. Even in small things you have big doubts."

"You are always calling me an idiot. I don't know why you belittle me so much."

"I'm sorry. I still can't seem to appreciate the fact that simplemindedness is your charm. It is not my doing that you have beauty and no brains," he said half-jokingly, and he tried to make it all up by hugging me. I didn't know how to react. Though his words hurt, his kisses soothed me. My anger subsided, and I said, "My love is stronger than I."

"Our love, I would say, is stronger than both of us. Remember what we promised each other, for life and for death?"

"Yes."

"But I will repeat our pact once more, so that both of us may remember: If one of us gains fame and money while the other gets kicked out of Hollywood, we will both return to Europe. Do you remember?"

"I remember very well."

"Sometimes I have the feeling that you would not keep this promise. But I'm talking nonsense. I'm sure we will both become famous and wealthy."

We were struck by the monotonous landscape of Missouri and Kansas—the flat space of huge farms with more and more animals and fewer and fewer people. When we grew tired of sitting in our compartment, we went to the back of the train to the three-room observation car. As we moved west, we would sit fascinated by the scene which changed slowly from very flat terrain into valleys and hills.

When we reached Colorado, I felt the impact of the mountains right away. The brown plateau slowly absorbed the red color of the sun, or perhaps it was stained by the dried-out blood of slaughtered Indians.

Before we left Colorado, we stopped in the little town of La Veta, which lies in the Sangre de Cristo Mountains. At the La Veta station, we got off the train to stretch our legs and breathe the delicious air into our lungs. Our eyes were filled with the colors of Blanca Peak; I will never forget the gold, silver, and red in which the peak was dressed. I called to Moje, "We must return quickly and spend a few weeks just to admire this miracle."

Suddenly the sharp whistle of the conductor called us back to reality. The train wound slowly through the Sangre de Cristo. A tired sun bled deep in the mountains and lost more and more of its strength. To our left we could see Costilla Peak, and on our right, a little town with the same name. We were entering New Mexico.

It was quickly swallowed by night. The train attendants switched the lights on in all the cars. The locomotive threw silver sparks on both sides of the track, which was now skirting the high rim of a canyon. Although we could no longer see New Mexico in its nude magnificence, we did feel its wildness through the windows, and the insignificance of a frail human being in confrontation with space.

"Let's go downstairs," said Moje suddenly. "Let's have dinner and admire our fellow passengers, if there is anyone to admire."

When we entered the dining car, the chief steward greeted us with a low bow. We were, as usual, trying to please ourselves, and so were the only people dressed formally for dinner, as though we belonged to the European upper class. The rest of the guests were attired in a variety of garments from cowboy suits to ordinary street clothing.

As we were eating, Moje said softly, "Look over there to your right. There is a tragedy going on."

Across the aisle sat a girl of about nineteen and a boy in his twenties. She was extremely beautiful, with dark hair and blue eyes. He had blond hair and a very regular profile. They were talking excitedly. The steward stood in the doorway staring at them; I thought that at any moment he would ask them to stop quarreling. Suddenly the girl jumped up from her seat and began running toward the front of the train. The boy followed her. They both disappeared. Only the two overturned chairs and the crumpled napkins on the floor told what had happened. The chief steward straightened out the tablecloth, picked up the napkins and the chairs, and was about to greet some new diners when somebody yelled, "She's jumped off. She's jumped off!"

Someone pulled the emergency brake. The dining car seemed to crack to pieces. The train had become a colorful mosaic of scattered food, broken dishes, and frightened faces. The passengers no longer thought of the girl—only of themselves and their soiled clothes. As the last broken dish stopped rattling, the chief steward said loudly, "Please stay calm. She has been found and everything is all right. Ladies and gentlemen, please be seated at your tables and we will begin serving a second dinner."

Moje whispered in my ear, "Our next stop is Santa Fe. Let's get married there."

"Why now?" I asked, taking my seat.

"Because I have the feeling that in America we shall experience many kinds of surprises, and it will be easier for us to swim through them as husband and wife."

"Why have you suddenly become such an enthusiast for marriage, when not so long ago you were indifferent and sarcastic? You might commit a big error by getting married to me."

"I prefer the error of enthusiasm to the indifference of the wise man."

I didn't say a word. Perhaps I was surprised to hear this particular statement from him in this particular situation. He sensed my reservation. "Why are you so hesitant? Don't you love me? Are you thinking of some Texas millionaire?"

"You know very well that I like you more than anybody else and that you will be my only love."

"So why are you reluctant? Let's get married in Santa Fe. Don't you think it would be very romantic?"

"Romantic, yes, but after this incident with these two young people, I don't feel like it at all."

"For that very reason we should get married now."

"In my opinion, marriage should be performed in more serene circumstances, when there is peace in our minds and souls."

"You are waiting for something, not knowing where and from what it will come." He reached for a cigarette, and silence fell. I didn't know what to say or what to do; I was lost. Silence seemed appropriate.

While we were still at dinner, our waiter told us that the girl had been obsessed by the desire to make a career in films. She was only eighteen, and against the advice of her parents and her fiancé she had decided to go to Hollywood. She had taken the California Limited in Chicago. At the last moment her fiancé had joined her. While they traveled, the young man was constantly on the attack, accusing her of selfishness, indifference, and betrayal. The girl tried to match his invective. I guess she suddenly lost her mental balance and jumped. We soon learned that the steward had lied—the girl had been found dead on the siding. Her body was put into a postal sack and transferred to a train going back to Chicago. Her fiancé accompanied her body.

I soon discovered that the crewmen of the train were not moved by the tragedy of this young couple. Rather they were concerned with proving, in the interest of the railroad and the insurance company, that they had not been responsible for this accident. I now became convinced that the dollar was the paramount value in American life. The girl and the boy were the products of such a society. And Moje and I were going with tremendous speed straight into the thick of this world.

The California Limited stopped for the first time in California at a town called Barstow. Then we moved quickly southwest toward Los Angeles. During the last leg of the trip, Moje and I sat in silence and avoided each other's eyes. We were both probably thinking the same thing—"me." It was a dull, deadly silence, especially for two people who were supposed to be in love.

At the Southern Pacific station in Los Angeles, we were met by photographers from local papers and MGM representatives. The only surprise was Victor Seastrom, who said to me that we had left New York in such a hurry that he had to greet us in Los Angeles. He had actually left a few days before and had not told us. Victor gave us one more surprise. He had brought a few children from a Swedish neighborhood, who greeted me with flowers. Victor convinced the photographers that it would be nice to take some pictures of me with the children and their flowers. While the shutters snapped, he walked over to Moje, who was standing to the side in a very somber mood. Victor hugged him. "Moje, my friend," he said. "Are you all right? It's me, Victor."

Moje's face did not change as he said, "Sir, naturally I

remember your name very well, but I don't remember your face." He gave a weak smile as if he were trying to be funny.

I was upset, even angry. I didn't know what to think about Moje's response. Was he sick or just acting stupid?

The reporters questioned me—"What are you going to do? Where are you going to go? Whom do you know here?" I avoided them in my usual fashion: "I am very tired. I would like to go to the hotel, take a bath, and sleep for a week."

I was actually frightened. A tired feeling overwhelmed me. I forgot how to move my legs and hands; I didn't know that I had a smile. For the first time I was so scared that I wanted to scream. I even tried, but nothing came out.

PART FOUR *Hollywood*

17

Into *The Torrent*

My first home on the West Coast was at the Miramar Hotel in Santa Monica. It was an attractive and serene spot not very far from the MGM studios. Moje rented a five-room beach house near the Miramar, and our life on the West Coast consisted of traveling between the hotel, the studio, and the beach house from eight in the morning to eleven at night. Although the scenery was beautiful and the weather balmy, our psychological state never matched the surroundings. We were pushed from office to office, from Louis B. Mayer to Irving Thalberg, the production manager of MGM. From him we were often shunted to the production supervisor, a skillful manipulator, Harry Rapf. Although Moje kept claiming that Sam Goldwyn was his relative, nothing improved our lot in the studio. We were shuffled between the fat Mayer, the young Rapf, and the handsome Thalberg. All three of them wore hats night and day and dressed in the European style. They also displayed a thoroughly crooked attitude toward business competitors and even their actors in their consuming drive to make money. Even Moje, who conversed with them in Yiddish, could not manage them.

We were supposed to start work on September 1, 1925, but my work first began with publicity. First they measured me. As I recall, I was five feet seven and one half inches tall and weighed one hundred twenty-seven pounds. Next they worked on my teeth, my hands, and my feet. They even instructed me on how I should dress on all occasions. After that, they took publicity photos, including one shot of me with a lion, another with the U.S. track team, and many other stupid ones that I can't remember now. I still recall my anger when I was given prints of them.

Moje was also annoyed when he discovered that the producers had turned down his scenario *The Affair of Lemberg,* which he had begun working on in Stockholm. They complained that his approach to filmmaking was too expensive. Mayer and his associates didn't like Moje's filmmaking methods because, according to them, it was just wasting money to photograph various scenes from different angles. Their original favorable opinion of his work was based on Moje's European films, on his written projects, and on conversations with him. They had not yet had a chance to see him in action in a Hollywood studio. They had never seen him spend money. And it was not their money that he had been spending in Europe. They were also fearful of involving themselves with his difficult genius, because they kept postponing his first project while allowing him to be paid regularly every week.

One evening Moje returned to our hotel loaded with books by the Spanish novelist Vicente Blasco-Ibáñez. "I have received inside information from the studio. You will be playing a leading role in a film based on the Blasco-Ibáñez novel *The Torrent.*" He continued excitedly, "You know Rudolph Valentino made his career on Blasco-Ibáñez' *Four Horsemen of the Apocalypse.* You must familiarize yourself with all his characters, and the best way to do that is to read as many of his works as possible. In that way you will catch the spirit of the characters. After that it will be easy to select the correct way in which to sublimate your way of acting into the actions of the women in the novels."

Taking the books from him, I asked, "And what will you do?"

"They don't want me," replied Moje, sitting down on an old soft chair whose squeaking reminded me of the sound of casket hinges. His face was ashen, and he re-mained quiet as he collected his thoughts. After moving around in the old chair some more, he said slowly, "I'll manage. Don't worry about me. What bothers me more than anything is that they want to make you into another Norma Shearer or Pola Negri. I hope it will be a new Pola, because even Thalberg's admiration can't make an actress of Shearer."

"Maybe I should talk to the studio bosses."

"Nothing will help. I have already told them all that you are not going to imitate anybody. First, it is not your nature to agree. And second, nothing important can come of imitating second- or third-rate actors. But they don't lis-ten to me; they just repeat their hackneyed ideas and cite their own financial statistics to prove that Shearer is making lots of money for the studio."

"Then I should talk to them."

"No!" yelled Moje. "If you go to them, they might break their contract with you. Let it be. We'll see what hap-pens. I am technically still under contract. Since they don't want to give me any assignment, I'll spend time with you, studying your role and discussing your dialogue and move-ments before the cameras. I've discussed the film with an excellent cameraman, William Daniels, and he'll do his best for you. What's more, he likes me, and I'm sure he will listen to my suggestions on how to photograph you. If MGM ignores my suggestions and ends up with a poor film, they'll know that to make a better one they will have to put me on active duty."

This reasoning was convincing for the moment, and I had nothing to add. Instead, I put all my energy into the study of Blasco-Ibáñez' novels. From a biographical sketch I learned that he was born in 1867. For many years he had been a member of the Cortes, or Spanish parliament. Why do I mention these two bits of information? Because I am trying to illustrate Moje's working method. He insisted that I learn not only the works of a particular author but also everything possible about the man himself so as to develop an inside view of each character.

Systematically, for many hours each day I studied and analyzed with Moje the characters, background, customs, and even minute mannerisms of the Spanish women in

Blasco-Ibáñez' novels. I had absorbed his radical political beliefs as well as the general content of his literary works. I learned to like and admire him because he was on the side of justice and freedom. Besides his love for the Spanish people, he admired Paris as Moje and I did, although I hadn't been there yet.

Our producer, Irving Thalberg, was the founder of the star system, which fashioned beauty queens from unknowns. The ideal virgin Norma Shearer, the shopgirl Joan Crawford, the sex symbol Jean Harlow appeared to the public as heavenly spirits, full of charm and femininity, surpassing any other woman living or dead. Thalberg's gospel asserted that with the right kind of publicity a girl without talent, but with beauty, could be transformed with very little training into an acceptable actress and capture the love and admiration of all.

Thalberg also believed that the director should tell the actor how to play his part down to the last detail. Moje disagreed completely with this philosophy. He believed that the actor himself should master every aspect of his role, including the dramatic reasons for its existence. Before even attempting to play the role before the camera, the actor should mime the character and memorize his dialogue to the last word. It was the actor's job to find an interpretation that would fit the character. Finally came the work of the director, who, after observing the actor rehearsing, would correct his dialogue, behavior, and movements before the camera. The emphasis in direction would be to praise the good qualities of the actor so as to enhance them, and thereby minimize irrelevant mannerisms or, if possible, turn them into positive assets. According to Moje, an actor and a director so trained to mutually refine their talents would create a fine film.

Despite my belief in Moje's intuitive approach toward acting, I continued to worry about his position in Hollywood. One day, without his knowledge, I decided to visit the MGM offices and talk to Thalberg. When I reached his office door, I suddenly became frightened. I turned around and rushed toward the end of the corridor. Then I heard Thalberg's door open; he called, "Miss Garbo! What are you doing here?"

"I would like to talk to you."

He went back into his office and returned carrying a large manila envelope which he placed in my hands. "Here's the script for *The Torrent*. Go to your hotel and study the role of Leonora."

I took the envelope from his hands obediently, almost as if I were dealing with Moje; I turned around and, without another word, went home. Moje was there to greet me at the entrance to my apartment.

"Where have you been? Shopping or taking a stroll?"

"Both, and on the street I met Thalberg, who took me to his office and handed me this script."

Moje grabbed the envelope from my hands. "You didn't say anything about me, did you?"

"I didn't have the chance."

"Good. I don't want you to interfere in my affairs."

Moje said nothing more, and we walked over to the couch and sat down to read the screenplay by Dorothy Farnum. It was the love story of a Spanish peasant girl, Leonora, who was beautiful and sang well, and Don Rafael Brull, the son of a wealthy landlord, whose domineering mother tried to prevent her son from even meeting this daughter of an ordinary scrubwoman. I don't know why, but I thought of my mother as we read the script. It was a simple, even banal story from the viewpoint of emotions, action, and psychology—like an old opera. I had no opportunity to avoid this role, so I determined that as an unknown Swedish actress in America I would show an Anglo-Saxon audience how well I could play. I pored over Leonora's role for weeks, from seven in the morning till seven at night. In a few days I learned from the studio that the role of Don Rafael had been given to Ricardo Cortez, whose real name was Jacob Krantz. My inner tensions subsided completely when I discovered that Cortez didn't know Spanish and had never been to Spain. He was a pleasant person with dark hair and dark eyes. He was also young and very popular with the Hollywood crowd. The studio paired us because in appearance and character we created a study in contrasts. If my acting or my physical appearance could not draw the public to the movie houses, then Cortez, resembling Rudolph Valentino, would fill them up. Thalberg always calculated every detail in advance.

Ricardo played the role of the weak lover very well. In

retrospect, this was the greatest performance of his film career. After he had played with me, everything went downhill for him. I don't know whose fault it was, but I am sure that the film's mediocre director, Monta Bell, who never had a real film success, could not have done even as well as he had if he had not been under the supervision of Stiller.

My photographic success in this film was achieved through the excellent camera work of William Daniels, who picked up my best angles. I guess I was very lucky, because despite Moje's perfectionist demands, Daniels never stopped admiring me, correcting my diction, and teaching me a few of his own photographic tricks. He was most patient and occasionally made Moje jealous by spending a great deal of time, not only in the MGM studios but also in his own house, taking thousands of pictures of me. But on the whole, his devotion had a soothing effect on Moje, who was at that time depressed. He thought that I would be lost among Hollywood people running after commercialism. Daniels also tried to straighten out some of the differences between MGM, Moje, and me. When he talked about us, he always did so in loving terms, and he always tried to do it before as large an audience as possible. In return for his large and small favors, I strove to please him in all ways. I accepted his suggestions and his criticism without a word, doing just what he wanted.

During the most strenuous period of our work, I lost weight. I ate only oranges, bananas, and grapes, and I smoked excessively. I had no appetite for anything except long hours of hard work.

The film was finished at the end of December. Thanks to Daniels, I knew it was going to be a success. When Moje saw the rushes he said, "Very good, even excellent. Everything works fine. You have elevated this very weak story, and have helped the other actors. Even Ricardo Cortez looks great." Moje was trying to lift my spirits. Later on, I found out that Moje had thought the film was awful.

The opinion of the studio executives was predictable. In their eyes I was a mixture of Norma Talmadge, Pola Negri, Alma Rubens, and Norma Shearer. In other words, a great money-maker who would make *The Torrent* a box-office hit. They weren't wrong. When the film premiered, in February 1926, in Los Angeles at Loew's State Theater and in New York at the Capitol Theater, the public was excited, and Moje's spirits lifted. He knew that the profits from this film would ensure that MGM would keep me under a long contract. After the opening, we began writing letters to our families and to our friends in Stockholm that bragged about the financial success of the film. As an actress, I didn't feel anything special, but as a commodity I was quite precious to MGM. So I decided I would ask the studio heads for a larger share of the gold that I was earning for them.

If someone were to ask me what I liked about California, without thinking I would reply: "Not the studio buildings; not the producers' games; not the overly friendly attitude of the film technicians; not even the actors and actresses as people. Rather the ocean; the abundance of citrus fruits, especially the oranges; and the sunny weather."

Because the MGM studios were located in Culver City, some twenty miles from Santa Monica, where I lived, I did have some privacy and peace at the beginning. I got up about seven, and if I was not working that day I would pack my basket with oranges, bananas, apples, and other fruits and spend the day at the beach with Moje. The salt water and the constant beat of the waves gave me the vitality and the desire to do something worthwhile.

In spite of the agreeable atmosphere of our simple life away from the studio, Moje stayed depressed and remained in his inner world, which was becoming more difficult for me to penetrate. From time to time the studio would send over some good-looking actor to try to break up my relationship with Moje. This made him even more upset. I begged him not to take the studio's strategy, and Thalberg and his group, so seriously. But Moje grew more upset and sometimes even violent, though he never once struck me. Afterward, he quickly lapsed into withdrawn silence.

I believe Moje's jealousy first arose over my relationship with Ricardo Cortez. While we were filming *The Torrent*, Ricardo played the role of a man deeply in love very well. He often tried to invade my privacy at the hotel or else in my studio dressing room, where he persisted in asking me to take walks, go to the beach, or even spend the night with him. So as not to endanger my delicate beginner's position with the studio, I accepted most of his innocent propositions, but I also always made sure Moje came with me. During such excursions we spent most of the time talking about Swedish film technique and especially about Moje's approach to filmmaking which I tried to explain to Ricardo in these few words: "Extract the maximum from the actor and think nothing of costs." This was the opposite of the Hollywood technique, which was based upon saving money.

Whenever Moje would leave us to ourselves for a few moments, Ricardo's conversation turned to personal matters. He was always trying to be the romantic. I pleaded with Moje not to interfere, promising him that I could handle Ricardo very well on my own. But Moje pressed on with his sarcastic observations: "They want you to become entangled in some sordid sexual affair with Cortez. That way they could eliminate me entirely from your life and then eliminate me from this country." I could say nothing, because I knew that what he was saying was true enough.

The handsome Cortez played his role in a masterly manner. He was a good swimmer, and because Moje was not good at all, he would lure me into deep water, where he would tell me how much he loved me and how he could not bear to live without me. I would then fill my mouth with water and blow it out like a fountain on his face. That was my only response.

After many similar encounters with Cortez, one day I finally said to him, "I like you very much, Ricardo, but I am getting tired of your put-on attitudes; I don't know who is behind this, or for what reason. I just don't care to pursue it any longer. I want you to leave me and Moje alone." And so this relationship was severed like a piece of meat by a sharp knife, swiftly, and without emotional mutilation on either side. After that, someone else stepped into the picture.

When I was filming *The Torrent*, my black servant girl overheard actors on the set saying that I was original, unassuming, fascinating, so that very soon all male actors shared the secret wish of being cast with Greta Garbo. My maid certainly possessed a strange love for me. Such overheard talk made her quite jealous. Every lunchtime she would bring me fruits and gossip. She printed most of the rumors she heard on a brown paper bag. Maybe it was from her that I learned to print, instead of writing, like normal people, as if I were trying to conceal my real character. From then on I printed everything, even my own name.

Dorothy Farnum introduced me to Antonio Moreno, saying that he would probably be my partner in the second film the studio was planning for me. The script would be based on another Blasco-Ibáñez novel, *The Temptress*. I was supposed to play the role of Elena, while Moreno, whom everyone called Tonio, would play Robledo.

Tonio was in every sense a typical Spanish type—handsome, athletic, romantic, and dashing. He spoke Spanish and English well, and for ten years or more he had been a well-known film actor whom women from all the world ran to see. Dorothy explained that he was rich as well as a good actor. I replied that I was not interested in him, because he was too short for me.

Dorothy told me that my objections would probably have no impact on the casting. She said, "Tonio is a money-making actor. He insists on playing opposite you, and he has considerable influence in the studio."

After my own talks with Thalberg, I finally decided to accept the situation as it stood. I didn't have much power in Hollywood then, and so for the time being I would have to accept whoever and whatever came along. During my conversations with Thalberg, I kept stressing that my next film must be directed by Mauritz, but I never received any written commitment from the studio.

One day while I was resting on the beach, Dorothy and Tonio came over to where I was lying. Before they had even said hello, Tonio started reading a piece from *Variety*, in his colorful tenor voice: "This girl has everything in looks, acting ability, and personality. She makes *The Torrent* worthwhile. Louis Mayer can hand himself a few pats on the back for having brought this girl over from the other side!"

Then he reached for a *New York Times* review by Mordaunt Hall, who told his readers that "she is never at a loss for an expression or gesture, and in most of the scenes she appears to be at ease before the camera. Miss Garbo takes full advantage of the numerous opportunities to display her ability as a film actress, and she easily captures the honors by her performance."

This critical observation from the *Times* pleased me very much. Moje, who had been lying next to me all the while, did not say a thing, but kept his eyes fixed on the ocean. Tonio noticed our passive delight and continued to read, this time from Richard Watts, Jr., in the New York *Herald Tribune:* "Greta Garbo, Swedish screen star, makes her American debut. . . ."

At that moment, Moje, still staring at the ocean, got up and slowly started walking down the beach and into the water. I watched him without blinking an eye. He did not turn back. He moved like a man in a deep trance. The waters first covered his legs, then his back, and before I had changed my position I saw that the waves were striking his shoulders. Still he walked. I jumped up.

"Moje! Moje!"

I started running as fast as I could toward the water's edge. Dorothy and Tonio rushed after me. I ran into the water and started swimming after him as fast as I could. His head disappeared under the waves, and I grabbed at his hair. I reached for his arm and tried to float him toward the beach, but he was as heavy as a log. I do not know where I got the strength to fight the waves, keep myself afloat, and pull Moje shoreward. But Dorothy and Tonio finally reached us and helped.

When we were safe in shallow water, Moje abruptly got to his feet; he looked pale but said in a strong voice, "I do not know why you interfered with my water communion."

None of us could say a thing. It was all quite crazy. We three just looked at each other in deep fright. To break this morbid silence, I said to Dorothy and Tonio, "Mr. Stiller swims a hundred percent better than you and I, but because he was too tired to listen to stupid reviews, he went to play with the ocean."

Dorothy looked once more at the ash-dead face of Moje and just as quickly turned away. Tonio asked, "If he knows how to swim so well, why didn't he keep his head above water?"

I was shivering, and my heart was swimming in my throat. I sensed Moje to be at the very edge of some kind of final tragedy.

18

The Temptress

When I walked into Louis B. Mayer's office, cluttered with expensive bric-a-brac, the self-made millionaire didn't get up from behind his huge mahogany desk. He adjusted his black-framed glasses and motioned with his cigar for me to sit down. The day before, I had worked out in detail the way I would deal with him. At this moment I was not at all scared or even slightly intimidated by his manner. I sank down into a comfortable leather chair and in order to give my argument as much force as possible, lied in a strong voice, "I do not want to play any longer. I want to return to Stockholm with Mr. Stiller."

He removed the cigar from a mouth full of saliva and once more adjusted his glasses. He had not lost his tongue, however.

"Miss Garbo, you're crazy. Already we have spent over a million dollars on publicity. Look at this photograph."

He took out a print from his desk drawer and tossed it toward me. It was a reproduction of the Sphinx with my head and the three words "The Swedish Sphinx."

I gave it a quick look and repeated, "I want to return to Stockholm with Mr. Stiller."

Mayer moved his small fat body around in his leather chair as he searched for words.

"It's true that my people have ignored you, maybe didn't even see you," he said; "but remember, Miss Garbo, I've changed all that."

"I know. You noticed me when *The Torrent* started to make money for you."

"Maybe, but you're going to get fame and money. You'll star in *The Temptress*." He took a few puffs on his cigar. "A few million dollars more in publicity, and you'll be the queen of Hollywood. And tell me, who else is going to have an opportunity like that?"

I ignored this question and said instead, "You have a great director in Mauritz Stiller, and I think you should give him all the support you can."

"I will, I will," he said, raising his voice as if he were annoyed with his butler. I grew more calm.

"For me, as an actress, it is not important how much money a film makes. For me it is important not to allow you to give the direction of my film to people who don't know my work or me, and whom I don't know anything about. Tell me, please, why must all of you act with such pettiness and stupidity toward Mr. Stiller?"

"For myself and my boys, I apologize." Mayer's voice mellowed. "Everything will change. No one will bother you or Mr. Stiller."

I felt good, because here was I, a simple Swedish girl, who for the first time in her life had bested a shrewd businessman. As if to rub in my superiority, I repeated, "I would like to return home with Mr. Stiller."

Mayer stood up behind his desk, which seemed to be a quarter of a mile square, and walked around it to pat my arm.

"I'll give you and Mr. Stiller a new contract for three years. What's more, he'll direct your next picture."

There was a long silence as Mayer returned to his huge chair. His piercing eyes seemed to grow larger behind his thick glasses. He removed the cigar from his mouth and asked, "Do you agree?"

I thought of how much money I should ask from him and of how I should present this conversation to Moje. I decided that I would make Mayer crawl a little longer.

Finally I said, "I will take this whole matter under consideration, I'll talk it over with Mr. Stiller, and then both of us will give you a reply. But one thing I should like to say right now. If anybody interferes with Mr. Stiller's direction or accuses him of extravagance, I will break our contract and leave for Europe."

Mayer now switched to an emotional angle. "Miss Garbo," he said, "you know Stiller is from my part of Europe. And I know he is a fine director. We really do know each other. But he's got to learn how to save money in pictures. Hollywood is to movies as Pittsburgh is to steel. Every business is based on profits. Here at MGM, we have our own way of making pictures."

"I see now Mr. Stiller and I will have to leave you to your great film productions and go someplace else."

"Okay, okay, okay." He got up from his desk, walked around it, and stood close to me. "I'll leave both of you in peace. I will not even *talk* to Mr. Stiller. He'll have a free hand. And I want to see what happens to your picture with your friend in charge."

I got up to leave his office immediately. He stretched out his hand and said, "Maybe you're right. In any case, *The Torrent* is making money, and we need friendship for the next success. I'll tell you a little secret: I want to triple your salary."

"How about Mr. Stiller's salary?"

"I'll triple his too."

I wanted to squeeze as much money as possible from him, and so I said, "I am most grateful for your generous offer, but please don't hold me to it, because final salary arrangements will have to be talked over with Mr. Stiller. We'll let you know in good time. I am sure we will be able to meet someplace in the middle on the problem of salary."

"What do you mean? Here I am, ready to triple your salary and you still talk more money."

When I returned home, I related the entire conversation to Moje and to Lars Hanson, who was visiting us. Moje yelled at me, "Who gave you permission to talk business with the studio? You are supposed to do the acting while I take care of the contracts."

Lars tried to appease him. "Look," he said, "it's actually good that Greta discussed the business side of her career, because she has the reputation of being a simple peasant girl who is controlled by a clever man."

"Is that true?" I asked both of them.

"Maybe it is true," replied Moje. "But I have given that impression in order to make you into a mysterious person. I want everyone to think that you are wrapped up in your film art and that nothing else matters to you. You are a great actress, and people should admire your creations, not your bank account."

Lars interjected, "But now the gossips will say that Greta is not only a great actress but a good businesswoman. Everyone will be confused, and that is good publicity."

"What are you saying? How will I look then? I, Mauritz Stiller, who created Greta Garbo?"

"But she must stand on her own feet. Everybody knows that Garbo has her own character."

Moje took my arms and kissed me on the forehead.

"Don't worry, Moje," I said. "It's true that you created me, but recently you have been very much upset. I thought it would be best if I cleared up some of our problems with the studio. I felt we could not go on any longer like this."

Lars, knowing Moje's character well, tried to bring us down from the emotional to the concrete. "Triple salary is not so bad," he said. "As a matter of fact, it is excellent."

"What are you saying?" screamed Moje. "They have to pay Greta a minimum of five thousand dollars every working week, and even more for me. I will split the difference between our salaries with Greta. She must have expensive dresses, hats, shoes, and the most exquisite silk undergarments."

Seeing that Moje's face was happy, I suggested, "At the same time, we ought to save. Who knows? Mayer might change his mind about us and after the film give us a return ticket to Europe."

Surprisingly, Moje agreed with me. "You're right. We can't trust a rag dealer who wants to play God."

I tried to appease the animosity of one Jew against another. "We're not yet a success in Hollywood," I said. "Especially you, Moje. But when we become a success artistically and financially, millionaires and the cream of European aristocracy will be running after us. Then we, and not Mayer, will have the upper hand."

As I said this, I realized how much I had adopted Moje's way of thinking. Lars must have had the same thought, for he said, "Who knows? Perhaps sometime in the future we will be running after you and begging you for all kinds of favors: 'O great and wise queen of world film! Look at us and grant us your benediction. Smile on us. Let a portion of your goodness and power flow to us.' "

I started laughing, and so did Moje and Lars.

"The role of Elena in *The Temptress* is not very different from your role of the simple girl, Leonora, in *The Torrent*," said Moje, nervously pacing the room and smoking a cigarette. "And when I finish, you will show the world that you can play a conniving South American courtesan as well as a beautiful honest girl."

Moje was overwhelmed by enthusiasm and repeated over and over, "I will show them how to make a film. What is more, I will show them that I can turn out a first-class picture which will generate tremendous revenue for the company."

I didn't mention to him that the studio people were gossiping about his deal with Charlie Chaplin. Chaplin had convinced Moje that *The Temptress* could use a circus scene. He had been working from the beginning of 1925 on his own film *The Circus,* with a production cost of over nine hundred thousand dollars. To lower his tremendous expense, he wanted Moje to hire his circus. He had also been forced to delay production a few times because of financial problems.

Chaplin's circus group had many top European and American talents. It was really a small zoo, with a big tent, wagons, animal trainers, and two specially constructed platforms from which shots could be taken of the high-wire walkers. Chaplin even promised to appear with this circus, which included Merna Kennedy, who was supposed to ride bareback on a wild horse.

For this entire show Chaplin asked Moje for one hundred thousand dollars. Moje appreciated Chaplin's acceptance of a role in his film, and he offered him twenty thousand dollars for his services and those of Merna Kennedy. In the beginning it looked as if there were no way to reconcile this difference of eighty thousand dollars. But

Moje was fortunate, because Charlie was having marital problems with his second wife, Lita Grey. Foreseeing long and costly divorce litigation, he agreed to Moje's twenty-thousand-dollar offer provided he would not have to act with the circus group.

When word of this contract discussion reached Mayer and Thalberg, they were furious. Moje tried to convince them that if Chaplin did appear in the circus scene of *The Temptress*, the film would be of greater commercial value. But Mayer and Thalberg could not be persuaded that Chaplin would act in somebody else's film. Didn't he almost always write the script, direct himself in the leading role, and retain financial control? They just could not believe that the famous Chaplin would consent to play a tiny circus part in a Stiller film. Nevertheless, Moje stubbornly persisted in his assertions that Charlie would play. If Mayer could be made to believe that Chaplin would be in his film, he could perhaps squeeze some more money out of Mayer to pay for *The Temptress*. This controversy between Moje and the studio was not generating good publicity for either. The two sides were moving further apart to their separate positions.

I tried to stay out of all of this. I continued to study the role of Elena, and Moje kept directing me. He would stand on a chair and pretend he was a camera shooting my solo performance. Seven pieces of furniture represented the other actors. I recall how much I enjoyed rehearsing with the carefully placed lamps, chairs, and tables. Moje was quite ingenious, often leaping from his perch to hurry behind a piece of furniture and imitate a particular actor. In such a fashion we acted out an entire film in one room. Moje worked with almost mathematical precision on all my gestures, my every movement.

Sometimes if he came upon an interesting approach, he would ask me to make a note to use it later when we were in front of the camera. Then Bill Daniels' manipulation of the camera would also be under Moje's strict direction. Years later people asked me how Bill could take such beautiful photographs. My reply was simple. Moje taught Bill how to photograph me *en face,* how to draw the visual maximum from my facial expressions in close-ups. This great cameraman followed Moje's advice scrupulously and became a devoted admirer of my acting.

But all contentment and optimism quickly vanished as soon as we began work on *The Temptress*. The first day on the set, the camera was arbitrarily handed over to Tony Gaudio. Gaudio was a good friend of Antonio Moreno, the male lead, who had tremendous influence at the studio through his financial investments. We quarreled, we argued, but Bill Daniels did not return to the camera. This was in spite of the fact that MGM had promised Moje that he would have complete control over the film, including selection of all personnel.

The studio had cheated him again; but Moje was so eager to make his first Hollywood film that he decided to teach Gaudio how to photograph me. For a while, it looked as though this new student were learning fast and everything would return to normal. But Moreno suddenly decided once more to interfere with Moje's work. He considered himself to be the most beautiful of male actors and knew that if he had the most close-ups the story would revolve around him. Moje managed to convince Mayer that the film would be a mess if Moreno and his cameraman were allowed to interfere with the director's work. Surprisingly, Mayer intervened on our side, and we resumed work in moderate harmony.

The next problem had to do with feet. Moje suggested that Moreno wear shoes two sizes larger than he normally did to disguise his small feet. Otherwise they would look ridiculous in comparison with mine, which were rather large. Moreno did not agree; but instead of going once more to the studio bosses, Moje decided to avoid shooting his feet.

It was nerve-racking work for Moje. He did everything imaginable to allow me to dominate each scene, as he felt that this film was very important to us both. But we tried as much as possible not to alienate my leading man, who was paying increasingly more attention to me.

Tonio dealt with me in the same fashion as Ricardo Cortez had. During shooting and during lunch or after work, he bothered me with various propositions. I related all his proposals to Moje, who decided to intercede on my behalf with Mayer and Thalberg. But I begged him to wait until my own position was stronger.

Moreno did everything in his power to have as many

technicians as possible on the set, all kinds of assistants to assistants, numerous writers, and a lot of others who were drawing their salaries from the budget of *The Temptress*. As a result, the cost of the film went way up. I suspected that Thalberg and Moreno were trying to get rid of Moje by piling up enormous costs and thereby proving his "extravagance." Yet despite the tension, quarreling, and petty maneuverings, work on the film progressed steadily.

I conveyed my inner tension by not speaking to any of the other people, by not even looking in their eyes—I knew that most of them were against either Moje, me, or both of us. Every free moment I spent talking to Moje. I begged him not to lose his temper, but to concentrate all his energies on producing a great film. Moje listened attentively, but he was not able to stop cursing at everybody and everything on the set. He cursed in Swedish, Yiddish, German, and English. People around him were always asking what he was saying. He stopped answering questions that did not explicitly concern the film. Under his direction, everyone worked a very hard, full day, turning out thousands of feet of film.

The studio bosses liked the results, but grumbled that he had already surpassed his budget. He had only begun to work and couldn't believe that he had already surpassed the budget. Rumors spread that he would be removed shortly. Moje was frightened. I thought that this would be the end of both of our careers. The powerful and the vicious seemed bent upon destroying the two of us, and I didn't know why.

At about eleven o'clock in the morning on our fourth day of work, with everyone on the set, I received a cablegram from Stockholm: my sister, Alva, had died of tuberculosis. My heart stopped beating. I lost consciousness and awoke in Moje's arms. I looked up at him and didn't have the strength to say a word. Moje was speechless too. For the first time in my life I wanted to be with my mother.

19

Alva

I recovered enough to ask Moje to take me to the ocean. He still hadn't said much. After all, what can one really say at such a time? He just did as I asked. All the way there, we said nothing to each other. Words would have had no meaning anyway. Our language, any language—even the language of the Bible and Shakespeare—would have been too poor to express the deep pain I felt. I would never again see Alva. I would never laugh with her or share sorrow. I would never see her bright face or her graceful walk. I would never again be buoyed by her optimism about life, career, and success. Although her life had been hard and beset by never-ending health problems, Alva had been brimming with hope. She had not needed money, because once I started making it I sent some to her. But she had never been interested in money. She wanted so much to make her mark in Swedish films; and she had struggled hard to gain recognition. During my years in Stockholm, people continually compared her to me and always predicted a great career for her. I was hurt, and our sisterly relationship cooled off. But that was not her fault. It was completely mine.

Jealousy has been a source of torment for me from early childhood. It still is. I have tried very hard through the years to cover up this jealousy with bashfulness or impulsiveness in my behavior toward other people. I didn't know how to express my jealousy without hurting them, if that is at all possible. So I remained speechless while the bitter jealousy ate at my insides.

Alva was not only more beautiful than I, but smarter, more honest, and above all, more straightforward in her relationships with other people. She was also very generous. But somehow nothing ever came from her sincere and strenuous efforts. Maybe she was in need of a man like Mauritz Stiller; but such a man is not born very often. She didn't know how to run after powerful people or how to beg, be crooked, play around, act deaf and dumb, be the bashful girl or the mysterious woman.

As I sat on the beach, I tried to communicate with Alva, or rather with her spirit, hoping that the ocean waves would carry my thoughts to Sweden where my only sister was resting. Moje stayed near me like a faithful dog. I paid no attention to him; I was talking to Alva—talking not with my lips, but with my thoughts. It was a monologue, a useless one at that, because I suspected Alva had known more about me and my attitudes than she could have expressed in a lifetime.

I felt the wet, salty breeze from the ocean on my face. I didn't have any makeup on, but I felt as if I did. It seemed to me that my mascara was melting and dropping down to the wet sand. And drop by drop, the mascara seeped into my soul, making it black and sticky. I was losing the exquisite shape of my face and my soul. The ocean loomed larger and larger. Waves covered all with their giant white feathers, which leaped rapidly toward the black sky. Suddenly it began to rain hard. I was losing strength; my legs were leaden and my thoughts dissolving. I was sinking in the sand as the rain beat me down. I was headed for some kind of catastrophe, but I didn't know what form it would take. As I stood facing the ocean, my legs gave way and I collapsed. I lay face down on the wet sand for what seemed to be a long time. Then I stretched out my hand and touched somebody. I knew it must be Moje. "If he's with me I won't die," I said to myself. And I lost consciousness.

When I awoke, it was morning and I was home. Moje was sitting on the edge of the bed.

With a rare smile he asked, "How do you feel?"

"It's difficult to describe. What happened to me?"

He quietly replied, "Nothing much. What were you dreaming about?"

"About oranges. There were millions and millions of them. Their skins had been ripped off. They had been quartered and were rotting. On every quarter I saw faces. I saw members of my family, famous actors, friends and enemies—all dead faces."

"And where was I?"

"Among them," I said without thinking.

I am superstitious; I believe tragedies come in pairs. Alva's death was matched by another tragedy, this one involving Moje.

After six more days of shooting *The Temptress*, I arrived for work and saw Fred Niblo sitting in the director's chair. For a long time I had heard rumors that Moje would be replaced, and had repeated these rumors to Mayer, who emphatically denied them. It was now obvious that Mayer had been lying to me. I was finding out that the top men in Hollywood were all liars and could not be trusted.

That morning Moje and I had arrived at the studio early as always. When I saw Niblo acting as director, I went looking for Moje in the director's quarters on the MGM lot. I found him sitting with his elbows on his knees, his head in his hands, and a cigarette in his mouth.

I shouted at him, "Why didn't you tell me when we were coming to the studio this morning? You didn't mention a thing!"

"To the very last moment I was trying to clear up this matter. I didn't want to tell you because you had had enough tragedy. I never thought they would do such a thing to me."

I said nothing, even though my head was swimming in thought. I was upset that the front office had decided to switch directors. I pitied Moje, but I was also scared.

Moje read my mind and lifted his head again. His cigarette dropped to the floor. "I am still under contract. That's why I came in with you as I've always done. Now I will sit on the side and with Niblo's permission give you directions."

Shivers ran through my body. Moje's face expressed the humiliation and indignation he was suffering. He was trying so hard to save me from catastrophe.

"When did this all happen?"

"Yesterday. Mayer called me to his office; Thalberg was already there. They told me point-blank that I could not work on the film anymore, but that I would draw the same salary."

"Why?" I reached for Moje's cigarettes and noticed that as I lit one my hands trembled.

"The reason is always the same. I have gone over budget, spent too much money. If the picture continues under my direction it will cost them an additional half million dollars."

"But they came to see our work and they were very happy."

"I think someone convinced them that to double expenses as they did on *Ben Hur* was simply not worthwhile."

"But they went even further than that. They tripled or quadrupled the original budget of *Ben Hur*."

"You are probably right, but *Ben Hur* has a tremendous mass appeal, while our film has only limited possibilities."

He motioned for me to sit down on a chair beside him. "Anyhow, the whole business is closed. I know contracts. I have no basis on which to go to court. Postponing *The Temptress* will only bring you grief. People all over the world are waiting for your new picture, while you and I wait for more dollars. When we get them we shall return to Europe, to culture, and to fair play. As you can see, we have no way out."

When I returned to the set, the good-hearted Lionel Barrymore told me that Niblo had decided to scrap all the work that Moje had done and begin again. He didn't want the credits to read "Directed by Mauritz Stiller and Fred Niblo."

I didn't confront Mayer or Thalberg with this information, but I did tell Niblo in the strongest words I could find that if he started all over he would have to find another actress to play Elena. I knew MGM would not allow him to do that, because my first film had made them money.

So Niblo changed his tactics and become so cooperative and pleasant that I could have vomited. He showered me with presents and let me play any way I wanted to. I had complete freedom in my interpretation of the role. When the others on the set saw Niblo's attitude, they were, without exception, most pleasant to me. They took care of me as a mother would take care of her child. They let me do anything I wanted.

I was determined to be punctual and hardworking. At a quarter to nine I was on the set, and with only a short intermission for lunch I worked until five. I worked extremely hard, with precision, and at a fast pace. Tony Gaudio imitated Bill Daniels' techniques and concentrated on extracting as much as possible from my face and from my figure. The actors, including Tonio Moreno, displayed a great deal of friendliness and understanding. They knew that after the death of my sister and the removal of Moje from the picture, I was working under terrific nervous pressure. They were afraid that I might collapse and then they would be forced to stop working. Even Moje, who was himself under great inner pressure, followed me on his tiptoes, producing clouds of smoke and throwing out praise for my acting. This flattery helped me return to normal. I didn't wish to disappoint anybody. I tried to finish the film as soon as possible.

Work on *The Temptress* dragged. When it was over, I went home and slept for an entire week, getting up only to take nourishment. The house was overflowing with bananas, grapes, dates, apples, pears, cherries, and pineapples, which I ate with cashews, walnuts, peanuts, and hazelnuts and washed down with water. I also smoked a great deal.

After a week of rest, I went for a walk on the beach with Moje. I didn't want to see anybody or talk to anybody except him. I even refused an invitation from Thalberg and later from Mayer to go to the studio to discuss my contract. Moje told me that they were going to make me an offer of more money and that they wanted me to start work immediately on a new picture. According to them, *The Temptress* would be a great success.

As we walked, Moje said, "It looks as if our roads are going in different directions."

"Why do you think so?"

This was the question I asked most frequently of him and of others. I always needed more explanation, more clarification, and ultimately more commitment from other people.

"A simple deduction," replied Moje. "They tossed me out of MGM, and you are still there. They will give you five thousand dollars a week if you sign an agreement with them and stay. As for me, I have no money and I don't feel good."

"What's wrong with you besides the usual things? You should go see a doctor."

"I know what's wrong with me, and a doctor can't help. I will drag myself along for a few months more, maybe even a year, in this Hollywood dust; collect a few dollars; and return to Stockholm."

I responded automatically, "I will return with you."

He was pleased that I remembered the promise I had made as we left Sweden, but he said, "You stay here a little while longer. You will have a fantastic career and earn a few million dollars. You will dance to the tune of their pleading and begging."

"But what about you? How can you make money when they don't want you at MGM?"

"Don't worry about me. I'll manage. Paramount has invited Erich Pommer from Berlin. They have made him production head at the studio. He's a great admirer of mine, and he'll give me work."

Although Moje had had many bitter experiences, he still believed in people and still tried to build his career on friendship. I didn't share his faith in people, but I knew I couldn't change him, so I held my tongue.

Moje began to plan. "I already have a scenario, *Hotel: Stadt Lemberg*, that I hope to direct for Erich."

"Is that the script you submitted to MGM under the title *The Affair of Lemberg*?"

"It's similar."

"But one studio has already rejected it. Do you think another will now accept it?"

"Yes. In *Hotel* I have included the very best portions of *Affair*. Besides, Pola Negri has read the script, and she likes it."

It shocked me to discover that Moje was considering other actresses behind my back. I saw that he was not as pure as I had been picturing him. But his telepathy remained a focus for my admiration. He sensed my indignation and said, "Remember I am a director, a film director. All actors and actresses are interested in me. I cannot sit without making films. And I need money too."

"But you are still on salary at MGM."

"I am. But they can remove me anytime they wish to. Besides, I am on salary only because of you. They want you for their next film. They have spent thousands and thousands of dollars on publicity for you. And those crooks at MGM are not spending that money because they love you. They would sell their own parents for a few dollars to make soap."

"Let's not go too far. Let's see how the public accepts *The Temptress*. There is a possibility that my career in Hollywood will end with this picture."

"I've seen the completed film."

"And?"

"From the viewpoint of art, it is a scandal. But you play extremely well. I am sure that the American public will call you 'The Beautiful Sphinx' from now on, or 'Dream Princess,' or 'The Mysterious Stranger.' I've seen the publicity prepared by the MGM lackeys. But don't let anyone influence you. Be yourself!"

After the premiere of *The Temptress* in October 1926, the press gave me excellent notices. I had tried to bring out the feelings of a woman who was being pursued by men who lusted for her body but did not love her spirit. I wanted to show the tragedy of a woman who knew exactly what was going on around her as she desperately struggled to find love. She never did, and the tragic ending gave an extra dimension to the film and to my acting. Audiences left the theater discussing the picture, quarreling over me and my acting. Some condemned, while others praised. The film's success made me feel more sure of myself.

For the first time in my life I felt that I could stand on my own two feet without anyone's help. Imagine—I was just twenty-one years old and I had both youth and fame.

20

"Speak Less, Say More"

I was never influenced by other actresses; I never tried to learn from them or imitate even the most famous. In spite of this approach, critics continued to compare me to Norma Talmadge, Pola Negri, Norma Shearer, Zasu Pitts, Gloria Swanson, Joan Crawford, Marlene Dietrich, Tallulah Bankhead, Katharine Hepburn, and many others. To name all of them would take a page or two. Yes, I did see them play, but I never used any of their particular professional tricks. From the very beginning of my career I believed that with my talent and my capacity for work I could play any role better than anyone else. I would like to say that three stage actresses—Helena Modjeska, Eleonora Duse, and Sarah Bernhardt—inspired and aided me in developing my own acting techniques. I read about them extensively.

Moje, above all, played a decisive role in my acting career. But I should not leave out the acting and directing methods of Mack Sennett, D. W. Griffith, and Charlie Chaplin, which I mastered through viewing their films countless times. Observing their work, I concluded that an actress should rely on her own intuition and ability to improvise on the set instead of slavishly following the written word. Directors did, of course, try to prevent me from doing things as I wanted to. Most of the time I was quiet and listened to the director, but I still managed to go my own way. In the beginning this was difficult. Gradually, with increasing fame, I succeeded in expressing completely my own peculiar style of acting and living.

Moje taught me many things. Each scene should be photographed from various angles so that the best angle could be utilized. And if the director is in love with his leading actress, he will concentrate on enhancing the face, figure, and movements of his beloved. In my case it happened that cameramen, especially Bill Daniels, were able to develop my "acting attitudes" through clever shots of eyes, lips, and even shadows of my profile.

My best teachers were ordinary people. I observed them carefully and memorized their movements and the facial expressions that resulted from confrontations with their surroundings and their inner emotions. All my life has been spent learning the secrets of behavior and *real* acting from ordinary people.

With my personality, directors worked best by needling me, but not to the point of drawing blood, for when I bled emotionally I could not act. I just stood there petrified. But a little needling, a little argument, usually brought forth a creative spontaneity.

Perhaps it is old-fashioned, but aside from learning my particular role by heart, I also studied the other roles in every film I made. If it was a period film, I liked to know everything about the history and way of life that were presented. A few days before I went before the cameras, I tried to forget my role and occupied myself with cooking, washing, sewing, taking long walks, seeing other films—anything but thinking about my approaching performance.

When, after such relaxation, I confronted the hot lights and the camera, my role immediately gained an extra dimension. My subconscious gave my words a different color. I moved as if to music, and my face acquired all kinds of interesting shadows that only a camera in an expert's hands could capture. During actual shooting, I disliked—or more accurately, I hated—people staring at me and making trivial comments. My work could not be evaluated properly if each scene was considered separately. If it were possible to make a film without directors, technicians, and hundreds of assistants, I am sure I would have played better, and such a film would have cost less money and less of my strength. Then film work would have been a pleasure for me. But it was a torture under the glaring eyes of hundreds of people. I was very jealous of my method, of my ego. I didn't like onlookers' forming wrong opinions about my imperfect initial acting and my relations with the technical crew.

Whatever I achieved came from my talent and hard work. To the last day of my life I will defend this achievement against those who try to minimize my efforts and destroy me. To defend my achievement, I choose as a weapon complete silence. You can use this weapon very successfully if you have enough money to maintain absolute privacy. I use money and silence to shelter myself from those who try to belittle or destroy me. It is not easy, for I must always be on my own.

When Moje talked about our life together, he always mentioned great lovers—Antony and Cleopatra, Dante and Beatrice. He always maintained that he loved me and that he admired my acting. But when he went to Paramount he chose Pola Negri and claimed that she was the actress best suited for his next film, *Hotel Imperial*.

She called Moje very often and left messages signed only "Pola" at the Miramar Hotel. In the beginning, I asked him who this mysterious Pola was. Like a good gambler, he replied, "The horse on which I am placing all my fortune."

I saw that Moje was trying to broaden his horizons and find a new artistic idol. Like him, I began to feel that our roads had come to a parting.

"Film acting, though it must not be taken too seriously, is nevertheless an important study in human nature," Charlie Chaplin said at the reception in his spacious home.

Everybody who was anybody in Hollywood was there. Among the guests were Mary Pickford, Douglas Fairbanks, and Sam Goldwyn. And there were others from the arts— novelist Upton Sinclair and Clare Sheridan, an English sculptor and writer. Clare was in love with Chaplin, as were many of the actresses present, like Lila Lee, Lenore Ulric, Josephine Dunn, Anna Q. Nilsson, and Pola Negri. Lita

Grey, who had divorced Chaplin but was still in love with him, was the only one besides Pola who claimed that the famous actor had built his huge mansion in Beverly Hills for her. The forty-two-room mansion was surrounded by trees which had been transplanted full-size because, as the story went, Pola loved to sleep with an open window and listen to the rustle of the branches in the wind, as she had been accustomed to doing in her native Poland.

Pola's real name was Apolonja Chalupiec. She had come to the United States after she divorced her first husband, Baron Popper, in 1921. Immediately she had, according to her account, become a hit in Hollywood. She had attempted to form permanent relationships with many actors such as Rudolph Valentino and Charlie Chaplin, to mention just two of the most prominent. In my opinion, her spectacular romances made more of an impression on the public than did her films. Even Moje was enchanted by her beauty and talent and stuck close to her.

That evening an organist was playing Bach in the huge living room with its very high ceilings. This beautiful music was corroded by trivial conversation. Discussion centered on the topic of filmmaking—control by one man versus the "factory method"; the relative importance of actors and the director; and the role of the producer. Naturally the Mayers, the Goldwyns, and the Thalbergs were most interested in box-office returns. The artistic achievements of Sennett, Griffith, Eisenstein, Von Stroheim, and Chaplin did not convince them otherwise. To them the dollar was a direct measure of art.

During the party, I discovered that Moje's method of photographing a scene many times until perfection was achieved had been employed by the producers of *A Woman of Paris*. Adolphe Menjou, who played Pierre Reyel in that movie, told me that some scenes had been shot sixty times and the most complicated were done over one hundred times. Edna Purviance, as Marie St. Clair, was photographed one hundred times in one scene. She had had the trying task of showing through kisses alone that she knew that Menjou didn't love her anymore but that this knowledge did not make her unhappy.

Speaking of a complicated love affair, it was here that I met for the first time John Gilbert and his business manager,

Harry Edington. Gilbert had black curly hair, a well-trimmed mustache under a long, slightly crooked nose, and black close-set eyes. When I shook hands with him, I noticed how strong his grip was and I also noticed his big ears. He was perhaps two inches taller than I and was dressed in a gray-and-white-checked jacket, black trousers, and a black tie. He was overly persistent in his attentions and told me that I should call him Jack. But I insisted on calling him Yackie. Hearing me call him this, he laughed and said that from now on he would call me Flicka. Moje was immediately jealous and doubled his attentions to Pola Negri. Yackie was not conscious of Moje's attitude or of anyone else in the room except me.

"Flicka, you will be my *femme fatale* in *Flesh and the Devil.*"

"I don't know anything about that," I replied without any interest, "and I don't care."

He ignored my mood as he ground out his own.

"You will die under ice trying to warn me of the dangers of my duel with Ulrich von Kletzingk, who will be your good friend Lars Hanson. And you will be his wife, Felicitas."

"And what is your name in this film?" I asked, not really paying attention and looking for Moje to rescue me.

"Leo von Sellinthin."

I suddenly became angry. "This whole business is a mystery to me. Everyone else knows what role I'm going to be taking, but I'm kept in the dark about everything. Why hasn't Thalberg or Mayer told me?"

"They'll tell you tomorrow, but right now let's go for a ride. My car's outside."

Yackie grabbed me by the arm. I shook him off and remained rooted.

"Who wrote the story?"

"Benjamin Glazer. It's based on Hermann Sudermann's novel *The Undying Past.*"

"Who will direct?"

"Clarence Brown. Do you see him standing over there in his perfectly pressed suit talking with Arthur Hornblow, Lilyan Tashman, and Edmund Lowe? All of them are my friends," he concluded with pride.

"I don't know any of them."

"You will meet them, Flicka. My friends will become your friends."

I said to Yackie half-jokingly, "I admire your optimism."

Moje had been talking with Pola Negri for the past half hour. Suddenly he appeared between the two of us as if to break off our conversation. He said nothing, but glared at Gilbert.

"I will see you later, Flicka the Swede," the smiling Yackie said, completely ignoring Moje's presence. "Or maybe," he added playfully, "I will call you Geebo. I don't know just yet." He shook my hand energetically and went off.

"Why did you involve yourself so deeply in conversation with him?" Moje demanded. "Is it because he makes ten thousand a week, or is it because he has been married twice and is now running after every girl in Hollywood?"

"I see you did your research for today."

"Yes I did. Eric von Stroheim, who directed him in *The Merry Widow*, told me that Gilbert is a third-rate actor produced by a second-rate pair of vaudevillians. He doesn't know acting, and he has no formal education—only a look which helps him to seduce women left and right. His marriage to Leatrice Joy was shattered because he brought teen-age girls to his house and organized drinking and sex orgies in her presence. Right now he is between wives."

"But his films must take in a lot of money if the studio pays him ten thousand a week."

"That's true. The American film industry doesn't need good directors or good actors. Everything is based on gimmicks and floods of well-organized publicity. In the opinion of most critics, Gilbert is emotionally shallow, and his interests lie not in film but in women. Escapades with them are touched up by the publicity department and sent to the press. His adventures have caused him to become an idol of the lonely American woman, and his poor acting is covered up by his so-called good looks. I think it would be best for films and for the public if the industry would leave him to his sexual exploits and let him die in obscure happiness."

"That is your opinion."

"Ask anybody in this huge house. Everyone will tell you the same thing. After a few drinks even he himself will admit it. I have nothing against him personally, but don't tell me I didn't warn you. He will entangle you in some cheap adventure which he or his stooges will then publicize all over the world so that eventually you will not be called Greta Garbo, the great actress, but Jack Gilbert's ex-girl."

"What can I do? I'm supposed to be playing with him in a film. You know they don't let me select my partners."

After a pause Moje replied, "That's true. Perhaps we should go to MGM and ask them to select a new partner because your temperament is such that you cannot act well in his presence. Your two films are making money, and you are regarded as a fine actress and a pleasant person. You don't want to lose that image by playing with him. I'm sure the studio will take that into consideration, and the profit from your films will support your wishes. Under no condition should you be involved in any scandal."

"That makes sense," I replied agreeably. But at the same time, I kept thinking about Yackie. I had met many intelligent, handsome men, but none of them had appealed to me. He was only the second man, after Moje, to possess such a magnetic personality. Perhaps it was his dynamic character, somehow opposite to mine, and his bursting desire for life that planted romantic notions in my mind. I felt I needed a new spark in my life, and Gilbert was going to provide it. He was eight years older than I and, as Moje said, had considerable experience with women. But when I met him I felt the freshness of a young boy, as well as the charm of the mature man. He was also no intellectual like Sinclair Lewis or Charlie Chaplin.

But Yackie could not soothe what bothered me most—the attitude toward me of MGM's studio bosses. They just ignored me. Everybody around me knew what I was going to do, but I never received this information first-hand from the studio. I finally decided that I would have to fight with the bosses for the privilege of selecting material, coactors, and directors, and above all, to get more money for my hard work. It is true that Gilbert was having a financial success with his film *The Merry Widow*. Later I learned that some of his other films, such as *The Big Parade*, brought in even more money. But I, with only two films to my credit, had received far greater critical acclaim. I tried to explain MGM's attitude to myself, by saying that the majority of American filmgoers were women, and Gilbert was the idol in their dreary lives, while to MGM I was a foreigner, simple and stupid.

The only solution left for me was to arrange a frank talk with my bosses. I didn't want Moje to be a partner in this discussion. He was busy trying to establish himself as a director, and that was going to be a difficult task even with his talent. I was thinking of going to Charlie Chaplin for advice, or Harry Edington, the man who had gotten Gilbert ten thousand dollars a week.

Then, as if my thoughts had willed it, Edington approached Moje, took him to one side, and whispered something. I saw that Moje was listening intently. When they returned, Edington, after being introduced, said that it was callous on MGM's part to exclude me from the discussions about my future projects. He instructed me to continue playing ignorant, while he, as a friendly gesture, would talk to the top MGM people. He would not even take the usual ten-percent agent's fee. Moje whispered in Swedish that I should agree to this proposition. The three of us then began to discuss the whole situation in English.

I discovered that Edington had been sent to us by Gilbert to convince me that I should play in the film with him. Moje knew this, yet continued to support Edington. I guess he thought it would be the best way to get as much money as possible. I made an appointment to meet with Edington at Gilbert's house on Tower Road the following day. Moje nodded approval. I didn't really want to go to this meeting, because I still felt I should go to MGM myself and discuss the whole matter. Slowly but surely, I was learning American business tricks. After fifteen more minutes, I left the party and went home to rest and develop tactics for my own surprise visit the next day to MGM. Moje returned to Pola Negri to engage in some banal conversation.

As I was leaving, a Swedish saying came into my head: "You should have less fear and more hope; you should eat less and chew more; you should sigh less and breathe more; you should speak less and say more; you should hate less and love more. When you do those things, all that is best will be yours."

So I changed my mind and did not go to either meeting. In spite of the late hour, Moje, when he returned from the reception, insisted on telling me the newest story about Yackie.

"Do you know that I introduced your Yackie to Bernard Shaw?"

"Stop calling him 'my Yackie.' We've both known him the same length of time, and equally well. Also, Shaw was not at the reception."

Moje insisted he had been there, and I tried to explain to him that he was a victim of hallucinations induced by his hatred of Gilbert. I never did check up on Shaw's where-abouts, so I cannot swear whether he was at the party or not. But the story was a good one.

"When I introduced him to Shaw, Yackie grabbed his hand and said, 'Are you the real Bernard Shaw?'

"Shaw answered his question with a question of his own: 'Mr. Gilbert, are you really an unbeliever?'

"Gilbert told him, 'Please forgive my suspicions, but last week at a party at Thalberg's, somebody introduced me to Julius Caesar. A day or two later, I discovered that I had been fooled.' "

Moje had probably told this story many times, but he still laughed when he told it to me. With laughter I replied, "Maybe Yackie's knowledge of history and literature is zero like mine, but this doesn't mean that he doesn't want to help me."

"There is a big difference between the two of you. You like to learn and make progress. But he was born a fool, and he will die one. Besides, I don't believe he wants to help your career. He just wants to help you into his bed. And because you're not interested, you pose a challenge for him. So he must work on a strategy."

21

Yackie

I remember Moje saying that life does not stop after the first kiss or after the last one, after victory or defeat. Right now I was at a crossroads.

I was born under Virgo. Women under this sign love to shop, yet are never certain what to buy, what to accept free, and how much to pay for anything—friendship, love, shoes, or a piece of furniture. They are always looking and bargaining, and so their lives are spent on trivial things.

I bought several dresses and suits, half a dozen comfortable pairs of shoes, and even a fur coat. All this shopping lasted a few months and took me to stores in Los Angeles and Hollywood. I looked, measured, and bargained; I noted the prices in one store and then went to a half dozen more, where I compared, touched, measured, looked in the mirror, and bargained again. I was afraid to spend money, because I thought money was the only security that I would ever have. On the other hand, as an actress, I knew that I should be dressed exquisitely, so I bought the best things on the rack. I loved luxury, because I had come from a very poor background.

I was hungry not only for luxury, but for friendship and new surroundings. I felt lonely and thought my life was without purpose. Although I had all the necessary ingredients for happiness, the addition of more ingredients only brought me discontentment and depression. I felt that everybody was bothering me and everybody was uninteresting. I kept trying to escape from people. I never once thought that I might seem flat and uninteresting to other people.

After my shopping spree, I thought of some excitement in love. I was tired of my relationship with Moje, who kept making unnatural demands. He was always trying to teach me new things in film and in sex. I was now financially independent, and I kept having the desire from time to time to exchange Moje for somebody else. This feeling arose not because of his adventures with Pola Negri, but because I was restless for new experience.

Inside, I was drifting away from Moje, but still there was never a moment in my life that I did not think of him in some way. I suspect that was only natural. We had spent so much time in the same bed, at the same table; I had learned practically everything from him. Yet I felt that in time I would think about him less and less because of my inner nature. I don't know how to be grateful for good things that are freely given by others.

Then there was John Gilbert. He was regarded in the film colony as intellectually primitive, as well as crude in his acting and his sexual behavior. He didn't possess an ounce of originality or inventiveness. People said that he was totally a creation of the MGM publicity department. But Gilbert, abetted by the studio, thought otherwise. The studio had asked Harry Edington and Carey Wilson to protect him in this unspoiled view of himself and to build and perfect him as the divine lover. His sexual and marital escapades with actresses such as Virginia Bruce, Leatrice Joy, Clara Bow, Mary Hay, Mary Pickford, and Beatrice Lillie and with the writer Dorothy Parker were publicized extensively. No one could separate the facts from the lies. It was rumored that his hilltop palace on Tower Road, which overlooked all of Beverly Hills, was the setting for drinking and sex parties.

I decided to see all his films, and I asked Bill Daniels to organize a private showing for me. Of all his films, I liked

The Big Parade the best—especially the scene in which Gilbert teaches Renée Adorée how to chew gum. Another scene I found superior was his encounter with a dying German soldier. After I saw those two scenes, I told Bill that Yackie had great talent.

Bill never said that Yackie was a bad actor, but he did comment that he was probably better in bed than in front of the camera. Those scenes, he added, had been wholly the creations of the director, King Vidor. They had been photographed without rehearsals, as was that great director's habit.

This was common in silent films, because the director could yell instructions to his actors without worrying about his voice's interfering with the actors' voices.

During the first day's work on *Flesh and the Devil,* when Clarence Brown introduced me to Yackie, I didn't mention that I had met him earlier at Chaplin's. I was cool and formal. He saw that and during the first two days of shooting decided to take a different stance toward me. He was polite, smiled often, was not at all persistent, and sometimes even ignored me completely. But I read his black eyes, and they contained sexual desire, perhaps even real love. In the scenes where kissing was required, Yackie kissed me with great passion, with an open mouth, and he whispered of love and marriage. Gilbert's kisses and caresses on the set excited me. I felt like a woman, something that I no longer felt when I was with Moje. Lars Hanson played my husband, and when he saw what was going on, he became indignant about Yackie's feelings toward me. Bill Daniels related a conversation to me between Yackie and Clarence Brown in which Gilbert begged him to tell Lars not to be so close to me on the set. He wanted to have me for his wife, and he detested seeing another man touch me. Brown replied that Lars was playing the role of my husband and must therefore act like one.

I knew at the start that it would be difficult for me to avoid Yackie, not only during working hours but also in my private life. Through my long association with Moje, I had developed certain psychological and physical patterns which suited Moje and eventually me. I had a tremendous fear of associating with new people, but at the same time, I desired such contact and was uncertain how to deal with

Yackie's persistent presence. Was I heading into something new and more beautiful, or was it just going to be one big headache?

In the meantime, the MGM publicity department anticipated my feelings and began publicizing the then nonexistent affair between Garbo and Gilbert as something out of this world, truly a great love adventure. This publicity made me uncomfortable. I didn't know then that I could object to it and that my objections would carry some weight. On top of all this, one day after work, Yackie came up to me and said, "Unreciprocated love is torture for the soul."

"And fulfilled love is a torture for my body."

"Who taught you to talk like that? Moje?"

"Maybe," I said. "But your sayings, your clever sayings, are created in the front office of MGM. Is that not so?"

Yackie had considered himself something of a god, especially in his relations with women. So he said nothing and left like a little boy who had just been scolded by his parents.

A few days into the film, I noticed that changes were taking place in his behavior. Perhaps he was going through some crisis, experiencing the first real love of his life. I knew that he represented golden love to every American woman, and I felt sorry for him. In conversation with me, he was so meek, so resigned. I read approaching drama in his eyes. But what could I do? I had lived so many years with Moje. His constant presence had had a lasting effect on my entire existence. I had to act in this film to make money, to establish my position. I had to play opposite a man who I felt was experiencing real love for the first time. I was not certain of his true feelings, and my confusion so blinded me that I could not analyze my feelings toward him or even toward Moje. I was compelled to examine my attitudes toward both of them. I thought that if I compared and evaluated my own feelings I might come up with some solutions. I couldn't sleep nights. I tossed feverishly, trying to place myself in the proper perspective regarding the two of them. Finally I said to myself, "Only an idiot would allow herself to be bitten by the same dog twice."

On the other hand, someone else might say that love is governed by its own law. I would have to agree with that too.

Hundreds of the most important film personalities came to the Hollywood premiere of *Hotel Imperial,* the film Moje had directed for Paramount. Moje and Pola Negri, his leading lady, did everything conceivable to make this premiere a grand social event. Hanson, Seastrom, Asther, and I represented the Swedish colony in Hollywood. Chaplin, Gilbert, Thalberg, and Mayer came, as did the most famous actresses of the day—Gloria Swanson, Norma Shearer, Marion Davies, Lillian Gish, Mary Pickford, and Edna Purviance. Moje didn't forget to invite Antonio Moreno, Lionel Barrymore, Clark Gable, Douglas Fairbanks, and Conrad Nagel. He also invited Cecil B. De Mille, even though he had had a violent argument with him on a Hollywood street a few days before over filmmaking. Negri was accompanied by Gable and the syndicated Hollywood columnist Louella Parsons. She had already been pronounced a success in the film by Paramount publicity releases. After the showing, we were all invited to a cold supper and drinks, where practically everyone was talking about Moje's film. During the reception, Moje received a promise that he would direct two new films for Paramount. The first film was to be *The Woman on Trial,* with Pola Negri and Einar Hanson. The second was to be *The Street of Sin,* with Fay Wray and Emil Jannings.

At the party Moje took me aside. "I am independent now," he said, "and you are no longer my protégée. You don't need me anymore. We are both famous, and we will soon have lots of money. After two years of hard work we will return to Europe together and work on our own films."

Moje was certainly under the influence of success and alcohol that night. Although I didn't want to cast any shadows on his happy mood, I said, "It is difficult to say now when we will go back to Europe."

Moje didn't become discouraged. "Everything will right itself. We have promised each other that we will return to Stockholm together. Remember my advice: Don't get involved with Gilbert. He is not worthy of kissing your feet, let alone your lips. Remember that."

"I will remember, but you should remember not to involve yourself with Pola Negri."

"She doesn't mean anything to me. I must keep up a front with her for business reasons."

"Gilbert means the same to me." I imitated his sour expression.

"But people gossip and columnists write that you are in love with him. My private investigation confirms that."

"You mean you are investigating me?"

"That's not important. What is important is that we love each other, and after those two films I would like to leave this Hollywood jungle."

To emphasize his commitment, he said very loudly, "I would like to leave with you!"

People around us stopped what they were doing to stare at us, but Moje didn't care and repeated several times, "I would like to leave this Hollywood jungle with you!"

I was irritated, and I left his side because I felt uncomfortable. Everyone seemed to be looking at us and thinking that we were quarreling. Suddenly Yackie appeared in front of me.

"I've had enough of this business," he said. "This whole show, here, there, staged very well by Stiller."

"This whole show, as you call it," I said, "was not organized by Mr. Stiller, but by the Paramount publicity department. Don't you remember what MGM did for you when you finished your last film?"

"You're right. It's no cause for argument. Let's go for a ride." He took my hand and we went out the door. I felt hurt. Moje always seemed to try to embarrass me in public, especially when I was trying to show him that I was a grown-up woman, an independent woman. Without thinking, I seated myself in Yackie's sports car, and we rode slowly through Hollywood. Yackie sang some Spanish melodies, and I gazed at the fields shining under the moon.

At one point he stopped his singing to say, "Felicitas, please don't be that close with Ulrich all the time. Get closer to Leo."

"You mean you're jealous even when we work on a film?"

"To tell the truth, yes, because for the first time in my life, I really love a woman."

"You mean after so many girlfriends, wives, and other kinds of women, you are still capable of loving someone?"

"The past means nothing in your presence."

I felt strong emotions brewing in his mind, so I said, "I'm very tired, and it's late. Please take me home."

"I'll take you home," he responded quickly, and he turned his car into a narrow side road.

"Where are we going?"

"I told you I would take you home, but with your permission, I should like to show you the beautiful view of Beverly Hills from my house."

"No, not tonight. Maybe some other time, during the day."

"But the view is best seen during the night under a bright moon. If you're afraid to go to my house, I can assure you we will not be alone. The servants will chaperon us."

"No, I'd rather not. Please take me home."

"Okay. I'll take you home right away."

He turned right and started going back. I began to reconsider my decision. I knew that there were many servants in his palace on Tower Road, and I knew that he would not molest me. The silence between Yackie and me was punctuated by the steady throb of his car. He was hurt, or perhaps he was only playing that way. I didn't have a deep enough knowledge of his character, and I took his silence as a positive sign.

After a few more moments of deliberation, I said, "Although I'm tired, I've decided I would like to see your famous view. I won't stay more than a few minutes, because I'm exhausted and do need the sleep."

He said nothing, but stepped on the gas and started driving like a madman. At the same time he returned to his Spanish melodies, singing them much louder than he had before. When we arrived at the entrance to his mansion, a servant leaped out and opened the door to the car. We went up the brightly lit steps, and a butler greeted us. I said to myself, "He was right. The house is full of people."

Upon entering, I noticed that his spacious quarters were filled with royal furniture.

"Did you select and arrange all these objects yourself?"

"No. I don't know anything about that sort of thing. I hired an interior decorator from New York, and he did everything. But that's not important. Let's go to the terrace."

He took me through many large, elaborately furnished

rooms. He seemed to be trying to impress me with his wealth. And I was impressed—the house looked like a museum with its well-polished furniture and gold-framed pictures. But the whole scene was overwhelming; I don't remember anything specific about it except lots of red, gold, and blue, vibrant in the bright light.

When we stepped onto the terrace, I saw a table set for two. Candles flickered, and a big silver bucket held bottles. Everything was like a fairy tale.

"Here," he said, seating me on a huge carved chair; "we will drink champagne and admire Beverly Hills. Here I do not serve sandwiches and unsophisticated drinks like those at Paramount parties."

Two maids dressed smartly in black uniforms brought us food on silver platters. I could smell the exquisite sauces, but I said, "Everything looks beautiful and expensive, but I don't see Beverly Hills."

"It's too late at night. All the lights are out. People are sleeping. Perhaps if we drink a few glasses of champagne we will be able to see Beverly Hills."

I wondered how he knew that I would accept his invitation to enjoy all this elaborate fare. Perhaps he had been expecting someone else. I knew it was too late to retreat, so I strove to prepare myself for anything.

Supper lasted for over an hour, but I enjoyed it all very much. I was hungry, and nothing tastes better when you are hungry than a pheasant in an exquisite French sauce washed down with champagne. I ate fast and drank plenty. Suddenly my head started reeling from the alcohol, and I looked for a way to excuse myself. I said straightforwardly, "I know I'm not being a polite guest, but I should like to go home now."

Before he could reply, an old servant woman appeared to ask if we wanted our coffee on the terrace or in the drawing room. Yackie said the drawing room, and the servant left. I certainly wanted coffee; I've never felt as tired and drowsy as I did then. I pulled together the remnants of my mind. Had he put something in the drink? My head was spinning, but I managed to hold myself together, hoping that the coffee would help.

"Let's go to the drawing room," Yackie said softly. "The coffee is probably ready." And in that same tone of voice, as though he were talking of the same things, he said, "I love you. I love you very much."

I said nothing. My mind was on the coffee, and I walked beside him trying to keep my balance. I didn't want to have him catch me.

When we reached the drawing room, I could smell the coffee, and I speeded up my pace, only to fall onto a big sofa. I closed my eyes for a moment and murmured, "I'm so very tired."

He sat down next to me and kissed my neck. With both hands he held my waist while my head rested on the back of the sofa. I felt nothing as he kissed me on the lips. His hands were working at my dress and then at my stockings. His mouth was soon traveling over my entire body. He did all of this slowly and with deliberation, using his hands and his mouth gently but insistently. It seemed little different from what Moje had done, but Yackie was more methodical, less nervous, and perhaps more experienced. I felt for a moment or so that my father was rocking me to sleep, and just for that moment I thought Yackie to be superior to Moje. I felt his warm body, and for the first time I experienced a different kind of love. Through my mind, steeped in alcohol, went the thought that Gilbert's love was different from Stiller's. I don't know why I use their last names, except perhaps to be more impersonal, more objective, to emphasize the physical and emotional differences between them.

Suddenly a noise woke me from this dream, and I heard Yackie whispering, "Get up quickly."

I sensed impending danger, and I grabbed my clothes and ran after Yackie. I don't know how long I ran, for I was in some sort of stupor, but I soon felt cold air on my body and I knew I was on the terrace.

"Get dressed fast," he said, half-dressed already.

"What's happening?" I asked, trying to put my clothes on with my trembling hands.

"I think I hear Stiller quarreling with my butler at the door."

And with those words he was completely dressed; he smoothed his hair and mustache.

"Stay here," said Yackie, regaining his composure. "I'll go and greet Stiller and tell him I am showing you Beverly Hills from the terrace."

He disappeared, and I finished dressing. The night air cooled my cheeks, and I thought the California breeze a most wonderful thing.

Clever Yackie took about ten minutes to bring Moje to the terrace. He took him on a tour of his mansion, pointing out every piece of furniture and every painting. After each description, I heard Moje direct the same question to his host: "Where is Greta?"

And Yackie kept repeating that I was admiring Beverly Hills from the terrace. Moje raised his voice. "It's time for her to go home!" he shouted. "Please don't take up any more of my time with your stupid possessions. Take me to her."

When I heard his angry voice, I left the terrace to greet them. As I entered the house, I saw that Moje had grabbed Yackie by the collar and was hitting him on the face and yelling, "It's time to go home. Time to go home!"

For a split second Yackie attempted to defend himself, but he gave up and took the beating stoically with his hands hanging at his sides.

"Time to go home! Time to go home!"

Moje's baritone voice shook the pictures on the walls. I jumped between them. Yackie turned his back to me, and Moje came toward me. He was still yelling that it was time to go home. He grabbed me by the shoulders, and I felt a terrific pain there. A few steps, and we were outside the mansion.

Later, I discovered that a beautiful view of Beverly Hills could be had from Gilbert's terrace. But that night there was fog.

22

Flesh and the Devil

The role of Felicitas was easy for me. I played a woman who sacrificed love for comfort and material luxury. I felt the role with every muscle of my body. Clarence Brown, my director, sensed this.

"You don't need my instructions. All I have to do is follow you and catch your superb acting, and we will make a great film."

Cameraman Bill Daniels was also excited about my work. "Your face changes during every scene almost as if the sun and stars influenced your features. Every move you make expresses the precise meaning of the words and the character of Felicitas. Your face is phenomenal in its depiction of feeling."

Lars Hanson, who had the role of my husband, was amazed by my commanding movements on the set. The same astonishment was expressed by Eugenia Besserer, who played Lars's mother. Gilbert too was pleased with my acting, and he tried to carry our lovemaking from the set to real life. We took long walks together, or swam in the Pacific, or had dinner in fancy restaurants. This activity went on during the weekends, because during the week I was working on the film ten hours each day and was extremely tired. I had only the strength to go home, take a cold bath, and go to bed. When sleep did not come, I would pick up a novel or a play written by Sudermann. I learned to enjoy and admire him as a writer, and I dreamed of starring in his play *Magda*, in which Sarah Bernhardt, Helena Modjeska, and Eleonora Duse had triumphed.

Although I was getting satisfaction and recognition from my acting, my health was suffering. I had pains in my chest, and I was deathly pale. I did everything I thought would help me. I rested, ate wholesome food, exercised, and soaked in hot and cold water, but nothing helped. I dreaded doctors and their probings, but I finally decided that I must see one. He gave me a thorough examination which lasted two hours and then told me that I had some peculiarities in my lungs, irregular beatings of my heart, and a touch of anemia.

"Really nothing serious. I had the same symptoms once," he said, clapping himself on his chest, "and look at me now—I'm still alive."

"You know why you're alive? Because a different doctor was taking care of you, not yourself."

He laughed so hard his bald head became red, and in a shaky hand he wrote me a prescription. I went home to sleep. The next day, as always, I had to be in the MGM studio at six o'clock in the morning to continue my work. On my way back home, I picked up a few newspapers and to my surprise found my name linked with that of John Gilbert in each one. It was our great love that fascinated the papers; we were compared to the greatest lovers in history. All the writers of those long articles stated that only Shakespeare could have captured the supreme passion of Garbo and Gilbert, that he alone could have written the appropriate sonnet. I noticed other curious similarities in all the articles, and I concluded that Yackie and the MGM publicity boys were responsible for spreading this gossip. Somebody had to be paying for the writers and the space in the papers.

I began receiving invitations from people who were unknown or little known to me. Arthur Hornblow, Jr., Edmund Lowe, and Diana and George Fitzmaurice, not to mention Hollywood executives, traveling princesses, and all kinds of aristocrats, invited me to dinners and parties. Even the Swedish Ambassador to the United States sent a letter asking to visit me in Hollywood. I was most surprised that actresses like Mary Pickford, Clara Bow, Norma Shearer, Gloria Swanson, and Pola Negri, who had always considered me a rival, suddenly started inviting me to their houses. After much deliberation with myself and discussion with Moje, I wisely decided not to accept any invitations. As a result, people started referring to me as an "alluring personage," as well as the "Swedish snob." I didn't think much about that talk at the time, but I have to admit it did bother me a bit. I began to say to myself, "Greta, be stubborn. Greta, have more courage." But I knew that courage is sometimes a mask that covers fear. You have to be very clever to cover cowardice with courage in such a way that people will not be able to sense your fears. It was difficult for me to master this psychology and successfully confuse everyone.

When *Flesh and the Devil* was completed and MGM gave a private showing, everybody was waiting to congratulate me. Instead, I left in the middle of the screening and went home. I reasoned that I had done my job in front of the camera and that I didn't need to exhaust myself in front of people who were unimportant to me. Besides, I didn't get paid for socializing with MGM's guests. The MGM bigwigs didn't like such behavior, but I had come to a point at which I just didn't care what they thought.

Flesh and the Devil premiered on January 9, 1927, at New York's Capitol Theater. I still remember by heart what the *Herald Tribune* said about me: "Never before has a woman so alluring, with a seductive grace that is far more potent than mere beauty, appeared on the screen. Greta Garbo is the epitome of pulchritude, the personification of passion . . . Frankly, never in our screen career have we seen seduction so perfectly done."

Yackie threw a big party on his two-hundred-thousand-dollar yacht, *The Temptress*, which was named after my second picture in the United States. Naturally, MGM paid for it. Mayer used every kind of persuasion to get me to go to this party. I finally yielded to his pleading, because I felt I had exhausted the patience of MGM and because I was still financially dependent upon the studio. All of the cast from *Flesh and the Devil* was to be at this party, including Marc McDermott, "Count von Rhaden," who during the entire filming had forced different foods on me, saying, "You should eat well so that you will have the strength to finish this film. Our futures depend on your efforts."

I debated whether I should go with Clarence Brown, who had been so patient with me during filming, or with Lars. I finally decided I would feel more comfortable on Gilbert's yacht with my compatriot, so I went with Lars. As soon as we arrived, Yackie pushed Lars aside and demanded of me, "Have you ever been in love?"

"Only once in my life. And it ended tragically."

"What happened? Did he marry somebody else?"

"No."

"So what happened? Did he commit suicide?"

"He is living."

"Where?"

"He is living with me."

Yackie dropped his glass and grabbed me in his arms, "Leave him! Marry me! Leave him! Marry me!"

I turned and fled *The Temptress*. I went home to cry.

23

On Strike

I had made a great deal of money for Hollywood, but I had not made much for myself. I began thinking hard about the entire situation. I came up with a brilliant idea. I would not go to Thalberg's office or his house. I would not accept any telephone calls or messages from Mayer. I would just simply disappear. I made this decision on my own and promised myself that I would stick to it and see what happened.

I was tired from my work on *Flesh and the Devil*. Then, without giving me a rest, the studio handed me a new script, *Women Love Diamonds*, which had yet another vamp role for me. Once before, I had not shown up on the set when I was supposed to; but I did not have the courage to stay out and went back to work after only one week. This second time was different.

The first person to call was Yackie. My maid told him that I was sick. When Mayer called the same day, my maid told him that I could not come to the telephone. She told Thalberg the same thing when he tried to reach me the next day.

When Moje discovered what was going on, he became very angry. "They want to discuss your contract, and you, like a fool, won't talk to them. You should listen to what they have to say. You don't have to agree right away, but you should listen. Otherwise you will lose work."

I noticed that Moje was upset and was hovering, cigarette in mouth, behind me. I reassured him: "Don't worry; everything will be all right. I just want to get the same ten thousand dollars a week that my partner in the film gets. After all, we both play leading roles."

"I like that, but we have to think the entire situation through. I think that if I were to go talk to Mayer and Thalberg, they might not accept my reasoning. They might even refuse to see me, because both of them hate me."

Moje and I stopped talking. Instead, we began thinking how we might obtain maximum results. Suddenly, somebody knocked on the door. The maid thought it was a food delivery and opened the door. When she saw an empty-handed man in the doorway, she said, "Miss Garbo is not at home."

"How do you know that? I am sure she is."

He brushed her aside and walked briskly straight into my bedroom.

"I'm Carey Wilson, a producer at MGM. I've seen you and Mr. Stiller several times, but I haven't had the pleasure of meeting you."

Moje shook his hand, and I asked him to sit down. Wilson came right to the point.

"Miss Garbo, Mr. Thalberg asked me to bring you a message. When can you see him in his office for the purpose of discussing a new contract?"

I answered coolly, "Mr. Wilson, when you return to your office, tell your paymasters that I will not play in their films unless I receive ten thousand dollars a week, the same salary as Mr. Gilbert gets. I am packing my belongings and going back to Europe."

Wilson became pale, while Moje broke into a smile. He was probably thinking that he had taught me well.

"Is that all you have to say, Miss Garbo?"

"Yes. I'm most grateful for your taking the trouble to hear me out. I hope that someday very soon we will have a more pleasant conversation."

"That's quite all right. I'm looking forward to a more leisurely exchange of opinion." He got up, shook hands with the two of us, and left.

Later on, I would see Wilson often at Yackie's home, where we became friends.

Two hours later, Harry Edington appeared at my hotel door. He was extra pleasant. "Jack Gilbert would like to play tennis with you, but he can't reach you by telephone. He asked me to ask you to accept his invitation."

"I regret that I don't know how to play tennis well."

"He also mentioned swimming."

"Please tell Mr. Gilbert that I have forgotten how to swim because there is no river here."

"But we have an ocean, and swimming in the Pacific is a delight."

Moje was listening to this conversation and appeared pleased.

"But I'm afraid I don't know how to swim in the ocean. I'm accustomed to rivers and small lakes."

Edington was persistent. "How about yachting?"

"I have no yacht."

"Jack does."

Moje saw that this conversation was leading nowhere. He decided to be blunt. "Miss Garbo is distracted because she is having contract difficulties with MGM. She wants ten thousand dollars a week from MGM. Otherwise she will not act in their next film."

"I understand. If you and Miss Garbo will permit me, I will communicate her desire to Thalberg and Mayer. I will act not as an agent, but as *amicus curiae*. I won't take any agent's percentage from her. The entry in my book will read 'Prestige.' "

"I agree one hundred percent," said Moje, and I echoed him. This proved to be a most intelligent move on my part, because Harry Edington got a five-year contract from MGM worth five thousand dollars a week for every week of the year. Most actors at that time were paid for only forty weeks. Each year the amount would grow until it reached a weekly six thousand. I would be getting two hundred sixty thousand dollars a year the very first year. True to his word, Harry didn't take a ten-percent agent's commission, and he became my friend and financial adviser. He helped me invest my money in real estate and stocks and bonds, to secure my old age. Discussion on this contract ultimately dragged on for six months. It was officially signed on June 1, 1927.

Rumor had it that I had dropped Moje after the violent encounter at Yackie's, and Victor Seastrom was supposed to have become our intermediary. The truth is that Moje, tormented by his growing jealousy and failing health, was trying to drop me. His tuberculosis had flared up, and he had developed circulatory problems. He complained that he could not feel his legs and hands—"They are numb, like pieces of dead wood."

Although he had no real reason to be jealous, he was drowning in this obsession. This passion, together with his poor health, transformed him into a tragic figure. It was about the time that I signed my contract that he told Victor, "She doesn't need me anymore. She is making money and is famous. I would only be a dead weight on her neck."

Although I am not known for my delicate conscience, I tried very hard to see Moje. I spent a good part of many days sitting in the lobby of his hotel waiting for him. But he always managed to slip out unnoticed, and he told his servant not to let me into his apartment. At Paramount, in those last days of *The Street of Sin*, he gave orders to the guards to keep me away from his office. I knew him very well. He was stubborn and ambitious, and if someone blocked his way, man or woman, he would become enraged and provoke a physical confrontation.

Moje's intake of nicotine and alcohol had become very heavy. He was even drinking during working hours. He made enemies left and right at Paramount, fighting with the actors, technicians, with everyone who didn't promptly execute his orders. When he had finished work on *The Woman on Trial*, the company claimed that it would be a financial failure. But he still had his contract for *The Street of Sin*, and he worked very hard to finish it as soon as possible, always pointing out to Victor that he didn't have much time left. Unfortunately, he became sick toward the end of the filming in the fall of 1927, and so was unable to complete the work on his own. Ludvig Berger finished it. But it was really Moje's film. This second film was graced by Stiller's unique touch and craftsmanship; but because it was not in the American style, it too was financially unsuccessful.

Then the day came when Victor told me that Moje was leaving for Europe. He begged me not to go to Moje and say good-bye, but I got on my knees to plead with him to give me a chance to talk to my so-called creator for the last time.

"If I take you to Moje, I will lose his friendship. And if I don't take you, I will lose your friendship. I don't know what to do. Is it worth it to take you to the railroad station and let you see the ruins of a man?"

I knew Victor was a good man and that he was in a dilemma. I also knew it was the incident in Yackie's house that had made Moje so unspeakably angry and that he had never explained what had happened to Victor. It was not in his nature to talk about his feelings. He was secretive and protective about anything that related to me. But Victor was convinced that Moje's reason for breaking with me was his Hollywood failure.

"For the hundredth time let me try to make you understand. Moje thinks he is a burden to you, and because of his physical and mental condition, he thinks he cannot help you anymore. But I don't feel you can break such a long friendship just because one of the partners is a success and the other a tragic failure."

I listened intently to Victor and took his every word to heart; but like Moje, I couldn't tell him of our secrets. The next day was rainy and gloomy, and Victor, who had yielded to my pleas, brought me to the station where the California Limited was being loaded for the trip to New York. To my surprise, Moje greeted me with a smile on his pale face, almost as if nothing had happened between us. And he said, "I am returning to Europe because Svensk Filmindustri"—and here he weakly waved a yellow cablegram in front of my face—"has invited me to make a great film over which I am to have complete financial and artistic control."

Although I knew this was all false, I nodded my head to give the impression I believed him. After a moment of silence and painful hesitation, he added, "You have to stay here, because Hollywood is your future. Don't think about the promises we made to stay together. They were childish and romantically foolish."

Victor looked at me and I at him, but he had no opportunity to discover the reality behind these words. He was a delicate and discreet man, careful not to intrude. Besides, he knew Moje very well, and to ask a personal question might trigger a violent outburst. Moje abruptly took up another subject: "I had a long conversation with Bill Daniels, and he knows just how to approach your face and figure with the camera. He knows how to capture your movements, your smile, your sadness."

I grabbed him in my arms and kissed him so fervently on the face and neck that I thought I might appear mentally deranged. He pushed me aside.

"Keep healthy and gain great fame," he said. "I am proud of you and I will never stop believing in you. I will never forget you."

I started to cry like a small child, and I saw tears in Moje's eyes. Victor turned his face away, and I knew that he too was trying to hide his tears. Moje then grabbed me in his arms, and I felt his tears fall on my forehead and roll down my face to mix with my own tears. Suddenly I felt Victor prodding us toward the railroad car. Moje took me by the hand and picked up his valise. I looked at the station's huge windows and saw that the sky was almost black. Then there was the whistle of the train, followed by the whistle of the conductor, and the train began moving. Moje let me go and jumped onto the steps of his car.

"We will see each other in Stockholm, dead or alive."

"Yes, yes, Moje."

"Don't hurry," he yelled. "You have too much work to do. Don't hurry."

"I will see you in Stockholm in a few months," I yelled to Moje. I repeated this several times, but I am sure he didn't hear because the train and people were making so much noise. I could only see his strong hands stretching up into the air. I felt weak, my head was burning, and I began to faint. Victor caught me and in a shaken voice said, "You almost went under the wheels of the train."

I started yelling, "This hand! This hand! This hand!" and I felt Moje's hand touch my face. But I lost the vision because my eyes had drowned in tears.

24

Anna Karenina, or *Love*

Victor Seastrom had yearned for a long time to direct me, but I was very much surprised when I learned that he had been trying to convince various MGM executives that only he was capable of doing so. He knew that I admired the writings of Lev Nikolaevich Tolstoy, whom Moje always referred to by his full name. Consequently, he told the MGM people that he would direct me in a screen adaptation of one of Tolstoy's novels. To reduce suspense, I can say that Victor never did get to direct me in Tolstoy, but thanks to him and Moje, I tried to learn as much as possible about this great Russian writer. I discovered that his philosophy could be summed up in one sentence: "Don't be wiser than nature and life."

When the MGM studio bosses decided to film *Anna Karenina,* they entrusted Frances Marion with the scenario. For the director's job they talked to Dmitri Buchowetzsky, who knew Russia and her history very well, but his directing ideas did not coincide with those of the bosses. Eventually they settled on Edmund Goulding. John Gilbert was to play Vronsky opposite my Anna. Brandon Hurst played my husband, Karenin, while the Grand Duke was George Fawcett and the Grand Duchess, Emily Fitsroy. Philippe de Lacy took the role of Seresha. The only consolation for me was the knowledge that Bill Daniels would be in charge of the camera. I was thus assured of his masterly photography. As so often happens in Hollywood, the title of Tolstoy's great novel was changed. The new title was *Love*. The publicists could then announce, "John Gilbert and Greta Garbo in *Love*." The press release exposed the mentality of Mayer and his helpers, who cheapened the story with their tidy sentimentality. "Anna is the wife of the Russian Count Karenin. She is a great and popular lady, much younger than her husband, who is more occupied with affairs of the state and business than with matters concerning his lovely wife. They have a little son, on whom the mother lavishes the love of a starved heart. One stormy night the Countess, returning to St. Petersburg from a journey, is forced to stop by the fury of a blizzard which blinds her horses. A young officer appears at her carriage and takes her to the inn where they spend some time . . . Next they meet on Easter morning in church. He begs her to forgive him for the incident at the inn, and she forgives him. During the evening of the same day, she asks her husband to take her away on a long trip, 'just we two alone.' "

The busy husband does not comply, and naturally she falls in love with somebody else. So much for the story; but the emotional setting and atmosphere are of tremendous importance to any actress. There is also something more. Despite a poor scenario, she can still present a quality of mystery, the stuff of which legends of feminine perfection are made.

The film premiered in New York City's Embassy Theater on November 29, 1927. It amazes me to think that the American press could praise me so wonderfully.

The cautious Richard Watts, Jr. of the *Herald Tribune* wrote: "She seems an excellent and attractive actress, with a surprising propensity for looking like Carol Dempster, Norma Talmadge, Zasu Pitts and Gloria Swanson in turn."

Ten years later, probably after seeing the film again, he could go even further. "I think that no actress has brought so much beauty and magnificence to any form of the theater within this generation, and the closest thing to a vision of ideal loveliness that is destined to be vouchsafed to us in this world!"

But the European press, except for Sweden, was not so lavish—I presume because MGM influence was not as strong on the Continent.

My creation of Anna brought me the New York Film Critics Award as the best actress of 1927. When the film came out, I was very much annoyed that Yackie insisted on receiving top billing. I remember how hard I had worked to bring to the surface all the delicate threads that would fully reveal the humanity of Anna without overwhelming a simple woman's sentimentality. I think I achieved this illusion despite a poor scenario. Because of my knowledge of Tolstoy's works, Moje's teachings about the Russian character, and Bill Daniels' photography, I felt I had fulfilled my obligations as an actress. But I would probably have given even more of myself if it had not been for Goulding's stupid instructions, which went completely against my nature and my acting habits. Yackie also prevented me from working at my very best. When I played love scenes with him, I shivered. I could not act the role of a real woman. I was like a swimmer who swims in the ocean and says to himself, "There are no sharks here. No sharks could be here. Sharks cannot be here." Yet one day he goes for a long swim and is destroyed by sharks. In *Love* I felt that I could have been eaten alive at any time.

25

No Wedding

Yackie was not in love with me. He was only trying to show to the world that any woman, half-woman—or anyone, for that matter—could not muster the desire to resist him, his "beautiful eyes," "luxuriant mustache," and "spontaneous actions." To him everyone was a tool with which to gain publicity. Love played on film is one thing, but to tie myself up with a man who was unstable and quarrelsome like Yackie was not for me.

Once, when my maid was on her daily shopping tour, Yackie suddenly appeared in front of my house in his shiny car. I saw him from my window on the top floor and, like a fool, went down to greet him. He asked me to go for a drive to Santa Ana, and I accepted because he hadn't insisted on coming in. As we drove, Yackie kept repeating, "I love you and I want you to be my wife."

I replied simply, "I cannot do it."

"Why? Are you not a woman? Or is Stiller still bothering you?"

Such talk annoyed me, and I let him have it with all my honesty. "I know you taught me how to play tennis, how to dance the tango and the rhumba, how to eat well and drink the best champagne; but you cannot teach me how to love you, and marriage with you would be a complete disaster. For you, marriage is just one more publicity stunt, while for me, marriage means love and peace."

"I will give you both. I think we will be a very much admired couple. And you will have peace and my love. Your love will come later."

"I don't believe in that kind of logic."

"Stiller is still entrenched in your soul and has tricked you into loving him by his return to Europe."

It was a sunny day; the world was green and gold; but his stupid talk gave me almost unbearable pain.

"We will organize our own film company." Yackie refused to let up. "We will produce films in which we will star, and we will divide the profits down the line."

"You're not proposing marriage, but a commercial undertaking for which you must have not only mutual understanding, but also a great deal of money."

"I have money, and if we need more, any bank in America will lend to us, provided of course, we go at it together. We are the most famous pair of lovers in the world, and on this foundation we can construct fantastic film careers."

"As you can see, this is a purely business proposition."

"Of which my love for you forms the base."

" 'From whichever side we approach this proposition, business comes out,' Nils Asther once said to me."

"So Nils is against me too, although the son of a bitch plays the friend in my presence."

"Don't be angry, Yackie. Everyone knows from your publicity everything about you and me. People come to me because they read so much in the papers about you, and they warn me. Even my maid is against my relationship with you."

"So you consult even your servants about our marriage."

"That's not true. I'll tell you just once more. I never ask anybody. To ask advice is against my nature. The people around us have eyes and ears. Not long ago, someone told me that at the same time you're asking me to marry you, you are seen in nightclubs with other women. Maybe I'm old-fashioned."

Yackie suddenly stopped the car and angrily said, "It's no secret that you like to sleep at night and that I prefer to spend my nights more pleasantly. I enjoy taking actresses to nightclubs. I don't kiss them, let alone talk of marriage. And if people talk about me going with other women, I will tell you that those same people very often say that you visit John Loder."

I was rather surprised by this remark. "Who said such a thing?"

"Jacques Feyder, the Belgian director."

"But did he tell you that every time I do see John, Feyder's wife is with us?"

"No, he didn't. But that's not important. Only that you meet other people besides me."

"Do you want to know why? Because John speaks very beautiful English with a British accent, and so I learn from him. And I meet with Jannings so that I can converse with him in German—in very good German, as a matter of fact."

"And do you meet Nils Asther because he speaks Swedish?"

"Are you being sarcastic? I'm speaking the truth."

Yackie dropped the personalities and began digging from a different barrel. "Clarence Brown told me that MGM is insisting that you and I play together in our next film."

"And what does film have to do with life?"

"If you hate me that much, it will be difficult for you to play love scenes."

"To play in film has nothing to do with our private lives," I replied quickly. As so many times before, I thought, everyone knew about my future film plans except me. "And what kind of film will it be?"

"You don't know?"

"If I knew I would not ask you."

"It is based on *The Green Hat*, by Michael Arlen."

"This is the first time I've heard of it."

"You see? If you marry me you wouldn't have such surprises, and the Hollywood set, including MGM, would treat you seriously."

"You have finally found the first sound argument for me to marry you."

"Aha! At last I've convinced you that besides love there

is something else between us, including the possibility of your having the same salary as mine."

Yackie stepped on the gas and sped recklessly toward Santa Ana. He suddenly asked, "When we see a church, should we have a wedding or a funeral?"

"At this very moment it would make no difference to me."

"All right, Greta Garbo. We will have a wedding."

A few more minutes of furiously fast driving and Yackie abruptly stopped in front of a small white house surrounded by tall palms. He opened the car door in a very dignified manner, took me by the hand, and led me down a narrow cement path that cut through a green yard.

Inside, we were greeted by an older man in a black suit and tie. "Wedding or funeral?" he asked.

I looked at Yackie, who enthusiastically exclaimed, "A wedding, naturally."

"Please follow me."

He walked rapidly, smoothing his gray hair with his hands. I wondered how funerals and weddings could have been held in this same building. I had never witnessed a wedding before, and I thought it would be an interesting experience to see one. Our destination was a nice clean room containing several chairs placed before a sort of lectern. The preacher said, "Please fill out these forms."

I looked at Yackie, and my heart started beating fast.

"Yackie, are you crazy? He's not allowing us to witness somebody else's wedding. He thinks we want to get married!"

I turned and ran outside. Yackie came after me. He grabbed the belt of my dress, spun me around, and tried to calm me.

"It's not a big deal. You can have a divorce anytime. Just think how much publicity there would be for you and me."

I looked around and saw several photographers aiming their cameras at us.

"Are you crazy?" I whispered.

"I'm not crazy, but maybe you are," said Yackie so that everybody could hear. "You know that you've told me many times you wanted to marry me."

The photographers began asking the obvious questions—"Has the ceremony been performed?" "Where is the honeymoon?" "When are you returning to Hollywood?"

I was surrounded by photographers and reporters hungry for the latest news about the "ideal lovers."

"If I had said something sometimes jokingly," I told them, "no one should now take my joke as a serious matter, especially marriage."

The nearest photographer asked me, "You mean there has been no wedding?"

"No!" I yelled. "And there will never be a wedding." I suddenly quieted down, smoothed my hair, and said to the same photographer, "Would you do me a favor?"

"With pleasure," he replied, taking my picture.

"Please drive me to Los Angeles."

This was the beginning of the end of my great romance with Yackie Gilbert.

26

The Divine Woman

As far back as I can reach into my memory, I have always wanted to be like Sarah Bernhardt. I even tried to imitate her acting, but my Shakespeare used to come out too realistic, and theatrical possibilities for me in Stockholm were rather limited. It was my meeting with Mauritz Stiller so early in life that put me on the film road. I grabbed at the opportunity, telling myself that whether on the stage or in film you had to be a good actress. Besides, theater has a limited audience, while films can be shown to millions of people. Naturally, I was also dreaming of great fame. I reasoned that with the help of my mentor, film would allow me to refine my acting and produce almost perfect performances. This way of thinking was shaped by Moje, but I have always been haunted by dreams of playing the great classical roles on the stages of Paris, Berlin, London, and New York. These dreams never materialized, and with age they intensified.

When Victor Seastrom gave me the play *Starlight*, by Gladys Unger, to read, I discovered that it was based on the life of Bernhardt. I was very much excited to have the opportunity to play this role. Victor also convinced MGM that I should receive top billing. He told me that it would be the perfect opportunity to play my greatest role in this, his most important directing assignment. For three months, several writers worked on the scenario. Finally, Dorothy Farnum added her touches to the script and thereby got her name into the billing. But all this elaborate literary work left nothing real from the great Sarah's life. Instead of presenting the interesting life of Bernhardt, *The Divine Woman*, as the film was called, told the story of a poor, beautiful girl who dreams about a great theatrical career and falls in love with a soldier named Lucien. This role was given to Lars Hanson. I, of course, played Marianne, the "divine woman."

I have to admit that working on this film was rather pleasant because I was able to spend my free time with Lars and Victor, with whom I could speak Swedish. Both were under Moje's influence and had a tremendous respect for his style of filmmaking. Because Moje refused to correspond with me, I had to turn to them for news about his struggles in Stockholm to reestablish himself as a director. I also learned that his health had deteriorated. This worried me more than his failures in the film business. To my surprise, in practically every letter Moje asked them about me and kept praising my talent and my determination to succeed. Reading these lines from a man who helped me without ever having any ulterior designs gave me courage. I was always thinking about returning home after the next film, after making some more money. But time slipped by, and my departure was postponed every few months.

The premiere of *The Divine Woman* was on January 14, 1928, in New York. The American press found my acting the only thing to praise in this film. At this time, the Hollywood careers of Victor and Lars were coming to an end. Victor longed to go back to Sweden. In his next film, *The Wind*, he directed Lars and Lillian Gish in what is now called a film classic. This did not matter to Lars. He went back to Europe, where he returned to the stage.

The way the press reported all this, I was a jinx for actors and directors who worked with me, especially if they were Swedish. It was said that anybody who acted with me was overwhelmed by the "garboesque" method, although it was never explained what that method was. Oliver Marsh, the cameraman for *The Divine Woman*, called me a "Swedish fjord." The end of Yackie's career was also predicted because he had been my leading man. Although it was difficult to pinpoint who was spreading such gossip, I felt very strongly that it was the work of MGM's publicity department, which was making me into some sort of vampire. I sometimes thought that perhaps there really was an element in my character that was detrimental to others. When such propaganda was added to these feelings, the only solution for me was to lock myself in my room and try to analyze my idiosyncracies. I decided to become more aloof and avoid people.

And increasingly, all kinds of people, from members of royal families to the teen-agers who invaded the MGM studios, begged to see me. I was very much annoyed and fled from all such encounters. My excuse was simple: "People don't expect to visit a bank clerk during his business hours and watch him count money. People don't stand over a writer's shoulder while he works on a manuscript. Why should my work be disturbed?"

But my statements and my anger did not prevent such goings-on. I sank deeper into the controversial publicity which not only distorted my character but also had a great impact on my day-to-day life and my psychological and physical well-being.

From time to time, I received letters from Mimi Pollack, my old friend from the Royal Dramatic Academy. She sent me bits of information about Moje, none of which was too cheerful. Svensk Filmindustri had decided that it didn't want to work with Moje anymore, so he switched to directing straight plays and musicals.

The Swedish financier Olle Andersson, who enjoyed backing plays and films, insisted on the title *The Good Old U.S.A.* for an upcoming production of *Broadway* because "It would please the American embassy in Stockholm"; but Moje insisted on controlling every detail of his work, and the title remained *Broadway*.

With every passing week he became more nervous, chain-smoking, drinking to excess, and constantly coughing. He alienated everyone with whom he came in contact. I was getting news from school friends like the actress Lena

Cederström, the director Alf Sjöberg, and the actor Karl-Magnus Thulstrup. They said they wrote to tell me about Moje, but I suspected the real reason for their letters was an interest in making millions in Hollywood, a pursuit in which they felt I could help them. But perhaps I am unjust in expressing such opinions.

After his return to Sweden, Seastrom also wrote to me about Moje. Pasting together his information and Mimi's, I developed a clear picture of Moje's activities.

In January 1928, before he entered a hospital, he sold his house in Lidingö, believing that he would not leave the hospital alive. But after four weeks of treatment he was able to return to the theater. And he resumed his film work. Although he had talked against British imperialists, he made contacts with the London film industry to produce a picture that would present the beneficial side of British rule in India. A second film was to have been financed by a French Rothschild, who specified that it be shot in Palestine and that it show the harmonious relations between the Arabs and Jewish immigrants. Scenarios for both films had been prepared by Moje and were ready for shooting. Only certain financial details remained to be settled. According to Victor, Moje had made plans to go to London and Paris and was even thinking of visiting Madeira to take a rest. His doctors advised that the balmy climate of Madeira was ideal for his tuberculosis, rheumatism, and nervous and circulatory problems. Such plans were realistic because his musical play had been a critical and financial success in Stockholm.

"The road is open again for me," Moje had told Mimi, who relayed this news to me. Her letter went on, "Then he said, 'I didn't worry about it. I knew I would succeed in Stockholm'—and here he began coughing and choking."

Mimi wrote that everyone was concerned about his health. From early afternoon to well past midnight, people swarmed about him, drinking, eating, and merrymaking— all things for which he bore the cost. No one knew where he was getting all this money: certainly not from the musical. Rumor had it that Rothschild sent him money because he liked his scenario on Arab-Jewish cooperation in Palestine. Others said that the British government had paid him in advance for his projected film on India. In any event, Moje was wasting money like water—throwing banquets and buying cars for friends, furs for women, as though he had no tomorrow. I worried about his health most of all. I had thought of him every day since he had left Hollywood. But after long and deliberate calculation, I concluded that it would be foolish for me to return to him. For what? To kneel before him? To beat my breast and cry? I have never been capable of doing such things.

I still didn't know why our relationship had ended so suddenly, although I did feel that I did not want to be anybody's satellite, even his. This was my dominant feeling. With the passage of years, I began to think that maybe I would never have succeeded without his help. But on the other hand, in the beginning, I was never allowed to sink or swim on my own. With Moje's help I knew I was a sure thing. I admit that Moje taught me the tricks of business; I learned how to be shrewd in dealing with people, how to smile faintly and say little. I don't think I did badly with Mayer, Thalberg, Gilbert, and their like—all of them shrewd and conniving. I had become a merchant of my own talents, a superb investor, and a skillful manipulator. I think I exploited my talents and my possibilities to the limit. The results are visible today. Everyone still mentions my name with reverence.

I was fortunate to meet and to receive love and help from a man like Moje. I was lucky that he had picked me, but I was also lucky that I had the capacity to learn quickly from him and work hard. I am not sure, honestly speaking, that other people helped me much, because I always despised them. I always felt they were not necessary for the success that I had achieved and secured more permanently than anyone else in the film industry, save perhaps Chaplin. I despise people even more today, because I don't need them to build my fame, and I don't need them in my daily life. I believe—perhaps illogically—that if I bring people closer to myself, they may discover my real character and through their maneuverings and gossiping I might lose my legend. My legend is everything to me now. I would not sell it for life, happiness, or anyone, including my sister, my father, or Moje. As a matter of fact, I would even sacrifice my own life so as not to jeopardize it.

27

A Triangle and a Duel

My arrogance increased in proportion to my growing fame, although to casual acquaintances I played sweet, scared, modest, and shy. Most of the time I simply followed MGM publicity suggestions, which presented a series of lies and half-lies about my private life, my acting, and my so-called philosophy. My "character" changed frequently, depending on the film I was working on or the ideas of the head of publicity. One month I was publicized as Joan of Arc, the next as Lucrezia Borgia, and the following as Queen Christina of Sweden or Salome. There were also the periods of Mata Hari, *La Dame aux Camélias,* Cleopatra. There was no famous woman in history to whom the publicists did not compare me. Their purpose, as I discovered, in mixing me up with all those famous female characters, was to confuse the public. I too became corrupted and confused, most of the time imagining that I was extraordinary. And they continued to feature me in unnatural roles. My next film, *The Mysterious Lady,* with a scenario by Bess Meredyth, was based on Ludwig Wolff's novel *War in the Dark.* The director was Fred Niblo, the man who had replaced Moje on *The*

Temptress. I played Tania, a beautiful Russian spy. The male lead was to be Yackie, but I went to the MGM bosses and explained that I did not have the physical and emotional stamina to play opposite him. So they chose Conrad Nagel to play the Austrian officer, Karl von Heinersdorff. The Russian general, Alexandroff, was played by Gustav von Seyffertitz, and his aide, Colonel von Raden, by Edward Connelly.

One day I overheard a conversation in which von Seyffertitz praised me by saying that I was "unassuming, yet strangely fascinating." I decided to make him my constant companion from that day on. Some people had started talking about my lesbian inclinations, and I felt Gustav, with his perfectly gentlemanly behavior, was well suited for me. The studio executives thought differently. They kept prodding Conrad Nagel to be my companion. They reasoned that it would be good publicity for the film if my leading man were in love with me. Because of this situation, a rivalry between Conrad and Gustav developed. I encouraged one, while the other was urged on by the studio. As a result, I became nervous and angry, and the whole affair almost ended in tragedy.

During the shooting of *The Mysterious Lady,* I often asked Gustav to accompany me home because I felt weak and had pains in my legs, hands, and chest. Because I didn't like doctors' poking at me, I told myself that the pains were caused by anemia, which I could cure through proper diet. I tried not to think about anything else except finishing the film as soon as possible. I was regarded by the public as a very healthy woman, so I avoided talking to anyone, even my servants, about my problems.

I had good reasons for my secretiveness. Very often Hollywood correspondents became fed up with stale MGM publicity and would try to gather new information about me. They were willing to pay plenty of money. My servants were not really any different from most people—they could be bought for a few dollars.

Gustav was a charming and intelligent companion. He knew the theatrical and film world in Europe and America as few others did. Very often we would spend hours talking. I would drink a glass of red wine, and he would drown himself in a sea of black coffee. He would describe his eventual triumphant return to Europe and would try to persuade me to join him. "In Europe there is more substance in art and in life in general."

Conrad was an entirely different sort. He spoke about loneliness, about love, about his sexual experiences. He was determined to create an atmosphere for a closer relationship; I tolerated this buildup because I didn't wish to upset MGM. Yet I was enjoying the companionship of Gustav more and more. I would pick his brain very often to learn something new.

Although I was systematic in building up my career, I hated to keep a record of anything. I disliked writing letters, signing my name, keeping a diary, or even putting on a calendar the names of people who visited me. Very often I would ask somebody to visit me a week or two in advance, and by a strange coincidence I would later make an appointment for the same day with someone else. Because of my aversion to writing anything down, I was responsible for the following very unpleasant incident.

One evening Gustav was sitting in my living room, discussing, as usual, the art of acting and the arts in general. Suddenly Conrad, who was known to my servants, burst into the room yelling excitedly, "We have a supper date. What's this Prussian doing here?"

Gustav jumped up and hit him in the face. Conrad retaliated in kind. They began to punch each other, knocking the furniture about and shrieking all kinds of obscenities. I stood quietly to one side, fascinated by this struggle of two men for my affection. Through my mind went the thought that I must be worth something if two men of different ages, backgrounds, and intellectual levels could battle over me.

Gustav grabbed a chair and threw it at Conrad, who jumped to one side. Conrad then took a small table and hit his opponent very hard on the shoulder. Gustav fell to the floor, and Conrad jumped on him. They rolled on the carpet tearing their jackets, hitting each other with their fists, biting each other like wild animals. I saw blood and smelled perspiration; I felt exhilarated. I wanted to say something, to persuade them to stop fighting, but nothing came from my mouth. Instead, I stood fascinated as I watched them struggle around the room. I was seeing a boxing championship for the first time. I wondered what would be the out-come of the match.

Instead of subsiding, it grew worse. Conrad and Gustav still rolled on the floor, kicking and hammering each other. Suddenly they lost their strength. Their movements slowed. I saw blood mixed with saliva on their chins. I didn't inter-fere because I had in my heart neither pity nor love for either one. Instead, images of Spanish bullfights, Mexican cockfights, and Roman arenas full of Christians and lions flooded my mind. At that point I couldn't tell which was the lion and which the Christian. I was so absorbed in my own thoughts that several moments passed before I noticed that the two fighters were lying motionless, except for their heavy breathing.

"Thank God they are still alive!" I said to myself. "I don't have to get the police involved." I exclaimed to them, "Get up! We can settle the problem by sitting and discuss-ing it on the couch."

Conrad dragged himself up and staggered to the bath-room. I went over to Gustav and helped him onto the couch. When Conrad returned, he sat down on the floor.

I said to his enemy, "Now you go get washed, and after that we will talk."

Because he was older and more battered, it took Gustav longer to clean himself up. When he returned, I asked him to sit beside me.

I began, "You tried to kill each other. My philosophy is very simple. Nothing is more sacred than life, and a woman's love is not worth sacrificing one's life for. I'll tell you something else." I searched for a different argument because I noticed they didn't feel like talking. "A woman who works in films should not think of marriage. In our profession, marriage is almost never successful."

I hadn't elicited any reaction from them; they still stared blankly at the floor. To break the uncomfortable quiet, I took still another angle.

"Take me as an example. When I work the whole day in front of hot lights in a jungle of voices, I come home dead tired. I don't have the strength to talk or eat. I can only sleep. I must save my strength for my work, for my ambi-tion. For me a husband would be a tragic encumbrance.

After a few months of marriage I am sure he would leave me or I him. I cannot live without acting, but I can live without a husband."

I stopped and looked at their swollen, bruised faces. They had not been touched by my words, so I said very frankly, "I think you are fools to fight over love. I don't think about love; I don't think about marriage; I don't even think about affairs with a man. Perhaps I am too egotistical or too ambitious; perhaps I'm not physically and emotionally prepared to live with a man. What is the matter with you boys? What is the problem? I won't live with either of you."

Then Gustav said, "Honor."

Conrad repeated, "Honor."

"Conrad, what you will have? Pistols? Swords?" asked Gustav.

"Pistols."

"Gentlemen," I interjected, "you mean you will duel? Please tell me, for what?"

"Honor," replied Gustav.

"Honor," echoed Conrad.

"Honor?" I asked them. "Are you willing to be injured or to die for such a silly thing as honor which has such an illusory meaning, and no meaning whatsoever in this situation?"

"Yes," said one, and after him the other.

"At least you agree on something." And I laughed. "Okay," I said, "honor. But before you duel, will both of you, because you love me, do me a small favor?"

"What?"

"Let's finish the film first. After that I will even act as a second for both of you, because I am completely impartial. I don't love either of you."

Saying that, I got up and waited for their replies. But I received not a word, only some strange stares. So I turned around and went off to the kitchen.

"I'll get some champagne and glasses."

The next day we were again hard at work on *The Mysterious Lady*, and never during or after this film—never in our lives, for that matter—did we ever discuss that violent night. The film had its premiere in New York at the Capitol

Theater on August 4, 1928. I received my usual excellent write-ups, but the critics ignored the story.

At the premiere, reporters surrounded Conrad to ask him just what is "the mystery of Greta Garbo."

"The only mystery about her," he responded, "is the title of this film."

28

Tragic News

A passage from the novel *The Green Hat,* written by Michael Arlen, has lodged itself in my memory to this day. I memorized it when I was working on *A Woman of Affairs,* which was based on this novel. I memorized it because this fragment captures very well the essence of my relationship with Moje, which I cannot better express in my own words:

> Above all things in this world I love the love that people have for each other, the real, immense, unquestioning, devouring, worshipful love that now and then I have seen in a girl for a boy, that now and then I have seen in a boy for a boy, that playmate love. It isn't of this world, that playmate love, it's of a larger world than ours, a better world, a world of dreams which aren't illusions but the very pillars of a better life. But in our world all dreams are illusions . . .

I recall another fragment:

> He has renounced his love, I thought to myself, as a man of honour should do, but he knows that a man of honour is not

worthy of the name unless he can also convince himself that there never was any love to renounce, for that would make him feel martyred.

These two passages are the best expressions of the attitudes Moje and I had toward each other. That is the reason that I have remembered Michael Arlen's words for fifty years.

I never grasped the mechanics of MGM and the reasons I was cast in films like *A Woman of Affairs,* which was about an English Sodom and Gomorrah of the early 1920's. Although in her scenario Bess Meredyth reshaped much of the novel, the substance remained. The name of the heroine was changed from Iris to Diana. I was truly looking forward to playing in this film. I was happy because Clarence Brown was again my director, and Bill was cameraman. I knew that with such a combination the film had to be a success.

Brown had high screens constructed around the sets so that visitors would not disturb my work. He knew that more and more people from the world of American millionaires and European royalty, not to mention the journalists and other males and females in love with me, would try to see me on the set. My male opposite, Neville, was Yackie again. Time had worn down my intolerance for him. The other major roles were taken by Douglas Fairbanks, Jr., Lewis Stone, Hobart Bosworth, John Mack Brown, and Dorothy Sebastian.

During the filming I was more nervous and tired than ever before, and I worried a lot about my health. Doctors suggested that I take a complete rest, but I said to myself, "You must endure; you must finish this film, because this is your most important role."

I avoided everyone and spent my free time resting; I took pills and ate vegetables and some meat. I thought constantly that catastrophe was about to strike me. One thing had become more agreeable: Yackie had ceased bothering me with his sexual advances, even though lots of stories still appeared in the press about our "immortal love." I know Yackie had decided that the best thing for him to do was hire a clever press agent to spread juicy stories. I suppose the MGM publicity department agreed with this change in tactics. The stories must have been believed, for I heard that

I was married to him, that we were living together, and that we even had a child. I didn't bother to investigate or even ask Yackie about these stories. My health was not good, and my only concern was to finish the film so that I could go to Europe. I had decided to take my money to Europe and invest it for my old age. Before, I had been using Moje to further my career. Now I was thinking of him as the one to invest my money so that I could live in Europe in peace. Money and fame were the most important things in my life, and Moje and Europe would help me to keep both.

I had received news about Moje, and none of it was good, especially concerning his health. But I couldn't worry much, because I had plenty of worries about my own health. I had no one to talk to, no shoulder to cry on. I knew that I had fame. I knew that I had money. I also knew very well that I did not have peace of mind. Only hard work and plenty of sleep made me feel better. Brown did not live far from me and was constantly asking me to his house. I always refused his invitations. Chaplin, Lionel Barrymore, Yackie, Mayer, Lillian Gish, and the Fairbankses invited me for suppers or weekends, but I always refused, because I was unsure of myself and suspicious that people were using me. I soon acquired the nickname "mysterious stranger." In my free moments, I reread *The Green Hat,* marking passages that I felt pertained to me. I felt that this novel helped explain my soul and my problems:

> I sat there subdued by the thought of the awful helplessness of men and women to understand one another and of the terrible thing it would be for some of them if ever they did understand one another, and how many opportunities the devil is always being given of making plunder out of decent people.

I played my role in *A Woman of Affairs* in much physical pain and tremendous emotional turmoil. I played the role of a brother, and I played the role of a sister, two inseparable souls, lost forever together.

In September 1928, MGM was already at work on an enormous publicity campaign to introduce *A Woman of Af-*

fairs to the public in January of the following year. At the same time, the studio bosses induced me to begin work immediately on a new film, *Wild Orchids,* based on an original story by John Colton and with a scenario by Hans Kraly, Richard Schayer, and Willis Goldbeck. If I had to judge humanity using myself as the standard, I would have to say that people are indestructible animals. Depite my illness, after a short, secluded rest I began memorizing my role of Lillie Sterling.

The story was set in Java. My leading men were Nils Asther and Lewis Stone, a man of beautiful character whom I remember very warmly to this day. Stone played my husband, John, an American businessman. Prince De Gace, played by Asther, was the owner of thousands of souls and many palaces, a man of great mystery and charm. He meets me on a ship sailing from San Francisco to Java. To convince me that "the relentless heat in Java sweeps aside all pretenses," he kisses me, although we are not yet in Java, but barely a few hours out of San Francisco. As a moral woman, I slap him in the face, but such treatment does not faze the prince. He pursues me with even greater fervor in the hope that I will eventually love him.

Bill Daniels took some exquisite shots of Javanese dancers, Prince De Gace's palaces, the tropical settings, and the rich costumes. Because of the powerful characterizations of the three players, a mysterious fable was created in spite of Sidney Franklin's weak direction. Stone's economy in acting was on the border of genius. Asther, although a good actor, had to play many unbelievable scenes. He was clawed by a tiger and shot by my husband—melodramatic episodes that were so necessary to Hollywood productions.

I will never forget my love scene with the prince. As the cameras were rolling, Louis B. Mayer came onto the set with a telegram from Mimi Pollack telling me of Moje's death. I collapsed, and I remembered nothing until I awoke in my dressing room. When I opened my eyes, I saw Nils kneeling beside me, and behind him stood Lewis Stone, Bill Daniels, Mayer, and a doctor. I looked at them keenly and asked for a glass of water. I sipped it for a few minutes while I made my decision.

"Let's finish the scene."

The others were dumbfounded, and I read contempt on their faces. But I said to myself, "Death will come to everybody, but the living must go on."

Of course, my behavior made a tremendous impression on the people present in my dressing room. I wanted to show them that I was strong, that I could stand on my own feet without anyone's help. The problems between Moje and me were our own, in death as well as in life, and nobody had a right to interfere. Besides, I knew these people. They didn't give a damn. They played sympathetic, but they were interested in finishing a film that would bring them much money.

That day when I came home from work, I sent my servants out for the evening, suggesting that they go to a movie and supper at my expense. I put two bottles of champagne on ice, opened a fresh pack of cigarettes, and put some Swedish songs on the phonograph. I lay down on the couch and listened to this folk music while I smoked and drank. I tried to remember my life with my family and with Moje, who came after my two dearest people, my father and my sister.

"I was dreaming of oranges," I said to myself the next day when I awoke, and immediately after breakfast I returned to work. I was probably physically and psychologically stronger than I felt myself to be, or perhaps I was completely rotten. There was a third alternative. Maybe my strong will and physical endurance were being gradually, systematically, eaten away by some indescribable disease. I couldn't think about it. And there perhaps lies my strength. I was never inclined to be a deeply analytic person about myself or about the world around me.

Letters from Stockholm soon told me the story of Moje's last days. Late one night Moje had collapsed on the street and had been taken to the Red Cross Hospital. The doctors discovered that he was suffering not only from tuberculosis but also from stomach cancer. When he had first returned to Stockholm, doctors had diagnosed lung cancer and had removed several ribs in order to cut out part of his lungs. He had survived this surgery, but against all medical advice he had continued his reckless way of life, sleeping a little during the day and spending all night working or talking or on walks through the city. He did not cut down on his smoking of cigars and cigarettes, and he didn't stop drinking.

"Alcohol and nicotine stimulate me," he would say. "If I cannot think, I cannot create. If I cannot create, I don't want to live. I should then be called not Mauritz Stiller, but a rat. And I hate rats."

In the Red Cross Hospital he required nurses twenty-four hours of the day. They pumped all kinds of drugs into him. But Moje continued to read and to plan revolutionary productions of authors from Shakespeare to Tolstoy. He dreamed of a theater in which the actors would play spontaneously without any rehearsals, and directing would be confined to the mere smoothing of rough edges. He barricaded himself behind his books, poring over them, taking notes, and telling all his visitors to believe in him because he was still a young man, not even fifty years old, and had terrific determination. They believed him and thought he would survive and return to theater and film.

Although his mind belonged to the future, his heart was in the past. Shortly before he died, Moje had abruptly stopped calling himself a Swede and had asked to be called a Jew. He felt strongly that he must be part of the spirit of his people.

Because Moje was so restless and could not sleep, the doctors prescribed sleeping pills and gave strict orders to the nurses to give him one each night. One evening a nurse whom he liked very much asked if she could go out for a while. He agreed readily. "I'm not a cripple," he said. "Just leave the bottle of sleeping pills and I'll take one myself." After a pause he added, "When I get sleepy tonight, I'll take the pill and dream of my theater, though I think I'd rather dream of sleeping with you."

The nurse took his proposition with a smile, and Moje was left by himself with his thoughts and his books. No one can say what he was thinking or what he was doing in those last hours. Maybe he thought of me; maybe about himself and his childhood.

When the nurse returned two hours later, he was lying on the edge of the bed. His big black eyes were open but sightless. She saw the empty bottle that had contained the sleeping tablets near his chin.

The doctor's verdict was that Mauritz Stiller died at 11

P.M. on November 8, 1928, of a heart attack. He was buried in the Stockholm North Cemetery a day later. Aside from his attorney, Hugo Lindberg, nobody attended his burial. Perhaps it was because Moje had not recently been speaking so interestingly about art; or perhaps it was because the world had only been playacting that he was liked and that he really had friends.

Right, Garbo and Mauritz Stiller arrive in New York, July 6, 1925. Below, Garbo photographed by Arnold Genthe shortly before leaving New York for Hollywood. Below right, with Victor Sjöstrom (left), the Swedish actor/director who worked in Hollywood as Victor Seastrom, and Stiller.

CULVER/ARNOLD GENTHE

CULVER

Opposite: Hollywood, 1926, in *The Torrent*, based on a novel by Blasco-Ibáñez.

This page: scenes from *The Temptress*, 1926. The Garbo image was taking shape.

Flesh and the Devil, in 1927, was the first of a number of films with John Gilbert.

Love, Garbo's first film based on *Anna Karenina*, was with John Gilbert. A picnic during the filming included one of her favorite cameramen, William Daniels (far left), and next to him, director Edmund Goulding.

CULVER

Left, filming *The Divine Woman* with Lars Hanson and director Victor Seastrom. Below, with Conrad Nagel in *Mysterious Lady*, and shooting a scene with Gustav von Seyffertitz at the head of the table.

On a trip to Sweden, photographed with her mother and Swedish actor Nils Lundell, in 1928. Right, shooting *A Woman of Affairs* with director Clarence Brown and cameraman William Daniels. John Gilbert co-starred in this film based on the novel *The Green Hat*.

Above, with Lewis Stone, "a man of beautiful character," and right, with Nils Asther, in *Wild Orchids.* Below, with Norma Shearer, Irving Thalberg and John Gilbert at a Hollywood premiere.

Book Two

PART FIVE

Garbo

29

To the Past and Back

To this day I cannot successfully explain to myself why I didn't return to Stockholm with Moje when he was alive. I did so only when he died. I decided to go to Stockholm in December 1928, and my main reason for the trip was to prove to everyone that I was no longer "Stiller's protégée." Perhaps if I went to put flowers on Moje's grave, I would demonstrate to the public eye my inner strength and my ability to live without him. Then people would stop calling me "Stiller's creation." This phrase was unbearable to me, and every mention of it on the radio or in the press had brought me pain and anger. I dreamed of friendships with ideal people whom I could trust, with whom I could talk, with whom I could cry. But in every encounter, sooner or later Moje's name would come up, and I would become annoyed, upset, and distrustful. Looking back, I sometimes believe that I was as scared of him as he was scared of rats, but kept this inside because I knew if he discovered my fear of him, he would stop loving me and perhaps even try to destroy me as I moved toward stardom. Eventually he, like a million others, came to accept my shyness and my avoidance of people and difficult situations. I convinced Moje and the rest of humanity that this was my nature. And eventually I too began to believe it.

After finishing all preparations, I secretly took the train from Los Angeles to New York, where I bought passage on the S.S. *Kungsholm.* Travel by train across country was not pleasant on this occasion. I slept a lot in my compartment, ate steak and vegetables, and didn't exercise except for a few brief walks in the corridor. I took a taxi from Grand Central Station to the pier where the ship was docked, all the while followed by gangs of reporters who confronted me at different points in my journey. Once aboard, I promptly locked myself in my cabin. Although no reporter bothered me during the voyage, I did notice that one from the New York evening press had managed to write that "Garbo is a thin woman with great big eyes, a collar that was almost up to her ears, a coat that was almost down to her ankles, a hat that was almost down to her shoulders, and a stride that was almost across the platform." I dreaded what I would face in Göteborg, where I would be smothered by Swedish reporters asking me about Moje's death.

One afternoon, after I had spent three days in my cabin, Lars Ring, who happened to be on this same voyage, persuaded me to take a walk on the upper deck. This walk was so enjoyable that the next morning I was out again. During these early-morning walks, the skies were unbelievably blue and the sea moved to the powerful music of its waves, but my conversations with Lars were so dull. He persisted in reminding me of how good he had been to me in Stockholm when I was a young actress, and intimating how thankful I should be for everything he had done for me. To this day I try to recall what he did do for me, and I don't remember a thing.

One morning as we were walking, I decided to drop him and stay in my cabin for the rest of the voyage. But Lars suddenly noticed some friends walking and chatting idly. He introduced me to the Count and Countess Wachtmeister, the Count and Countess Bonde, and the twenty-two-year-old Prince Sigvard of Sweden. I became friendly with them, and the rest of the voyage was very pleasant.

Only the prince presented problems. He followed me around telling me how much he admired my films; how in love he was with me, my figure, and my eyes. One day he even knocked on my cabin door and announced that as soon as we docked in Göteborg, we would go to the royal palace, where he would introduce me to the entire royal family. Then we would take a long trip through Sweden, because I must learn everything about my native land. I finally realized that the prince was sincere, but I had no desire to become involved sexually with anyone, even with a prince. I led him out of the cabin under the pretext of going for a walk. After our walk, I returned to my cabin and locked myself in. All my meals were served me there, and I told the steward that I would see no one. Only at five o'clock in the morning, when everyone was sound asleep, did I emerge for a solitary walk to maintain my health.

When I arrived in Göteborg, I announced to the crowd of photographers and reporters, "In Hollywood I work. I have come to Sweden to rest."

Wilhelm Sörensen, a friend of Prince Sigvard's who had come from Stockholm to greet him, then asked a stereotyped question which annoyed me.

"What do you think of America?"

I wondered how such an intelligent man as Mr. Sörensen could ask such a stupid question.

I replied, "In the rest of the world, people change tires more often than cars. Only in America do people change cars more often than tires."

Everyone laughed, including Mr. Sörensen, who later became a friend of mine, although I had probably lost Prince Sigvard.

While greeting the reporters and other strangers, I almost completely forgot about my mother; my brother, Sven; and Mimi Pollak, who waited somewhere in the crowd. I was rather upset with Mimi, and I thought, "Why has she gotten married and had a child?" She was even calling herself Mrs. Ludwig Lundell.

Among the crowd of reporters, autograph hunters, and curiosity seekers I saw Max Gumpel, the millionaire house builder and an old friend.

I said to myself, "Max still has some love for me and deep confidence in my integrity. Moje used to say that Max has confidence in old friends but no patience for them."

When I saw him pushing aside other people while

trying to reach me, I felt a warm glow in my heart. Max, almost completely bald, looked like a head of cabbage with a monocle in one eye, but always smiling. He once offered me a ring, which I accepted, saying that the ring looked like one of the English crown jewels. I told him that even if I did accept his ring I could not marry him. He didn't get mad, and now after so many years he was here at the ship to greet me.

After giving me a big hug and many kisses, he told me he had a car waiting, so that I could slip away from the reporters. He advised me not to stay in a hotel or at my mother's house, but in a private apartment.

"Whose private apartment? Which private apartment?" I exclaimed, suspecting a scheme of his.

"I've taken the liberty of renting you a beautiful apartment where you can have lots of privacy."

"In Stockholm?"

"Yes, on Karlbergsvägen."

"I'll think about your offer, dear Max, but right now please help me reach my mother. You have strong arms. Push the crowd aside."

"Where is she?"

"Over there." I pointed to the edge of the crowd. "The plump woman in a black hat and fur coat carrying flowers. Sven is standing beside her."

Max took my orders literally and started shoving people aside. I followed him. In half a minute I was in the arms of my mother. We kissed each other and cried. I don't know what she was thinking, but my mind was filled with scenes from my ugly childhood—my parents' quarrels, and the fights marked by physical violence. Then the quiet voice of my father spoke in my heart: "I love you, Keta. I love you, Keta." Suddenly from my subconscious arose still another voice: "You are a drunkard."

It was the voice of my mother, an ugly voice. But as if to soothe me, my father said again, "I love you." Then I felt his spirit leave me.

Max sensed that something strange was going on and approached me saying, "Let's get out of here. Where do you want to go? To a hotel? To your mother's? To Karlbergsvägen?"

"First let me go to the cemetery. I would like to talk to my father and Moje."

But I changed my mind and decided to go the next morning.

That December day was sunny, but very cold. I dressed myself warmly in a sweater, woolen skirt, fur coat, and black hat. On my feet I put high boots. I prepared for the sad journey to the North Cemetery. I went in a car with Mimi Pollak and Hugo Lindberg, Stiller's attorney, who after Moje's death had been trying to satisfy his creditors and take care of other legal matters. On this ride I thought that a woman will call a man her friend if he allows her to degrade him and deny him pleasures. On the other hand, men don't like women who consider themselves superior in any way. I don't know what relevance this has to my visit to Moje, but it was the only observation my blank mind registered on this solemn trip.

It took us an hour to find Moje's grave in the Jewish part of the cemetery. The headstone was not very impressive. It had been placed there by the Jewish community, because Moje had no immediate family in Sweden. I decided right away to remedy this and erect a suitable monument. I felt pain grip my heart, because Moje had had so many friends, yet there was not a single flower on his grave.

I recall that Moje had very often said to me, "I am a cynic, and a cynic is the kind of man who tells people what he really thinks about them. But you, to some extent, resemble a clever sentimentalist, because you think only what others say. Maybe you are smarter than I am."

When he had first uttered these words, I had become angry. But now as I knelt at his grave in the snow, I said to him, "You were right."

From the shimmering bushes I heard his voice: "Never mind that. Tell me, why can't you sleep at night?"

"I'm afraid. I am afraid of you, and I don't want to die yet. Perhaps it is through your influence that I have recently developed such a craving for alcohol, tobacco, and sleeping pills. Are you driving me to these excesses?"

"How stupid you are! I love you. From the first day I saw you I knew I would make you a great actress. But I loved you in spite of myself. Even now I travel all over the world and hunt down all the critics and whisper in their ears that they should always link our names. No one must forget that I created you and that I live on in you."

A sharp wind blew, and his voice faded. I felt pain in my knees as the snow where I was kneeling melted.

He returned. "There is only one thing I did not succeed in doing for you."

"What?" I asked, shifting because gravel was biting into my knees.

"To give you a real intellect. The desire to build up your own legend has occupied your entire brain and has not left any room for logic, honest thinking, or the sheer pleasure of pure thought. You have become the merchant of your talents."

I listened and nodded in agreement.

In my own defense I said only "I am what I am."

"And those sleepless nights—there is a reason for them. You have never loved anybody except yourself. You have never done anything for anybody simply for the sake of doing it. Your only pleasure has been to establish and admire the Garbo legend. Now go home. Go away. Don't visit here again. I will come to you in California or wherever you may go."

"Are you all right?" asked Mimi as she helped me up.

"I'm fine. Now I would like to go to my father's grave."

As I slowly walked away I thought of Moje, and how he had never changed during life or after death. He was not afraid of yelling at people or at God. That was the real Moje. I know that I will recognize him instantly among the billions of wandering souls I will encounter after death.

During his lifetime my father had been a man of few words. But now as I stood before his grave he complained in bitter tones that I had been sending too much money to my mother and my brother. He said that Sven, who had always overestimated his talents for acting, producing, and business, was now wasting money on idle pleasures. He had been playing the wealthy man, moving in the bourgeois circles of Stockholm and doing nothing worthwhile. My father went on, "And your mother, although she still lives in our old home, spends your money on fancy dresses and on fooling around with elderly men."

"So what?" I asked.

"So what, you say? I could understand if they were strangers. But they are my old comrades, like Hjalmar from the city sanitation department, and Halvdan, the one who was a janitor on Götgatan. Once she even took in a drunkard named Karl like me. She sat drinking with him in the restaurant not far from Djurgården where I used to work. This scum Karl still owes me money, yet your mother now drinks and laughs with him. She gossips about me and says that she made you into a great actress. But what hurts me more than anything else is her saying that you resemble her when she was young. Everybody knows very well that you are the very image of me."

"You're right, Father. I resemble you completely."

He liked this very much, and he laughed. The wind carried laughter to the tops of the spruce trees, and then he whispered, "I know that you love me, and I would like to ask you for a favor. I've never asked you for one before."

"Anything, Father. Please just tell me."

"Do you see this grave marker? It is not quite twenty centimeters by twenty centimeters."

I looked, and I felt ashamed.

He continued, "Please erect a nice-size stone with the inscription 'Here lies the father of Greta Garbo.' "

"That would not be right, Father. I don't want to make publicity for myself in the cemetery."

Suddenly the sharp wind sent down sheets of snow and carried my father's voice away. Now the wind whistled without interruption. But I didn't mind. I acquired extra strength, and I started walking all over the cemetery looking at the headstones, while Mimi and Hugo followed me like shadows. They didn't say anything to me. I didn't care to talk to them. I was thinking about my father and Moje and talking to them. Everything was normal in behavior and in words among the three of us—the line between life and death had disappeared. Suddenly I stopped and asked myself, "Am I going mad?"

I forced myself back into the "real" world. Glancing at the epitaphs, I said to Mimi, "To judge by the sentiments on these headstones, all the people who lie here must have been very, very noble."

Mimi and Hugo began laughing, and hearing them

laugh, I discovered that I must be normal and that there was nothing strange in talking to people who had died. We walked toward the cemetery gates. The dry snow made ugly noises under our feet, and above our heads the whistling wind was gaining in intensity.

Suddenly, I recalled something Moje had said to me a long time before: "Don't look back. Love is like religion. It is easier to be a martyr than a holy man. People don't understand you. And it is good if they don't understand you, because when they start understanding you they will say that you are barbaric or just plain stupid."

Suddenly I covered my ears with both hands and started crying. Mimi and Hugo took me in their arms and helped me to the black car that waited for us. The chauffeur, in his fur coat and hat, looked like a Cossack. Moje had told me lots of stories about Cossacks. I silently screamed, "My God! Why is Moje always in my mind?"

I spent my vacation in Stockholm sleeping and walking. In Hollywood I had gotten up early, but I reversed my pattern now. I slept until noon or later. Curiosity seekers knew of my early-rising habits and looked for me in the morning and early afternoon. But I went out as dusk fell. I wrapped myself up in the worst-looking old coat I could find and completed my drab costume with a shabby hat and high boots. I would go to Blekingegatan, and other streets in the Söder district where I was born and spent my childhood and youth. I looked for the faces of people I used to know. I even visited the little tobacco shop where Mrs. Agnes Lind had been proprietor and where my father had bought me magazines and candy.

Snow was falling, and as it grew steadily thicker I said to myself, "God gave the Swedes so much snow for only one reason—that they might talk about it all the time."

I went into a shabby café and asked for a cup of coffee. At the next table a woman sat with a young boy. She said to him, "Did your mother teach you to be unpleasant in a restaurant and ask the waitress for an extra piece of pastry?"

I knew she was thinking of the price, and I was amused by the boy's answer: "No, but Mother didn't tell me that one piece would be so small."

I asked the waitress to bring four pastries to the boy's table; I paid the bill and left.

Then I went to the barbershop that Einar Widebäck had owned. It was still open and quite busy. I looked inside and didn't see any familiar face. So I went on, this time having no idea where I would go. Suddenly I felt the presence of my sister, Alva. We walked together quietly, without words, to Götgatan, where there was another barbershop, owned by Mr. and Mrs. Arthur Ekengren, and where I had worked as a *tvålflicka*. Even with Alva at my side, I didn't recognize anyone whom we had known in our childhood. From there we walked to the PUB department store, where I had had so many unpleasant experiences. The huge store was packed, and the street outside had a holiday feeling because people were emerging loaded down with packages.

"Let's go to the theater," I distinctly heard Alva say.

We went to Södra Teatern and later to Mosebacke, where Carl Brisson used to play. No familiar face, not even one. Even the doorman was different, although I am sure the new one was wearing the old one's uniform.

We walked to the Strand Hotel, and I decided to take a taxi back to my brother, Sven's, home, where I was staying during the Christmas holidays. I said to Alva, "Let's ride home, because I'm very tired."

And Alva replied, "My home is in the cemetery."

I had tears in my eyes.

During the last days of December I decided to visit the office of Hugo Lindberg and ask him if Moje had left anything for me as a farewell token. I wanted to have something he had used every day, something that had lit up those black eyes of his. When I appeared in Lindberg's office unannounced, he sat me in a comfortable chair. I looked around and saw that his office was stuffed with furniture and papers, and concluded that this chaos demonstrated poor business talent, extreme absentmindedness, or else just plain carelessness. He wasted no time. "Moje loved you," he said, "as he loved no one else. He talked of you on many occasions, and I learned that he believed his love was not returned. I didn't try to change his opinion of you. How could anyone know more than he did about your heart?"

I listened intently, with my heart beating hard. I

thought that no defense or explanation would change his opinion of me. So I said only, "Can I have something, a small thing, that would remind me of Moje?"

"I'm sorry, but he ordered me to sell all his possessions, and with that money to buy him a black headstone and chisel on it this sentence: 'Here rests Mauritz Stiller, a human who did nothing in his life except rest.' "

"But I never knew a man who worked harder than Moje."

"I know he worked very hard, but for other people. He did nothing for himself."

Three months had passed since I left Hollywood, and a miracle happened. I felt lonesome for the American film center. Or perhaps I was lonely for work on a new film. In Stockholm I would not escape the past, so I decided to leave as soon as possible. I said good-bye to my family and friends, and Willie Sorensen, the friend of Prince Sigvard's, who had been kind to me, took me in his car to Göteborg. On March 10, I boarded the S.S. *Kungsholm.*

My sudden departure was explained to everybody in one sentence: "I must return to work."

The real reason, of course, was Moje's ghost. I felt that the long trip across the Atlantic in privacy and seclusion would help me settle down. Then some hard work would dissolve my mental tension. But I soon realized that I would never be rid of him. My conscience kept repeating, "You took everything from him, perhaps even his life, and what did you give him in return?"

Once aboard the S.S. *Kungsholm* I locked myself in my cabin, determined not to leave it until I reached New York. There was so much to think about and to read. Although I had a stack of plays and books, I always returned to *The Green Hat.* I imagined Moje as the hero of this novel, while I became the heroine. So fascinated was I by the characters in Arlen's story, I developed a desire to die, like the heroine, in an automobile accident. I have always become excited by reading or hearing about unusual love affairs, different ways of life, different deaths. Although there were moments when I wanted everything to be normal, I kept returning to the character of the woman in this novel. I felt her tragedy and tried to relive it. The moral of the story was simple: there is no place in our world for great love, and one has to pay with one's life to experience it. *The Green Hat* fascinated me, and I was upset because I believed that *A Woman of Affairs* was a very poor adaptation of the novel. Now, on my way back to the United States, I knew very well how the role should have been written and played. But it was too late. *A Woman of Affairs* had premiered in New York at the Capitol Theater on January 19, 1929. The Swedish press acclaimed the film as a success, but I knew my Diana was a poor rendering of the Iris in the novel. The American critics were lukewarm.

If an actress in films has great talent, she doesn't need a director, only a good dramatist—or, more precisely, a good scenarist and an inventive cameraman. The three of them working together can put together a great film. For me, the camera was the most important element. I behaved more naturally before it than in front of my best friends. Usually I found the start of a film difficult, but as soon as I became accustomed to the people around me, I forgot them and concentrated on my relationship with the camera. My personality, which is really flat in relation to people, grew before the camera, and dimensions of my personality submerged in everyday life were evident in every word and movement.

When I confronted the camera's eye and spoke my lines, my mind floated out through villages and cities and to people I had never met; I felt as if I were trying to impress the camera with the activity of my brain and the movements of my body. My face had its own rules and regulations and developed shadows and angles to show my spiritual state. My face told about the life that I portrayed. I didn't need much makeup to emphasize the nuances of love, hate, and sorrow. I cared very much about the coordination not only of my hands and my legs, but of my whole body and especially of my facial muscles. Sometimes I imagined that the camera was trying to act too. So there would be a rivalry or perhaps a collaboration. The camera was for me an integral part of my life, my career, and my fame.

I had been fortunate in having Bill Daniels as my cameraman for nineteen pictures. The secret of his success was that he was in love not only with the camera but also with me. And this relationship, so pure and so free of ulterior motives, was one reason for my continued success.

During my transatlantic return to my career, I read book after book, play after play, all of which had been given to me by Willie Sörensen. I was most impressed by the play *Anna Christie*, by Eugene O'Neill. I liked this work because it was both realistic and symbolic. It was not a sexual play in the literal sense of this word, but a drama of life in which the sea stood for human existence and the fog for everything that obscures our vision so that we don't know the direction in which to sail.

I felt that the role of Anna had been written for me, and after I read the play a second time, I became obsessed by it. I thought it would be very interesting to meet Eugene O'Neill. During my days on the *Kungsholm*, I said to myself over and over, "Anna is a challenge for Greta." I wanted Greta and Anna to reverse roles.

30

Femme Fatale

We reached New York safely even though the crossing had been very rough. For two days I was nauseated and completely exhausted. Friends in Stockholm had said that in New York I would encounter a rough press. My last film and my attitude of not saying anything important to reporters might have had something to do with it. I also heard that MGM was planning to send Howard Dietz from Hollywood, along with several others in publicity and advertising. On my arrival the MGM publicists rushed to prevent the press from getting to me, but I was more lenient then. I was eager to have even greater success in new films, and I thought I would be pleasing myself and pleasing the reporters. I had a few ideas about how to handle my future plans, but when the moment came to confront the crowd, I forgot everything. In any event, the first thing I was asked was my reaction to Moje's death.

I replied cryptically, "What is there to talk about? A tragedy can make some people sad and others happy. It depends upon where you stand."

The reporters quickly dropped this subject. Photographers scurried about snapping pictures, and the reporters asked other personal questions, to which I answered, "Sometimes I am ashamed, sometimes I am afraid to talk about my personal affairs."

"Why?" asked one. And so I repeated what Moje had said to me a long time ago: "You feel timid, you feel shamed when stupid people don't praise you."

The reporters were puzzled and retreated to safer ground. "What will you play in next?"

"I would like to play Joan of Arc or Anna Christie. But the question is meaningless, because I am under contract to MGM and I have to play what the studio tells me to."

Mr. Dietz took me by the arm and led me to a limousine. As we drove to the hotel, I asked him to arrange for me to leave on the next day's train for Los Angeles. I sent a telegram to John Gilbert asking him to meet me with his car in San Bernardino; in that way, I would avoid an unpleasant confrontation in Los Angeles with the press and studio officials who would be waiting for me there. I knew I could depend on Yackie. During my stay in Europe, he had been sending me letters and telegrams asking me to get in touch with him because he had something important to discuss. I had ignored them all, knowing there would be plenty of time to talk in Hollywood.

In San Bernardino, the smiling sun and Yackie Gilbert greeted me. He grabbed me and started hugging and kissing me, professing his deep love. I felt good, not because of his passionate welcome, but because I had fooled Louis B. Mayer. I had not forgotten MGM's neglect of Moje and me when we first arrived in New York.

After his warm embrace, Yackie took me to a restaurant where the two of us ate a steak and drank champagne in a private room. Between bites of steak and sips of champagne Yackie managed to kiss me and tell me how much he wanted to marry me.

I thought that perhaps I could use a husband—a man who could help me in my battles with the studio, in getting a new house and a new car, and in a hundred other petty things for which I didn't have any talent. For such things, Yackie would be a good man. But he was definitely not cut out for marriage—he was always flying from flower to flower.

I then deliberated on a make-believe marriage. We would make a few pictures together, and MGM would make a fortune because the publicity would be so fantastic. But I was sure that such a union between Yackie and me could not last because every young girl in Hollywood would become his lover. Also, every old actress would come out of hiding and testify that before sleeping with her Yackie had promised her marriage. Anyhow, I would not marry a quarter of an actor even if he was handsome. But in this private room where we sat on a comfortable couch, I let him do everything with me. During his hugging, kissing, and undressing, I was thinking that I would prefer to have him not for sex, but as some sort of messenger boy and manager.

Finally, as he kept pressing me more and more about marriage, I told him, "If you are interesting during our sex, maybe I will think it over."

"I will go crazy, mad from love for you," he whispered. "Let's get down on the floor. The carpet is soft."

He slid to the floor and pulled me to himself.

"Everywhere we have a floor," I said, "and everywhere we have a sofa."

"You're joking. You're making a fool of me."

"A good lover," I said, "is one who can read the woman's mind." I saw the surprise on his perspiring face.

"Does that mean you do not want to have normal sex with me?"

"I can't even think about sex, because I'm very tired after my trip. Besides, you have already deposited your semen on my dress and I'm sure you have had enough. If you did not brag so much about your sexual powers, perhaps you would do better and go farther."

"It is very difficult with you. You give in without any feeling, as though you were made of wood."

"And you profess that you are on fire. So burn this wood and make embers. Don't think that when you leave your semen on me you can merely pay for the cleaning of the garment and think you have done plenty."

Yackie stopped and looked at me. "You need to learn some new sexual methods," he said, "and not follow the old paths that our grandparents walked on." He attacked me once more, and I gently pushed him aside. "You are tired, and the time has now come to go home. Let's put away your new methods for another day when I'll be rested. And remember one thing. A slow-moving elephant can go farther than a fast-running horse."

Yackie jumped to his feet and yelled, "God damn it! Stiller is dead, but you are constantly pulling out his smart-ass sayings. That means only one thing—you can't free yourself of him."

"Get dressed," I said quietly. "He did not invent proverbs and clever sayings. To be truthful, at that moment I was thinking about no one but you."

He bent over and kissed me gently on the cheek. We dressed quickly, left the room, and got back into the car. As he turned the ignition key, he again asked, "Will you marry me?"

The car was moving quickly before I answered, "Right now I really haven't made up my mind, but for a start, I think it would be a pleasure to be your friend."

"That's not enough for me."

"It has to be until I can arrange my thoughts and some other areas of my life." The car was traveling very fast. Nevertheless, he took one hand from the wheel to bring forth a book from under the seat.

"Here are the critics' opinions of you as an actress."

"I didn't know you kept a scrapbook about me."

"I have this scrapbook on your film acting and another scrapbook in my head about your sex acting."

"Which one is more impressive?" I asked, smiling at him, hoping he would get me home safely.

Without looking at me he replied, "For the time being, the film one is more impressive, but taking under consideration other factors, I think the sex scrapbook has potential too."

The premiere of *Wild Orchids* was in the Capitol Theater in New York on March 30, 1929. Almost all the American critics praised the performances of Lewis Stone, Nils Asther, and me in this lush romantic drama. To MGM the most important thing was always that the company made money on my films. And this one was to be no exception.

Feeling more secure financially, I decided to leave the Miramar Hotel for the Beverly Hills Hotel. My cottage there was surrounded by a gray wooden fence. Behind the fence grew seven-foot hedges, so I would have some privacy and no one from the neighborhood would be able to peer into my house. What I liked most about the cottage was the porch, whose roof was supported by white columns. I hired a Swedish couple, Gustav and Sigrid Norin, to clean and cook. During my free time I worked on slipcovers and re-styling my dresses. The job that took me the most time was the selection of furniture. In a few months, I collected a mixture of eighteenth- and nineteenth-century English and French furniture which gave my living space a certain style and elegance. I don't know why I occupied myself so much with the house, because I didn't think of inviting anybody.

Shortly after I moved in, the director John S. Robertson came to my cottage with a scenario titled *The Single Standard,* written by Josephine Lovett and based on Adela Rogers St. Johns's novel. I was to play Arden Stuart, a woman rebelling in vain against the conventional morality that a man may play with many women but is right in expecting virginity in his future wife. The male lead was played by Nils Asther.

It was very pleasant to work with the actors and technical personnel on this film. Much of the action took place on a boat, and we worked on board a yacht moored about seven hundred feet from the coast of Catalina. Nils and I took our lunch together, and we conversed in Swedish most of the time. On many occasions I shared snacks with the technical crew. When the days were cloudy and we were unable to film, I amused myself by shooting revolvers at targets. Emil Ploen, the set electrician, was an expert gun-smith, and he asked me if I would be interested in learning how to shoot. I agreed, and he taught me how to handle a revolver, how to aim at the target, and how to pull the trig-ger.

My first target was a five-gallon can sitting on the rocks. To my great surprise, I hit it. Ploen was also very much surprised, and the next day during lunch he called in every-one from the crew who claimed he was a good shot. I think about ten people showed up. He first gave everyone a chance to shoot three bullets. And when each one missed the target, we blamed it on the wind or an unfamiliarity with the gun. Finally Ploen gave me the gun, and I shot my three bullets. I hit the can each time. In a short time everyone on the set knew that I had won the competition in fair contest. They were all amazed. But Ploen said to them, "Why shouldn't she win a shooting competition? She's a real American girl, playing an all-American role."

During the filming, I also formed a close friendship with Dorothy Sebastian, who had played the role of Constance in *A Woman of Affairs*. In this film she was Mercedes. She and I had similar characteristics, especially our sense of humor.

Dorothy considered me a real genius and admired me without any reservations. She thought I was most original in my acting and was fascinated by my style of life on stage and off. One day she commented, "I think you would enjoy children. Have you ever thought of having a child?"

"How can I have children," I asked her, "if I cannot find myself a real man?"

"How about John Gilbert? He's handsome and virile."

I didn't want to commit myself, and so said nothing. The next day, while we were working, word spread on the set that Jack Gilbert had gotten married.

During lunch Dorothy asked, "Have you heard that Gilbert has gotten himself a new wife?"

"I don't know anything, and I don't care."

"He's married the Broadway actress Ina Claire."

"I wish them lots of luck," I replied, getting up and going back onto the set.

The evening papers announced that Miss Claire had met Yackie just after my return to Hollywood. According to the columns, it had been love at first sight for both of them. During the next few days, when many reporters tried to storm my hotel, I was very much disturbed. My only recourse was to look for a home with a higher fence and lock myself in. Harry Edington, whom I had originally met through Yackie, helped me find just such a house, at 1027 Chevy Chase Drive in Beverly Hills. It was eight rooms, done in the Spanish style, with a fruit garden and swimming pool. Trees, shrubs, and a very high fence protected the house on all sides. I was very happy that I had found such a place to live. I gave my Swedish servants, Sigrid and Gustav, strict orders not to give information over the phone and not to let anyone in. If someone wanted to communicate with me, he or she had to write a letter.

I gave my servants one hundred dollars every month with which to buy groceries, and I spent another thirty dollars monthly on the car and dry cleaning. I made sure that my servants gave me a receipt for every cent spent. I had learned my thriftiness and the importance of receipts from Moje. Gustav knew how to drive the car, and on my free days I would sometimes accompany him and his wife while they did the shopping. Sometimes in the evening I would drive with them to Pasadena, Long Beach, or Los Angeles to do some window shopping or sight-seeing. I did this to show people that I was not always by myself but did go out with those who could protect me from questions. I was very close and very friendly with this Swedish servant couple.

Later I discovered that to get some extra cash, they had sold stories about me. Some of them were true, but some of them were not. It was said that I spied on them when they made love; that I liked garlic; that I wouldn't buy newspapers but read theirs; that I asked them to eat vegetable dinners, while later I consumed caviar and other expensive gourmet foods in the privacy of my room. When I mentioned this gossip to Sigrid she denied being the source of the rumors. Eventually, however, I concluded that my servants were guilty of spreading stories about me.

But they were not alone; John Gilbert and hundreds of others added to the gossip that swirled around me. They were all jealous of me and my money. Even in my own house I could enjoy no privacy and peace of mind. I could escape nowhere. I swam in my pool only when my servants were out shopping. If I wished to sunbathe in the nude, I would send them on errands for a few hours. When I did my morning calisthenics, I would lock myself in my bedroom. I had become a prisoner in my own home. And when I was afraid that I was losing my mind, I began worrying about Nils Asther.

Although his acting in *The Single Standard* had been very good, after the premiere at New York's Capitol Theater on July 27, 1929, reporters wrote that perhaps this was his last film. All of them were saying that I had placed a jinx on his career. MGM didn't want to give him a role in my next film, *The Kiss*, although he still had a contract.

To this day I don't know why they gave the role of André to Conrad Nagel instead of to Nils. My humiliating pleas to MGM had no influence on the casting. I played Mme. Irène Guarry, while my husband's role was undertaken by Anders Randolf. Lew Ayres played Pierre. Holmes Herbert took the role of Lassalle, and George Davis played Durant. I begged the studio to give Nils any kind of acting job. But my pleas fell on deaf ears. Nils was bitter. He blamed me and even dead Moje for his misfortune.

In Hollywood, in New York, and in Europe, more and more people were saying that I was an evil character who destroyed every man who worked with me. It was very unpleasant to hear about the Garbo jinx, but it was impossible for me to control such vile talk. I could live without men, but I certainly didn't believe that I was a jinx.

During this time in my life, animals were the only companions that eased my loneliness. I know I alienated many people, but I still don't know how and why. Some of my friends left for Europe; some left for another world. Others turned against me. I think all the misunderstandings and broken friendships were caused by malicious gossip. It was said that when my servant was sick, I left her alone and went to fetch a doctor. I had a telephone at home, but it was said that I would go to any lengths to save on my bill. And I was said to have told the sick servant, "When you feel the end is coming, please turn out the light, because we must save on electricity."

A parrot, a dog, and three cats became my real companions.

My interest in animals reached back into my early childhood. I was probably not more than five years old when my mother and father took me to the village where my mother's kinfolk were living.

One day I noticed in the rabbit warren a chicken's egg. I ran very happily to the house shouting, "We will have rabbits very soon. We will have rabbits very soon."

My mother, who was always quick to scold me, asked, "How do you know?"

"Because I saw an egg in the warren."

"You're really stupid," said Mother in her strong voice. "Rabbits are not born from eggs. Their mother bears them live."

When I heard this, I was really confused and asked her, "Then could you have a rabbit?"

Naturally this question brought not only scolding but also a few slaps.

During the lonely days in Hollywood I spent a lot of time with my cats and dog, playing with them in bed or during my meals. The dog would swim with me in my pool, and after that I would play with all of them under the trees in my garden. I also enjoyed horseback riding.

One day I noticed, to my great surprise, that my dog, whom I privately called Moje and in front of my servants, Doc, and whom I took to bed all the time, resembled me to some extent. I was really shocked when I started dreaming that this dog was helping me with my daily chores, talking to me, and playing in my films. I pulled myself together and decided to keep the dog out of my bedroom, telling the servants to confine him to the kitchen, where I couldn't see him.

But my loneliness grew, so I turned my attentions to my parrot, whom I taught to call me "Geebo." She was a very quick learner. One day she cried out, "Geebo, go to hell. Geebo, go to hell." She had picked up this expression from Gustav and Sigrid, who had been cursing me in the kitchen. I was enchanted by my parrot spy, so I decided to buy her a mate, thinking that eventually she would have young and fortify the whole apartment with little spies. I could never shake my weakness, especially at night, for my dog, but during the day when I had free time, my parrots kept me occupied.

This love for animals I shared with my friend Paderewski, whose house in Switzerland was full of animals that he adored. Once he said to me, "Man is better off when he has stupid animals for friends instead of smart people." I could agree with him at that particular moment in my life, because I was so lonesome.

My other great pleasure was the massages performed by Sigrid in my bedroom. She was really an expert, and I enjoyed her work on me very much, even though at times she was a bit rough, so that I felt pain—although pain can be pleasure too. Sigrid did this work without her husband's knowledge, and I secretly paid her extra. When she was sick, her husband took me to the Turkish baths, but the massage there was not the same. The bath employees were upset when I tried to teach them how to massage. Finally I abandoned my trips to the Turkish bath and determined to take care of all my physical needs at home.

I even stopped going to the beauty parlor, because the professionals there used a variety of chemicals on me and my skin became irritated. I was also exposed to comments and stares from the staff and the other clients. So I settled for simple soap and water. Sometimes Sigrid would set my hair, and after she had finished, we would drink chamomile tea and eat dates. We would discuss the sexual problems of the modern woman. When her husband was out, we would cook and eat together. She became more understanding and even told me what her husband thought about me. Perhaps the money that I gave her in secret had done the trick, or maybe she had lesbian inclinations.

I have never had a satisfactory experience with doctors. Since I had been feeling rather exhausted, I thought I should go for a general checkup. I went to a well-known Hollywood physician. He peered and poked for an hour or more, and seeing a blank expression on his face, I knew he hadn't found anything.

"But Doctor, I have pains in my chest. I have pains in my hands. I have pains in my legs. I often feel faint. What's the matter with me? Something must be wrong."

"I don't know," he replied phlegmatically. "Maybe if we performed an autopsy we could find it."

All of Hollywood was full of quacks like this doctor, and they flourished in every conceivable human endeavor. Hollywood bubbled with mad people.

My tenth film in Hollywood, and my last silent one, was *The Kiss*. The scenario, written by Hans Kraly, was based on an original screen story by George M. Saville. The studio gave me "a young Belgian genius," Jacques Feyder, as director. I was again lucky to have Bill Daniels as my cameraman. The story line was dramatic and, in my opinion, well written. I played the wife of a rich old man whom I murdered. My defense was successfully conducted by a young lawyer, well acted by Conrad Nagel, who was in love with me on and off screen. Pierre, another of my lovers, was played by Lew Ayres, then a nervous newcomer.

Because I tried to help Lew with his acting problems, he developed the impression that I was in love with him and started calling me his "peach."

After I had invited him once or twice to my house, he asked me point-blank, "Why are you doing all these helpful things for me?"

"Because you are young and talented, and you need the help."

"But you are the great actress," he protested, "and I'm only a beginner. Yet you make it appear through your actions that I dominate the scene. Why?"

"You just think so because you're not familiar with the camera," I said.

"Yes, but it's very generous of you to want to share the spotlight like that."

I became impatient. "When you see the finished picture, you will know that I did the right thing."

"Well, I like you very much, and I'm very grateful to you for showing me how to relax before a master cameraman like Mr. Daniels."

Often I would go for a walk with him, and we would talk about the injustices suffered by workers and peasants all over the world and about war. Lew was a pacifist and detested war, which he believed was started by the wealthy. During such conversations I would suggest that he go into politics and organize people to work against war and social injustice.

And he would reply, "You need fertile soil for the seeds of change, and today's working people are complacent—they have been very cleverly misled by propaganda. And what can I do without a name and money? How can I get into politics? Besides, I don't feel I have any talent for politics. I must learn to express my philosophy in other ways. Right now, I would like to find a good script and a good director with whom I can make a good antiwar picture."

"Who will give you money for antiwar films? The capitalists surely will not, and to make such a film you need a lot of money."

But Lew's optimism was indestructible.

I have to admit I was enchanted with his enthusiasm and his love for humanity. I tried to help him any way I could. I took him with me everywhere I went, including Jacques Feyder's house, where people like Pola Negri, Lewis Stone, the Barrymores, the Fairbankses, Norma Shearer, Gloria Swanson, and even Charlie Chaplin were regular guests. But Lew, with his antiwar and anticapitalist tirades, alienated them, and important people avoided him. The one exception was Chaplin, who liked Lew and engaged him in discussions. However, he never asked him to play in his films, because he thought Lew did not have comic talent.

When Willie Sörensen arrived in Hollywood, he monopolized my time to such an extent that I didn't have a minute for Lew. He saw what had happened and, being very sensitive, completely disappeared from my life. And since I never pursued anybody, I didn't make any inquiries after him.

The New York premiere of *The Kiss* was on November 15, 1929, again at the Capitol Theater. The critics repeated over and over, "a sensitive actress" and "a genius *femme fatale.*" Lew Ayres was warmly received.

Soon after the premiere of *The Kiss,* I ran into Lew on a Hollywood street and asked him to my house. During dinner, all he could talk about was my supposed jinx on actors. It appeared that someone had told him everything bad that had been said about me. My defense was "Maybe I am a jinx for actors without talent, but not for you. I'm sure you will come up on your own and play great roles."

"And I will never abandon my beliefs in pacifism and socialism," he responded with determination.

"You don't have to. You must not. In films, talent is the important thing. If we have that, we can lead private lives and fight for our beliefs."

For the first time in my life, I had been clear and determined in expressing myself. But I was to be proved wrong. Years later, during the Second World War, Lew was blacklisted because he refused to serve in the army.

31

Anna Christie and Others

For me Eugene O'Neill was the most interesting American dramatist. His rebellion against the empty cultural life of his country inspired me. Once, he had said of himself, "I am a submarine waiting beneath the surface of life to torpedo merchant ships wallowing with obese assurance, too sluggish to fear or wonder."

His *Anna Christie* poses a challenge to an actress with its difficult yet picturesque language. Anna's character holds great truths about life. For the first time I was enthusiastic over a role the studio had proposed. I immediately began refreshing my knowledge of this play. I went even further—I read everything O'Neill had written. Frances Marion did a fine job in writing this scenario. I was doubly fortunate because the studio gave the camera to Bill Daniels. *Anna Christie* was my first talkie and, I sometimes think, my best film. Before I even began to rehearse, I learned the role by heart, with the help of the director, Clarence Brown, who with great understanding tried very hard to take Moje's place.

I poured all of my soul into Anna's character. My husky

voice aided me immensely in creating an immortal representation of this great dramatic character. Because I had studied Eugene O'Neill, I was able to feel not only the author's philosophy but also the independent life of his characters. And for the first time I felt that I received sincere cooperation from my fellow actors. I underline sincere. I really felt that way. Perhaps the tragic spirit of Moje was directing me and the others to create a masterpiece of *Anna Christie*. My first talkie was an artistic triumph and, what's more, a great financial success. Although MGM was paying me almost six thousand dollars a week, the company was making more than enough for itself. And for the first time the American press began referring to me as "the greatest living actress."

After the success of Anna Christie, MGM immediately pushed me to work on more films. In less than two years I acted in six new creations without a minute of real rest.

The first was *Romance,* based on the play by Edward Sheldon. The story was similar to my own in some ways—the heroine climbs from material deprivation and early sexual abnormality to the summit of fame and riches. Only the desire to spend the rest of my life with the man I loved never materialized in real life for me. Lewis Stone, in the role of Cornelius Van Tuyl, attained near perfection in his acting. But the performance of Gavin Gordon as Tom Armstrong was acting in diapers. I had problems with him off the set as well, because he kept trying to date me.

Somehow it happened that on the first day of shooting he broke his collarbone. From then on he acted in a cast, which was concealed by his costume. As a result, our love scenes were stiff and rather comical, and again the rumor spread that I was a jinx. As I recall, I never saw him on the screen again after this film. I also had a few problems with Clarence Brown, who didn't want to consult me in the selection of actors.

The premiere of *Romance* was on August 22, 1930, and it didn't make much of a critical stir. My next picture, *Inspiration,* was made with the same director and cameraman. The original screen story and scenario were written by Gene Markey. Lewis Stone, who took the role of Delval, said to me one day, "This is the fourth film I've made with you.

You are a good artist, and your enthusiasm on the set communicates itself to me and to the other players. You are a person of many moods, all of them interesting."

"Why are you saying this? Is this a trick or something?"

"I don't understand," said Lewis.

"As you probably know, the studio is saying that in some mysterious way, I'm gaining power over actors, directors, cameramen, and even technicians. With so much praise and admiration from my co-workers, I'll be able to demand a half-million dollars per picture. Mayer says I don't have the courage to approach him myself and am using everyone else to pressure him."

Lewis was very much upset and said nothing. He just turned around and left me. It took me some time and much persuasion to convince him that everything I said was the truth. For the first time I believed what people were saying about my jinx. It seemed to me that now I would put my jinx on Lewis Stone. From then on our relations cooled. He left an impression on my memory as a good supporting actor possessed of a spiritual character.

In *Inspiration*, André was played by Robert Montgomery, who showed more enthusiasm than talent. I liked him very much and tried to help him as I had helped Lew Ayres. Bob was enchanted with my acting and talked to everyone about me.

But I had had enough of men and the problems they brought me, and so I decided to avoid him. But the more I avoided him, the more he pursued me. After the premiere of *Inspiration* on February 6, 1931, the critics didn't like his acting, and one of them even said he had given "an uninspired performance, the worst of his career." I thought a young actor like Bob did not deserve my jinx, and I helped him get a role in *Strangers May Kiss*, in which the leading lady was Norma Shearer.

My so-called jinx was widely discussed in the press and on the radio. All this publicity exhausted me mentally and physically and led me to astrology, occultism, and magic. I read books and magazines on these elusive subjects. Later, when reading alone could not satisfy my interest, I began searching out mediums, fortune-tellers, card readers, and anyone else with extrasensory perception. I struggled to solve the secret of my character and the reasons for my constant anxiety over my emotional and physical well-being. Very often I had nightmares about my father, about Moje, and about a tragic, early death.

I didn't have any one to whom I could talk freely, so I went to occultists, devil worshipers, mind readers, and those who occupied themselves with the summoning of spirits. Because I believed in life after death, I kept trying to talk to my father and Moje. During my dreams I heard their voices—terrible, angry voices, warning me not to involve myself with any other men.

My attitude toward my environment and people in general became more and more chaotic and irrational. I became so suspicious and so confused that I didn't know my friends from my enemies. Confusion ruled my mind and soul.

The first person to notice my inner turmoil was Bill Daniels, probably because he was spiritually sensitive and believed in mysticism. He told me that reading Pirandello, the Italian mystical dramatist and novelist, would do me a lot of good. At that time this writer was popular in Hollywood among so-called intellectuals. Though I had gone through some of his plays before, now I read him with more care. I greatly admired his opinions on the arts; some of them I copied, while a few I even memorized. Pirandello's philosophy, with its deep supernatural overtones, expressed my thoughts better than I could express them myself. I had an absorbing interest in the reasons for the existence of man and in the peculiarities of character and behavior. I thought that by reading Pirandello I might find the key to my own existence. Systematically studying this Italian author was for me like taking a hot mental bath, followed by a cold shower. I felt confused, but somehow better.

My films brought MGM so much revenue that Louis B. Mayer and his crew of profiteers kept draining my energy and artistic imagination in film after film. My next two works were *Susan Lenox: Her Fall and Rise* and *Mata Hari*. They were conceived and produced in such a hurry that I did not have much time to digest the stories or to develop my personal attitudes toward the characters. *Susan Lenox* was based on a novel by David Graham Phillips, and here again fragments of my own life showed up—especially in the scenes that touched on misery, quarrels, and physical violence. There is a happy ending when I am reunited with my lover, Rodney, played by Clark Gable. Gable's interpretation was most undistinguished, but in my association with him he proved to be a pleasant young man. He knew his own shortcomings, which I had spotted right away, including a stiffness that was close to the quality of wood.

The film was a two-dimensional melodramatic yarn. I blamed the flaws not on the acting, but on the poor scenario written by Wanda Tuchock and on the unimaginative directing of Robert Z. Leonard, who could master detail but couldn't handle multidimensional scenes. Only Bill Daniels' photography saved me from complete critical annihilation. The premiere was on October 16, 1931, at the Capitol Theater in New York. The critics were devastating.

Mata Hari was based on the life of the beautiful spy of the First World War. The story and scenario were written by Benjamin Glazer and Leo Birinski, and the film was directed by George Fitzmaurice. The handsome but untalented Ramon Novarro was Lt. Alexis Rosanoff. Lewis Stone played Adriani very well, and Lionel Barrymore was quite good as General Shubin. Bill continued his miracles with photography and saved me once more from catastrophe. But after the film's East Coast premiere on December 31, 1931, at the Capitol, I came in for some harsh criticism.

Reporters camped around my house, waiting to question me about my inferior performance. I hid inside or stayed concealed behind the bushes in my garden, giving orders to the servants to let no one in. Sometimes I would climb the cypress trees and scan the faces of the photographers and journalists from the West Coast, the East Coast, and the world over. I didn't have anything to say.

I spent many nights without sleep trying to figure out what had happened. I had worked with inferior material, inferior actors, and inferior directors in the past and had succeeded. Why had I failed now? My inner torment probably had something to do with my uninspired performance. Yet no one recognized my spiritual turmoil, and almost no one defended me. One exception was Gustav von Seyffertitz, who had played with me in *The Mysterious Lady* some three years before. In an interview, he said, "I don't believe she has changed her style materially. She was a star when we made *The Mysterious Lady;* the producers merely hadn't realized it yet. Garbo has her own methods of portraying characters; her technique is individual, and so I don't believe she has changed much. She is essentially the same actress: original in her art and possessed of that magnetic attraction, mystery."

I will never forget his noble defense, because it came at a time when practically everyone was criticizing me. I spent many hours every day going through piles of newspapers and magazines, looking for and clipping favorable reviews, which at the time gave me a tremendous lift. I felt helpless; I believed that having been born under Virgo, I was the captive of a past that would prevent me from developing a happy present. It was difficult for me to collect my thoughts and make a decision. Should I stay in Hollywood, or should I go back to Stockholm?

During this painful time I accepted an invitation from Jacques Feyder to go on a picnic with him and his wife and Willie Sörensen. While we were sitting on the beach, an old man came up to us and asked for something to eat. We invited him to share our ham-and-cheese sandwiches. I was fascinated by the old man's tanned and wrinkled face, his burning black eyes, and his heavy eyebrows, which cast shadows on his cheeks. His gray mustache covered thick lips and big rotten teeth, which bit savagely into the sandwich. His wrinkled hands were big and strong and covered with gray hair. I shivered as I felt the presence of Moje. Yet so occupied was he with eating his sandwich that he seemed oblivious of our presence. But when the others weren't looking, he stared intently at me.

This mysterious figure, who had popped up from nowhere on the deserted sands, finished his sandwich quickly, got up with the agility of a young man, and said to me, "Too bad I am not young."

"Why do you say that?" I asked, my voice trembling.

"Because I would marry you."

"How do you know that she would like to marry you?" asked Jacques.

"Oh, I know."

"But I don't feel that." My words came out more confidently as I noticed everyone supporting me.

"Deep inside your heart," said the old man, "very deep

in your heart you are a good woman and you have love there. But life has ruined that, and the people around you have turned you into an empty shell. But I can save you from destruction." Saying this, he moved away slowly. He turned and faced the ocean; he spoke louder to be heard over the surf.

"I could save you," he said. He was walking quickly and with purpose toward the ocean. With each step he appeared to be getting younger. I was transfixed as he moved closer and closer to the shoreline. The beach was totally deserted as I watched him go into the Pacific waters. My eyelids grew heavy.

I don't know what happened to him. He disappeared somewhere between the waves and the horizon.

Clouds gathered over our heads, the sun disappeared, and we started home. On our way back to so-called civilization my companions didn't say anything to me. They probably knew what I was thinking; Willie certainly did— he knew my past very well. But words could not convey my fear, so I remained silent. Some years before, Moje had said to me, "A man likes a woman who understands him, while a woman likes a man who does not try to understand her."

I thought everything was now too late. When I returned home, I took a hot bath, went to my room with a bottle of champagne, and locked myself in. I undressed, pulled out Moje's photograph from the bottom drawer where I kept it under my lingerie, and for the first time placed it on the night table in front of me. I drank some champagne and talked to him. But he would not answer. When the silence became too painful, I played with my body.

Irving Thalberg cooked up the idea of collecting as many stars as possible in one picture. He knew such a film would have a fantastic financial success. Because he was vice-president and chief of production at MGM, he could determine the allocation of money for film projects he personally selected. One day he called me into his office and told me that MGM wanted me to play a leading role in *Grand Hotel*, with a scenario by William Drake that was based on Vicki Baum's novel. Thalberg contracted Edmund Goulding, who had directed *Love*, to direct this picture.

Baum was quite impressed with my acting and after

observing me from some hideout, reported to Thalberg, "My admiration for Greta Garbo is great. I saw her tired, tragic face in the opening scenes and her extraordinary vivacity of expression and action as the happy woman." At the same time, she commented that John Barrymore acted as though his collar were too tight.

I consider my work in *Grand Hotel* my best performance after *Anna Christie.* I found after the premiere in the Astor Theater on April 12, 1932, that Robert E. Sherwood shared these feelings. He sent me a telegram: "You're the greatest living actress." For him it was my acting that saved the film, Thalberg, and the group of distinguished stars.

My work on my next film, *As You Desire Me,* went on simultaneously with *Grand Hotel.* Pirandello was for me an unsurpassed master of moods and philosophies. His play *Come Tu Mi Vuoi* had had a tremendous success in New York. The role of Zara was rather difficult, and I didn't succeed in presenting this character in any great depth. Perhaps I had too much knowledge of the author and too much respect for him. As a result, I was overanxious. Or maybe it was the fault of Gene Markey's script, which failed to capture the spirit of the original. Although Melvyn Douglas and Erich von Stroheim were fine actors, their performances, in my opinion, were mediocre.

After such artistic ups and downs, I began to lose confidence in myself and for the first time in my life didn't know what to do. Willie Sörensen suggested that I see the films and evaluate the work of my competitors, if I may call them that. Among the many films I saw in Beverly Hills was *The Love Parade,* directed by Ernst Lubitsch, who was a great admirer of Moje's and my work. The leading role was played by Maurice Chevalier, and although I had considered him just a vaudeville performer, he came across very well. I also was very much surprised that such a film could be produced in Hollywood. I remember I saw it with Willie, and immediately afterward I asked him to take me to Lubitsch's house. On the way there I bought a bouquet of yellow roses as a way of complimenting him for such a great achievement. But now, after many years, I can admit that I did such things in perfect premeditation because I was constantly searching for new directors and new scripts that would allow me to express myself freshly and in novel dimensions.

Ernst greeted me warmly when I handed him the roses. "I would like to direct you in a comedy," he said. "I think you have great talent in that area."

I was surprised and replied, "Some time ago Chaplin was thinking of playing opposite me in a film, but after analyzing my talent and my figure, he told me I would be no good for comedy."

"I'll convince you," Lubitsch said. "I'll bet a million dollars that if you play in a comedy under my direction, you will have your greatest triumph since *Anna Christie*."

Such talk lifted my spirits, and I never regretted the money I'd spent on the roses.

Another person who helped me survive this critical period was the anonymous soul who sent me a clipping from *The New Yorker* in which John Mosher wrote of *Grand Hotel*:

> In spite of the brevity of her appearances, against what many a star would call ground odds, Garbo dominates the picture entirely, making the other players merely competent performers, in my opinion; giving the tricky, clever film a lift, a spring, such as pictures without her, without that intense, nervous vitality she's got, cannot possess. By her walk alone, her gait, Garbo is exciting, and it doesn't need the folderol of grand dukes and pearls that this story gives her, the so conventionalized role of the beautiful premiere danseuse, to lend her that exasperating enchantment vaguely described as "glamour."

After reading such an opinion, I felt that my life's effort was not lost. But I thought it would be a good idea for me to reinforce this belief in Europe.

32

Mercedes

I have always believed that ever-present God wants us to be free people; but I also believe that he has decreed that great loves will turn us into slaves. So if I could not choose between love for a man and love for a woman, I thought, I would remain free and spend my time pleading with God to help me achieve an important position in life. If I achieved that position, I would spend the rest of my life thanking Him. But instead, it happened that I became a slave to both sexes—not because I was afraid to make a final selection, though that task was painful, but because I could never be decisive, and because from my earliest childhood various people had confused me. In my career, through some miracle, I had learned to make the correct decisions, but I was never able to transfer this ability to other areas of my life. It was beyond me to realistically evaluate the actions of other people and then draw accurate conclusions and act accordingly. That was my weakest point. Yet on the other hand, this confused approach to such matters was perhaps the cornerstone of my legend.

From early childhood, I was equally fascinated by both

female and male bodies and their sexual functions. The first time I was aware of such matters was when I peeked at my parents from under the covers and concluded that their lovemaking was never harmonious. There was so much violence that I did not understand, and I grew to abhor this violence between naked male and female bodies. I came to the conclusion very early that the differences between male and female are the sources of this violence.

Later, when I visited my relatives in the village, I noticed almost the same thing happening among domestic animals. Slowly, I was driven to the realization that this was not real love, but only a way to relieve oneself, to relax. Also, it represented a desire to dominate—one being over another. I discovered that the mutual caressing and delicate handling of two people of the same sex was more soothing than the activities that took place between the two different sexes. I even found that masturbation is more rewarding than sexual intercourse between male and female.

I have tried everything at various times of my life, but my body and my thoughts were never satisfied completely. I tried to tell myself that this failure was caused by my nature, my physical makeup, or my mental attitude. But I think that most of the responsibility must fall on my parents who were such ill-suited lovers. But whatever the cause, my physical and emotional needs were never satisfactorily met.

I finally came to the conclusion, after collecting bits and pieces of information on human behavior through the years, that probably everybody is directed by similar emotions, but we try to cover them over. I do know that Moje shared these observations. Very often I discussed with him various sexual experiments in and outside of marriage. His observations on married life itself were rather cynical, and even scornful.

After Moje's death I was more lost and confused about many things, especially sex. I often tried to visualize how my life would have been if I had married him. Maybe we would have destroyed each other, or maybe we would have looked at life and art differently, more realistically. Who knows how our lives would have arranged themselves? Perhaps I would not have been able to become a legend; I might have spent my life as an insignificant caboose on Stiller's huge train to fame and wealth.

Sometimes I think that if I had stuck with Moje every one of our days, I would have saved him from ruin and an early death. But that is just idle speculation. I believe that whatever has happened, God directed that it should happen. Everyone has his road indicated by God, and he must follow it. We exist to go forward. God's hand directed me to Stiller, who molded me into a good actress and eventually into a famous and wealthy one. If Stiller had not discovered me, I would probably have remained a simple Swedish girl. I would have gotten married, had two or three children, and spent the rest of my life bringing them up and making a living through physical work.

Reaching into the past, I must conclude that women pursued me more often and more persistently than did men. And women were of more consequence to me, perhaps because of their motherly feelings and deeper friendships. There must have been something in me that drew women toward me. I was not as fascinated by their intellectual capacities as I was by their bodies; in each woman I would find something different and uniquely appealing. I became excited by observing the different functions of their bodies and comparing them with my own. I required a great deal of psychological preparation for my friendships with men, but with women this preparation was shorter and smoother. It is difficult for me to explain all these feelings any more clearly, but I am trying to do my best.

The first woman I knew well was my mother; although my attitude toward her was sometimes friendly, I never trusted her. I greatly admired and trusted my father, but I later came to mistrust men. I observed lots of men and became close to some of them. As a result, my wariness deepened. One exception was Moje, and looking back with sadness on the cold facts of our relationship, I did come out better than he did, physically and sexually. My relations with women never gave me as much satisfaction as I had with Moje. I was capable of bringing out the best from women, but many times I discovered that this was not enough. So I looked forward to the next relationship with stronger hope. There was a sexual base to all of this activity, but it never lasted long. I became bored easily and began to look for someone new, although I didn't realize until much later that the new love would always be the same as the old.

I can count my long friendships with actresses on the fingers of one hand. Among them was my relationship with Marie Dressler, who played Tillie in *Tillie's Punctured Romance.* I will never forget her warm body, simple love, wisdom, and perceptive, friendly attitude toward me. She was the first person to convince me that I should play Queen Christina of Sweden. She gave me the opportunity to meet other women and displayed great love for all her friends. She taught me not to be ashamed of this kind of love.

When I was sad or emotionally exhausted, she would come to me, sensing my need for her. Standing on my doorstep, she would sing, "Heaven will protect the working girl." This song would mark the beginning of our evening. And when she was ready to return home the next day, she would sing her good-bye with the same song. To pay her back in a small way, I persuaded MGM to engage her to play Marthy in *Anna Christie,* a role for which she was perfect. Who knows?—maybe Eugene O'Neill had Marie in mind.

I was also friendly with Dorothy Sebastian, who appeared with me in *A Woman of Affairs* and in *The Single Standard,* though our friendship was not as deep as the one I had with Marie. I had similar relationships with the actresses Barbara Kent, Paulette Duval, and Florence Lake, all of whom I met during my professional life.

But my most original friendship was the one with Mercedes de Acosta, a woman with a small figure, a sharp nose, and a great appetite for the arts and for life. Naturally, I underlined life at that point. I was living in Brentwood, on San Vicente Boulevard. I changed houses often to avoid uninvited guests and people who were no longer my friends. Sometimes I would not even give my new address to my studio, only my telephone number.

I became aware of an elegantly dressed women who often walked by my house, especially when I was going to or coming from work. I became rather upset because she would simply look me over, say nothing, and go away. I was on the verge of changing houses when she finally approached me.

"I am not a thief, and I am not an autograph seeker. My

name is Mercedes de Acosta, and I'm working in Hollywood as a screenwriter."

"That's good," I said. I went up the steps thinking about her odd face and rapidly moving hands. I remembered that I had seen her face in some magazine or newspaper.

But before I could place her, she said, "Although I know how to live, I am lonely, and I would like to share my knowledge with you."

"Why with me?"

"Although we don't have any physical similarity, we share a great spiritual kinship."

"Maybe some other time," I said, reaching my door. "After a long day in the studio, I am tired and must rest."

"Yes, perhaps some other time," she replied, not pressing me, though I detected a determined tone in her voice. "We have several friends in common: Bill Daniels, Lionel Barrymore, Jacques Feyder, Mayer, Thalberg . . ."

She mentioned only men's names. Then, after a pause, she added, "Check up on me, and we'll meet later." With those words she turned and left, and I went into the house.

During the next weeks I didn't see her on the street. Such behavior intrigued me. Delicately I made inquiries among various people. To some I even divulged the whole story. I discovered that she was a member of a well-known family. She had traveled much and wrote verses and plays. Everyone admired her vast, original wardrobe. She had so many clothes that although she had been living for some time in Hollywood, no one had seen her twice in the same dress, suit, or shoes. And all her garments were made to order, including shoes, hats, and handbags. She had been married to a New York artist, but had dropped him and taken up Buddha and vegetarianism as substitutes. She had traveled through Asia to absorb the wisdom of the Far East. But what intrigued me most of all was her dropping from view as soon as she had presented herself to me. I thought often about her face, her hands, her walk, her entire body, her original way of dressing.

After a few months, Mercedes sent me an invitation to a reception in her home and *en passant* mentioned a group of well-known people who would be there. I thought that she must have an enormous house to hold so many people at one time. I decided to go, but at the last moment I called up to tell her I could not come because I was sick.

"If you're sick, I would like to visit you," she replied. I agreed, but asked her to postpone her visit until the next day because I was afraid she would catch my cold.

"I'll come and cure you immediately," she replied, not believing me. I had no way out, so I agreed to see her that day. Within the hour, she appeared with two bags of oranges and lemons and said, "I'll cure your cold if you take me to the kitchen."

She walked into the kitchen and straightaway began squeezing oranges and lemons. She gave me a large glass of their juices to drink. She continued to mix the juices, increasing the amount of lemon juice. The third glass was ninety percent lemon juice. When I had finished it, I said, "Three glasses is quite enough for me."

She didn't insist, but convinced me that she should stay and later repeat her cure a few more times. I discovered that the melody of her speech cast some sort of spell over me. When she almost chanted that fresh oranges and lemons were gifts from Buddha, full of sun and vital energy that would cure me completely of all my ills, I began to believe her. I felt that I was falling deeper and deeper into emotional involvement with her. She said that people could easily be cured of physical maladies and mental distress. She believed that besides a healthy diet, a person requires meditation, sensible exercise, and a love of humanity. But above all, meditation and love.

"I'd like to stay with you longer," she said, "and show you the proper attitude toward life."

"You mean I will live forever?"

"Not forever, but very long, until your life will have no sense for you and no excitement for others. Then you will pass into immaterial immortality."

Mercedes' whole philosophy was much too deep and too confusing for me, but I decided to begin with the oranges, which I consumed every day in enormous quantities. This fruit was again the link between my past and my future. In dreams I would sometimes see on them, as before, the faces of people known to me from my life or from history.

That first day, when I related those early dreams to her,

Mercedes told me, "This is a very good beginning. But have you seen Queen Christina in your dreams?"

"Yes, but why do you ask? And how did you know?"

"You resemble her, perhaps not so much physically as spiritually. Queen Christina was a fascinating person, and I believe you are a reincarnation of her."

I asked her point-blank, "Is reincarnation possible?"

"Of course. Sometime in the future I will appear in this world again as a little bit of myself, a little bit of Sarah Bernhardt, and a little bit of you." She said this with such power and conviction that I felt I must believe in this complicated philosophy.

We moved from the kitchen to the living room and sat across from each other. Mercedes continued to talk about her philosophy of life.

"When we stop eating meat and live wholly on vegetables, when we meditate, exercise, pray, and work for the good of others—then everything will be possible, including love between enemies. Everyone will be our brother and sister, and love will be not mere love between man and woman, but between woman and woman, and man and man. We will have marriages between people of the same sex, and lovemaking will become intensely exciting. The people who want to have children will have them, and sexual intercourse will have God's approval. Sex between people of the same gender will be a form of prayer. Happiness shall rule the world."

Then, for a moment, she stopped pouring out her thoughts, and I tried to grasp the meaning of her words. She sensed my intense interest. "That's the reason I was searching for you," she said. "I felt that you are going through some sort of inner torment, and I would like to help you to the road of sun and happiness."

"I think that would be most difficult for me."

"Nothing that is beautiful is easy or simple, but if you take the right road, everything is possible. My own life is an example of what can be done if you have goodwill and accept the wisdom of Buddha and that of simple people."

She started talking about her family; about her poetry and plays; about her marriage; and about her road from atheism to belief, from the first Christians to Saint Francis of Assisi, and finally to her vegetarianism, meditation, and Buddhism. I listened spellbound, and I interrupted her only to ask, "Why do you dress so peculiarly? Why do you travel all over the world?"

"I dress the way I do to attract other women. First they admire me, and then they ask questions. This is my way of meeting women. Then it is an easy matter to turn the conversation to religion and sex. Of course, you are the exception. I have seen you many times and you have seen me too, but it was very difficult for us to get in touch. We are both very suspicious and rather closed to others.

"As to traveling all over the world, I do that to meet other people and to evaluate them to see if they would be good material for the community of real religion."

I was very much excited by everything she said. I knew nothing of the subjects she had talked about. "You are very convincing," I said.

She jumped up and started hugging and kissing me. "We are spiritual sisters. I knew this would happen between you and me. I knew it every moment, from your walk, your look, and your opening of the door—the door to an empty house which we will now fill with meditation and love. We are created for that . . ."

There seemed no end to the flow of her words and her kisses. She was now exciting me more physically than spiritually, and I thought that in spite of her eloquence, she was still looking for love and happiness, although perhaps she gave them different names. But maybe I could learn something from her, if not about Buddha and sex, at least about elegance and vegetarianism.

She returned to her home the following morning, and I knew she was almost as excited as I was, although she was five or six years older than I and possessed vivacity, charm, and a great knowledge of love. She had excited me in everything she did.

As I recall, Mercedes whispered to MGM officials that I should play Queen Christina, a role that she said would be my greatest achievement.

Looking back, I can see that my relationship with her gave me not only new sexual experience and spiritual peace for a time, but above all the foundation on which to base my interpretation of this great queen.

My friendships and my tragic and secret tribulations have never completely deprived me of a realistic approach toward life. After each emotional storm, I would quickly regain my balance, my practicality, and my colossal hunger for fame. Next to fame, the second most important thing to me is money. I love it, sometimes more than living people. But it did not give the independence I imagined it would. My struggle to stand on my own feet brought pain and tears which I shed while locked alone in my room.

The seventeen MGM films I had starred in had given me a world reputation and allowed me to amass plenty of money, part of which I invested successfully through my old friend Max Gumpel in Sweden. No one should blame me because I invested abroad the money I made in the United States. America during the Depression underwent an economic catastrophe, and everyone would agree that it would have been stupid to invest my money in a country where millions of people were without work, where lines formed in front of food stores, and where banks had gone out of business. I don't know how President Hoover learned of my foreign investments, but he sent an emissary who asked me to announce that I was investing money in the United States. I told the emissary, gently but firmly, that I had more trust in Max Gumpel than in Herbert Hoover.

The emissary, who was tall and bald, scratched his ear and replied, "What should we expect from a foreigner?"

And he was right. Although I was working and making money in Hollywood, I was not an American citizen. But to justify my attitude I said to myself, "I am not taking anybody's work. With my talent I can work in Europe too. And my success is thanks to Mauritz Stiller and not to President Hoover."

Besides, not being an American citizen was useful to me in negotiating a new contract with MGM. The contract signed five years before would expire in June 1932, and I told myself, "The foreigner will go to Europe and let Mayer worry until he is willing to pay me more money." Mercedes would spread the rumor that I was not returning to Hollywood.

I was tired, physically and mentally, and in June 1932 Mercedes and I left Hollywood for New York, from where I was to take the S.S. *Gripsholm* to Sweden. Before we left, I had a copy made of the *Queen Christina* script and returned the original to the studio bosses, hoping they would become worried that I had rejected their offer and would stay in Europe.

Each time I went east, I thought what it would be like if Moje were alive and I were traveling with him. The intensity of such thoughts grew as I neared New York. I dreamed about him and about the arguments I had offered him for remaining in America. I am sure when we meet in the other world he will forgive me, because a man like him who knows how to love will know the meaning of forgiveness. Mercedes suggested that we get off at Newark, the stop before New York City, in order to elude photographers and reporters. She booked a suite for the two of us in a small hotel. Before I sailed, we went into Manhattan to do some shopping. I bought three suits—one gray, one dark blue, and one a very light blue—two hats, two berets, four pairs of shoes, two bags, four pairs of gloves, and many undergarments.

During this buying spree, an incident occurred that disturbed me very much. A man approached me on Fifth Avenue. I thought he was going to ask me for an autograph. I stepped aside to avoid him, but my feet felt leaden and for a moment I could not move. I looked at his face, and he resembled Moje.

As I struggled to recover myself and move away, the man said, "Yesterday I was talking to my brother and he said you should return to Stockholm and commit suicide on his grave."

He spat on the sidewalk, turned around, and left. Mercedes, who had stopped to look at a window display, saw my distress and rushed forward. She grabbed my arm and asked, "What happened? You are deathly pale. What did that man say to you? Should I call the police?"

I stood riveted to the sidewalk. I felt a tremendous emptiness inside me and a numbness in my hands and legs. People and buildings spun before my eyes. Mercedes put her arm around my waist; she guided me to the curb, where she helped me into a taxi. I don't know how long we drove around looking for our limousine—perhaps ten minutes, perhaps an hour; I lost any sense of time. Perspiration flowed over my body and my numbness grew. When Mercedes spotted our limousine waiting at Fifty-seventh Street and Madison Avenue, we changed vehicles and returned to Newark. Mercedes questioned me, but I didn't say one word during the trip back. When we reached our hotel, she took me to my room and put me to bed.

I don't know how long I slept, but when I awoke, Mercedes was sitting on the edge of my bed, bathing my face with a cold towel. Gradually I returned to reality and told her the whole story. She listened without saying anything, and when I had finished, she got up, went to the next room, and came back with small statues of Saint Francis of Assisi, the Virgin Mary, Saint Theresa, and Buddha.

"We must drive the bad spirits away through exorcism," she said, placing the figurines beside me on the bed.

"I don't understand."

"Your Moje is now suffering in hell and has sent a devil to meet you on Fifth Avenue to convince you that you should commit suicide. But you must not kill yourself and deprive yourself of life because somebody wants you from beyond the grave."

She picked up the statues and placed one in each of the four corners of the room. She again went into the other room and came back with four tiny glasses full of herbs mixed with oil. She placed one in front of each of the four statues and then put a match to each one. I smelled a heavy, nauseating aroma.

Mercedes said, "I will now perform the exorcism and, in performing it, chase the ugly spirits from you and from this room. I will be successful if you listen to me and do what I ask you to do."

She knelt in the middle of the room and began to undress. "Come here, kneel beside me, and get undressed. Let the fragrant smoke and my prayers touch your naked body and protect you."

Influenced by her words and by the setting, with the smoke making me not only nauseated but also drowsy, I got up from the bed, knelt beside her, and undressed. Suddenly she began whispering in a strange tongue. Although I understood nothing of what she said, her words made me feel free and unworried. From time to time she directed her invocations to the Virgin Mary, Saint Francis, Saint Theresa, or Buddha. The spell of her words and the thick, fragrant smoke made me very sleepy. I felt that I would like to exist like this forever. My eyes were closing and opening regularly, and I lost feeling for my body. I was in a trance—the first time that I had experienced this state. From a distance I heard Mercedes' voice, which now became a song that I had never heard before but that enchanted me as it floated on grayish clouds. The voice soon became a chorus of voices. My eyes were closed, yet I saw myself floating in a beautiful church, around me the faces of thousands of young girls. I didn't want to move. I didn't want to do anything, not even open my eyes. I just wanted to remain forever in this ecstasy. I didn't know whether I was alive or dead. It didn't make any difference to me, because time and space were nonexistent and I was happy with things outside and inside of me. When I awoke, I was lying naked on my bed, and beside me was Mercedes, also naked.

"From now on, the ugly spirit of Mauritz Stiller will not persecute you." Mercedes patted my breast gently.

I was confronted by a ticklish situation when Mercedes decided to accompany me to Europe. As delicately as possible, I explained that it would be very bad for my career if she went with me. Yet at the same time, with every passing day I felt myself to be under a satanic spell that she would use to mold me. Her response to my predicament was direct: "Your career is making a slave of you, and because of it you are unhappy and ready to sacrifice the happiness of others, especially those who love you. For you the only important things have become fame and money. Everything else is worthless."

I was stunned by her judgment, but had enough strength to reply, "God accepts me as I am; so should you."

"I'm sure you're afraid of being accused of having Sapphic inclinations."

"You're right. That would really hurt my career, because I always play women who are entangled in love with great men."

She saw my logic, and she compromised by stating she would follow me on the next ship. I was rather pleased; I had not expected it would be that easy to escape from her clutches.

Early in the morning of July 30 I went to the ship, locked myself in my suite on the upper deck, and determined not to see anybody from the press. Two representatives from MGM brought me the draft of a contract and a few presents from friends, including an expensive watch from Mayer with the message that I should know the time when I had to return to work. Bill Daniels sent me a gold cigarette case; Yackie Gilbert, an antique bracelet with a note in which he said that this old bracelet would "bind" his love to me; and Marie Dressler, a few cartons of cigarettes because she had smoked mine so many times. Marie had been chosen by the Motion Picture Academy as best actress for 1930–31. I was pleased and thought about her as I smoked her cigarettes. Perhaps I was also jealous.

The MGM executives, worried that I might never return, had sent me a contract. To confuse them I told their New York representative that I would need a lot of time to consider their proposal. I also received a package from Marie containing books on Queen Christina. The wrapping made me suspect that Marie had been asked by the studio to send me those books, but they proved to be such pleasant companions on the lonely stay in my pine-paneled cabin that I didn't mind. I learned that Queen Christina was a most unusual woman, enchanted by French and Italian arts, and that she carried on an extensive sexual life with men and women.

As I read about her life, I kept comparing myself with her and identifying with her, although I was only a descendant of the peasants whom she strove to help. I didn't have a drop of royal blood in me, but I felt that if I had been Queen, I would have behaved just as Christina did. What fascinated me most was her private life. Although she was raised in the strict discipline of the royal court, she managed to preserve her individuality, her intellect, and her integrity in affairs of state. She succeeded in maintaining her position for ten years. But eventually the conniving nobles overwhelmed her; they did not wish to share their wealth with the poor. Her personal life had been based on impulse and on a terrific appetite for adventure and love. She was only twenty-eight when she abdicated, and although the aristocracy had deprived her of influence over affairs of state, they never succeeded in changing her way of life.

On my way to Europe, somewhere in the middle of the Atlantic, I decided I would play Queen Christina. This role was as much a challenge for me as anything in real life. And I reveled in the thought that I, the daughter of Swedish peasants, would live, for a while, the life of a great Swedish queen, that I would immortalize her. The MGM executives' tricks were succeeding, and I was almost certain that after a rest in Europe I would return to Hollywood and accept their proposition.

There is something else that influenced my decision. A few hours before my departure from New York, the MGM representatives timidly mentioned that Mayer might agree to my conditions: that I make only two pictures a year and that I receive two hundred fifty thousand dollars per picture. But until I received a contract with these terms, I didn't think much of Mayer's "promises."

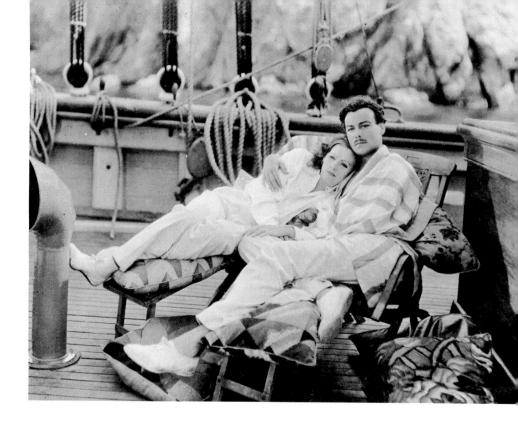

Two films from 1929: above, *The Single Standard* with Nils Asther; left and below, *The Kiss*.

The Face in films from
Peter the Tramp (1922) to
Two-Faced Woman (1941).

The bar sequence in *Anna Christie* as filmed for the American version . . .

. . . and as it was shown in Germany.

Anna Christie, with Clarence Brown directing (above), and Marie Dressler (below), was the first film in which "Garbo Talked," and the husky voice became as famous as the face.

PART SIX   *The Legend*

33

An Interlude

I have been as sincere and truthful as possible in recalling the story of my life. I have revealed many facts about myself and other people whom I have known. It has become clear that my moves in life were not dictated by idealistic thoughts. Ambition and egoism drove me to achieve fame and money.

I achieved these things early in my life because every step was made with great premeditation and yet in such a natural way that everybody around me believed in my morality, in my honesty, and in my shyness. As a matter of fact, I believed in those things myself and became a slave to them. People who intentionally or unintentionally helped me in my career later became burdens. In my own way I was always looking for new people whom I could enchant and whom I could use to further my career, to enlarge my fortune, or just to play with me.

At the end of March 1933, I boarded the freighter *Annie Johnson* to return to America. I looked forward to the five-week voyage; completely isolated from the outer world, I would sleep well and eat good food.

And the voyage began so simply. When the freighter, loaded with Swedish glass, furniture, and steel, had just left our European port, the steward knocked on my cabin door to ask if I needed anything. He was tall and blond, with blue eyes, and had a soft voice. He didn't look like a sailor, but rather like a Swedish girl. He was, or maybe he was merely pretending to be, a bashful creature, but he enchanted me straight off. The engines were running full as the setting sun threw less and less of its girlish gold into my cabin to illuminate the rich brown wood of the paneling. The steward was captivating. Maybe I was tired of Europe and worldly people like Max Gumpel and Mercedes. In any case, I told myself that if I acted cautiously and did not frighten him, he could become a source of beautiful experiences for the next five weeks.

So like a bashful girl, I turned my eyes away and said in a quiet voice, "I would like a piece of good steak and some champagne."

When his eyes moved from my feet upward, I was sure he was thinking that the steak would give me vigor and the champagne romantic notions. He nodded politely and disappeared, maneuvering his muscular behind.

"Like a girl, like a girl," I thought when he had closed the door.

Perhaps a half-hour later it was already dark. I put the light on. At that moment there was a knock on the door, and the steward appeared with a tray. He placed it on the table and hesitated before walking slowly out the door. He had brought two glasses, so he was probably waiting for me to ask him to have a drink. But I did not invite him this time. Instead I poured myself a drink, took several sips, and began eating my steak. The delicious smell of fried onions mingled with the strong scent of seawater. I ate and drank slowly, thinking that he hadn't yet brought me dessert.

When I had finished my meal, I lay down on the bed and began to read the script of *Queen Christina*. But I couldn't concentrate on my reading; I could think only of the steward. He was somehow very peculiar, and at the same time fascinating in his quiet politeness. My brain, soaked in champagne, turned to dreams about perfect love on the ocean. Memory took me through all my encounters with men and women. I again realized that none of them had brought me lasting pleasure, and for a moment I thought of locking my door from the inside. Instead I started to get undressed and postponed locking myself in until after I had completed preparations for bed.

Suddenly the door opened and the steward stepped in. I was lying on my bed. He pushed the door closed with one leg and started removing his clothes. His body was muscular and brown. The statues of Apollo and Minerva flashed through my mind. My beautiful steward said nothing, nor did he smile. When he had removed everything, I whispered, "Lock the door with the key." I couldn't take my eyes off him. He smiled, revealing sparkling white teeth. He turned the key and came over to my bed and began kissing my feet. I lay motionless, shivering a bit. I turned off the light, I didn't have the strength to do anything more. The salt air and the darkness covered my body and permeated my mind. I could not hear the engines. A mysterious silence reigned over all. I felt I was floating on the waves and wished that I could float forever.

34

Queen Christina

MGM met my conditions, and I had no major problems in negotiating my new contract. But I was not at all satisfied with the script of *Queen Christina*. The screen story was written by Salka Viertel and Margaret F. Levine, and Salka and H. M. Harwood wrote the script. But this did not satisfy me. Over the objections of the authors, my director, Rouben Mamoulian, had dramatist S. N. Behrman polish the dialogue. The touches of this seasoned writer made the script acceptable to both me and Mamoulian. The sets and costumes were magnificently ornate and historically accurate.

Mamoulian worked with great enthusiasm and inventiveness; his directions were very simple and logical but highly effective. He asked for my complete trust in his method of directing, and he proposed that we spend some time together to develop a deeper knowledge of each other.

My response was straightforward: "If I do that, people will immediately say that we're romantically entangled."

"That would be an honor for me," he replied. "The film will be successful, not only artistically but also financially. As director I would demand the maximum of myself because I will be involved with you totally."

When, during weekends, we took trips to Los Angeles or canyons in the area, reporters swarmed around us like bees after honey. When I visited his home in Beverly Hills to discuss technical details, gossipers said that I was sleeping with him and that we were contemplating marriage. Mamoulian was not my type physically, with his wild hair and thick-rimmed glasses, but I did have tremendous respect for his talent. He did not like the way other directors had me face the camera. Instead he let me behave as I wanted. This kind of freedom made me relaxed and composed and allowed me to walk around the set as though I were in my own house. He was in agreement with Bill Daniels, again my cameraman, and together they took many shots of the same scenes, selecting only the very best. As a result, MGM spent thousands of dollars on celluloid and extra pay for the technicians. But even I felt we were making a superb film.

I have often been asked why I chose John Gilbert for my male lead. It is a reasonable question, but in fact I did not have much say in selecting the people who worked with me.

Our first day on the set I told Yackie, "This will be your last film with me—maybe even your last film ever." The Garbo jinx had finally reached Gilbert.

When I recall my work on this film, one thing stands out in my mind: how comfortable I felt in my role. I felt most like myself playing Christina. I could relive my youth, not as a poor girl, but as a princess caught up in royal splendor and intrigue. I always wanted to be an aristocrat, and this film allowed me to show my talent for such a role. It was not difficult to shine, for the actors playing with me didn't have even a fraction of my talent. Most of them overplayed, and I was confident that when future generations viewed this film I would glow even more. Even the press picked up on these secret thoughts after the New York premiere on December 26, 1933, at the Astor. To them my acting was "inspirational, full of poetry and the genius of a great actress."

I kept up my friendship with Mamoulian after I completed this film. During filming I also struck up a friendship with the young actress-writer, later house decorator and dress designer, Barbara MacLean. She was at that time, if I am not mistaken, Hollywood correspondent of the *New York Morning Telegraph*. I liked her appealing face and her praise of me. It was she who called me the "frightened gazelle." I made an exception in her case and allowed her on the set.

After one scene where I was dressed as a man, I could see MacLean was fascinated by me. She did not seem to know how to respond, and instead left. I followed her and explained that she should not be bashful, because this was only a film and not real life. I enjoyed her companionship and invited her to my home. Later, because she had such exquisite taste in clothing, I took her shopping for my dresses and shoes. Sometime after this she helped me to decorate my house. After my return from Europe I did not see Marie Dressler because I became quickly attached to young Barbara. I did not know that Marie was quite sick and in need of my friendship and help. Later, I discovered that she died in Santa Barbara on July 28, 1934. But perhaps I somehow sensed her impending death and searched for another woman with similar qualities.

Speaking of people to whom I never returned, I would like to say something more about John Gilbert. His performance in *Queen Christina* was catastrophic. He began drinking more and more. He lost his money and his house, just as he had lost four wives and countless girlfriends. He tried to commit suicide several times but finally died of a heart attack in 1936. His funeral was arranged by a neighbor, the actress-agent Noll Gurney, and John Barrymore. Both had struggled to pull him from ruin. I will never forget Yackie's tragedy. And I will never forget the gallantry of John Barrymore, with whom I had worked in *Grand Hotel*. On seeing me for the first time, he kissed my hand and said, "My wife and I think you are the loveliest woman in the world."

The Painted Veil, based on W. Somerset Maugham's novel about a love triangle, was my next picture. Richard Boleslawski, who was to direct the film, persuaded me to play in it. Like Moje, he had received his theatrical training in Eastern Europe. He had just directed the film *Rasputin and the Empress*. His working method was like Moje's; their views regarding how an actress should learn dialogue, directions to the cameramen, and even ways of talking were similar.

Boleslawski urged me to read *The Painted Veil*. I did, but was not moved by it. To me, the novel seemed overpolished and even cynical, which is a difficult feeling, even for an accomplished actor, to project. What upset me most was the shallowness of Maugham's characters and the emptiness of their lives. They were two-dimensional and purposeless. When Mayer tried to persuade me to play the role of Katrin, I said no, so Dick Boleslawski and three screenwriters—John Meehan, Edith Fitzgerald, and Salka Viertel—were mobilized for the effort. The three authors produced a scenario which the studio asked me to read. Besieged by everyone, I finally agreed, but only under the condition that the role of the sacrificing doctor, Walter Fane, be given to Fredric March. The studio then informed me that Herbert Marshall had already been signed for the part. I protested, but Dick and the three writers again went to work on me. I knew they had put in a lot of effort, so I was inclined to accept the part. I finally agreed when George Brent, whom I had met sometime before and who had become a constant companion, said that he would play Jack Townsend, one of the characters in the triangle. During the filming I felt that none of us was working well. The critical reaction after the premiere, on December 7, 1934, at the Capitol Theater in New York, proved me right. I thought that I, like Yackie, was sinking into a quicksand of poor acting and human deception. Only my work saved this film.

I was depressed and humiliated for a while, but with my good sense of self-preservation I decided that from now on I would follow my own instincts, not others' advice, in choosing roles. I reread *Anna Karenina*, on which my silent film *Love* had been based. I enjoyed reading what Tolstoy had said to his wife: "Oh, let me hurry and finish this book. . . . If a book is to be any good, you have to love the central idea it expresses. In *Anna Karenina* I love the idea of the family . . ."

I was lonesome, without a family, without anyone on whom I could depend, so this novel gave me rest and tranquility.

Anna Karenina occupied not only my heart but my

mind. I was absorbed in thoughts of playing her once more, as no one else could ever play her, this time in a spoken part. I would like to be worthy of Tolstoy. Who could help me to do that?

35

Hazel Washington

A great body of water excites and fascinates me much more than does the human body. It brings me a different feeling from that evoked by people—a combination of admiration and fear. And when I looked at the ocean's waves, I always shivered as though I were receiving some extraordinary sexual stimulation. I have always felt that the simplicity of the water and the simplicity of my body and my soul communicated in a special language. Very often when I was thinking of ending my life, I thought to end it in the furious waves of the ocean.

Anytime I had a free moment, most often on the weekends, I told my chauffeur to drive me north toward San Francisco or south toward San Diego. I would ask him to stop when I spied a deserted spot on the edge of the Pacific. Carrying a basket of fruits, vegetables, and cheeses, I would go far away to brood and watch the waves. The chauffeur would sit in the car and sleep, awaiting my return. Sometimes my wanderings lasted a day or two. On such occasions I slept overnight in the nearest hotel. From time to time I took with me the man or woman with whom I was then keeping up a friendship. I would tell my companion that our party would include only the two of us and, of course, the ocean. On such excursions I took Yackie, Lars Hanson, Nils Asther, Marie Dressler, Ramon Novarro, Jean Hersholt, and others. It depended on my fancy. Very often I would take Harry Edington, who was my financial agent with MGM. Such excursions were a reward for him; he had helped me to get from the studio three hundred thousand dollars per film. On our return Harry was usually so excited that he doubled his efforts to manage my financial affairs.

On certain days an inner voice would tell me that I should go by myself to experience life with the ocean; odd days of the month were for me the most exciting.

Once I went out on a very cloudy day. I didn't notice many birds over the Pacific, only the overwhelming noise of the waves. I was walking on the edge of the ocean, holding my shoes in one hand and my basket of food in the other. My mind was empty, as if preparing for some tremendous experience. I walked a few miles and saw no one. My eyes scanned the empty shells thrown up by the waves. Suddenly I lifted my head and saw a black woman in front of me. Her dress had been faded by the sun. Oily black spots were the only color. I stopped and thought, "Why didn't I see her before?"

She didn't turn toward me but continued to look across the ocean. Perhaps she hadn't heard me or couldn't see me. Or perhaps she didn't want to talk. Her muscular body was shivering, from the cold breeze off the water or from some emotion. I tried to pass her by, but I thought if I only said hello, nothing could happen to me. I walked closer and did just that. The woman turned her eyes toward me. I looked into them. They were black as coal, and they shone with tears. My heart trembled, and my mind said to me, "Don't bother with her. You might get into trouble." But my heart won out, and I said, "I'm looking for a place to have lunch. Are you hungry?"

My cautious mind burst in, warning me, "Don't be foolish. Tell her you are not alone, that your car is waiting not far away."

The woman didn't respond; she only continued to pierce me with her sharp eyes.

My mind, now in accord with my heart, told me to say,

"The best way to cure troubles is to talk with another human being."

"Too late," she answered.

"Why is it too late? If a person is still alive, there is always time to talk."

"Maybe it isn't too late. But white people don't want to bother. They always make more trouble."

"Why do you say that?"

"They use you. Then when they don't need you, they throw you out with the garbage."

I said, "You're right. Most of the time, it does happen like that."

She tried to wipe away her tears. She bowed her head, turned to face the ocean, and said softly, "Ma'am, I always tried to take care of my own troubles, but today everything is finished."

I picked up my basket and shoes and stretched a hand to her in a gesture of friendship. She didn't move, so I withdrew my hand. I offered her the basket. "If you don't want to go with me," I said, "take this, because you must be very hungry."

"Where I'm going, I won't need food."

"And I will tell you that suicide is not going to solve your problems. I have thought many times about getting away from myself, but you know it is useless to try. You are a woman and I am a woman. Although we have different skin colors, we have the same heart."

Suddenly she turned from the water and began walking tiredly up the beach. I felt the trembling electricity of her body, and I said, "You can't walk to the city. I have a car; I'll take you wherever you want to go."

She turned her face and said quietly, "I don't have nobody to go to. For me any direction is all right."

I was encouraged and continued, "At least change your wet dress. I have some clothes in my car."

We walked together in silence, but when she saw my black chauffeur, she started talking. Her name was Hazel Washington. She was the thirteenth child of a Southern white farmer and his black mistress, and her traveling had brought her to Los Angeles, where she had been working as a maid in a wealthy home. When some jewelry disappeared, suspicion pointed to her. Although her employers had no proof, they turned her out. I said to myself, "This is unbelievable. Because she was accused of theft, she decided to commit suicide. She must truly be an extraordinary person."

I took her to my home, although I was debating with myself whether I was doing the right thing. I reasoned that the least I could do was give this woman a dress and a night's rest.

But the story didn't end the next morning. Hazel not only stayed in my house and became my servant, but became my trusted confessor and the only person whom I allowed to walk unannounced into my bedroom at any time. She went to the studio with me and spent the day in my dressing room. I learned about her and she learned about me. We were as close as any two people can be. I trusted her as I did no one else with the exception of Moje. She knew more about me than any other living person. The ocean had brought us together.

36

Anna and Marguerite

After its premiere, in New York's Capitol Theater on August 30, 1935, *Anna Karenina* traveled all over the world. Critical and public opinion was most favorable. The New York Film Critics Circle bestowed on me its award for "best feminine performance of the year." The Venice International Motion Picture Exposition announced that *Anna Karenina* was "best foreign film of the year." And the seventy-seven-year-old King of Sweden, Gustaf V, after seeing the picture, crowned me "Garbo the genius!" He suggested that I receive the *Litteris et Artibus* award for artistic achievement, which I did receive two years later. The studio even saw fit to raise my salary. Everyone was soon asking me to star in new films and to endorse products, which I refused to do. If I had had enough courage and more business ability, I would have made millions of dollars a year. Instead, my income was about half a million.

My career was reaching new heights; perhaps it was already at its summit. I already had twenty films behind me and had attained perfection through hard work and discipline. Although I didn't feel that I played any better than I had in some of my other films, world enthusiasm was greater than ever before. Why had this happened? Perhaps because so much hard work had gone into *Anna Karenina*.

When Sam Behrman received the draft of the scenario from Clemence Dane and Salka Viertel, he worked diligently rewriting scenes and dialogue. After I read what he had done, I suggested some revisions to the studio. Sam didn't like them and went to Mayer with his complaints. The boss told him, "Sam, don't worry. You're a bad press agent for Garbo, but you write great plays. Go back to work."

I was lucky to work with talented actors like Fredric March as Vronsky, May Robson as his countess, and Maureen O'Sullivan as Kitty. Karenin was created by Basil Rathbone.

The camera was operated by Bill Daniels, who knew the lights and shadows of my body and my soul. Before we had started to work on the film, Clarence Brown, the director, said to me, "We have an intimate relationship. I am not afraid of you and you are not afraid of me. You are the best actress in the world to direct. I love your art and love to work with you."

This was a straightforward definition of our cooperation by a very competent director who was constantly encouraging me to work harder and better. He also set up screens around the set to shield me from the stupid comments and curious eyes of outsiders. Only people working directly on the film were present. Even carpenters, electricians, and other technical people were warned not to peek through and watch me at work. This arrangement allowed me better concentration, since I knew there would be no interference. When it came to dialogue, I was always perfect. I learned every word of my script by heart and rehearsed it before my mirror countless times. I even practiced with chairs, sofas, and tables which stood for my leading actors.

Only Hazel observed these crazy performances. Once just before bed, she asked in her melodious voice, "If you use the furniture as partners, why don't you use me?"

I agreed and let her take part in those home rehearsals. In one scene she was Vronsky, in another the Countess Vronsky, and so on. I discovered that she possessed unusual talent and that she liked my direction. She was excited about working with me and even memorized various roles. Hazel knew that she was helping me and that I needed her. This feeling gave her happiness and brought us closer together. I often wondered why I was so successful with simple people like Hazel and not with educated ones. I came up with a simple answer. I too was a simple, uneducated person, and although such feelings as love, hate, and betrayal are basic to everyone, in educated people they are more camouflaged or suppressed completely.

In almost every woman there is a bit of the prostitute. At some time in her life she dreams of having any man she desires. I am sure every woman who has read the novel or seen the play *La Dame aux Camélias* secretly admires the heroine, Marguerite Gautier. Most sympathize with, and perhaps even envy, this idealized courtesan.

The novel and the play have been popular for more than a century. The greatest actresses of their time, such as Sarah Bernhardt and Eleonora Duse, played this immortal courtesan. Dumas in this play, as in many of his works, occupied himself with the problem of the "eternal feminine." I cannot go into the complexities of the author's thesis, but I will admit that after reading the scenario, *Camille,* prepared by Zoë Akins, Frances Marion, and James Hilton, I greatly desired to play Marguerite. There were other reasons aside from the artistic and sexual elation I would experience before the camera. One was personal: My sister, Alva, had died of tuberculosis, as Marguerite does. And I suffered from a touch of tuberculosis as well as pernicious anemia and arthritis.

I also wanted to play Marguerite because I felt that my presentation of her character would be unique. The dramatic interpretation of this role by great actresses had always been confined to the sentimental. This revealed more about their own attitudes toward men than it did about the character of Marguerite, for these actresses had been victimized by men in their private lives. I wanted to give my Marguerite a dose of realism. What I mean by that is quite simple: I believed that Marguerite loved her work. She loved dresses, corkscrew curls, and the cultivation of a deliberate attitude that was different for each lover. Her dance, walk, and other movements varied accordingly. Her persistent cough became the means of guaranteeing sympathy.

Her realistic, perhaps cynical, attitude in her first encounter with young Armand Duval, played by Robert Taylor, is gradually transformed into a protective attitude. I stress "gradually" because Marguerite eventually feels she loves him. The scene where Marguerite accepts the visit of Baron de Varville and asks him to play Chopin becomes the mirror to reflect her real feelings for Armand. Her loud laughter during the music and the Baron's fury as he slaps her in the face brings out the pure love of Marguerite for Armand. This is my own interpretation, and I don't know if it coincides with that of literary experts, critics, or historians.

I determined that even my hairdo had to support my interpretation. So my hair was fluffed over my forehead to give me a frivolous look and to emphasize a kinship of character with similar girls on the boulevards of Paris.

I was going to prove that the "cold Swedish girl" was able to play a French courtesan better than Modjeska, Duse, or even Bernhardt; in fact, better than the three of them put together. George Cukor, my director, told me, "You have conquered every difficulty in re-creating this role. No actress will ever surpass you."

My involvement in Marguerite was so complete that I was unable to maintain emotional contact with people whom I met during work on this film.

Robert Taylor was most attentive, trying without success to make me respond to his love. I noticed his ardor, and I became especially patient with him in explaining how he must act, since he was young and inexperienced. But I never spent any time with him in the evening after work. In the same fashion I also accepted the gallantries of the experienced actor Lionel Barrymore as Monsieur Duval. The energy I needed for this role drained me of any social or sexual desires, and to my surprise, I was content with my own acting.

The premiere took place in New York's Capitol Theater on January 22, 1937. *The New York Times* wrote that I was "as incomparable in the role as legend tells us that Bernhardt was." Mary Cass Canfield, an American playwright and perhaps the only critic who made a religion of following my career, raved, "If a death has ever been played with such absence of bathos and such bitter truthfulness, the history of acting does not remember . . . Garbo is a genius." And the *New York Herald Tribune* added, "Her sensitivity throughout and poignantly moving portrayal disclose the finest contemporary actress at the height of her power . . . Garbo challenged comparison with all of the great actresses of the last eighty years, and she can do so with triumphant assurance."

For this film I received an increase in salary from MGM, the *Litteris et Artibus* award from the King of Sweden, and from the New York Film Critics the award for "best feminine performance of the year." Therefore I was eager to play in another film.

37

Stokowski

It is probable that most of my problems have been rooted in my character—I am highly intuitive, but have great difficulty expressing my ideas and feeling. As far as I can detect, these traits came from my peasant upbringing, my minimal education, my early ventures into film, and my tremendous appetite for money. I never had the incentive to learn in school, and I will remain, to my last day on earth, nothing more than a simple peasant girl. I gained my fame and money through hard work, and I still worry about losing these two commodities. My attitudes and behavior toward people were based on my instinct, a quality I could never define or control. Sometimes I think I am like a child who reacts to her surroundings suspiciously and indecisively. Even with a simple problem like citizenship, I deliberated for the longest time whether I should become an American citizen or retain my Swedish birthright. I moved from place to place to escape from real or imaginary intruders. Although my permanent residence was Hollywood, I maintained a home in Stockholm at 10 Artillerigatan. I also planned to build a house on an island that would offer me seclusion.

As a famous and wealthy personality, I could approach anyone I wanted sexually without scruples and with guaranteed success. I never took seriously the professions of eternal love by my partners. As a young girl, I had observed my family and friends, and I saw that their so-called love never measured up to the ideal that I believed in stubbornly. As a result, I was fearful of emotional involvement or sexual entanglement.

To illustrate my feelings I should like to offer an account of my romantic adventures with Leopold Antoni Stanislaw Stokowski. He was twenty-three years older than I; when I was just a baby, he was musical director of the Cincinnati Symphony Orchestra, and from 1914 to 1936 he had been in charge of the Philadelphia Orchestra. In the mid-1930s he had come to Hollywood as a musical arranger and conductor. He had parts in several films, among them *The Big Broadcast of 1937,* and made many recordings. He was present at all kinds of social and public gatherings in Hollywood. He also was trying to meet me. In 1937, as I recall, the writer Anita Loos invited me to her house for dinner, saying that we would be alone and could discuss an exciting literary property. But when I arrived, I also found Stokowski, who straightaway insisted that I call him Stoky. He made a very pleasing impression on me with his elegant bearing and a distinguished quality that rivaled Paderewski's. His romantic manner toward women also brought Paderewski to mind. I spent the whole evening talking with him of mysticism, lost souls, and life after death—about all those things which puzzled me so much. I tried to explain my past and future in terms of dreams whose meaning he grasped immediately. He had probably done extensive research on me, or perhaps he had great intuitive powers.

As he was taking me home after this pleasant evening, he told me that he had seen all my films many times, that he had read everything about me, and that he had listened intently to everything his friends in Hollywood had to say about me. All this had caused him to fall in love with me. I thought this gentle approach, invoking historical comparisons, was quite original, but I said, "I will be happy to return the money you paid to see my films. I have nothing against continuing our social contact, but let us begin our relationship *sans* emotional entanglements."

Such talk didn't discourage him. He started in about how two similar souls could work together and create masterpieces. I soon discovered he had been considering a film with me and his music. But all his plans were out of the question, because I was about to begin work on *Conquest*, a film based on the historical novel *Pani Walewska*, by Waclaw Gasiorowski. My role was that of Countess Maria Walewska, while her lover, Napoleon, would be played by Charles Boyer. Although he was perhaps too tall to play Napoleon, he was a good actor. Stoky immediately told me that for the sake of my film, we should go to Poland and visit the villa in Walewice, near Warsaw, where the Countess lived and where she bore Napoleon's son on May 4, 1810. Not wishing to offend him, I said that although his idea was interesting, time would not permit me to visit Poland. Besides, the scenario had been written by three authors, one of them being Salka Viertel. She had been born in Poland and would therefore be qualified to bring historical truth to the film.

But he immediately attacked this idea, asserting that unless I knew the soul of this woman and her surroundings, it would be impossible for me to portray her. I deflated his argument easily: "You have praised my Anna Karenina and my Marguerite, but I have never been to Russia or to a French bordello."

He had no answer; he kissed my hand, smiled, and left. I was confident that despite my strong rebuke, this was not the end of our acquaintance. Again the soul of a simple Swedish peasant girl had triumphed in me.

Moje once said to me, "Listen to your conscience or even your most primitive logic, or just plain simple hunch. Follow it. Don't listen to anyone except yourself." I did this when I refused to go with Stoky. But I made a great mistake by ignoring my conscience, which told me to resign from my role in *Conquest*.

I had wanted very much to play the beautiful Maria, whose love for Napoleon, and his for her, survived despite political intrigue and the eventual downfall of the Emperor. But the scenario of Salka Viertel and Samuel Hoffenstein, with the final touches by Sam Behrman, did not succeed in presenting the emotional and historical truth. Everybody tried to improve it and ended up destroying all real sentiment in the script.

Finally MGM, which had a budget of four million dollars for the film, decided it could wait no longer for a better script. A huge cast had already been hired, costumes made, and sets built. After reading all available material on the subject, I felt strongly that the historical facts were more dramatic than the work of the dramatists and scenario writers. I wanted to see included in the film the scene where the son of the Emperor and the Countess Walewska is born. I also wanted the film to show the tragedy of Maria's husband and to depict the corruption in the Emperor's court and the conniving of the Polish aristocracy. In short, I was thinking of portraying the tragedy of a troubled nation through the story of two people in love.

Needless to say, no one listened to my suggestions, and the result was a mediocre product. I seemed to have no allies in my struggle to make a good film. Even director Clarence Brown went along with Mayer, whose only consideration, as always, was money. The cameraman, Karl Freund, betrayed me. Whether this was intentional or not I do not know. What I do know is that he didn't know how to photograph. As a matter of fact, I even think the usually good actors Charles Boyer, Henry Stephenson, Alan Marshal, Leif Erickson, and Reginald Owen let me down.

I didn't wish to attend the premiere on November 4, 1937, at the Capitol Theater in New York. I knew it would be a critical disaster. It had been an unfortunate moment in my life when I decided to stay in this film.

When I look at my relations with Stoky from the distance of all these years, I see more and more clearly that my work on *Conquest* influenced our relationship. I don't want to draw any ridiculous parallels between the love of Napoleon for the Countess Maria Walewska and Stoky's infatuation with me. But all my life I, like the Countess, dreamed about having a great love. Years passed; my days were full of anguish and hate. But gradually I grew further and further away from romanticism. The feelings of Stoky and his golden eloquence influenced me. I thought, "Maybe there is not much time left for real love. Maybe now it will come."

In my naive soul I felt that I might be able to have a child like Maria. But I was already thirty-two, and there was not much time left for a great love and especially a healthy child. After the failure of *Conquest* I needed a radical change in my life, relaxation in different surroundings, not on the West Coast.

When Stoky got his divorce from his second wife, I accepted his invitation to spend some time in Europe. In December 1937 I went to Sweden to spend Christmas with my mother and brother and to settle affairs in connection with my estate. This was on a beautiful lake some miles southwest of Stockholm in Sörmland province. The estate was named Hårby and included over one thousand acres of the most magnificent forest. In the very center sat a twelve-room house which I had purchased earlier for almost sixty thousand dollars. I loved this place despite the mosquitoes.

At the time, because of Adolf Hitler's and Benito Mussolini's policies, I sensed an impending world holocaust. I considered selling the property, but I thought that if I got married, I would want to settle in this beautiful spot. In such material transactions as selling property, I have never been able to make quick and final decisions. After long deliberation, I decided that I should sell because Europe was on the brink of war. I could not put out of my mind some bizarre information I had received from highly placed Swedes. I had been told that Hitler loved my acting and was anxious to meet me because he felt that I was an extraordinary specimen of the great Nordic race. The thought came to my mind that I could go visit Hitler, carrying a revolver in my purse, and kill him very easily. I said to myself, "This is the way to solve the problem of my estate, prevent a new war where more people will die than in any earlier one, and become a great heroine, maybe greater than Joan of Arc."

Such simplistic notions traveled through my mind, but not having a political education, I didn't then realize that war could be started by the Germans without Hitler, because all you need for war is generals.

The real reasons for my going to Europe in December 1937 were to take a rest, distribute money among my relatives, and do some shopping. But on the day of my arrival, the Countess Wachtmeister invited me to her estate. This invitation marked the start of a continuing series of receptions, horseback rides, long walks, theatergoing, and movie viewing.

When my life in Sweden began to bore me and my arthritis, in spite of the diet prescribed by Mercedes, became more painful, I went to meet Stoky in Italy.

I stayed with Stoky at the Villa Cimbrone in Ravello. I was enchanted by the balmy climate, and with Stoky's help I learned to admire Italian art. Most of our time was spent sleeping, doing yoga, eating delicious Italian fruits and vegetables, and taking excursions to the neighboring town of Amalfi. Once or twice we went to Rome to see the historic buildings and to visit the Vatican Museum. But we couldn't stay there for very long; the reporters discovered us, and we were forced to return to the Villa Cimbrone. We enjoyed this place because the servants treated us like members of some royal family. They always referred to me as *una grand' artista*. I spent much time with Stoky discussing the arts and other human achievements that had flourished among the Italian people. How could I talk to somebody about my artistic achievements in film after seeing the Sistine Chapel? I was bashful when anyone called me *una grand' artista*. What kind of artist was I when I had to repeat my film scenes a dozen times or more to achieve some sort of perfection?

And Stoky didn't dispel my doubts by saying, "Your eyes are more beautiful than the waters of Amalfi Bay during sunset."

"Let's not be like children enchanted by first love. We are speaking of great people and immortal works, not of my eyes and the dirty waters of the bay. If you have something worthwhile to say, please say it. If not, let us be quiet and ponder our insignificant roles."

He was hurt by my remarks and said, "The treasures of Italian art represent the contributions of artists through the ages, just as the treasures of film art represent the achievements of actors, directors, photographers, composers, and other people working in this medium. Every one of us contributes something to culture, depending on our talents."

"And how much do you contribute with your conducting?"

"Not much. But I want to compose great music," he said, beginning to defend himself. "I've told you before that

I would like us to create a film about Chopin and George Sand and also one about Richard Wagner and Cosima Liszt. I've already written music and a scenario."

"Would you play in the film?"

"Why not?"

"And you would like to be the director too?"

"Yes," he replied with deep conviction.

I began to laugh, but my laughter did not discourage him. He continued, "Together we could create a film masterpiece."

"Let us assume I agree with you. Where will we get the money for such a tremendous enterprise?"

"A combination like Garbo and Stokowski would make every financial speculator want to invest his money . . ." Here he stopped as he thought about something else. "But the best way would probably be to invest our own money so we can harvest the profits ourselves."

This observation made me nervous, and I said coolly, "It would not be right for me to play in a film in which I'd invested my own money."

"But if we split the costs, we will split the profits."

I said nothing. He stared at me and ran his long fingers through his hair. It was clear he was waiting for my reply, but I stayed quiet. One thought dominated the many that ran through my head. I had thought this evening would begin with some sort of sexual experience, but the financial problems crowded out all such matters. After a longer silence I finally said, "Tomorrow let's go to Capri; now it's time to get some sleep." I got up and left the room, and looked back to see him sitting motionless and pale. Evidently he had spent some time analyzing our financial cooperation, while I with a single sentence had destroyed everything.

"If love cannot blossom in Capri, there is no chance of love." Such sayings were very popular in Europe in my time.

The island itself, situated on the south side of the Bay of Naples, was full of sun, flowers, and tropical fruits. Caves, like the famous Blue Grotto, were ideal places for lovers even back in Roman times. Not having abandoned my hope for real love, I arrived there with Stoky. He was quiet and didn't talk about personal affairs, but I knew he had not given up calculating how to squeeze money from me. He stayed away from that subject and talked about the history of the island. During our many days there I learned about music, about the art of directing orchestras, and about art—particularly Italian art, which he enjoyed most. Although flowers generously dispersed their fragrance as in ancient times and the grapes tasted like no others, he didn't speak of love. During a visit to one of the grottoes he did make a sexual advance, but was unsuccessful. He became so nervous that he started to cry. He reminded me of a hungry baby unable to grab hold of its mother's nipple. I was also frustrated and disillusioned by his ineptness, and one thought continued to dominate all others with me: his desire for my money. I regretted that he had proposed this financial venture, because I had had hopes for a lasting relationship with him which would give me a protector and interpreter of my thoughts for the rest of my life. Now everything around and in me appeared to be in ruins. Disgust took over, and I felt I should be having normal sexual relations. Everything had disintegrated just when we were so close to happiness.

From Capri we returned to Rome, where reporters besieged us. They asked if I was already married to Stoky. My reply was direct: "Mr. Stokowski is my friend. I have many friends, and I have married none of them." When they asked me if I was expecting a baby, I said, "If I have no man, how could I have a child?"

All this made Stoky angry, but he didn't say anything. I knew that the incident in the grotto had been very painful for him. Later, when we were together, he spoke of his masculinity and asked me to give him a second chance. I didn't have any inclination to do so, and I replied, "Sexual feeling must come for me in a natural way. I cannot order it as I order a meal."

He replied apologetically, "Forgive me for my mistakes, but I have already written to the States that we are getting married. And now nothing has come of it."

I wasn't angry but said, "You should have consulted me and not written before the event."

He said nothing. I saw that he was in a depressed mood and went on, "Maybe I am not suitable for marriage. Let's be friends, and perhaps with time something will come of our friendship."

"We don't have much time," he replied with resignation. On that I could not comment.

He begged me not to leave abruptly, because that would make him look very foolish. I agreed with him, and we stayed a bit longer in Rome and then sailed to North Africa. Later I asked him to go to Stockholm, where I would join him after stopping off in Switzerland for a few days to take care of my financial affairs. So Stoky went to Stockholm while I left for Geneva and Riond-Bosson to visit Paderewski. I fell in love with Switzerland. What happened there was the logical outcome of my stay in Italy. My circle had closed.

When I returned to Stockholm, I dreamed of oranges. In these dreams Capri was a rotten orange. Stoky tried to persuade me that we should return to the United States together. I convinced him that I had to stay a bit longer in Sweden to reorganize my financial affairs. He returned by himself to his own work; he plunged into the orchestration of Chopin, Bach, and Wagner. Before he left, he had told me, "The American people are waiting for my music," and I had urged him to return and fulfill his obligation. When I promised that I would meet him in New York, he left right away.

I kept reading in the papers about our great romance, and I kept thinking about how my relationship with him had collapsed and our so-called love had dried up. I kept telling myself, "You did the right thing in breaking it off, because you would never have been able to have a happy marriage with him." There was another thought: If I married him or someone else, my husband might conceivably persuade me to cut off my mother and brother from the substantial income they received from me. They would no longer live in luxury, because I would have to spend the money on my spouse. After keeping these thoughts to myself for some time, I decided to share them with the Countess Wachtmeister. When we met, she said, "I've read in the papers about your great love for Stoky, and I'm curious as to who was giving out the information."

"Not I."

"So it is probably he. I don't know who said it, but a very loud love is not very deep. Great love is silent."

"So why did Stoky do this?" I asked naively.

"For publicity reasons. A typical American approach. He needed publicity. He probably thought that the love between a great actress and a musician would lend him a special aura."

"I don't understand."

"There's nothing to understand. Such publicity is worth a million dollars for Stoky."

"But I don't think Stoky would do that," I said, trying to defend him. "It's not in his character."

"In the United States everything is based on the dollar. Even love has material foundations."

I was very much surprised that the Countess was so brutal in evaluating the situation. But I couldn't refute her statements, so I listened to her.

"You know, I am sure, that some women are not created for marriage. You are one of them. You, Greta, are satisfied with yourself and with your artistic achievements. Besides, you don't know how to select people. For you to select with your egoistic nature is to miss out on the things which you ought to select."

I was upset. "I have had enough of your aristocratic philosophy," I said. "It does not solve anything for me or settle my problems."

But the Countess was not moved by my strong words. Perhaps she sensed that I thought she was right. After a moment she went on: "Look into your own soul and back to your early upbringing for the answers to your problems. And if you want I will tell you what I really think about you."

"I would like to know."

"You are not a full woman and you are not a full man. Everything depends on the season of your soul. One day you are a woman, and the next day you are a man, but above these forces that dominate you, you are also a prisoner of your art and money. These are the sources of your inner conflicts and explain all the things that you do."

I listened attentively to these words and repeated them to myself so as not to lose the melody of her voice. I couldn't move from the chair as she concluded her highbrow philosophy: "The genius is the person who doesn't know how to shoot at something that everybody else sees, and though he lands on the left or on the right he is always on target."

This was my last conversation with the Countess Wachtmeister about Stokowski. As for Stoky, I was one hundred percent correct in relying on my intuition. It didn't take him very much time to find himself a younger and richer girl. Her name was Gloria Vanderbilt, and she was said to have an inheritance of more than twenty million dollars.

38

Ninotchka Triumphs

In October 1938 I returned from Europe to New York. Physically I felt fine; on the ship I had slept twelve hours a day and spent the rest of my time on exercise, walking on the deck, and reading books supplied by the captain from the ship's library. Most of the reading material consisted of Swedish novels, because I thought I might find something suitable to play, something on the scale of Queen Christina or Anna Karenina.

As we neared New York, I visited the ship's hairdresser and asked him to cut my hair in front so as to make me resemble Joan of Arc, for I wanted to appear simple as well as beautiful. My hair had a natural luster, and when I wasn't working I wore no makeup except a touch of mascara on my eyelashes. When the ship docked in New York, I courageously met the reporters and told them straight off that I was happy to return to Hollywood. When they asked me what I had done on the ship, I replied spontaneously, "During the voyage a child was born, and I was so fascinated by it that I spent lots of time with the child and its mother."

This led to a new question: "Would you like to have a child of your own?"

"Every woman would like to have at least one child, but before that she should have a man."

This again led to the question of my relationship with Stoky.

"We are friends, nothing else."

They then asked me what I would play next.

"Some great woman who will inspire others of my sex" was my answer. I sensed that up to now I had talked convincingly and logically, so I stopped at that point to prevent myself from becoming entangled in the reporters' verbal snares. At that moment, Mercedes appeared and got me out. The next few days were spent with her in New York, buying clothes and shoes and seeing new films and plays. But I must say with regret that nothing stayed with me, nothing worthwhile.

On the way from New York to Los Angeles, Mercedes told me about her new discovery, the "doctor of natural science," Gayelord Hauser. I had never heard of such a degree, but I accepted this information without question. She told me that this doctor performed miracles by using only juices, yeast, wild rice, celery, carrots, blackstrap molasses, oranges, grapefruit, bananas, and other fruits of the South Seas, where a strong sun gave extra vitamins and minerals to this "living" food. Hauser's motto was "Look younger! Live longer!" In his brochures and books, he suggested various methods to attain health and beauty. From Mercedes I learned that Adele Astaire's husband, Lord Charles Cavendish, was also enchanted by the new methods of this handsome doctor. And Clara Bow, the Duke and Duchess of Windsor, Archduke Franz Joseph, Barbara Hutton, and Baron Philippe de Rothschild, among thousands of others, were great believers in this new dietary religion. Taking my silence as a response, she said, "You have to meet him and taste his dishes."

I had had enough of European dishes, so I decided to try this new regimen. Naturally suspicious, I kept my decision to myself, because I thought that this nutrition doctor might have urged Mercedes to capture me for his stable of prominent people. He required a continuous flood of publicity for his "health methods."

Shortly after Mercedes' speech, Gloria Swanson also told me about this "healthy method of nourishment and cure." She suggested that Hauser was capable of performing wonders on rheumatism, stomach pains, anemia, migraine, melancholy, and loneliness. He could cure almost anything with his dietary technique. I could never be stingy when my health or happiness was at stake. The doctor's work was exciting.

Mercedes soon took me to supper at Hauser's home, Sunrise House, in Beverly Hills. It was, as I recall, a big house, pretentiously furnished and decorated. There were many people there that evening, and everyone Mercedes mentioned or introduced to me had some aristocratic title.

I quickly realized that the whole affair had been set up so that Hauser could pay special attention to me and my health. First I drank a "sunshine cocktail" which tasted of beets, oranges, celery, and carrots. After that, I ate "hamburgers" made of nuts, wild rice, eggs, and soy sauce. For dessert, I had a baked banana and grapefruit with blackstrap molasses and afterward tea that smelled of acacia and roses. I must admit it all tasted very good, although I doubted that such a diet could save me from illness or improve my mental health. And I was disturbed that this doctor of herbs and foods used various people including me to publicize his products. When I made some remarks about this, Mercedes told me, "He is not dangerous for women like us."

Hauser soon began dressing in a beret and suits similar in design and color to my own and met me often under the pretext of teaching the "good and healthy life." I began to ponder the entire business. In my life, many different women and men have sought my friendship or my heart, always with love, admiration, jewelry, or other things of value. Now someone was trying to win me through my stomach. I tried Hauser's "naturopathy"; although it was basically boring and prosaic, for a time it held my interest. I decided to be passive and wait to see what would come of it all. In the meantime, I evaluated several MGM film offers and gently tried to push aside this "doctor of natural science."

With every passing day, I thought more and more of playing Madame Curie. Her life fascinated me. Her stubbornness and her scientific genius were qualities I admired, and I felt that to capture her character on celluloid would be a wonderful event. Regrettably, as had happened many times before, I could not find a script that expressed my thoughts. Maybe later, I said to myself. In the meantime, Ernst Lubitsch, who was fascinating as a man but even more fascinating as a director, talked to me about his plans. He was always full of ideas, and he was elegant and witty, wise even—almost like Moje. He also had a fine European schooling in the making of motion pictures. I learned some history from him, especially the history of Communism. I discovered that in the twenties and thirties Communism had become very attractive to intellectuals and to theatrical and film people. The Soviet Union was the example of how to solve economic, political, and artistic problems. Soviet film was realistic and powerful, and Soviet literature provoked European and American cultural workers to engage in experimentation. At the same time, fascism was growing fast, and Hitler's and Mussolini's admirers were making progress in the international arena.

The admiration for the Soviet Union in intellectual circles stirred a fighting spirit. But in the governing circles of Europe, fascism or Hitlerism was making progress too, and some European leaders developed the idea that it would be good if fascism and Nazism got together to annihilate the Soviet Union. Their line of reasoning was very simple: Let Hitler and Stalin fight and destroy each other. Then there will be peace in Europe and the world. Then democracy will have a better chance to survive and develop. A few intellectual circles in Europe and America picked up this idea and decided to propagandize it through the arts.

After my second or third meeting with Lubitsch, I discovered that he thought that way himself. He had bought an original screen story by Melchior Lengyel and asked me to read it. Because I greatly respected his professional abilities, I began reading right away.

After completing the story I told Lubitsch, "This is just propaganda, and I don't feel I'm suitable for it. It's a comedy, and I don't know if I can handle it."

"I agree with you, but wait with your final refusal until you read the scenario."

That was logical, so I agreed. In the meantime, I spent many days with Gayelord Hauser, meeting his social circle and trying his culinary concoctions. He even gave me a diamond ring, while I consumed a tremendous quantity of juices.

I did not have to wait long for the return of Lubitsch, who presented me with a scenario, written by three specialists in this type of work: Charles Brackett, Billy Wilder, and Walter Reisch.

"If you don't like something in the script, these three writers are on the MGM payroll, and they'll work long and hard to tailor the role of Ninotchka so that it will be just perfect for you."

His attitude and logic pleased me, and I was happy that the studio was being so cooperative. But I still felt strongly that I should not involve myself in anti-Soviet satire.

I knew that the international political situation demanded anti-fascist films, because there was real danger to humanity from the fascists. Also, I was under great pressure from the studio, as well as Lubitsch, to play in this anti-Soviet picture. He would say to me, "I will do anything for you. I will change the dialogue. I will change the actors. I will rewrite the scenario completely. But you must play in this comedy, because it will be your greatest success."

The next time I saw him, he presented me with a complete list of co-workers. Ina Claire was to be the Duchess Swana, and Melvyn Douglas, who off camera was in love with me, was Count Leon d'Algout. And there were an old European actor from the Stanislavsky school, Alexander Granach, as Kopalski; Sig Rumann as Iranoff; and Felix Bressart as Buljanoff. Bela Lugosi had been selected to play Commissar Razinin, while Count Rakonin was to be played by Gregory Gaye. Since Ina Claire didn't like me and I didn't like her, I thought it was very creative on Lubitsch's part to cast us as rivals. Ernst promised me that Bill Daniels would have charge of the camera. But the most important factor in my decision to play Ninotchka was the gossip that I could not play a comic role, let alone such a complex character as Ninotchka. I was accused of not knowing how to smile—so how could I play in a comedy? This gossip was undoubtedly instigated by the studio to make it impossible for me to refuse.

During the next three weeks I memorized my lines and acted them out before Hazel and the furniture. My never having done a comedy made the work very difficult. After long hours of rehearsal in my home, I informed Ernst that I was ready. Work with him was also difficult, because he was a perfectionist. He was not as inventive as Moje, but instead tried to convince me that I should be more inventive. As a result, we did the same scene over and over again with a little changing here and a little changing there. He liked my scenes, especially when I laughed. Everybody was especially pleasant to me on the set, and I appreciated it, because there I was, beginning my new career as a comedy actress. I felt very good.

The scenario was very well written. The dialogue was crisp and full of humor. The situations between the male comrades and the female comrade Ninotchka were comical, and her masculine clothing and beautiful face and figure plus her realistic language mixed with Marxist jargon underlined the satiric tone of the film. It required tremendous talent to express the soul of a woman brought up in Marxist schools, now spending some time in Paris. Ninotchka proved to be a challenging character for me as an actress. I tried to express not only present reality and the differences existing between so-called capitalist and communist moralities, but also the soul of a young woman.

After the premiere of *Ninotchka* in New York's Radio City Music Hall on November 9, 1939, the critics proclaimed me not only a great dramatic actress, but the mistress of comedy. I didn't have much time to digest my Hollywood success, because Gay Hauser took me to New York for a whirl of parties. We went to an elaborate banquet at the mansion of Mrs. Cornelius Vanderbilt, who was said to be a great admirer of my acting. At this sumptuous reception were half a dozen of the various Vanderbilts and other dollar aristocrats, including Axel Wenner-Gren, the Swedish millionaire who in the very first minutes of our conversation informed me that he was returning shortly to his yacht, the *Southern Cross*, which was docked in Nassau. He said that he would like very much to have the pleasure of Gay's and my company on a Caribbean cruise. I'm sure this was all Gay's doing, but I thought I had nothing to lose and accepted, thinking that such a trip would lend further publicity to my films.

At the same time I was deliberating with myself about

whether it would be a good thing to go to Europe for a rest or perhaps even back to the West Coast in order to rid myself of my male companion. I decided instead to drift with the situation, and I agreed when Gay suggested we go to Palm Beach for some swimming before we joined Wenner-Gren. Perhaps he had had a second thought about Wenner-Gren and was jealous, for his marriage offers increased in frequency. My nerves were on edge, and I had had enough of rhumbas, foxtrots, warm words of love, and the theory that "every woman should have a child for health reasons."

On the *Southern Cross*, Gay subtly altered his methods to the "doctor of natural science in love." Because the sea was so beautiful under the bright moon, at night I sat on the top deck of the yacht to admire and contemplate nature. I did not have any thoughts about sex, but at every available opportunity Gay tried to lure me into his cabin. At that time I loathed any kind of intercourse. I don't know the reason; perhaps his diet turned me against sex, or maybe it was his annoying persistence.

"You arrange all those tricks," I said, "and now you ask me to pay for them."

Here he tried to convince me how much he wanted to marry me and that having sex before marriage is a good thing.

"To me," I said, "everything appears heavy-handed and organized down to the finest minute detail including the ready beds. If this continues, I'll become hysterical."

He was dumbfounded, and he left me alone for a few days. But I found the situation so tense that I finally told him, "I must return to Hollywood."

I had to repeat my declaration many times before the *Southern Cross* finally changed course and headed for Miami. I was absolutely sure that we were indeed going to Miami only after speaking to the captain.

And here again I discovered the precision of Gay's "courtship." When I arrived, I learned that he had arranged to allow a friend of his, a reporter with International News Service, to get the first exclusive news about his marriage to me, which was to have been performed by the captain of the *Southern Cross*. I was really incensed when I found out, and I immediately left the yacht without saying good-bye.

A group of reporters followed me, asking, "Mrs. Hauser, how was the honeymoon?"

I responded, "Ask Mr. Hauser. My name is Greta Garbo. And will be forever." Those were my last words in this comic vaudeville.

39

Reunion

Although I have spent many restless nights in my life, one night stands out. I tossed from side to side, racked by anxiety mixed with vague, undefined premonitions. I tried to collect my thoughts, but I was unable to. I was gripped by fear—fear that many people, including me, were facing disaster. Finally I succumbed, or I thought I did, to sleep. Suddenly I woke up, perspiring and shivering. Dawn was breaking. Ugly dreams from my childhood were lurking in my head. I don't know how long I remained in this mental and emotional state, but when I opened my eyes wider I caught a glimpse of the sun, and I said to myself, "Now I have a light." I thought I would scream so that I would know I was alive. Instead I said to myself that I would scare somebody by screaming. So I reached for the radio and turned it on to hear these words: "Today at dawn the German army crossed the Polish border and engaged the Polish army in a fierce fight . . ."

It was September 1, 1939, the day the Second World War began—a tragic day for humanity. As I've said before, I don't know too much about anything, and I know perhaps least about politics, but I had felt in the early thirties that those two butchers Hitler and Mussolini would bring only death to humanity.

A few days later, I met Mayer. He began our conversation with these words: "War has begun in Europe, and I think it will be a long war. In Europe there is no more market for us. It is very bad to lose such a profitable market for your pictures. . . ." He peered at me through his thick glasses and tried to evaluate my reaction. I didn't respond, so he continued, "Right away, we have to begin work on a new picture. You will play a glamorous girl. American. Fun-loving."

"Here," I thought, "is a typical American businessman. He is not worried that because of Hitler many people will die. All he can think about is his film market." I was boiling with hatred for such people and I didn't have words to express myself. I was forced to listen.

"I don't want you to decide now. Think it over and let me know. We have to stick to our contract. You've got to play, war or no war."

With those words he got up, walked around from behind his huge desk, and escorted me to the door, saying with the look of a prophet, "The Nazis will fight the Communists. They will end up destroying each other, and then we will have peace. Democracy will come to Europe once more."

He took my hand and squeezed it hard. I was already out the door as he added, "Then we will have the whole European market in our hands. European pictures will be no more. The public will be hungry for entertainment, the kind of pictures that show off your wonderful talent . . ."

He had more to say, but I turned around and left. I was shocked by the ugly logic of this American millionaire whose hands still clutched for bloody dollars. The most fragrant of soaps could not have removed the stench from his hands.

On my way home I thought of going to Charlie Chaplin, or to someone else with antifascist leanings; at that time in Hollywood there were many such groups composed of actors, writers, directors, and other film workers. But I didn't know how to approach those people or how to talk to them. Many times they had asked me to join their groups, but I had always avoided them. So I went home, went to my bedroom, fell face down on the bed, and started crying. After an hour or two I turned over on my back. I spoke to the ceiling: "What can they do, these antifascist people? What can Chaplin do? Should they organize a picket line around the MGM studio and should I march in the first line? Would that help stop the war in Europe? Lots of powerful Americans are waiting for this fight of fascists and Communists. This political philosophy rules American business, press, and radio. They will laugh at me for engaging myself in politics, which I don't know anything about."

Reading the papers the next few days convinced me that Germany was ready to make her next move. My thoughts shifted to Sweden, because I felt it might experience the same fate as Poland. I thought of my mother and brother. Then I jumped out of bed and went to the telephone to call Stockholm. The connection with New York was all right, but from New York the telephone operators had a problem in reaching Europe. I would have to wait, because the telephone company was overwhelmed by an avalanche of orders for transatlantic calls. So I decided to send a radiogram instead, insisting that my mother and my brother, Sven, and his wife drop everything and join me in Hollywood.

I concentrated on saving my own family. To appease my conscience, I gave five hundred dollars to the committee for the victims of Nazi persecution. With great shame I have to admit that although I was emotionally against fascism, I really did nothing concrete to fight it. My colossal egoism was the main reason, as well as a head empty of any good ideas. In such a situation even the most beautiful or most powerful person is not useful if he or she is not prepared to sacrifice all.

My mother arrived in California wearing a black seal coat, which didn't hide her stoutness, and a black hat that shaded her small eyes. I immediately rented a house in Inglewood for her and my brother and his wife. But as it turned out, Mother spent much time staying at my house in order to give Sven and his wife some privacy. When she saw the interior of my house, she told me that she didn't like mahogany furniture and asked why I didn't have Swedish light. I replied that because of the war I couldn't bring any Swedish furniture from Europe. Later she looked all over Los Angeles but couldn't find anything to suit her.

For a time she took charge of the shopping and cooking. I gave her money, and although she spent very little, her food receipts were very high. Once she brought home a receipt for three dollars' worth of fish that we never saw. Practically every second day we ate *smörgåsbord* and *knäckebröd* with butter, accompanied by inexpensive *schnapps*. I like fish of all kinds, and I like *smörgåsbord,* but not as often as she served it. On Christmas Eve we ate the same food we had been eating all year.

My brother became upset at these goings-on, but it was difficult for me to talk to her and ask her why she forced her habits upon us and what she was doing with the money I gave her. What could I do? Mother's attitude when she was questioned was the same as it had been when I was a girl. She would attack; she would start with little things she didn't like about me and go on to bigger and more important ones. She was especially angry that I had never married. She even gave me a list of Swedish men whom I should consider marrying, among them members of the royal family. When I told her that I didn't want to get married, she would reply, "A woman without a man is like a hunting dog without a scent."

I became upset and nervous. Once I told her that I hadn't married because I didn't want a life like the one she had had with my father. After that remark she did not talk to me for days and avoided me by locking herself in her room. I was worried, because she was an old woman with half a dozen serious ailments, including very high blood pressure. Since this was not the first time we had disagreed, I did what I usually had to—I asked her to forgive me and placed a couple of hundred-dollar bills in her handbag. And so we had peace for a day or two.

Once, after another argument in the kitchen about marriage, she said, "I hate you." She repeated this sentence several times with madness in her voice. I was extremely upset. Although I knew she didn't like me, I had thought her hate had died down after so many years. This encounter in the kitchen made me see that no feelings of love existed between daughter and mother.

Our relationship went from bad to worse. Sometimes I

tried to talk to her about Father, but she referred to him as though she were talking about a stranger. During one of our sessions in the kitchen, she expressed her feelings for my father in one sentence: "Better to lose something sometimes than to never have had it at all." But she said this with such indifference and disrespect that I felt even more hurt than I did when she attacked me.

The atmosphere in the house was definitely not suitable for her, and she was homesick for Sweden. But what could I do? I could not send her to Europe while a war was going on there. So I suffered. My brother and his wife suffered, and she suffered too. She hated the California climate. Maybe that was natural, since she had been brought up in a cool climate and was in love with snow. She began to cough and spent weeks in bed. And she was losing weight rapidly. This loss of weight was accompanied by a loss of strength and even of the desire to talk. I felt the end was near.

When I called the doctors, they examined her and shook their heads, saying that she had so many illnesses that they didn't know where to begin. Later she refused to see any doctors. She became apathetic and remained silent most of the time. I knew she was thinking of the past; she took photographs from her trunk and spread them out on the bed to gaze at them. When I sat on the edge of her bed, she would not meet my gaze and would say nothing.

Early one morning I got dressed quickly because I had some work at the studio. I looked into my mother's room. It was quiet. The shades were pulled all the way down, although at their edges some light was piercing the gray atmosphere of the room. I looked at her face. It was motionless and the color of honeycomb. I touched her outstretched hand. It was cold. I tried to say something. I tried to yell. My voice remained somewhere deep down and did not come out. I fell to my knees and put my head on her chest to cry without words, without motion.

40

The Last Stand

I know that some people ridicule me and others hate me. But I also know that the great majority worship me. No one can understand how a simple *Svensk flicka* could create a legend greater than Sarah Bernhardt's and Charlie Chaplin's together. I was not able to go anywhere in the world without using a pseudonym like Karin Lund, Harriet Brown, Mary Holmquist, Emily Clark, Gussie Berger, Katharine Cooke, or many others. When I walked on the streets or sat down to eat in a restaurant, people would stare at me, ask for autographs, or try to engage me in conversation. Although I tried to run away and hide from strangers' eyes, admiring glances made me shiver with pleasure. I was happy that royalty, aristocrats, prime ministers, and other important people sought my friendship. I felt important, and my heart was bursting with happiness at my success. The reasons for my success, as I have said, were hard work and Moje Stiller. After his death I was in daily contact with his spirit, and before making any important decision I would talk to him as I would talk to God. Whenever I went to Stockholm, I would go immediately to the North Cemetery. I would place flowers in front of Moje's monument which Hugo Lindberg had erected. My inner consciousness demanded it. The new stone was a square gray rock, on whose top lay a globe cut in half, and whose face bore only Moje's name and the dates of his birth and death. I would kneel and speak to him. When I would ask him for the hundredth time to forgive me for anything wrong that I had done him, he would reply, "You don't have to explain yourself. I understand you." He would give me advice, especially about taking care of my health and living long, because death is boring.

When I visited Moje's grave in the fall of 1938, he was occupied with something more important than me. He said, "A whirlwind is approaching. They are calling me. I must go . . . I don't know if I will return. You will be by yourself . . ." He didn't finish. A wild wind shook the trees so violently that I was afraid they would fall on me. During the next few days I brought flowers and prayed, but no word came from Moje. I was left to myself in this world, perhaps because I didn't trust anybody, sometimes not even myself.

Just before I began *Two-Faced Woman*, my mother was still alive but was in a state of physical and mental collapse. Her condition had a negative influence on me. I didn't have anyone whom I could trust, so I tried to get in touch with Moje. I locked myself in my bedroom with the same kind of flowers that I had brought to his grave, lit some candles, put Moje's picture between them, and knelt and prayed. Nothing came of this attempt. He didn't want to talk to me, although he knew I could not go to his grave because of the war. I could not understand his silence. So I started visiting mediums in Hollywood and Los Angeles. Nothing came of it. I had lost Moje and was losing money on mind readers and fortune-tellers. I was depressed. I also heard people whispering to one another around the MGM lot, "She is crazy."

The studio pressed me to accept *Two-Faced Woman*, and George Cukor, who had shown his directing skill in *Camille*, kept reassuring me: "You have played tragedy, you have played comedy, and now your genius should portray the typical American girl."

I had read *Two-Faced Woman*, a play by Ludwig Fulda, and I was not happy with it. I didn't know it at the time, but this play had been filmed in 1925 as *Her Sister from Paris*. Constance Talmadge had played the lead, without success.

When I told Cukor that I didn't like the story, his reaction was predictable: "The studio has hired S. N. Behrman, George Oppenheimer, and Salka Viertel. They are seasoned film writers, and their scenario will clear up your objections."

He was right. As I read the scenario, I forgot my original misgivings and became absorbed in thinking about women in general—that all of them have in their souls some feeling for prostitution and some feeling for virginity. Who knows? I began to think maybe I could play Karin successfully. She was an American woman who loved sexual fun with all the trimmings while at the same time she remained a loving wife. But I saw that the script needed some work. Karin's character was far too shallow. When I complained to Cukor, he gave me the front-office line: "A great deal of money has already been invested."

"So what? They've made a lot of money on me."

"Don't worry about it. The hairdresser will give you a new short, neat hairdo. You will learn a few new dances, such as the chica-choca, and will have some truly beautiful costumes, designed and made specially for you by the top people in the country."

"So what? That does not make for a great picture."

But he persisted: "We know from *Ninotchka* that you can smile. And I will teach you how the American glamour girl behaves. And given your genius for improvisation, we will easily have a great picture."

While I was still refusing to do the part, the studio sent Melvyn Douglas to me. He was to play Larry Blake in the film. He came at me from a different angle.

"This film will be a real challenge for you. You can show the world that you can play any role with enchantment and flair."

I was still relying on my inner feelings and refusing to agree. But Melvyn kept up his pressure: "You have an excellent supporting cast in two experienced actresses, Ruth Gordon and Constance Bennett."

I didn't object, because I knew they were very good. Instead I said to Melvyn, "I might reconsider if they give the camera to someone like Bill Daniels."

"I think you can arrange that with the studio without any problem," replied Melvyn.

But to my great regret I was not able to arrange anything with MGM. Joseph Ruttenberg was engaged as cameraman, and Cukor as director insisted on him. I sensed that I was going into a shaky, muddy situation; I felt uneasiness coursing through my body. At the same time, I didn't have anyone whom I could consult, and my friends like Salka Viertel were trying to persuade me to take the part because they were getting paid for their work.

Meanwhile, MGM's publicity department was feeding press and radio with wisdom like "The world is waiting for a new Garbo. She will bathe almost naked. She will make love. She will hate. She will cry. And she will dance and dance."

Pressure was now being applied from all sides. Somehow thousands of letters arrived at my home and thousands more at MGM. In every letter I was praised for undertaking the role of a fun-loving American girl, with the emphasis on "American." And I was getting more and more nervous and upset because my original reservations were growing stronger. Mayer called me into his office to tell me that I had to play because everything was ready, especially an eager public, and MGM was losing thousands of dollars every day the film was postponed. I answered back very openly: "I will not play because this film will be my creative grave. I have no logic to back up my opinions. I just feel that way."

Then Mayer tried to use my family to persuade me that I should play. He told them that if I didn't my career would be ruined completely. Finally I gave up and agreed. As always, I went to work with tremendous energy. I spent much time and talent and worked very hard on this film. But when it was finished, I was left with a bad taste in my mouth.

After the premiere on December 31, 1941, in New York's Capitol Theater, the critics pounced on me. They called *Two-Faced Woman* ridiculous trash and attacked MGM, saying the studio had miscast me and was trying to make a sweater girl out of me. To the attack of the press was added that of Archbishop Francis J. Spellman. In addition, the Catholic Church's Legion of Decency condemned the film as "dangerous to public morals." The attacks on me, on the film, and on MGM were stupid and vicious. MGM's bosses then decided to defend themselves and announced that they would rewrite and reshoot the picture to remove the objectionable scenes.

The New York Times, which had always intelligently praised my films, called *Two-Faced Woman* a piece of "shoddy workmanship" and said, "Miss Garbo's current attempt to trip the light fantastic is one of the awkward exhibitions of the season." *Time* wrote that "it is almost as shocking as seeing your mother drunk."

Such was my twenty-fourth film in America. And I have no regrets that it was the last film of my life.

With Lewis Stone in *Romance,* and with Beryl Mercer in *Inspiration.*

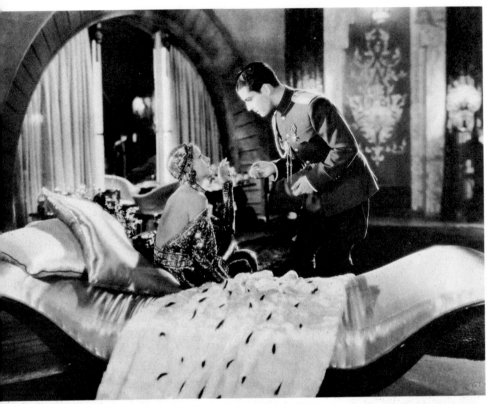

One of the femme fatale roles of this period was as the beautiful spy in *Mata Hari*, in which the co-stars were Lionel Barrymore and Ramon Novarro.

With Clark Gable in
*Susan Lenox: Her
Fall and Rise.*

As the unhappy ballerina in *Grand Hotel* with John Barrymore. "I consider my work in *Grand Hotel* my best performance after *Anna Christie*." Far left, Garbo on shipboard in 1932. Left, arriving in Göteborg (1932).

Opposite, with Erich von Stroheim and Melvyn Douglas in *As You Desire Me*, which was based on the Pirandello play.

Right, in *The Painted Veil* with Herbert Marshall.
Opposite and below, *Queen Christina*, one of Garbo's great successes, was directed by Rouben Mamoulian. Left above, the famous love scene with John Gilbert; left below, with Ian Keith, the well-known stage actor, in the role of Magnus. Below, the dramatic final shot.

 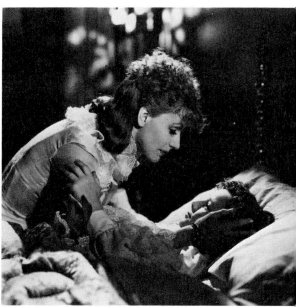

Many critics feel Garbo's performance as Anna Karenina has not been surpassed. Basil Rathbone was Karenin, Fredric March was Vronsky, Freddie Bartholomew played her son. William Daniels was again camera-man, and Clarence Brown directed.

Camille was one of Garbo's triumphs. Left, George Cukor preparing the scene in the theater box; below, the scene as it was filmed. Bottom, with Henry Daniell as Baron de Varville.

George Cukor working with Garbo and Robert Taylor on the scene of the arrival at the country house. Below, with Lionel Barrymore as Monsieur Duval. Right, talking with cameraman Hal Rossen. And the famous death scene.

With Charles Boyer in *Conquest*. Above, working with director Clarence Brown. Below, Garbo strolling along the Strandvägen in Stockholm in 1936 with Count and Countess Wachtmeister and Fredrik Nycander.

Ninotchka was Garbo's first attempt at comedy. The deft and polished Melvyn Douglas afforded a perfect foil for the female commissar.

Director Ernst Lubitsch "liked my scenes, especially when I laughed." A trio of European actors—Alexander Granach, Sig Rumann and Felix Bressart—were Ninotchka's "Comrades."

"Work with [Lubitsch] was . . . difficult, because he was a perfectionist."
Publicity for the film played up "Garbo Laughs."

Scenes were done over and over until Lubitsch achieved the desired
result.

With Gayelord Hauser in Palm Beach in 1940.
Garbo played a double role in *Two-Faced Woman*.
George Cukor working out a scene with Constance
Bennett, with Roland Young at the right. The man
ensnared by both "sisters" was Melvyn Douglas.

Garbo dances the "chica-choca" in *Two-Faced Woman*. This was her last film.

PART SEVEN   *Silence*

41

Aftermath

America and Europe were locked in bloody war. The world was exploding in hatred and murder. I had no allies in my own sufferings. Friends, who had always been few throughout my life, were now scarcer than ever. The only thing left for me to do was occupy myself more and more with personal affairs and my clairvoyance. I should add that this clairvoyance saved me several times from suicide. I became more superstitious, selfish, suspicious, and shrewd. In the presence of people I met by accident I played the innocent Swedish girl, while in the presence of others I played the mysterious Mona Lisa with the shadow of an ironic smile.

After almost two months of complete isolation and emotional and physical exhaustion due to the publicity connected with my last film, I gradually became a bit more normal and tried to analyze my situation in the new world created by the world war. I didn't need much time to convince myself that America and the rest of the world would not return to the morality of the 1920's and the 1930's. I knew also that neither my films nor I myself would fit into this new world. I thought of transforming myself and going along with this new world. But I did not know what path to follow. The only thing that remained solid and real to me was a few million dollars made through hard work and my now-exhausted talent.

Money had given me material independence but ruined me spiritually because I didn't know how to use it. The question of keeping my money occupied my mind more than anything else. Throughout my entire life in Hollywood I had listened to the MGM bosses, and I had done what they had asked me to do. When they asked me to cut my hair, I cut it. When they asked me to make curls, I made curls. I colored it, parted it on the left, parted it on the right, combed it up, wore bangs or didn't wear them. My head actually began to hurt from all these various cosmetic treatments, but I suffered in silence. My face was constantly being molded by somebody else's hands. The same thing was true of my figure. Masseuses worked on it, using different types of massage on each area to make me slim and more beautiful. MGM controlled everything—my clothes, my speech, my walk, my every move. I became a mannequin in the hands of financial speculators. I suffered, I bit my nails, I cried, and I listened. Although inside I rebelled terribly, I always did what they asked of me. People might say that because of my devotion I gained fortune and fame. I would say, "Not true." At the beginning, Mauritz Stiller helped me because of his great love for me. But Hollywood destroyed him and nearly destroyed me, giving me money to wipe away my tears. Now everything was finished.

I decided that I would never return to face a camera, any camera. I knew that my films had created the legend of Garbo. I decided that I should work to sustain this legend, because I felt my films would find a proper place in history and gain in value. As a still-living personality, I could enhance the Garbo legend. But I knew the world quickly forgets the actress who stops playing. The whole history of theater, opera, and film is a big morgue full of forgotten stars whom no one would now recognize. Would I be the exception? Doubts filled my mind. But after them came thoughts about scandals or attempts at suicide. This was not for me. With scandal and suicide attempts it would be difficult to support a legend. Many examples in history exist to prove that.

So one method was left to me. I would change my way of life. I would desert the Hollywood scene and become part of a different circle of people who constantly collect around themselves reporters, gossipers, and all kinds of underground informers. But for this I would need much money and courage. The first I had—I was completely independent materially. But courage I lacked. Then a very clever idea came to mind. If I played a person without courage and everything else that went with it, perhaps then something miraculous would happen. Many politicians, scientists, artists, I knew, were running around with tremendous amounts of courage and not gaining a thing.

What if I played a person confused by the world—one whom the world doesn't understand even though she has given it a dozen excellent films? I was still good-looking, and my strange beauty still possessed great appeal for the general public. I also had a singularity, which Stiller had fostered through the years and which I myself had nurtured. To mold all those things into a public image I would need time; but it looked as if I would have plenty of that in preparing myself for an original role in my new life.

For long weeks I lay in bed or walked in my garden, planning action on a world scale. To change my personality, I decided first to change my physical appearance. I cut my hair short and let it hang naturally like that of a young girl. I continued to use no makeup at all except for a touch of mascara. I cut my nails short, and I didn't use any nail polish. Then I considered my clothing and decided that I should look like a schoolgirl. I would dress very simply, but my clothing would be exquisitely tailored from the finest cloth. To achieve this look I decided to select some well-publicized dressmaker in America. I selected Valentina, who had her salon in New York and who was a leader in American *haute couture.* Her full name, I learned, was Valentina Nicolaevna Sanina, and like Moje, she had been born in Eastern Europe. She ran her business with her husband, George Schlee, and their clients included the titled and the wealthy from Europe and America. Actresses like Lili Palmer, Judith Anderson, Lynn Fontanne, Katharine Hepburn, and Pola Negri wore Valentina's clothes. I liked even better than her designs her saying that "Through designing women's clothes I am striving for a total effect, as in architecture or sculpture. The lines must be perfect. I love Greek sculpture, and every dress produced in my establishment has to have sculptured proportions and must be perfectly fitted to the individual woman. Clothes should reflect the individuality of the wearer."

I became convinced that only she could clothe me in a way that would emphasize my temperament, my psychological and physical structure, and my *tour d'esprit*. I decided in the meantime to change this *tour d'esprit* too in order to become more natural and more appealing.

I needed a different, more natural and sophisticated approach to what was around me, an approach that would give positive and lasting results and develop my psychic powers. For this I would have to do more thinking, more planning, because there was always the problem of my character and the limited range of my intelligence and education.

I made up a list of everyone who was in love with me or who played at being in love. I immediately crossed off all the females. I had had enough of the gossip about my lesbian inclinations. Because I was no longer in films, I decided that the group of admirers I would cultivate should come from the world of the aristocracy, like Prince Sigvard; from the world of business, like the Baron Erich Rothschild-Goldschmidt; from the world of politics, like Winston Churchill; and from the intellectual and social worlds. I felt that to complete such a list would take some time and some very delicate acting on my part. I also determined that the stage for this acting would not be Hollywood, but New York, Paris, and London, where the social life of the world's upper classes was concentrated.

New York City was the logical place to begin, since I knew New York the best and I was well known to all strata of the American public. I wanted to rent an elegant apartment which would be the base for my travels. I considered suites at the Waldorf-Astoria, the Pierre, the Plaza, and the St. Moritz, where I had stayed many times in the last ten years. But I decided that those places were too pretentious and not suitable for my new character. I wanted something more quiet and domestic, as well as elegant. My choice was the Hampshire House on Central Park South. Many theatrical and film actors stayed there, and these were the people

I best understood. It took me some time to come to a decision. Finally, after months of deliberation, I took a four-room apartment. The location of the Hampshire House was suited to me because it was only a few steps from Central Park, where I loved to stroll and feed the squirrels and pigeons.

42

Seeking to Belong

During the war, I spent a great deal of time in the modest home in Beverly Hills I had purchased from the singer Gladys Swarthout in 1943. In the garden I planted flowers and vegetables, and I enjoyed this work very much. My house was enveloped by the fragrance of flowers. I stopped buying vegetables in the market because I grew all I needed. From time to time, I invited some people from the Hollywood colony so that I could listen to them. Among my first guests were Clarence Brown, Constance Collier, Clifton Webb, and George Schlee. We discussed film, theater, and the other arts, and I specifically avoided any conversation about the ravages of war. In fact, the war so upset me that I refused to read about it in the papers.

Almost every evening ended with a plea by my guests that I resume acting in films. I also received concrete suggestions for possible film vehicles, most of them concerned with famous women in history. It was recommended that I play Bernhardt, Duse, Curie, or Catherine the Great. Clarence Brown suggested I play Saint Catherine of Siena, who had an important role in politics and religion in the fourteenth century.

I rejected all advice and even concrete offers, because I felt I could not portray anyone better than I had in my previous pictures. Anyway, I no longer had the strength to work eight hours a day in front of the camera. Some of my guests then suggested that I have a few dozen photographs taken to prove to the world that I was still beautiful. I agreed. And so the British photographer Cecil Beaton and the fashionable American photographer Anthony Beauchamp came to torture me by taking hundreds of shots. People spread the usual gossip. I was said to be in love with Beaton and about to marry him. I knew that he in fact did entertain such notions, and I made sure to dispel them immediately. Articles also appeared in which major studios other than MGM announced that I would perform in their films. I never deigned to reply to these rumors; I patiently waited till they died successive deaths. That had been my method previously. It was my method now. To calm myself, I spent much time sunbathing and working in the garden.

Among my friends, George Schlee was the most consistently faithful, and a person with whom I enjoyed spending my time. The first time I met George, I spent three hundred and seventy-five dollars buying a dress from his wife, Valentina. What I noticed first about him was that although a shrewd businessman, he always managed to look like a well-groomed aristocrat. He really was quite elegant, with his hair so perfectly combed that it hugged his scalp. I also noticed that he was about three inches taller than I. After our first meeting, I began comparing him with Moje, and to my surprise I discovered many similarities. That was the reason I kept up my friendship with George and his wife; it was not because of their clothes. George did, however, help me to make my decision to drop my tweed and corduroy and dress more smartly as befitted someone with an international reputation.

I spent thousands of dollars on clothing by Valentina. I thought Valentina would like that and would not mind my friendship with her husband. Although she was very friendly toward me and always tried to make me feel comfortable when I visited her salon, I would always search for jealousy in the eyes of this delicate and intelligent woman. I generally felt that in Valentina and George I had two great friends at a time when I was really hungry for friendship.

George was especially helpful because of his knowledge of the arts, business, and politics. He was eager to help me expand my environment. I was quite happy with him—with his character, intelligence, and politeness and the charm that affected everyone he came in contact with. He represented a new world of experience for me. Valentina also helped me in this way as well. She said once to me, "You should wear clothes for giggles. Never take them seriously, because if you do, you will capitulate to convention."

To the Schlees' salon came the wives of multimillionaires and world politicians to select their clothes; and in their apartment at 450 East 52nd Street famous actors, composers, and writers got together for dinner parties or soirees. Leland Hayward, who served as my agent when he could spare time from his theatrical and marital situations, once remarked, "Valentina and George are two angels who were let go on the earth to learn American business."

Fred Brown, Gayelord Hauser's manager, from time to time gave me tips on how to invest money. He used to say, "George will take my job very soon and I will have no chance to advise you on finances. What is more, George will take the place of Stiller in everything."

Naturally I brushed aside these remarks, and I plunged deeper and deeper into my friendship with Valentina and George. I sold my Hampshire House apartment to Greer Garson and bought a cooperative apartment in the building where they lived. George helped me furnish this new apartment, and we spent many days shopping in antique shops. Once he discovered a charming rococo chest of drawers from the first half of the eighteenth century. But I thought the price was too high, and I refused to buy it. So George called me "a peasant girl."

"I don't mind if you call me that, but I will not spend three thousand dollars for a piece of furniture."

He knew that he had hurt me, and from then on I don't recall his ever saying a harsh word to me.

To this very day, I love to visit antique shops and delight in the art of the eighteenth and nineteenth centuries. George taught me how to look at paintings, especially painters such as Renoir, Modigliani, Soutine, and Picasso, whom he loved best. His knowledge extended to the art of the Ming dynasty and Etruscan bronzes. In his opinion the

Etruscan bronze statues of Athena in a museum in Florence resembled me—or perhaps vice versa. He also never insisted that I return to films. "Your performances in *Anna Christie, Queen Christina, Camille,* and *Ninotchka* were the performances of a genius. No one can play them better, not even you. Now you should spend your time on self-education. You should live, travel, look, and play."

I felt very good when he talked to me like this. I felt that I had found a man who not only evaluated me properly, but was also very understanding of my peculiarities and weaknesses.

"I think we should plan to travel around the world. Together we should visit the most important and beautiful spots in Europe, Asia, Africa, and America."

"And what will happen with Valentina?"

"Don't worry. She's not the jealous type."

Although George assured me Valentina was not jealous, I was afraid she would accuse me of alienating the affections of her husband. As a consequence, I decided to expand my circle of male friends. Besides George, I began seeing Cecil Beaton. In addition, I accepted invitations from other men, including Baron Rothschild and Aristotle Onassis, for weekends and excursions in Europe or America.

I don't know why, but after the end of my screen appearances, I lost interest in sex. I needed a great incentive to return to it. I began to think that sexual partners should really be in love, in great love, in order to generate truly positive affection. And I observed that men and women tried to be close to me not because I was a sexual being, but because I was a great and legendary actress. Most people knew that I was not capable of love, and I was treated like a marvelous Greek sculpture which everyone looked at, admired, and tried to touch. But they knew that they could not receive love from marble. I seemed indifferent to all these attentions, because I was afraid of displaying emotion, thinking that I might somehow be punished for it.

The press stories, which I suspected were leaked by Gayelord Hauser, Cecil Beaton, Fleur Cowles, John Gunther, Clare Boothe Luce, Baron Erich Goldschmidt-Rothschild, and a hundred others, amazed and amused me very much. Although I didn't know any of these people very well, by which I mean that I didn't have a special affection for them or any kind of special relationship with them, it seemed they knew every thought of mine, past, present, and future. Everyone was saying something different. There was talk of my "inexhaustible spiritual assets" and, of course, of my physical beauty. I was compared to practically everyone in history, including Saint Francis of Assisi and Salome. These people became the propagators of my legend, although they also disoriented the public by spreading untrue stories. But I knew that my legend grew each time my name was mentioned on the radio or in the press. Surprisingly enough, the general public believed these stories because the people who originated them were highly placed in the worlds of the arts, literature, and finance.

I did not confirm or deny any of the rumors about me. Instead I would return home, lock my door, and laugh until my stomach hurt. I could not imagine how a simple woman like me was able to occupy the minds of outstanding writers, artists, and millionaires. If somebody engaged me in serious conversation about social, cultural, or political affairs, I did not know how to respond. Any man or woman who induced me to have sexual relations became disenchanted because my impulses were false and my reactions to physical stimuli were superficial. People who told exciting stories about me didn't know me and actually were hoping to have closer contact. I knew what they wanted, so I deliberately postponed closer relations, hoping that the hide-and-seek would go on longer and I would profit from the publicity. It was a game between a cast of powerful and clever cats and a little mouse, me. My legend was the nourishment of my life; I had no deeper interest. Even war and peace did not interest me much, although I once ventured to say in a social gathering that the Soviet soldiers who were beating back Hitler's army were courageous and beautiful. This story reached the press, and I received praise and invitations from Communist groups all over the world. So even Communists created publicity for a confused woman. Somehow people had a total belief in me and were willing to sacrifice their reputations and time to publicize me.

When I decided to go to Europe in 1946, the rumor spread that I was disenchanted with America and was going to Europe to stay and make films. I saw Europe destroyed and working very hard to get back on its feet; nobody asked me to make films. On my return to America, the reporters confronted me and were hostile. I told them, "I hate to be stared at. I know how the animal in the zoo feels when unfriendly people poke it with sticks."

I think this comment was admired by the humble readers of the many daily papers because they too are pushed and poked all the time during their lives. It was reassuring to know that everyone sympathized with me and liked me, not only the upper class.

I received another offer to play George Sand in a film about Chopin, but I refused. I can only guess that the same Hollywood circles had convinced John Gunther that he should write a scenario about a woman spy and foreign correspondent. MGM agreed to produce this film, but I didn't like the scenario, in which the character was a cross between Mata Hari and Joan of Arc. I refused the role and suggested some other actresses like Pola Negri or Greer Garson. Walter Wanger offered me a part in a film version of *La Duchesse de Langeais*, a novel by Honoré de Balzac in which I would play a character based on the Countess Éveline Hanska, who transformed the life of this great French writer. Walter said that if I could play Camille, I could play Hanska. He tried to convince me again and again that if I could play the Countess Walewska I could play Balzac's love too.

"A picture concerning Balzac and his great love would surpass your previous films, both artistically and financially," said Walter convincingly.

Although I had many doubts, I went as far as making a screen test for this film. Perhaps I just wanted to prove to myself that after nearly ten years of retirement I would still look good on the screen. Anyhow, Wanger could not raise the funds, and the project was cancelled.

George Cukor also approached me, to play the leading role in *My Cousin Rachel*, written by Daphne du Maurier. I told George, "I admire your directing, but I do not admire myself anymore in film ventures."

If I mentioned all the roles offered me, I would have to write another book. Every day of the year some producer, director, or writer would write me to offer "a great role in a great film." Some of the offers were genuine and financially very attractive. Some of them were not. But my reply to all of them was the same silence.

Then the American press began to attack me for not liking this country although I had made millions here. I don't know who had really started this or why, but it made me sad. I think it was this vicious press attack that made me decide to become an American citizen in 1951. After the ceremony I said to the papers, "I am happy to be an American citizen. I am as happy as the millions of other immigrants."

This comment was especially fortunate because everybody in America is an immigrant or has come from an immigrant family. The common people liked the fact that I was identifying myself with them. To take a breather from all the harassment, I packed my suitcase and went to Europe to rest on the island of Capri. From the Countess Madina Arrivabene I rented a "dream villa" nestled in the Anacapri Mountains from which I could see the azure Bay of Naples in the golden sun. I gave the Countess money to build a high fence around the villa, so that no one could see me sunbathing naked on the terrace. I rested peacefully, and perhaps the sun softened the "masculine" elements in my manner that were so often commented on.

43

Another Woman's Man

In September 1953, I returned to New York from Europe on the *Queen Mary*. My companion on this trip was George Schlee, and during this voyage I gradually came to realize that I was in love with him. It was a strange feeling, almost the same as the one I had had for Moje at the beginning.

George was extremely attentive and took wonderful care of me on the trip as he had done before. It was not the attention of a businessman but that of a man who was truly in love—tender, caring, without a trace of selfishness. I felt the same trepidation that I had experienced with Moje when I was just beginning my career. But now my career had ended, and I had gotten into social life. I was healthier then, psychologically and physically; now I was on my way down. Nervous pains ran through my body. And there were arthritis, mysterious stomach pains, headaches combined with hallucinations, plus other maladies real or imaginary. I felt all of them. I went to physicians and psychiatrists, but no one could help me because I didn't believe what they said. The best doctor for me was George, with his friendly words that acted like a miraculous ointment. He took care of my business affairs, and his kisses made me a young girl.

And always I kept comparing George with Moje. This was the first time Moje had found a competitor in my affections.

Many similarities existed between them, but George was more delicate with me and very correct toward others. Considering only exterior appearances, George was more polished, elegant, and truly handsome, while Moje had been attractive in his romantic rudeness and careless elegance. I had tremendous admiration for them both. If you want to call that love, you are probably right.

As we sat on the deck of the *Queen Mary*, George said, "I realize that I am a continuation of Stiller. I cannot do anything about that, because I cannot compete with a dead lover."

"What can I say to you?" I replied in a conciliatory tone. "I have to admit that he is in my mind very often. But you are also there. And you have a superior position because you are alive."

"I would like to have all of you for myself."

I began to praise him and assure him that I felt more toward him than toward anyone else alive, that I believed in his sincerity and would like for us to be great friends for the rest of our lives. My confession seemed to please him.

Several passengers came out onto the deck, and we went into someone's cabin to continue our conversation. Suddenly he changed the subject.

"Why have you twice refused an invitation from Buckingham Palace?" he asked me. "Such a visit would create very prestigious publicity for you."

I was taken aback by the word "publicity," and I replied, "If I didn't accept an invitation from the Swedish royal family, why should I accept an invitation from the British royal family?"

"You should accept both of them."

"What would I talk about?"

"The usual pleasantries. They don't talk of philosophy or mathematics. At their receptions you have good food and, after that, prestige."

I saw that he was as much concerned about my legend as I was. I said, "If they invite me again, to please you I will accept. You can please me by not talking about the 'masculine' element in my manner."

"I didn't mean to upset you, but I very often see that in the papers. They are doing an injustice to you."

"What should I do?"

"You should dress more femininely. You should not be so abrupt and harsh with people you meet. Naturally I am not asking you to change your husky voice or to stop taking those long strides or to slow your fast walk. But—"

I interrupted him: "If I do not walk like Garbo, if I do not behave like her, if I do not possess her voice, I would not be Garbo."

"You forget that your films transformed Keta Gustafsson into Greta Garbo. Your acting created the public legend, while your private behavior followed just a step behind. So if you improve your behavior by doing the things I've just mentioned, I'm sure you'll create a sensation in the highest circles of society."

"And when should I be myself?"

"In between," he replied with a smile as he embraced me.

So as not to lose him, I strove to follow his suggestions despite my stubborn nature. I laughed more often in conversation with people whom he introduced. I changed my appearance in line with his suggestions. But to alter my voice and my walk was impossible.

Almost every summer I traveled all over Europe with George, and I met those people whom he insisted I should meet. The base for our summer escapades was the villa Le Roc at Cap-d'Ail on the French Riviera, which he and Valentina had decorated "in the Spanish fashion," as he would say. From there we traveled to Paris, Rome, and London, where I met Princess Margaret. On first impression I regarded her as an overly plump, simple English girl who had a most charming smile. One summer we accepted an invitation to spend a weekend on Aristotle Onassis' yacht, which was moored off Monaco. On board we met Sir Winston Churchill, who was so pleased to meet me that the two of us consumed a bottle of Napoleon brandy which the kindly yacht steward supplied. For the remainder of the weekend I played cards and waltzed with Sir Winston, while George fished. Finally, Sir Winston decided he was going to teach me how to paint. I had had too much of him by now, so I asked George if we could return to Cap-d'Ail. He became very angry at me for the first time.

"How could you do such a thing?" he said on the ride to our villa. "Sir Winston was most angry, and instead of painting, he was scratching the surface of the benches and decks with his brushes and mumbling to himself. In his mumbling I caught your name."

As George said this, he held his head in both hands and kept his elbows on his knees. He was upset because he thought we would never be invited aboard Onassis' yacht again. What was even worse, perhaps the entire English aristocracy would condemn us. I moved close to him, put my hand on his head, and said, "Do you want to know what made me leave the yacht so abruptly?"

George did not reply, but still sat in the same position. I waited a few moments and then said, "Under the pretext of teaching me painting, the old man tried to molest me, saying, as he did it, 'I would like to see how the real Garbo looks.' As you may know, George, many people in their old age develop some kind of sexual fixation. Churchill's advances were not detrimental to my chastity but were very detrimental to my psyche. I am sure you noticed that he spent practically the entire day following me everywhere I went. Finally he grabbed me when I was off in a corner and tried to rip my dress off, saying, 'Everybody thinks you have no breasts. Let me see if that's true.' He was almost in a rage, with saliva dripping from his chin, as he pushed me to the wall. I finally escaped. And that is the story."

George lifted his head and began laughing and declaring how the old bastard would die without ever having seen the legendary Garbo's breasts. I had never seen him so much amused. And again between laughs he said, "He will die and he will never know if she has breasts or not. The poor bastard will know everything when he dies except the shape of Garbo's breasts."

George's jolly mood infected me, and I started laughing myself. We embraced each other, laughed some more, and held each other tight. We kissed, and when the car finally stopped before our villa, we rushed inside to make love.

And now I reach the end of my great hope for love and a new life. During the summer of 1964, George and I again stayed at Le Roc. During the day we baked in the sun, reading and talking, and in the evening we swam in the nude in the Mediterranean. George was very happy that my films were being revived all over the world. At Garbo Festivals in London, Paris, Rome, and New York, people stood in line to see my old works. And on television all over the world my films were being shown. I often thought that George was the instigator of this revival. Sometimes I was even sure that he had talked to various motion-picture entrepreneurs about my films. This was perhaps the result of my saying to him, "I have no plans for life . . . I am drifting . . . I am drifting toward death . . ."

After moments of such great happiness with him, moments of greater depression clouded my mind, and very often I lay in bed thinking that I was dying. I sometimes dreamed that I was a rotten orange with eyes burning with fire. And I dreamed that while I was lying with George in bed, I touched my head and discovered that I had four heads with ugly eyes. When I put my hand to my stomach, I discovered that I had four vaginas. In another nightmare I was a big cow with many nipples. Young boys came to take milk from me, but young girls were plunging knives into me from all sides. I was very much upset by those dreams, and when I related them to George, he would take me in his arms and rock me like a little baby.

But the summer of 1964 was more peculiar and more nightmarish than any other summer in my life. I felt that something dreadful was about to happen. I kept accepting the soothing words of George, and I told myself that I had to control my terrible anxieties. The sun was shining brightly outside, and the flowers were spreading their fragrances, and the water was blue and quiet around us. The world was singing with the voices of birds and bees, to the accompaniment of the happy fish splashing their tails in the water. I knew that I should not be so sad. I should be happy and gay in my relations with other people and in my relations with my conscience. But I didn't have sufficient resources to convince myself. Neither could George help me with his tender words and caresses. In more lucid moments I told him I would like to return to New York. It was almost the end of September, and it was time to leave the Riviera.

"Let's go to Paris," he suggested. "We'll go to theaters

and restaurants. We'll walk on the boulevards and go to see the treasures in the Louvre again. Maybe that will cheer you up."

George then insisted I go see a good psychiatrist as soon as we arrived in Paris. When I refused, he changed his tactics. "Maybe it would be better for you to go to the hospital and have a complete checkup to see that you're completely healthy physically." I didn't agree to that either. I thought that I might instead go once more to Stockholm. But at the last moment I changed my mind, and we went to Paris and checked in at the Hotel Crillon. We visited museums and restaurants and spent hours walking the streets of the beautiful French capital. It was already the beginning of October, and again I changed my mind and decided to stay in Paris. As the autumn leaves began to fall, George grew very sad. We talked of our love. We discussed the sense and nonsense of human existence. George kept repeating the words of Paul Gauguin: "At my age, a man feels good or he is dead." Not this sentence of Gauguin or any of our other words held meaning for us, and we drifted apart emotionally, although physically we remained close.

One night before George went to sleep, he turned to me, and said, "Divorce creates circumstances where the faults of the first husband bring suffering to the second wife."

"What do you mean?"

"The stupid person does those things at the end which a wise person does at the beginning . . ."

And again I did not understand what he was saying, but I didn't have the heart to ask him for an explanation because he was so pale. So I got up and slowly, with difficulty, walked to the next room. I looked back and saw through the open door that he had fallen down on the bed. I thought, "He is sleeping now. Maybe I should sleep also and tomorrow will look brighter."

The next day when I went to his room to wake him up, I could not. He was dead. I was panic-stricken, and I fled from the hotel and from Paris. I had lost my senses. I didn't have the courage to notify the hotel authorities or the police. I just left him there, alone.

By the time I arrived in New York, I had somehow regained control of myself. The first thing I started thinking about, as always, was myself. I decided not to see Valentina anymore and to avoid our mutual friends. My first thought was to sell my apartment on Fifty-second Street and move back to the Hampshire House or the Ritz Tower. It would be difficult for me to avoid Valentina in the elevator or the lobby. I knew I would go completely mad if she asked me about George's last days, or if I sensed that she held me responsible for her husband's death. I am sure she loved him very much, and that day after day, she had imagined George and me in different situations. I remember that at the beginning of our relationship he told her he loved both of us and would like to divide his time between us. This was his choice, and a free choice at that.

I never ran after anyone's love. I never encouraged George's love or any love. That was how I was, and this is the truth. I suffered and waited, but at the same time I remembered that diamonds had been pieces of coal a million years ago. And I knew how to wait for coal to transform its dull appearance into the bright shine of diamonds. Nobody can say that I don't know how to wait and that I don't know how to suffer. Perhaps our love was more on George's side than on mine, although we received equal shares of contempt from Valentina and our other friends. We waited passively for some sort of miracle. But a miracle in this age and with my nature turned out to be impossible. Naturally I liked it that someone was devoted to making me happy and doing everything possible to help me. Later this someone got tired and went away, or I got tired and disappeared. Then somebody else would come and take his place. Or die.

My character, my physical appearance, and my fame were attractive at first, but later became repulsive. People claimed this was due to the Garbo jinx. I too believed that I was endowed with special powers. I was even proud of them. I tried to explain it all to myself and put it all into some sort of perspective, but I was unable to.

After George's death, only the Baroness Cécile de Rothschild, who knew so much about the arts and about people, could soothe me. Once she said, "It looks as if you have learned nothing from life. You always worry or are surprised or astonished about everything. That's good. Because you will live a long time."

"But what value has such a life?" I asked.

"What value?" repeated Cécile. "Look at your hands. Those hands created the biggest legend I have ever known."

"But what of it?" I repeated the question I have been asking my whole life. "I would like to have happiness. Why don't I have happiness?"

"Who has this happiness?"

"Somebody must have," I replied. "Everybody everywhere talks about happiness, about love . . ."

"Yes, they talk, but they don't have it. You at least have your great fame, and you should be happy with that. What's more, you created it by yourself and you don't have to be grateful to anyone for it."

"But I am. I am still grateful to Stiller."

"I can't help you if you think like that. For a dead man a bunch of cut flowers placed on his grave is enough as a symbol of gratitude."

I disagreed but didn't press the point. Instead I showed her a clipping from a Swedish newspaper, which said that the old house at Blekingegatan 32 where I grew up was to be demolished. Cécile comforted me: "But your fame will not be demolished. Your films are being shown right now in Stockholm. I saw them when I was in London at the Empire Theater. If you like to see yourself, go to any large city, and I'm sure they're showing your films there. If they aren't, you can inquire at the Museum of Modern Art in New York and a private showing will be arranged for you."

All this Cécile said with conviction, but I also detected some pity in her voice. I decided to return to Stockholm to place some flowers on Moje's grave and try to restore spiritual contact with him.

44

Reflections

After my bath each day I examined my naked body in the mirror, and every day I noticed new wrinkles. So I underwent massages, dieted, and performed strenuous gymnastics to hold off age. But I was not successful.

Getting old is a very painful process, especially for a woman. And most especially for a woman who was once a great and original beauty. Neither I nor anyone else has found an antidote for aging. And nobody will find a way of avoiding the "blessings" of old age. On the other hand, I was aware that only one method exists for attaining a long life, and that is old age.

I was never happy with my age. When I was young I wanted to be old in order to cope with life's problems like a grown-up. Now I want to be young and I don't care if I can cope with my problems or not. All I want is to be young and vigorous again. But no one can ever have this wish fulfilled.

Throughout my life I have tried to base my moves on realistic calculations. Perhaps that was the reason that when I did follow my intuition I was sometimes confused and even made dreadful mistakes. I recognized the more beautiful and idealistic affairs of my life when they occurred, but I always continued in the same pattern of ultimate failure. I did not feel guilty about that, for I always placed the guilt on God, who created me, letting Him take full responsibility. Very often now I talk to God. I have to admit that I talk not only to Him, but to people who have gone to other worlds. Once when I talked to God, he told me in a cryptic manner like a general of the army, "Where it is difficult to find the guilty one, we should at least have one whom we can punish. Later we will look among the punished for the truly guilty parties and punish them doubly, while we will reward the innocent for their sufferings."

Sometimes I consider myself a wise person who was afraid to disclose herself before the eyes and ears of others who would soon discover her to be an ignorant person.

"Nothing is left to me," I whisper to myself. "Only to treasure in my mind as long as possible the lively memory of the people whom I loved."

This causes me tremendous pain, but my enemies and "friends" are happy that I have no one real to love and must, of necessity, reach back into the past. My memory about people and happenings from the past gets more readable and understandable. I recall now not only the expressions on faces and in eyes during numerous conversations, but also precise dialogue and actual emotions. Memory flows like a river through my head, a beautiful, crystal-clear, fast-moving river. Only death can stop that river. And who knows?—after the death of my body, my memory may flow on. I find it very curious that my head can hold so much crystal liquid memory.

God? Who is He? What roads does He travel? Why do we talk all the time about Someone whom no one has ever seen? True, I have heard Him many times, but I have never seen Him. Now, as I advance in age, His voice is becoming clearer. Yet I cannot allow myself to follow His voice, for if I do, I will not be myself. I would like to meet Him face to face, because I would have many questions to ask Him. Questions only He can answer, burning questions for me.

He is supposed to be wise and just in everything. But why has He given to people the idea that the artist is inspired by God and that artists are cousins of God who try to make interpretations of His beauty? Why is the artist, more than other people, tortured by life? Is this the doing of a just god?

Why did God create in me the great desire to act? And why in film? Why did a wise God push me into the hands of Mauritz Stiller, who, as I look back, was most likely an instrument of Satan? I can remember what Stiller said to me: "For us film is a miracle created by Satan—the greatest miracle, which can capture human emotions and happiness faithfully, more faithfully than any other medium. And I am sure film is more suited for the art of depravity than for the art of godly justice."

I am so confused now, because, though he was anti-God, it was through Moje that I became famous. Then he left me without reaping any reward for his work on my talent and on my spiritual and physical appearance. I was abandoned in this world like a corps of leaderless soldiers, like a tiger without a head. Yet other thoughts tell me that I don't need a leader anymore, that I don't even need a head.

I have lost a belief in people, in a God who put me in this situation without replying clearly to my questions. I am floating on the waters of life without direction, without a goal, without the knowledge of why and how long.

More and more I live in yesterday. Only memory is left, and a cluster of live people coincidental to my life who insist on moving around me in a macabre dance. I do not ask them for anything. I do not encourage them to do anything for me. But they still play the game of faithful friends, and I don't ask them why, because that question would lead nowhere.

Among these acquaintances are several writers desperately trying to establish themselves; some merchants of wine or real estate; old women who have been trying all their lives to become actresses or writers; photographers whose hands now shake with age; hotel men and grocers whom I pay well for their services; and financial speculators who persist in insisting that I invest my money in their schemes. All the great celebrities whom I knew have stopped seeking my friendship—they are dead or are waiting for a telephone call from eternity to join the others.

On the streets of Paris, London, Rome, or New York, passersby do not recognize me anymore. But if by chance some old man recognizes me, he doesn't have the strength to follow. In restaurants the new managements don't recognize me or ignore me. I think those restaurants belong to a different era and will be closed forever very shortly too. Yet my films are still being presented in theaters and on television all over the world. But I have nothing to do with them anymore spiritually and financially; they are in the hands of international speculators. No one asks my permission to show those films, and no one pays me when they are shown. Sometimes when I see them, I do not recognize myself. I am now so far from those times.

New generations and new problems appear very quickly on the surface of the world and nobody remembers an actress from the 1920's and 1930's. Most people are even surprised to find this old woman still cruising around the world. Not so long ago I received a few letters marked by the post office "Address Unknown." I received them only by accident. It looks as if even the United States Post Office doesn't remember me.

Looking for a piece of the earth where I would meet as little fauna in human skin as possible, I found a village called Klosters in Switzerland. The first time I heard of this place was from my little, insignificant cluster of friends. I have always been enchanted by the Alps, for the first time I saw them it was in their beautiful summer and fall. I also liked the flora of Klosters and the neighboring regions. I learned to differentiate and admire the beauty of the crocus, pheasant's-eye, narcissus, snowy anemone, Saint-Bruno's-lily, larkspur with spurred calyx, edelweiss, oxeye daisy, bellflower, Turk's-cap lily, and alpine rose. I became very well acquainted with them and knew where they lived and how high in the mountains they flourished. I loved to watch the growing flowers—watch their breathings, smell their fragrances. Now flowers capture my heart more than people or animals. In their company I feel free and talkative. Very often I explain my troubles to them and listen to theirs. Like me, flowers have most of their troubles with people, and after that with animals or changing temperatures. They suffer the most from human hands, because these hands mutilate and murder them.

I change my house in Klosters quite frequently, most of the time because of people. I didn't want to buy something permanent because I didn't know whether I would die in Stockholm, a Swiss village, or the Hotel Crillon in Paris, where George had died. Anyhow, I decided not to die in New York or Hollywood. Since Alpine flowers so charmed me, I thought it would be nice to place my spirit to rest in some corner of the Alps and have flowers under my head and a blue sky overhead.

My time in Klosters was spent in the private homes of various intellectuals from all over the world or in the dining room of a hotel, the Chesa Grischuna, where the main course was intellectual masturbation with a side order of trivial gossip. I kept quiet, because I knew I would just be generating material for more gossip and less peace for myself. When I had had enough of conversation, I would get up and walk away.

Most of the time a man or woman from this group would follow me and try to convince me that I should write my autobiography, or that if I wouldn't, he or she would. Quite often I would be approached on the street by strangers claiming to represent international publishing houses, or journalists who tried to bribe me with a million-dollar advance for a book. When this did not succeed, they would follow with a plea that I must put my thoughts on paper for posterity. The situation became so unbearable that I couldn't go out and buy a pair of shoes or a piece of steak because even the shoe-store clerk and the butcher would turn out to be literary agents.

Once, the manager of the Chesa Grischuna invited me to supper saying that he had a chalet which he would like to sell me, or rather that he was representing a friend who owned this beautiful and inexpensive chalet. I thought that perhaps I should buy a chalet in order to attain complete privacy.

When I appeared that evening at Chesa Grischuna, the manager led me to a table set for three. Two bottles of champagne stood cooling in a bucket. When we sat down, I asked him right off, "Where is this chalet?"

The manager, instead of replying, opened the champagne and poured for me and himself. I noticed he was stalling. I repeated my question, and at that moment a second man appeared whom the manager introduced as the London representative of MGM. I was furious. I got up and said to the manager, "Good-bye. You will never see me again."

With those words I left the hotel. I thought immediately of returning to New York, but on my way home I decided to walk for a while, although it was already dark. I wanted to say good-bye to my flowers. I felt cold, but I walked anyway in the direction of the mountains to see them for the last time.

My pace grew faster, as if I were attempting to shake off the cold that was trying to capture my body. Soon I was in darkness among the shimmering trees. I was frightened, but I continued onward as if in a trance.

Suddenly I noticed a light, and in the light an old man with enormous eyes. In his hand was a big stick. I opened my mouth to call out to him, but I was frozen and my voice wouldn't come. The old man was standing a few feet in front of me; with his long cane he pointed back to Klosters.

I felt hot currents going through my body. I tried to say something, but was still unable to. The old man again shook his cane in the direction of Klosters and slowly moved toward me. I didn't know if he was going to strike me or take me back to Klosters, but I felt that my body had regained some vigor.

I tried to communicate once more, but I abandoned my attempt. Instead I turned around and with animal power ran back toward Klosters. Wind swooped down through the trees and pushed my body. I ran as if I had wings. . . .

Garbo in Sweden in 1932, photographed with her brother, Sven. Los Angeles, 1951, Garbo signs for her citizenship certificate.

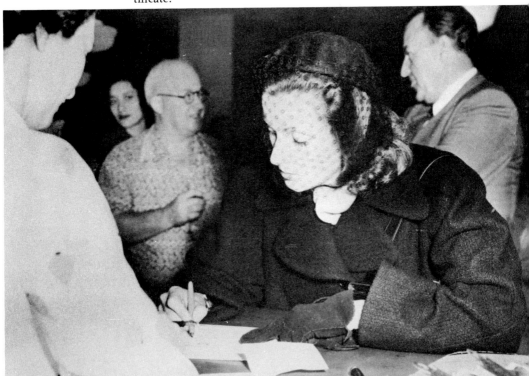

Above, in 1956, with Aristotle Onassis.

Left, walking in London with photographer Cecil Beaton.

Right, followed by George Schlee, Garbo strolls in the Mall in London. Below, again with George Schlee, she walks along the harbor at Portofino.

THREE PHOTOS: WIDE WORLD

UPI

THREE PHOTOS: PUBLIFOTO/PHOTOREPORTERS

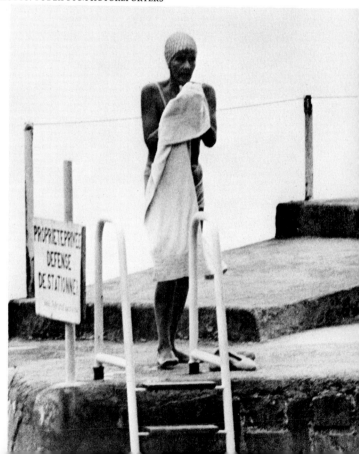

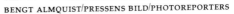

Opposite and below, Garbo caught by a tele-lens while bathing at Roquebrune, near Monte Carlo. She was a guest of a Russian princess at the Villa Soulico in September 1966. Right, at Arlanda Airport (Stockholm) on a visit to Sweden in 1961.

PLAGE PRIVEE
AUTORISEE À PARTIR de
15 30 SEULEMENT MERCI

Left, at the time of her seventieth birthday, Garbo visited with a long-time friend, the Countess Kerstin Bernadotte, at Villa Kungsberga in Sweden, September 1975. Right and below, on a trip to Greece in the 1970s.

Publisher's Afterword

The Legend as Actress
by Richard Schickel

Now she is gone altogether, but at some point in the early forties Greta Garbo and I decided to go our separate ways. Her decision was apparently a conscious one. Mine, alas, was entirely unconscious. But both were consequential acts. Her withdrawal from the screen obviously affected her subsequent personal history and it had portentous effects on the later history of her medium as well as the social history of her times. My decision was, of course, predicated on hers, and it is important only because it was multiplied by that of millions of moviegoers of my own and succeeding generations. Because we were unable to gain any firm sense of her presence as an actress, unable to re-create the allure she had once exerted on the older audience, she was a source of a curiosity for us that became more idle with each passing year. As a result, both parties missed out on something: we on the full power of a singular screen presence; she on posterity's highest regard, perhaps on the immortality that was obviously a matter of some concern to her, however little she cared to admit it.

By chance, I played an extra's role in an insignificant

scene in her later life, but my role in this essay can only be symbolic. Since I imagine myself to be quite typical of her latter-day audience, I also imagine that by consulting my responses to her image after she left the screen I can say something useful to readers—by now the vast majority—who, like me, know her exclusively as a legend. Those of us who were not present at the creation of her screen image have to reimagine the singular hold, both unprecedented and unduplicated, she exercised on audiences of the 1920s and 1930s. We have to do that, of course, with any star who does not make an impression on us in our most impressionable years—roughly between the ages of ten and twenty, when we are most innocent, therefore most open to the raw power of a screen image. But Garbo's silence and withdrawal —and the lack of resonance most of her films have for a modern audience—make that task peculiarly difficult in her case.

One of the many surprises in Mr. Gronowicz's account is Garbo's insistence that her retirement was not, as many believed, a course into which she had accidentally drifted, but a carefully calculated decision. *Two-Faced Woman*, which was to turn out to be her last film, had failed commercially and critically; the onset of World War Two convinced her (quite correctly) that both the kinds of films she had played in and the type of character she had portrayed were going to go out of fashion permanently; therefore, withdrawal from the screen was certainly an alternative worth contemplating. And, as she said, it was now within her means economically and, given the state of creative exhaustion in which she says she found herself, in her interest psychologically, to vary the elusive and enigmatic character she had been playing for over a decade and a half and project it not as a highly stylized cinematic fiction but as a living reality.

If this decision was as rationally thought out as she later claimed to Mr. Gronowicz, it was an extraordinarily bold one. She was, in effect, seizing total control of her image, eliminating from the process of tending and trumpeting it the studio functionaries who had participated in its creation. She would now test whether or not stardom could be converted into a pure idea. Or perhaps one should say, a pure ideal. She was asking, Could it be kept alive by *not* working at her profession, by *not* submitting to the hubbub and degradations of performance, publicity and promotion, but simply by relying upon what David Thomson once called "the self-perpetuating mechanics of stardom"?

As for me, I was coming to movies just as Garbo was leaving them in 1941. I might have seen *Two-Faced Woman* that year, but it was not the sort of thing on which a hearty American boy of the time would choose to spend part of his weekly allowance. Romantic comedies involving upper-class swells were not for us. Romance was a matter to be avoided and, if accidentally encountered, something to be hooted at. Comedy, for us, was farcical (Abbott and Costello made their first appearance on the box-office top ten list that year) or wisecracking (Bob Hope was high on the list, too). We were into action—westerns, crime stories, and, with war drawing near, the military adventure and espionage tales that were starting to proliferate. To us, Greta Garbo was a rumor circulated by our parents, her "mystery" subsumed in the all-encompassing mystery of adulthood. Like cocktails and cigarettes, sweetbreads and the "Voice of Firestone" radio program, she was a taste we imagined—if we imagined anything at all about her—we would acquire when we "grew up," and attained the rights, privileges, and fantasies appertaining to that remarkable status.

I'm sorry she decided not to wait for us. But she may have sensed that we were unlikely to be worthy of her. Or that she was unlikely to be able to survive, on screen, in a form worthy of her legend. As a matter of fact, as I look back on her movies now, consciously attempting to isolate and analyze the essence of her appeal, it occurs to me that she had been drifting away from us for something like a decade, so out of tune was she, as were those movies, with the prevailing spirit of American film; for that matter, of American life in the 1930s. Another way of putting it is to say that she was at this point shrewder about her past and the limited prospects it proposed for her future as an actress than anyone else, including M-G-M, the independent producers who for over a decade continued to tempt her with projects, or the press, which avidly, innocently, speculated about these enterprises.

Her screen character was totally irrelevant to most people by this time, of course. During the war we had been to Europe by the millions. After the war we continued to go there as tourists in even greater number. It didn't look like the world she had inhabited, and we found no females of her sort there. Even if we did not travel abroad, the European movies we imported showed us in the persons of Bardot, Loren and their ilk an erotic exoticism of a kind quite different from hers. There was now an exemplary overtness —a boldness, symbolized by the willingness of these younger women to do skin scenes—that was quite different from her more romantic (but also more furtive and guilty) sexuality.

But these changes merely made obvious what was implicit throughout Garbo's career in sound pictures. For looking back on them with the objectivity of the years, it now seems close to miraculous that she survived the eleven years from her first, somewhat belated, talking picture, *Anna Christie,* in 1931, to her final film. Indeed, the strain of finding vehicles that were at once suitable for her and reasonable commercial propositions for this era became clear to at least a few observers during that period. Graham Greene, for example, serving a five-year term as a movie reviewer, twice likened the prospect of attending a Garbo movie to picking up a work by Carlyle—not something to thrill the heart with anticipatory joys. "Retarded" was his word for the typical Garbo sound film, as it awaited "the slow consummation of her noble adulteries." If that was true for a man of Greene's sophisticated and patient interest in sin, sinning, and sinners, think of the impatience such a movie would have engendered in us of the forties generation. We had been raised on fast-moving, contemporary adventure yarns of the war years, and were untutored in any other movie tradition, particularly the high romantic tradition of the silent film, the manner of which her sound productions for the most part aped. The movies as we came upon them were stylistically far removed from that older mode of presentation. And the women in them were uniformly seen as peppy good sports, loyally, chastely standing by men deeply preoccupied by the military necessity and by their own problematic heroism. Subsequently, to be sure, in *films noirs,* the movies introduced a more fatal sort of *femme,* the spiderish creature luring males, often seen as psychologically weakened by the war, to their doom. But they were domesticated sophisticates, and the motive for their dark doings was always money, never love. If, as a rule, they came to ends as gloomy as Garbo's generally were, they uniformly deserved them. One cannot imagine her playing one of these roles any more than one can imagine her as a pinup girl. In short, one cannot quite imagine where she might have gone had she decided to continue working.

All of this supports the logic of her withdrawal from the movies, even if it is a somewhat suspect *ex post facto* logic. And it demystifies it as well. Is it possible to do the same for her screen image? Is it possible, at last, to blow away that cloud of gaseous speculation, much of it generated by intellectuals of a temperament less brisk than Greene's, and more anxious to claim their iota of immortality by definitively solving her famous mystery? Is it possible, in short, and at this late date, to see her plain? Not entirely, perhaps, but it is a salutary and stimulating exercise nonetheless.

She was always a creature of withdrawal, of silence—thus, ideally, of the silents—an actress who from the first moments she appeared on the screen defined herself by her refusals. This was an inescapable condition for her, a point Mr. Gronowicz's chapters on her childhood and adolescence vividly reinforce, though they are by no means the first writings on Garbo to suggest this.

She was not astonishingly beautiful in her formative years—"nice-looking," one thinks, glancing at photographs of the young Garbo. The chubbiness of her early years had to be melted away by maturity before the classical fineness of feature, inherited from her father, could emerge. Her body, long, slender, uncurvaceous, was her mother's genetic contribution, as was her odd gait, rather mannish, rather predatory (at least to some observers). In other words, there was nothing about her appearance in her early years that would inspire her with notable confidence or outgoingness. And, as she testifies, the relentless poverty of those years, encouraging withdrawal into dreams of success, obviously made its contribution to the formation of her essential shyness.

Yes, shyness. After so many decades of complex and

fanciful writing about Garbo, one hesitates to introduce consideration of such a commonplace condition into the discussion. But it was, indeed, the most basic element in Garbo's character, both off the screen and on. It is a basic element, ironically enough, in the characters of many performers. In fact, Josef von Sternberg, the director whose film career began around the same time Garbo's did, claimed he never met an actor who was not inherently shy. Perhaps he meant to say "a narcissist." Certainly that would be the term—the virtual synonym—that a modern observer, better versed in psychobabble, would employ to describe her.

Film, it should be noted, is the perfect medium for performers afflicted by this condition. For one thing, you can do your work in near-privacy, surrounded by the familiar, supportive faces of a relatively small cast and crew—your trusted colleagues; you do not have to face an unpredictable audience of strangers night after night as the stage actor does. Garbo was, of course, notorious for her insistence on closed sets and on working with people she had come to trust (Clarence Brown, a man of no more than routine gift, directed six of her movies; William Daniels photographed no fewer than eighteen of them).

Equally important, the screen performer is free to study her work as long and as often as she likes, for film is, among other things, a mirror, capable of reflecting back its subjects' self-images. Actually it is an improvement on a mirror, for it retains those images permanently, permitting one to study them at leisure—for a lifetime if one likes. As, in fact, Garbo did: Even after her withdrawal from the movies, she was known to book screening rooms at New York's Museum of Modern Art in order to run her old pictures.

Returning to her first feature, *The Saga of Gösta Berling*, for purposes of his distinguished "Portrait" of Garbo (1980), Alexander Walker, the English critic, found her "somnambulistic power" already fully developed. Drifting through a garden, gliding through the halls of a castle, lit only by the lamp she was carrying, she suggested, in Walker's words, "an infinity of emotion while registering only abstraction." Perhaps "self-absorption" might have been a slightly better word, but no matter—the point is made. Even at the beginning of her career she felt no obligation to the reigning traditions of movie acting, which in silent days necessarily involved the physicalization of very basic emotions in the broadest imaginable terms. Nor did she feel an obligation to the lunatic narratives of the films in which she appeared, these tales of forbidden lusts and awful retributions, no obligation, that is, to the conventional hyperactivity of their plots. Her business was to illuminate the effect of all those comings and goings on her "spiritual interior," as Walker would have it.

Narrative, one feels compelled to add, is a public matter, a composition of events even humble journalism, not to mention routine movie-making, is capable of adequately rendering. It is also an essentially masculine concern. Men are always hurrying heedlessly past the emotional nuances of a story in order to reach its point. They want to know who won and who lost—in love or war, in sport or business or politics. Women, as Garbo never tired of reminding us, prefer to linger over the state of their feelings, are, indeed, quite willing to risk everything they have in order to experience the rush and glow, the fervor and avidity of the romantically heightened moment. To experience such moments *is* the point of the story. And if the narrative conclusion of experiencing them is death or disgrace or poverty, so be it.

This escape from narrative, which also implies an escape from the ruling generic conventions of the movies when Garbo came to them, is of enormous significance in analyzing the grasp she exerted on both the popular mind and the critical imagination. Until Garbo, women in the movies were always the playthings of plot; their characters determined by its requirements, their fates worked out by its usually melodramatic, often implausible, always conventionally moral dictates. They were good (Lillian Gish and Mary Pickford) or they were bad (the vamps, from Theda Bara onward), and everyone they encountered in the course of the stories they appeared in was as conscious of their moral condition as they themselves were—and so was the audience. It was the fate of the good woman to assert her goodness against all manner of assaults until all challenges had been defeated. It was the fate of the bad woman to assert her badness until her victims recognized her evil intent and she received her comeuppance. No exceptions were allowed, no special dispensations were permitted in these tales.

Until Garbo claimed the right to both. Oh, all right, she would accept whatever punishment plot and morality demanded of her character. But it was a matter of supreme indifference to her. Indeed, from the start, she always seemed to know instinctively that she would eventually have to pay the price of death or exile for her passions. Therefore these final exactions came as no shock to her, and so the idea of a last-minute recantation never seemed to enter her mind. She merely smiled—a secretive, ironic, inwardly directed smile—at the final fadeout, and accepted whatever fate morality and the screenwriters doled out to her.

Fresh from reading her story, we can now see that this acceptance of fate's blows was a remarkable achievement in integrative psychology as well as the actor's art. For consider what we have just learned about the two most significant men in her life, her father and her discoverer-mentor-lover, Mauritz Stiller. The former was obviously shiftless and unreliable as well as emotionally withdrawn—not a trustworthy repository for a young girl's affection. And his sudden death in the ugly circumstances Garbo described for Mr. Gronowicz constitutes, psychologically speaking, the most brutal kind of desertion to deal with.

As for Stiller, who was obviously a substitute for her father, his masculine failures were equally serious: He could not defend her against M-G-M's rather crass and often peremptory management of her career; he could not defend himself against the studio's unmanning contempt for his gifts; he abruptly deserted her in America in order to try to pick up the pieces of his shattered career in Europe, whereupon he died, if anything more untimely than Garbo's father had.

After such experiences, cynicism, and of a rather coldly self-protective sort—true vampishness—might have become her romantic essence. And indeed, there was in her silent films an element of what Alistair Cooke once called "disdain." For her to have evolved a screen character based on the opposite quality—on compassion—to have become, by the time she was making such later sound films as *Anna Karenina* and *Camille,* the great exemplar of a near existential acceptance of the pain and loss one must absorb in the name of love, is nothing short of astonishing.

Assuming we are correct to believe that she was drawing deeply on her own history, her own feelings, to project this complex of emotions, we may perhaps have stumbled on a simple, partial solution to the enigma of her early retirement. Both here and elsewhere she spoke often of the exhaustion that visited her when she was making a film, which is odd considering her physical stamina. Obviously this was psychological in origin, the result of intense confrontation with herself in order to play her parts. It is akin to the debilitation that modern method actors like Brando have spoken of, and responsible, in his case—as in hers—both for the self-protective evasiveness of some of his work and for his premature withdrawal from acting.

Be that as it may—and obviously other factors were at work in her case—what she was doing may well strike us, from today's perspective, as unremarkable, as no more than good, realistic, psychologically acute acting. We now see it all the time. But in the context of her moment, it struck critics, and the ordinary audience, with something like revolutionary force. Pola Negri and the rest of the dark, vampish crowd, the only types to whom Garbo could logically be compared, took things much harder. The effects of their ups and downs were visibly manifested in unmistakable terms. Garbo couldn't, and wouldn't, indulge herself so broadly.

This was the source of her mystery. Very simply, no one had seen anything like her before on the screen. And the initial response to her was puzzled. Reviewing her first American film, *The Torrent,* Richard Watts, Jr., wrote, "She seems an excellent and attractive actress, with a surprising propensity for looking like Carol Dempster, Norma Talmadge, ZaSu Pitts and Gloria Swanson in turn." Having thus misdefined the indefinable, he added: "That does not mean she lacks a manner of her own, however." With that breathtaking analysis behind him, he turned in haste (and obvious relief) to the work of her costar, Ricardo Cortez.

There is, at least, a commendable modesty in such retreats from judgment. For after *The Torrent*, the deluge. For the remainder of the silent era, and most of the rest of her career as well, she was condemned either to a life of adultery or to wistful dreams of it. In the former category are: *The Temptress, Flesh and the Devil, Love* (which was an adaptation, but with a happy ending, of *Anna Karenina*), *A Woman of Affairs* and *The Kiss;* in the latter we may list *Wild Orchids* and *The Single Standard*. In only two of her American silent films —*The Mysterious Lady* and *The Divine Woman*—did she avoid this fate. But the former involves her in a sort of symbolic adultery. She plays a spy who must finally betray her spy-master (or husband surrogate, if you will) because she genuinely falls in love with the soldier he has assigned her to seduce. It appears that only in *The Divine Woman* (no print or negative of which now exists) does she avoid messy romantic entanglements. In it she plays a Bernhardt-like actress who rises from the peasantry to greatness on the Parisian stage. But even this story, as almost all Garbo stories had to, involved a renunciation: She must give up the stage career for which she struggled so hard in order to claim permanently the man she loves.

To be sure, her talking-picture debut was something of an anomaly. In *Anna Christie*, her surroundings were uncharacteristically inelegant. And all of her bad behavior (as a prostitute back home in Minnesota) occurred before the main action of this adaptation of Eugene O'Neill's lugubrious and risible drama began (in a New York dockside saloon). But from here to *Ninotchka* she was, in effect, making silent movies that merely replaced subtitles with dialogue. She continued to suffer in her well-established, increasingly old-fashioned way. If she was required less often to die for her sins—she did so only in *Mata Hari,* in her second try at *Anna Karenina*, this time with Tolstoi's tragic denouement intact, and in *Camille*, of course—her renunciations are legion.

She gave up a young clergyman *(Romance)*, a young diplomat *(Inspiration)*, and Napoleon himself *(Conquest)* rather than blight their promising careers. To maintain her better self, she gave up John Gilbert in order to claim a throne *(Queen Christina)* and George Brent in order to save her marriage and fight a plague *(The Painted Veil)*. In this decade she was allowed only two more-or-less happy reclamations: In *Susan Lenox, Her Fall and Rise,* she was permitted to flee an arranged marriage with a brute and find happiness in Clark Gable's arms; in *As You Desire Me* (based on a work by Pirandello, no less) she was an amnesiac who recovers her memory and, as a result, her first, true love.

Are we talking tosh? Yes, we are talking tosh. Though, of course, the productions were all first class, in the M-G-M manner. That is to say, the decor, the costuming, the hairdressing were ravishing, much of the acting talent the best that money could buy. The air of *luxe* surrounding these productions was quite overpowering. But the scripts were essentially semiliterate reworkings of subliterate forms and ideas. These, in turn, were staged by directors who knew what Mr. Thalberg and Mr. Mayer wanted, which was no expression of individuality, but rather restatements of the one great message the M-G-M organization wanted to impart to the public in those days: that it, unlike its rivals, spared no expense to please its customers.

In the broad flow of American film history, M-G-M in the thirties and forties represented a cultural and intellectual backwater, saved from total stagnation by the forceful personalities of its star players and by the occasional freshening influence of talents acquired after they had developed elsewhere (The Marx Brothers, for example, or Spencer Tracy and Katharine Hepburn, or Ernst Lubitsch, who, of course, enters Garbo's story too late). M-G-M continued to concentrate heavily on adaptations of second-rate literature, historical spectacles, and romantic melodramas, and it was not until Arthur Freed was permitted to establish his musicals unit (after the success of *The Wizard of Oz*), and his people proceeded virtually to reinvent the form, that Metro finally created a body of original, innovative work of lasting value.

The best directors of the day, the liveliest writing talents, the craftsmen for whom the coming of sound released enormous creative energies, and whose work gave the best American movies of the time their fizz and spunk, did not, by and large, work at M-G-M. Paramount, whence Lubitsch came and Preston Sturges developed, was throughout the thirties the great purveyor of romantic comedy. Warner Brothers, peopled by the ever-rebellious likes of Cagney and

Bette Davis, was the place where something of the fast-paced spirit of an urbanizing America was caught in brash, darkly witty melodramas. Fox, under Darryl F. Zanuck, was half M-G-M, half Warner Brothers, but without the glitz of the former or the brooding energy of the latter in its films, which had a rather hasty, rootless air about them. Columbia, economically downtrodden, had no compunctions about taking a chance on Capra's social-commentary comedies and the screwball cycle, since it had no dignity to defend. RKO, the other economic fringe dweller, was an important contributor to that cycle, and, like Columbia, it became a place where independent spirits such as Howard Hawks, George Stevens, Leo McCarey, and briefly, Orson Welles (not to mention such stars as Cary Grant and Fred Astaire) could find shelter for their quirky projects and singular talents. Indeed, it was often on loan-out to these studios that M-G-M's contract people did their most memorable work in this period (Gable, in *It Happened One Night,* for example).

Out of this ferment, which was highly verbal, in response to the new sound technology, a new woman—usually a woman with a job—smart of style and of mouth, able to hold her own with man dialogically and sexually, emerged. She might be brassy like Harlow, ironic like Colbert, dizzy like Lombard, elegant like Dunne, intelligent like Hepburn, but she was never a victim—not for long, anyway. Even Dietrich, in a sense the new era's successor to Garbo, since she too projected a slightly androgynous subtext, stated her desires with a boldness and a wit that would have been quite foreign to Garbo. (In her first major scene in her first American movie Dietrich wears a man's white tie and tails and before the sequence is over has boldly seized and kissed another woman lingeringly on the lips.) Moreover, the movement of the typical Dietrich movie was not from virtue to fall, but from fall to regeneration through a new or reclaimed love—quite different from that of the typical Garbo picture.

That Garbo continued to give herself to her films with characteristic intensity, that she was often very effective in them, is not in question here. But contemplating the full Hollywood context of the 1930s leads one to consider what now seems to be the central issue of Garbo's career as an actress (as opposed to her career as a celebrity). Namely, would she have prospered better had she not been so closely bound to M-G-M? Is it possible that under contract elsewhere, or as a free-lancer, she might have found projects that would have extended her range, stimulated her imagination, thus encouraging her to extend her career? Most important of all, is it possible she would have obtained immortality as an artist rather than as a curiosity, a phenomenon, if she had not been locked into films that, as Graham Greene implied, were anachronisms as they were being made?

These questions are not simply answered. However unhappy Garbo was with M-G-M's management, it was mainly money, rarely roles, that sent her into sulks and suspensions. And if its father figures sometimes distressed her, the rest of the studio "family" was invaluable to her, providing her with the friendly, familiar faces she needed to see around her when she worked. Moreover, given that self-absorption which only grew more intense the longer she resided as a stranger in a strange land, it is doubtful that she was aware of the alternatives available to her elsewhere in the movies. And even if she had been, the likelihood is that she would not have availed herself of them.

For one cannot help but speculate now that the silliness of most of her movies may have served what she imagined —with what degree of conscious calculation it is impossible to say—a larger purpose, which was to allow her to utterly dominate her texts and contexts. This, of course, began with the phenomenon we have previously observed: her lack of obligation to her films' story lines. But it finally went much further than that. There was literally nothing in these pictures to distract the audience from contemplation of "The Divine" (as the catchphrase of the day, doubtless adapted from the title of her 1928 silent film, had it). All their great moments are unequivocally hers. No line from any of the screenplays ever permanently attached itself to memory. No strong directorial hand ever asserted itself in her movies, no male lead or, for that matter, powerful supporting performance, ever challenged her domination of the screen. It was —seemingly—a perfect arrangement: she evaded all responsibility for the twaddle surrounding her, yet all eyes were always focused on her, because there was no place else they could comfortably rest for very long; all minds were constantly fixed on her, because there was nothing else to think about profitably.

As a result, her career became, finally, a little anthology of treasured moments, assertions of her "genius" against a lowering background of mediocrity. Thinking back, one recalls the communion scene in *Flesh and the Devil* where, presented with the chalice, she solemnly turns the cup so that her lips will touch it at just the place her secret lover's lips recently vacated. Or the moment in *A Woman of Affairs* when, sick unto death, she physicalizes forbidden passion by embracing a bouquet of flowers exactly as she would the lover who sent them. Of course, the moment in *Queen Christina* when she wanders the room she has shared with her lover, touching the objects it contains, committing them to tactile memory because she knows she will never see them—or her lover—again is justly celebrated. *Anna Karenina* is full of such moments, wonderful bits of business at a ball, at a race track, on a croquet ground, as slowly she acknowledges the fact that she has fallen into a forbidden love. Then, too, because the renunciation she is called upon to make in this film is of her son, her scenes with him (he is played by Freddie Bartholomew) have a natural poignancy which she realizes through the most delicate underplaying. A typical moment: She is in a garden, where her son disappears up an alley of shrubs in one direction, her lover, Vronsky, played by Fredric March, disappears in the opposite direction, and the camera catches and holds her, twisting and turning amidst the greenery, like an animal befuddled by a maze, her conflict symbolized by the anguished flutter of her movements. Her next film, *Camille,* is similarly rich in unforgettable actor's moments; the most notable, perhaps, the one in which to drive away her young lover, Armand (Robert Taylor), she pretends decadent attachment to an older man. The way she throws her head back in wild laughter, the way she sustains her merriment, at once persuading the youth of its genuineness and the rest of us onlookers of its brave falsity, the way she brings it to near-hysterical pitch, but does not lose control of it, constitutes great and subtle acting.

Camille's director, the wise and tasteful George Cukor,

would later comment that it was precisely her refusal to play the title courtesan as a victim, her insistence that the character be the self-aware author of her own misery, that redeemed the film from its origins as romantic popular nineteenth-century fiction (and drama). He believed that Garbo, like a handful of other great stars, had an instinct— an instinct supported by the medium's great tools, the close-up and the montage—that enabled her to find, as he put it, "the human truths, the human experience" that always exist beneath highly conventionalized material, no matter how hoary it is, how laughable it may seem to literary sophisticates.

So it seemed at the time, certainly. The moviegoers who had grown up with her, or were growing up with her, found her mere presence sufficient to animate a respectful attention to antiquated dramas and to an antiquated vision of a woman's lot they would have hooted off the screen if another actress had attempted them. They were joined with her in the agreeable, unspoken conspiracy that she bore no responsibility for the nonsense in which she habitually appeared, and that her presence on the screen in anything at all conferred on the vehicle dignity enough to make it worthy of their time and trouble. In any case, they could be pretty certain that she would, for a shot here, a sequence there, transcend whatever it was that had brought her out of her famous seclusion, them out of their houses.

In this view, the best critics concurred. Or maybe they invented it—impossible to say at this late date. In any case, if one goes back to sample the critical response to her career, one discovers, after their initial puzzlement over her had worn off, an astonishing lack of specificity about the films themselves. More often than not, in reading the typical review of a Garbo film, one is left in the dark as to what, precisely, its story might have been. But about the actress herself there are always several paragraphs of dubious generalities.

One day in 1932, for example, Stark Young, unquestionably the leading drama critic of his day, lowered his eye from contemplation of the then lofty (in its own eyes, anyway) theater world and fixed it upon Garbo. Possibly influenced by her appearance that year in a film adapted from a play by a certifiably great writer (Pirandello's *As You Desire Me*), he found that "She presents an instance of the natural and right progress of the poetic: from the concrete toward ideality." What he meant by this is what we have just been talking about—that air of removal from the contexts in which she was presented. "Elevation" and "distillation" were words that occurred to Young in contemplating her work, and he spoke of "the remote entity of her spirit, a certain noble poignancy in her presence" as well as "a sense of mood that is giving and resisting at the same time." All of this, he claimed, combined to "defeat and break down the poor little common theory of naturalness and prose method" which, as he said, ruled the reviewing of theater and movies at that time.

Young established, in this piece, what amounts to the main line of professional Garbo-watching. Some two decades later Kenneth Tynan was still saying the same thing, though in livelier, more sexually charged prose: "What, when drunk, one sees in other women, one sees in Garbo sober. She is woman apprehended with all the pulsating clarity of one of Aldous Huxley's mescalin jags. To watch her is to achieve direct, cleansed perception of something which, like a flower or a fold of silk, is raptly, unassertively and beautifully itself. Nothing intrudes between her and the observer except the observer's neuroses." And so forth, with the usual dismissal of her roles ("Through what hoops, when all is said and done, she has been put . . ."). Around the same time, Roland Barthes brought to our subject his highest mandarin manner, that uniquely Gallic blend of shrewd observation and woolly generality. Garbo, he wrote, "belongs to that moment in cinema when capturing the human face still plunged audiences into the deepest ecstasy . . . when the face represented a kind of absolute state of the flesh, which could be neither reached nor renounced." She offered, he wrote, "a sort of platonic ideal of the human creature . . . descended from a heaven where all things are formed and perfected in the clearest light." And so on, with no clear indication that he has lately seen anything but a rerelease of *Queen Christina*.

We might term writing of this sort "impractical criticism," criticism as detached from context as its subject was.

It does more than free Garbo from responsibility to her vehicles; it implies that no vehicle made by man could ever be worthy of her. Tynan, to be sure, moons regretfully that she never essayed Masha in *The Three Sisters,* but there is something obligatory in the remark. It partakes of the ritual regret men of the theater, even as late as the 1950s, felt they had to express over the way movies wasted and misused talent, as if the stage were never guilty of that sin.

Be that as it may, gush of the sort we are contemplating here has its dangers. Especially for its recipients. The more their singularity is insisted upon, the more they tend to isolate themselves, not only from the world, but from the original sources of their talent. And the more abstract their work tends to become, the more detached from reality. This was both true and untrue of Garbo's work in sound pictures, and there is a certain irony to be found in this dichotomy. It is certainly true, as Barthes observed, that as the years wore on, her makeup tended to grow thicker and whiter, more masklike, which reinforced everyone's sense of her as woman idealized. At the same time, though, there grew in her work, in her attitudes, that new compassion that we spoke of earlier. So far as I know, the first critic to remark on this fact was a highly practical one, Alistair Cooke, doing some youthful service as a weekly movie reviewer. Engaging with her 1935 *Anna Karenina,* he found not the "old, bold slick disdain" of her previous work, but rather "a sort of amused grandeur." In this film, he thought, she became "a tolerant goddess" wrapping everyone "in a protective tenderness." He added acutely, "She sees not only her own life, but everyone else's, before it has been lived."

Fatalism Cooke thought this might be; knowledgeability of a simpler, more instinctively acquired kind I think it might have been. He seems to have thought it might have come upon her of a sudden in this film; I think I detect hints of it even in such otherwise goofy enterprises as *Mata Hari.* But it doesn't really matter. It is there, it is the good side of maturity (as opposed to makeup masks), and it is surely the quality that enabled her to achieve the transcendence that Cukor spoke of in *Camille,* for is it not precisely "a protective tenderness" that she constantly extends to Armand in that film?

It is also a source of frustration. For this achievement of art is swaddled, muffled, in yards of period costume, trivialized by the fake historicism and the turgid literariness of the films in which Garbo appeared, and further distanced by the growing Garbo legend. As early as 1929, in *The Single Standard*, a subtitle had her repeating a variation on the "I want to be alone" theme that she had first enunciated to importunate newsmen who cornered her in New York as she was about to leave for one of her trips home to Sweden. "I am walking alone because I want to be alone," the title card read, and the film emphasized her solitary nature; in it she was often seen taking long walks in the rain. Thereafter the famous phrase, twisted this way and that, turned up in *Grand Hotel* and even in *Ninotchka*. More important, almost all the stories concocted for her stressed her isolation. As Tynan pointed out, it was generally necessary, given her accent, to cast her as precisely what she was: an exile, arriving alone in some strange port of call, either escaping from or in pursuit of love. If she survived whatever amorous adventure the script took up, she was then typically seen at the end departing as she came—alone. The famous last shot of *Queen Christina*, as she stands alone at the prow of the ship carrying her into exile, is the emblematic shot of her career, the one by which future generations, encountering it in compilation television shows or picture books, know her. To put the matter simply, everything possible was done to mystify, to obscure the plangent, poignant human truth—that reality beneath convention that Cukor was talking about—that Garbo was constantly illuminating in her work. Tosh scripts, in short, encouraged tosh journalism and a tosh legend.

And, as the 1930s wore on, a price began to be paid for this. Through *Camille* her films continued to be profitable, but apparently at diminishing levels, and with ever-increasing reliance on the foreign market for the largest share of that profitability. Then, in 1937, disaster struck. *Conquest*, the story of the doomed love of a Polish countess, Marie Walewska (by whose name the film was known outside the U.S.) for Napoleon, ran catastrophically over budget. According to Alexander Walker no fewer than seventeen screenwriters took whacks at a project that eventually cost over $3 million to produce, only a million less than *Gone With the Wind* (which was twice as long and incalculably enriching to the studio two years later). Obviously it was finally time to bring Garbo into the twentieth century. It was also time for her to embrace, as well, what were by now the established conventions of the sound film.

Hence *Ninotchka.* By this time Garbo's long-term M-G-M contract had run out and she signed a one-picture deal with the studio for less than half what she had received previously. But Ernst Lubitsch, whom she later—correctly —described to a friend as the only first-class director she ever had in Hollywood, had been wanting to make a picture with her since the early thirties. It was a happy collaboration and, as it turned out, one that restored her to favor at the box office.

The script, a collaboration between the great comedy-writing team of Billy Wilder and Charles Brackett and an old friend of Lubitsch's, Walter Reisch, represents a brilliant adaptation of her screen personality to the purposes of comedy. She plays, of course, a Russian commissar come to Paris to investigate the bumbling and bungling of a highly comical trade commission which has fallen under the spell of the city and of a womanizing con man (Melvyn Douglas). He, in turn, seduces her out of habit, then genuinely falls in love with her. As she is a new Russian woman, it is, of course, natural for her to travel alone on business and to conduct it in a mannishly independent manner. In the film this becomes an almost parodistic comment on the solitary ways of her former characters. It is the same when it comes to sex. When Douglas goes into his seductive routine she eyes him coolly and calls it "a natural impulse, common to all," thereby openly stating the calm acceptance of the physical act which previously she had only been able to imply in her earlier roles.

Thereafter, in a speech much quoted since, she makes, if you will, her most famous plea for privacy, for the individual's right to surcease from exactions of public responsibility in the age of megapolitics: "Comrades! People of the world. The revolution is on the march. Bombs will fall. Civilizations will crumble. But not yet, please. Wait. What's the hurry? Give us our moment." Again, this is an open statement of one of the most common implications of her previous screen incarnations—a deployment of her image for witty, as opposed to lugubrious, effect. And somehow the more touching as a result. *Ninotchka* even contrives to give her a renunciation that cheers instead of depresses. For in order to claim her true love it becomes necessary for her to abandon that which has heretofore sustained her, her political beliefs—and this, too, represents a distinct improvement on her former sufferings.

All of this says nothing of the lovely context in which she appears: the funny low comedy of comrades Iranoff, Buljanoff, and Kopalski, the trade commissioners she comes to chastise and stays to indulge; the sharp satirical thrusts at communist, aristocratic and capitalist habits of thought and manners; the combination of worldliness and sweetness, so characteristic of Lubitsch, in the romantic interludes; the sheer smartness and pace of the whole enterprise. In a single, gracefully sweeping gesture, its creators lifted her out of anachronism and placed her in the center, at the height, of what history now correctly sees as one of the great American filmmaking traditions. In sum, Lubitsch and his writers did for Garbo what has had to be done for so many actresses—names like Harlow and Marilyn Monroe come to mind—who make their initial impact as a sex symbol of great and exotic force: they gave her the opportunity to practice humanizing self-satire. For though distance lends enchantment to such figures in the beginning, it creates estrangement as time goes by.

Unfortunately, however, *Ninotchka* turned out to be a signpost on a road not taken. To be sure, the studio executives saw what it had accomplished for a star who represented a huge investment and who was still youthful, therefore still valuable to them. So they tried to find something in a similar vein for her. Unfortunately they came up with *Two-Faced Woman*. It was a scrimpy production, put into work after the outbreak of World War Two in Europe had effectively cut off almost half the studio's market (and more than half of Garbo's), with a budget that was minuscule by her standards (she took another, more modest, salary cut to make it). And though Cukor, who was effective with romantic comedy *(The Philadelphia Story, Holiday, Pat and Mike)* was assigned to direct, he was certainly not Lubitsch. Far worse, the writers, S. N. Behrman and Salka Viertel, who had worked on many of Garbo's heavier romantic epics, and George Oppenheimer, who hadn't, could not compare to the *Ninotchka* team. The result was not, perhaps, as bad as its reputation. Indeed, it was not unlike hundreds of other studio products, capable of generating mild pleasure and instant amnesia—nothing to work yourself up over one way or the other. Otis Ferguson, who was the only great American movie reviewer of that moment, shrewdly noted that the difference between this film and its predecessor was that the director had patiently shot everything the writers had churned out instead of pruning and pointing their work, as Lubitsch, who always worked closely with his writers, did. The result, as he observed, seemed draggy despite a lot of good lines and despite Garbo's "nice, dry" talent for comedy. As he said, "Unless you are determined to be grumpy you will probably enjoy it."

But *Two-Faced Woman*—in which Garbo plays a wife trying to rekindle her husband's flagging romantic interest by pretending to be her sexy twin sister—was greeted by a chorus of critical outrage. The goddess might laugh, but only in the hands of an acknowledged master of sophisticated wit, and only in a film the budget of which clearly reflected the artistic status to which the critical community had long since elevated her. Or as Ferguson also noted, "Serious people naturally want Miss Greta Garbo to be serious," and the relative insubstantiality of this movie led to an outcry about the shame and waste of their idol. Or, again to quote Ferguson: "Serious people object with high contempt to what they call Hollywood typing, and then turn around and issue the exact sounds that make shrewd movie producers keep as many actors as possible in as nearly the same part as possible, to keep the paying dumb public from squinting and shuffling its feet. Serious people of the kind I mean feel themselves above the dumb public, but cannot be differentiated in the matter of squinting and shuffling feet."

In other words, one might be disappointed to a degree by something like *Two-Faced Woman*, but it was not a cause for vast alarm or a great reexamination of everyone's premises. Alas, however, the outcry over it reached the star's ears. As we have read, she had always had her doubts about the project, and the denial of her request for her trusted cameraman, William Daniels, was typical of the minor stupidities Hollywood executives are always insisting upon in order to assert their petty authority over "talent." Now the excesses of outrage visited upon her by the critical press seemed to confirm for her the studio's lack of gratitude for past successes as well as its long-standing habits of patronization and erratic minginess in its dealings with her. Worse, this failure obviously loomed larger to her, an actress who made a picture only every year or two, than it might have to a performer who made, as most did in those day, three or four a year. Her films had always been events; she was not in the habit of forgetting the easily forgettable and pressing on to the next project. Still worse, it seemed to cancel out the promise the similar *Ninotchka* had held out to her. Perhaps that had been just a one-time sensation. Perhaps there was not, after all, a future in lighter, more contemporary romantic vehicles. Perhaps she had better reclaim her distance while yet she could. Perhaps she had better increase that distance, if possible.

And so the consciously planned withdrawal into everdeepening mystery. One can, of course, see other appeals in this strategy. Shall we put it mildly? She cannot have been unaware of her extraordinary beauty and the fact that sooner or later she would have to either withdraw its "maturing" charms from the crowd or consent to letting them observe its inevitable decline. Barthes puts this matter very well: "The essence was not to be degraded, her face was not to have any reality except that of its perfection, which was intellectual even more than formal. The essence became gradually obscured, progressively veiled with dark glasses, broad hats and exiles; but it never deteriorated."

In one way, however, she miscalculated—disastrously. There is a clear implication in the Prologue to this book that Garbo counted on her films to buttress the legend that she had created around herself, counted on them to bear interestingly enigmatic, endlessly reinterpretable evidence on behalf of her life and her achievements. Isn't that precisely the kind of gnomic material other people we are pleased to think of as gods, heroes, exemplars leave behind? Even if she were not thinking quite as grandly as that, she certainly had reason to suppose that the films would serve as her legacies—as books and poems and paintings had served other artists. Indeed, she was of the first generation of performing artists on whom film conferred this gift of concrete immortality. Nor did she have, at the time of her retirement, any reason to suppose that later generations would receive this work of hers less rapturously than her contemporaries had.

But the movies failed her. Or perhaps, in fairness, we who came along later failed her, in that we could not make the imaginative backward leap her work required of us; could not dig the reality of her achievement out of the antique dramatic and emotional conventions encrusting it. In any event, there is this irony to consider: Of all her movies the only one that remains alive for us today, the only one that is not the property of her ever-dwindling cult, the only one we can contemplate reseeing with pleasure or recommend to younger people with confidence is the movie in which she and her colleagues so artfully satirized her screen persona: *Ninotchka*.

It is not enough. Maybe in the end memory reduces all great star careers to the dimensions of a televised tribute, a compilation of film clips, reminiscences, antique critical opinions, and second-hand gossip. And, heaven knows, every movie actor's life includes many films—generally a majority—that he or she might wish evanesced like a failed stage play. But the fact remains that all of Garbo's contemporaries who might be considered her peers left behind at least a half-dozen movies that we can profitably and pleasurably return to at any time. These pictures are the anchors of their immortality, works that retain their freshness across a half-century and more, permitting newer generations to see not just their high moments but the full range of their personalities and gifts in enhancing—not to say delightful—contexts. These movies allow us to take stock of these players at leisure, to form our own impressions of him or her, free of legend, free of the cultist's odd enthusiasms, the historian's opinions, or the clip–show producer's tastes.

Garbo, in short, paid a price for her self-absorption, for her egoism, for her curious passivity when it came to choosing roles. Useless to complain, years later, that she had only one great director in her career. She was in Hollywood when it was at the height of its creative energy, and she had the power, if she had used it, to insist on its greatest directors, its finest writers. But she fought only for money and the minor prerogatives of stardom—such as the cameraman whose light bathed her most attractively. Many performers, with far less clout than she, struggled for, and got, parts that sustained their careers not merely into middle age, but onward into a future that is not yet finished. Sadly, one concludes, she had a peasant's shrewdness, but not an artist's high instincts. She became a legend in her time, but not a legend for all time. With each passing year she becomes more and more . . . a curiosity.

Think of it! Something like a half-century's existence as —to vary Daniel Boorstin's famous formulation—someone known for her unknown-ness. Or perhaps one should say her unknowability. The public saw much of her in the newspapers and magazines during the early part of that period, until the press lost interest in her, and age slowed her down. She was wraith to the world, glimpsed slipping in and out of airports, restaurants, theaters, hidden behind dark glasses, swathed in a veil, her hat pulled down low on her forehead. Some cultists took to following her about on her walks in Central Park or her strolls through the shops of the neighborhood where she lived, on Manhattan's East Side. Occasionally enterprising journalists joined in these stalkings and reported the unilluminating comments of the tradesmen who did business with her. For years, New Yorkers reported to one another their chance encounters with her on the streets, though few, if any, dared to speak to her. "Miss Brown," the pseudonym under which she booked airline and steamship tickets, became almost as well-known as her own name.

Those who knew of her only through the gossip press assumed she was a recluse, but she was not. In the forties and fifties, producers could reach her with scripts and ideas, and more than once word was passed that she was about to come out of retirement, but she was, apparently, teasing them—and testing her power to command the interest of press and public. Be that as it may, she had until her death a fairly wide circle of friends, and she exposed herself to the ever-lurking paparazzi mainly because she wanted to join them at their play. She constantly to-and-froed to Europe. Indeed, she was something of a freeloader, always glad to accept an invitation to the south of France or the Caribbean, as long as someone else was picking up the tab. Once ensconced in villa or exclusive resort, she participated freely, if quietly, in her friends' activities.

It would have been nice if in those years she had carried out the plan she mentioned to Mr. Gronowicz: making and sustaining relationships with the best minds and spirits of her time, world figures in the arts, politics, intellectual life. As she surmised, her status would have assured her access to these people, just as she might have had access to Hollywood's best and brightest in her active years. But the evidence is that the only artists she saw were those she naturally encountered in the social circles she preferred— Tennessee Williams, Truman Capote, Cecil Beaton. Many of them were homosexuals, therefore safe escorts for her (though, famously, she lured Beaton across the line into a brief, and on his part, impassioned, heterosexual affair). There is no evidence whatsoever that she reached out beyond this quite narrow cut of life toward a wider artistic world, let alone toward the world of politics or social awareness. She remained, one may kindly guess, too shy, too insecure intellectually, to make that effort. Unkindly, one may speculate that she remained all too conscious of her legendary status and dared not risk placing it too close for comfortable comparison to legends of comparable standing in other fields. In any event, and for whatever reason, she passed most of her time not just with the idle rich, but the stupid rich people who continued to defer to her stardom as hurrying youth, preoccupied with new fads, could not and would not. Her set's interests in ideas and art were confined to those which were comfortable, settled, approved by all the right authorities. And, of course, its members could provide her with those comfortable, carefully controlled environments where she could rest from her restless travels. Little that was new, youthful, challenging was permitted to penetrate their lives—or her life.

For all her comings and goings, her life after she left the screen—and it consumed by far the majority of her years— was an empty one, unrelieved by altruism or by any sense of obligation to culture or to history. It was, truly, among the most selfish lives ever lived by a public person in modern times, and one that is not redeemed by any posthumous benefactions, aside from this book—grudgingly submitted to by Mr. Gronowicz's own account, quite often mean-spirited in tone, and sullied by her repudiation of it while she lived.

Late in her life she seemed to sense that she had misspent much of it. At any rate, she complained to Mr. Gronowicz of the trivia of her existence, and the record testifies to the bitter truth of that remark. But still she did nothing to relieve her condition, to connect herself with the life of her times. She remained in life what she had been on screen, "raptly, beautifully, unassertively" herself. And one can read her last years as analogous to the last reel of so many of her pictures, that is to say as a renunciation, mournful and noble, this time not of a man, but of a woman—her former self. This creature, half-fiction, half-fact, was (largely) Garbo's invention, and so she had a perfect right to do what she wished with it—to protect it from time's ravages, to protect us from witnessing that inevitable decline. (I suppose, if she spared such a thought for our sensibilities, one cannot call her totally selfish.) But she forgot that life is not a movie, that it has a way of drifting on past its emotional high points, its logical climaxes, carrying us into the becalmed absurdities of age. So, though she avoided the pity we sometimes feel for the idols of our youth when we glimpse them in their late infirmities, all her efforts could not prevent Garbo the idea, Garbo the ideal, from deteriorating into a kind of silliness—on those rare occasions when we thought about it.

Yet there was still a kind of magic in her presence, if you could penetrate to it. I said at the outset that I played a walk-on role in one of these entirely forgettable scenes from her leftover life. Despite her disparagement of him in these pages, it was her habit to spend a month or so every year with the late Gayelord Hauser, the eccentric nutritionist. He was another homosexual she had enticed into a heterosexual fling, maintaining a friendship with him after their ardor had cooled. Clever with money, Hauser was generally rumored to have been responsible for guiding her investments—notably in Rodeo Drive real estate—so that she had reason to be grateful to him for the comfort in which she was able to maintain herself during her retirement. He lived in Los Angeles, just off Mulholland Drive, in a handsomely decorated house built around a pool, and often entertained Garbo, complaining about her exigent ways when she was his house guest (she was fussy about her meals and their timing). We had a mutual friend, and one day he called her to ask if I would like to join him and Garbo at a small party other friends were giving, and this was, needless to say, an offer we could not refuse.

She was introduced under her "Miss Brown" pseudonym, but naturally she was fooling no one. She was then in her seventies, her face remarkably unlined, her body slender, her movements calm, graceful, vigorous. Predictably, she did not have much to say, but on the other hand she was very much a part of the party, following the banal conversation with perhaps more alertness than it deserved. I felt, or thought I felt, a slight impatience in her, an unspoken hope that she might hear something she had not heard before, some news or gossip from the outside world. But even if these people had been capable of providing that, the constraint her presence imposed on everyone precluded any ruffling of the surface. At one point, though, I found myself involved in a conversation about investment strategies far too technical for me to follow. My eye wandered and caught hers across the room. She smiled broadly—and winked. I winked back. For just a second I was Armand or Vronsky, a whole generation of males, caught in that all-knowing glance, our otherness, our waywardness, our peculiar devotion to plot and ploys at the expense of the infrangible moment, exposed, accepted, indulged.

In the lengthening history of the movies only this woman had the gift for imparting this gift. It is a sadness that she made it so difficult for the future to find it.

Index

Index

Fitsroy, Emily, 238
Fitzgerald, Edith, 337
Fitzmaurice, Diana, 227
Fitmaurice, George, 227, 303
Flesh and the Devil, 211, 218,
    226–30, 266
Fontanne, Lynn, 405
*Four Horsemen of the
    Apocalypse*, 182
Franklin, Sidney, 259
Franz Joseph, Archduke, 360
Freshman, The, 147
Freudlose Gasse, Die, 113, 116,
    127
Freund, Karl, 351
Fulda, Ludwig, 373
Furth, Jaro, 114

Gable, Clark, 220, 303
    *Susan Lenox: Her Fall and
        Rise*, 303, 379
Garbo, Greta:
    acting techniques, 207–9, 285
    advertising films, 53–54
    American citizenship, 414
    animals, love for, 294–95
    awards, 239, 343, 347
    barbershop, work in, 43
    birth, 31
    childhood, 32–38, 125
    contract with MGM, 120–21
    department store, work in,
        52–53, 64, 66–71
    dramatic education, 64–66
    dreams of oranges, 39–42,
        201
    father, death of, 38
    first film part, 52
    Hollywood, early work in,
        126, 181–90
    jealousy, 200
    legend, importance and
        enhancement of, 249, 404–
        407, 412, 416–17

name, changing of, 96–97,
    170–71
New York, arrival in, 139–42
occult, interest in, 301–2, 373
publicity, 182, 250
retirement, 404
Royal Dramatic Academy,
    entrance exam for, 76–80
Stiller, Mauritz, meeting and
    early work with, 77–80,
    92–107
Stockholm, 1928 visit to,
    275–84
Sweden, departure from,
    131–38
theater and films, early
    interest in, 43–51
    See also Criticism and
    reviews; and names of
    specific films
Garson, Greer, 410, 413
Gasiorowski, Waclaw, 350
Gaudio, Tony, 197, 203
Gay Cavalier, The, 52
Gaye, Gregory, 363
Genthe, Arnold, 148–55, 159,
    169, 263
Gert, Valeska, 114
Gide, André, 14
Gilbert, John, 217–29, 232,
    240–44, 249, 251, 270, 288–
    290, 293, 320, 340
    death, 336
    first meeting with Garbo,
    210–15
    Flesh and the Devil, 218, 226,
    266
    Love, 237–39, 267
    marriage, 292
    Queen Christina, 335–36, 382
    Woman of Affairs, A, 257
Girl from Sevastopol, The, 109,
    113
Gish, Lillian, 220, 246, 258
Glazer, Benjamin, 211, 303